THE LAND BEYOND PROMISE

To Andrew
with best wishes
Colin Thundler

THE LAND BEYOND PROMISE

*Israel, Likud
and the Zionist Dream*

COLIN SHINDLER

I.B.TAURIS
LONDON • NEW YORK

Paperback edition published in 2002 by I.B. Tauris & Co Ltd
6 Salem Road, London W2 4BU
175 Fifth Avenue, New York NY 10010
www.ibtauris.com

In the United States of America and in Canada distributed by
St Martin's Press, 175 Fifth Avenue, New York NY 10010

Cover design by Steve Leary
Front cover illustration courtesy of PA Photos

First published in 1995.

ISBN 1 86064 774 X

A full CIP record for this book is available from the British Library
A full CIP record for this book is available from the Library of Congress

Library of Congress catalog card: available

Typeset in Monotype Bembo by Q3 Bookwork, Loughborough
Printed and bound in Great Britain by Mackays of Chatham plc,
Chatham, Kent

IN MEMORY OF BARRY SHENKER, 1944–1992

Each time a man stands up for an ideal,
or seeks to improve the lot of others,
or strikes out against injustice,
he sends forth a tiny ripple of hope,
and crossing each other
from a million centres of energy and daring,
those ripples build a current that can sweep down
the mightiest walls of oppression and resistance.

Robert Kennedy,
South Africa 1966

CONTENTS

Acknowledgements		ix
Glossary of Hebrew Terms		xi
Introduction		xvi
Prologue: Half-Forgotten Memories		1
1	The Long and Winding Road	7
2	The Advocates of Revolt	20
3	A Jewish State in the Land of Israel	36
4	Looking for Partners: Revisionism in Transition	49
5	The End of the Socialist Zionist Dream	62
6	The First Begin Government	83
7	The Cost of Camp David	96
8	Lebanon: The Escape of the Golem	109
9	Defeat from the Jaws of Victory	128
10	Begin's Holocaust Trauma	145
11	The Massacre at Sabra and Shatilla and its Consequences	159
12	Shamir: The Man from Lehi	171
13	Above and Below Ground	187

viii   CONTENTS

14   Outlawing the Palestinians   206

15   Between Information and Propaganda   220

16   The Year of Reckoning   235

17   The Shamir Plan   249

18   Forward to the Edge   262

     Postscript: Into the 21st Century: Enter Sharon 282

     Notes   291

     Select Bibliography   305

     Index   311

ACKNOWLEDGMENTS

The election of Ariel Sharon in February 2001 and the destruction of the Trade Center in September was the impetus in producing a second re-titled edition of *Israel, Likud and the Zionist Dream: Power, Politics and Ideology from Begin to Netanyahu* which was first published in 1995. A few weeks later, in November 1995 Rabin was murdered and subsequently replaced by Netanyahu. The hopes expressed at that time now look like wishful thinking. This edition has provided me with the opportunity to analyse recent events through a new introduction, postscript and afterword. I would also like to thank Shalom Lappin for his friendship and astute comments on reading the additions.

Many busy people in Israel, gave up their time to see me, to answer my questions, and to explain the subtleties of a particular situation which has eluded me. They included Moshe Arens, Benny Begin, Yossi Beilin, Eliahu Ben-Elissar, Boas Evron, Aloof Hareven, Shulamith Hareven, Moshe Katzav, Avishai Margalit, Dan Meridor, Aryeh Naor, Yuval Nee'eman, Ari Rath, Tom Segev, Zalman Shoval, Benny Temkin, Ornan Yekutieli and Dedi Zucker. Nitza Ben-Elissar of the Jewish Agency organised my schedule brilliantly and I am grateful to my friend John Levy for the connection. The Greenbergs of Baka gave me the warmth of their friendship and the run of their household.

Dan Leon, the managing editor of the *Palestine-Israel Journal*, and 'John Cecil' read the entire manuscript and made many pertinent suggestions. My respect and admiration for 'John' has deepened by the remarkable manner in which he has fought serious illness. I have not been as good a friend as I would have wished at this difficult time. I hope that a discussion of recent events will strengthen his spirit and aid his recovery. I would also like to thank Aryeh Handler – who was actually present when Ben-Gurion read the Declaration of Independence in 1948 – for reading drafts of the earlier chapters. Rabbi Jonathan

Wittenberg read sections on the Lebanon war and helped once more to ensure a logic existed in the transliteration of the Hebrew. As in the past, I have employed a system designed for the convenience of the English reader rather than the precise requirements of the academic scholar.

I would like to thank the library staffs of the Royal Institute of International Affairs, London; the London School of Economics; the School of Oriental and African Studies, London; the Truman Institute for the Advancement of Peace at the Hebrew University, Jerusalem; Metzudat Ze'ev – the Jabotinsky Institute, Tel Aviv; the Knesset Library, Jerusalem. I must also thank Anna Enayat, Deborah Susman and Emma Sinclair-Webb of I.B. Tauris for their encouragement, goodwill and professionalism. I am also indebted to my copyeditors, Robin Gable and Lucy Morton, for their astute questioning. Any errors of fact or interpretation are mine alone.

Nothing would have been accomplished without the support and humour of my wife Jean. Our children have now reached the age of reason and are only too aware of the problems of the Israel-Palestine struggle. My in-laws, Goldie and Derek Pollock have always taken a real interest in my work and a great delight in our family. They have always been deeply concerned for the future of Israel. I would also like to say thank you to Judy Keiner whose faith in the standard of the first edition persuaded me to embark on an academic career in Israeli studies.

The peace process between Israelis and Palestinians is at its lowest point. Only enemies can make peace but the outbreak of the second Intifada while explicable is still a numbing occurrence. Many Israelis and Palestinians are exhausted intellectually. They now struggle to maintain a dialogue as opposed to conducting negotiations. Although each side's tribalists accuse their opponents of original sin, at the end of the day, they will sit down and talk once more. How long that will take and whether such discussions will be meaningful are open-ended questions. Even so, it is still relevant to quote Eleazar Ben-Azariah whose words come down to us over eighteen centuries:

'Where there is no wisdom, there can be no reverence and where there is no reverence, there can be no wisdom. Where there is no knowledge, there can be no insight and where there is no insight, there can be no knowledge.'

Colin Shindler
September 2001

GLOSSARY
OF HEBREW TERMS

Achdut Ha'avoda	Pioneering left socialist Zionist party, characterized by maximalist policies towards the Arabs. Part of the Labour Party since 1968.
Agudat Yisrael	A-Zionist ultra-orthodox party influenced by Hassidism.
Al Hamishmar	Left-wing daily newspaper, often associated with the policies of Mapam.
Aliyah	Emigration to Israel – literally, 'going up'.
Ashkenazim	Jews from Central and Eastern Europe.
Askanim	Term of abuse for party apparatchiks.
Betar	Revisionist youth movement, later affiliated to Herut.
B'ezrat Ha'shem	'With the help of God.'
B'machteret	'In the Underground': publication of the Stern Group.
Bnei Adam	Worthy person.
Bnei Brak	Ultra-orthodox neighbourhood of Tel Aviv.
Brit Ha'Biryonim	Union of Zealots: neo-fascist group, active in the early 1930s.
Davar	Labour movement daily newspaper.
Degel Ha'Torah	Non-Zionist ultra-orthodox party, influenced by the Lithuanian school of *mitnagdim*.
Ein Vered Group	Maximalist Labour activists, some of whom were associated with Techiya.
Eretz Israel	The Land of Israel.
Gahal	Gush Herut Liberalim, the Herut–Liberal bloc formed in 1965.
Gush Emunim	Religious settlers' movement in the Territories.
Ha'aretz	Leading intellectual liberal daily newspaper.
Hadar	Jabotinskyian concept of honour and dignity.
Haganah	Jewish defence force in the Yishuv, predecessor of the IDF.

Halakhah	Religious Jewish law.
Ha'mefaked	The commander of the Irgun.
Haolam Hazeh	Radical campaigning magazine.
Hasbarah	Explanation of events.
Hassidim	Adherents of a popular ultra-orthodox movement, characterized by devotion to its rabbinical leader and fervent concentration on the relationship with God.
Havlagah	Policy of self-restraint.
Hazit Ha'Moledet	The Fatherland Front, a Lehi front which carried out the Bernadotte assassination.
He'Hazit	The publication of Lehi.
Herut	Party formed by Menachem Begin in 1948 and political successor to the Irgun Zva'i Leumi; now part of the Likud.
Histadrut	The General Federation of Labour in Israel.
Im ba l'horgach hashkem l'horgo	'If someone comes to kill you, rise up so as to kill them.'
Informatzia	Information.
Irgun Zva'i Leumi	National Military Organization: founded by Jabotinsky and led by Menachem Begin in the struggle against the Mandatory authorities.
Irgun Zva'i Leumi b'Israel	The first name used by the Stern Group.
Kach	Far-right party, led by the late Rabbi Meir Kahane, barred from running in Israeli elections.
Kollel	Religious learning community.
Kupat Holim	The sick fund, the health insurance scheme of the Histadrut.
Lehi	'Fighters for the Freedom of Israel', formerly the Stern Group.
La'am	One of the constituent groups of the Likud, formed from the State List, the Free Centre and the Labour Land of Israel Movement.
Likud	Right-wing bloc, inheritor of Revisionism. Dominant party in Israeli politics 1977–92.
Lishkat avoda	The employment exchange which provided labour for employers.
Ma'apach	Upheaval – applied to the change of government in both 1977 and 1992.
Ma'arach	Labour Alignment with Mapam: 1969 until the formation of the National Unity government with the Likud in 1984.

Machteret Yehudit	The Jewish Underground.
Mafdal	National Religious Party.
Malchut Israel	The sovereignty of the Land.
Mapai	Centrist Labour Party led by Ben-Gurion. Dominant party in early Israeli governments.
Mapam	Dovish leftist Zionist party.
Masigai gvul	Trespassers.
Mechdal	The lack of preparation for the Yom Kippur war.
Meimad	Dovish religious Zionist party formed to fight the 1988 election.
Meretz	Left-of-centre peace alignment: secular grouping consisting of Mapam, Shinui and Ratz, which joined the Rabin government in 1992.
Meshiach	The messiah.
Milchemet mitzva	Obligatory war.
Mishnah	First subject-ordered codification of the oral law.
Mitnagdim	Ultra-orthodox opponents of the Hassidim.
Mitzvah	Commandment, good deed.
Mizrachi	Religious Zionist movement, central component of the National Religious Party.
Modi'in Ezrachi	Israeli polling organization.
Moledet	Far-right party, characterized by the policy of 'transfer'.
Moshav	A cooperative agricultural settlement of individual owners of home and land.
Nekuda	The publication of Gush Emunim.
Netivot Shalom	Religious peace movement.
Palmach	The leftist assault companies of the Hagana.
Pikuach nefesh	The saving of Jewish lives: the principle of the primary importance of the saving of life.
Porshim	Dissidents: the name applied to the Irgun and Lehi by the Zionist establishment.
Rafi	Reshimat Poalei Israel, the Israel Workers' List: Mapai breakaway party, 1965–68, led by Ben-Gurion.
Rak Kak	Revisionist slogan: 'Only Thus!'
Ratz	Civil Rights and Peace movement, founded and headed by Shulamit Aloni.
Rodef	Assailant.
Rosh Betar	The head of Betar, Jabotinsky's post and honorific title.
Sephardim	Jews from the 'East'.

Sha'atnez	The Biblical term used by Jabotinsky to prohibit a mixing of ideologies such as socialism and Zionism.
Shas	Ultra-orthodox Sephardi party. An integral part of Rabin's 1992 government.
Shechem	The Biblical name for Nablus.
Shefichut damim	The shedding of blood.
Sheli	Small leftist, pro-peace group with origins in the Communist Party split of 1965; one of the earliest to call for negotiations with the PLO; won two seats in the 1977 election.
Shinui	Dovish centrist non-socialist party.
Shiurim	Religious study sessions, usually given by a rabbinical authority.
Shlemut Historit	The historic 'completeness' of Eretz Israel.
Shlemut Ha'moledet	The 'completeness' of the homeland.
Shlomzion	Sharon's short-lived party for the 1977 election.
Shoah	The Nazi Holocaust.
Shofar	The ram's horn.
Shomer Shabbat	The keeping of the Shabbat.
Ta'amula	Propaganda.
Tami	Sephardi breakaway party from the National Religious Party; won three seats in the 1981 election.
Techiya	Far-right party, formed in 1979 after Camp David through a split in Likud; obliterated in the 1992 election.
Telem	Party formed by Moshe Dayan for the 1981 election.
Tenuat Ha'Herut	The Herut Movement.
Tenuat Ha'Meri Ha'Ivri	The United Resistance Movement of the Haganah, the Irgun and Lehi, 1945–46.
Tohar Ha'neshek	The purity of arms.
Torah	Traditionally, the five books of Moses. In a wider sense, the entire body of religious precepts, learning and life.
Tsadikim	Wise scholars.
Tsomet	Far-right party of former Labour movement people; won eight seats in the 1992 election due to a strong stand against disproportionate religious influence in Israeli politics.
Yahadut Ha'Torah	The United Judaism list formed for the 1992 election by Agudat Yisrael and Degel Ha'Torah.
Yated Ne'eman	Ultra-orthodox weekly newspaper, generally supporting the views of Rabbi Schach.

Yediot Aharonot	Popular Israeli daily newspaper.
Yefei nefesh	Do-gooders.
Yeshiva	Religious seminary.
Yesh Gvul	Organization of reservists who initially refused to serve in Lebanon in 1982 and then extended their refusal to the Territories.
Yishuv	The Jewish settlement in Palestine before 1948.
Yom Ha'atzmaut	Independence Day.
Zarim	Foreigners.

INTRODUCTION

The victory of Ariel Sharon in the 2001 elections for Prime Minister of Israel catalysed a renewed interest in the Likud. The Netanyahu years had taken the Likud in a different direction, based on territorial compromise and effectively downgrading the dream of incorporating the West Bank into a Greater Israel. Netanyahu also presided over an unravelling of the Likud union of ideological tendencies, which Begin had forged through shrewd coalition building over thirty years. Netanyahu's defeat by Barak in 1999, moved Sharon from a position of increasing irrelevance to centre-stage, though in a caretaker capacity. The second Intifada produced a vote against both Barak and Arafat, which allowed Sharon to emerge from the shadows – as a tainted political figure and war criminal for some, but, as the strongman and protector of the Jewish people for others. He thus inherited the mantle of Vladimir Jabotinsky, the founder of Revisionist Zionism.

Sharon's standing in Israel was enhanced by his conduct in waging war against the Palestinians during 2001. Although many dissented from his maximalist politics on the future of the West Bank and his demonisation of the Palestinian Authority, his tactics of selected incursions into Palestinian territory and targeted killings of planners of suicide missions into Israel garnered strong support from a majority of Israelis according to countless opinion polls and despite international criticism. This was further accentuated by a sense of vindication in the long held Israeli stand against terrorism following the destruction of the Trade Center in New York and the attack on the Pentagon by Islamic militants in September 2001. The Americans, they argued, having experienced suicide missions on their own soil might now finally come to terms with the harsh realities of seeking a solution.

The modern Zionist movement was in part a consequence of the great changes brought about by the French Revolution. This bequeathed the Risorgimento to a renascent Italy and it was this spirit, which the young Jabotinsky imbibed during his student days at the turn of the century. If Jabotinsky was seemingly fashioned by Italian nationalism, then his disciples were moulded by Polish and Irish nationalism. The Third World Conference of Betar in September 1938 in Warsaw produced a defining moment in the history of the Revisionist movement, but also for the future of Israel. Here, the youthful Menachem Begin clashed with Jabotinsky over the proposed next phase of Zionism – military Zionism. Jabotinsky's inspirational declamations to be strong and proud were translated into reality by the succeeding generation but much to his own vehement opposition. With his death in 1940, his successors reinvented Jabotinsky to meet a new situation.

Following the victory of the Likud in the election of 1977, writers on the Middle East conflict began to turn their attention to the Israeli right. This spawned numerous biographies of Menachem Begin and the recent memoirs of Yitzhak Shamir. While many works added pieces to the jigsaw puzzle, my motivation in writing this book was to examine the phenomenon as a whole through the rise and rule of the Likud. The book sets out to explain where leaders such as Begin and Shamir were coming from ideologically, and how they shaped the Likud to become a party of natural government; and to record and detail their road to power and how their world outlook came to define far-reaching and seemingly unfathomable decision-making. In order to do this, it was important to go beyond propaganda and hagiography on one side and blinkered opposition on the other.

My original intention was to write a political analysis of the Likud in power from its election in 1977 until its defeat in 1992. It soon became clear that a brief introduction to Begin's Herut movement and the Revisionist Zionist heritage would not suffice. In order to understand what made the Likud tick, it was important to explain its historical and ideological background. I therefore chose to begin the study in 1931, the year in which Vladimir Jabotinsky and his followers first made a breakthrough at the 17th Zionist Congress and established the Revisionists as a force to be reckoned with.

In one sense, any examination of the Likud is a reflection of an ongoing process of fragmentation and coalescence of the Revisionist movement. This began shortly after its establishment with the evolution into the New Zionist Organization and continued into the split between the Irgun Zva'i Leumi and the Stern Group. The reasons for the split were many, but a central one was the desire to initiate a military revolt against the British authorities in Palestine. While the Irgun waited until the war against Nazism was over, the Stern Group – later Lehi – began 'The Revolt'.

Avraham Stern was a unique figure in that he was the first to openly ditch the central Zionist idea that the British were the only power that would bring about a Jewish state. Unlike the Revisionists, he believed in Zionism as a national liberation movement and that the Jewish state would be attained through armed struggle. He looked to the IRA, Garibaldi, the Russian Social Revolutionaries and the Jewish revolt against the Romans as models and sought to learn the lessons of their failures. This led Stern to approach in turn the Colonels' Poland, Mussolini's Italy and Hitler's Germany as potential allies in place of Britain. In Stern's eyes, World War II enhanced the possibility of assistance from the Axis powers, the premise being that 'the enemy of our British enemy must be our friend'. Stern's successors, the triumvirate of Eldad, Yellin-Mor and Yitzhak Shamir, looked similarly to Stalin's Soviet Union.

Begin, in contrast, continued the legacy of Jabotinsky while altering and reinterpreting his mentor's approach – such as Jabotinsky's pro-British orientation. Despite the fact that the original Revisionist movement still existed, Begin successfully posed as Jabotinsky's anointed heir and through his Herut movement enveloped most of the right-wing fragments. This process was ingeniously continued by Begin for the best part of 30 years. He proved adept at forming alliances with other parties and at establishing political coalitions with breakaway groups from the Labour Zionist movement. Thus Herut became Gahal in 1965 and the Likud in 1973. Likud policy was anchored in the original sin of the partition of Eretz Israel, the Land of Israel, and mainstream Zionism's acquiescence in that. Despite the promise of a larger Jewish homeland in the Land of Israel, the British gave the East Bank of the Jordan to the Emir Abdullah in the early 1920s, while the United Nations offered the West Bank to the Palestinians in 1947.

Begin never forgot Jabotinsky's claim to both sides of the Jordan and indeed he was the only Israeli Prime Minister who refused to meet King Hussein – even clandestinely. During both his governments, Begin balanced a Jabotinskyian pragmatism with a fundamentalist attachment to Judea and Samaria – the West Bank, which Israel had conquered during the Six Day War. Begin's sponsorship of the Camp David Accords and his decision to return Sinai to Egypt, however, resurrected the dormant far right in Israel. This was in a way reminiscent of the original opposition to Jabotinsky and the Irgun by the Stern Group.

Begin was a deeply emotional man, haunted by the Holocaust and its possible recurrence. He believed deeply in Jabotinsky's concept of an 'iron wall' of military might which would protect the Jewish people from hostile adversaries. His attempt to delegitimize the PLO by branding them a purely terrorist organization akin to the Nazis, and his aim to provide security for population areas in Northern Israel, were central to his initiation of the invasion of Lebanon in 1982. His original acceptance of the 'big idea', whilst leaving the details to underlings, allowed Sharon to develop the war to unthinkable proportions.

Yitzhak Shamir exhibited little of the passion and none of the charisma of his predecessor. He was chosen because he came from the same background as Begin. He was perceived as a safe pair of hands to receive the Revisionist legacy. But was Shamir really a Revisionist and a disciple of Jabotinsky? Shamir may have fought the British, but he espoused a different ideology. Unlike his former comrades from Lehi who had remained on the nationalist right, he did not join any of the small far-right parties. He understood that real power resided only in the Likud. As subsequent events showed, he allied himself with the pragmatists of Likud such as Moshe Arens to produce acceptable answers to domestic, Palestinian and American pressure, but beneath the surface he followed his own individualistic path. It was one thing to propose solutions, but quite another to implement them.

Avraham Stern's mystical inclinations led him to the Bible rather than to the British Mandate when defining the parameters of the new Jewish state. The Land of Israel would stretch from the great river of Egypt — presumably the Nile — to the Euphrates in Iraq. Thus for Shamir, there could be no compromise on the issue of the borders of the Land of Israel. He strongly opposed the Camp David Accords. Shamir's broad approach was based on a coupling of Stern's maximalist philosophy to Ben-Gurion's perception of political reality — of what was possible under current conditions and what was not. Although Shamir meandered his way through the morass of Israeli political life, he was still at heart a loyal member of the Stern 'Gang', albeit in Revisionist clothing, even as the head of the Likud. As in the Lehi days of assassinations and military attacks, all decisions were carefully considered. There were no Beginesque dramatic gestures, but rather a movement forward when it was safe to do so and a movement to the side when it was not. Standing still while opponents exhausted themselves in sheer frustration was always an option.

In 1989, he helped to marginalize his own Shamir Plan, which proposed Palestinian elections, when he refused to stand against a vociferous minority of 'Constraints Ministers'. Arik Sharon often remarked that 'the only Constraints Ministers in the government are Shamir and myself'. Shamir was perceived as tough and stubborn by his own colleagues and by the Israeli public. Yet by the autumn of 1991, he had resisted sufficiently all pressures to secure reasonable terms from the Americans for the opening of negotiations with the Palestinians and the Arab states. Judging by his inferences, Shamir regarded the Madrid Conference as purely ceremonial – a fig leaf for the arrangement of bilateral agreements with moderate opponents such as Jordan and the Gulf states. As he claimed after the 1992 election, he could have dragged out negotiations for another ten years.

Shamir's essentially immobile approach, which was applauded in earlier years, eventually led to severe dissension within the Likud, and many colleagues blamed him for the erroneous tactics which led to their electoral defeat in 1992. Yet these tactics – the art of political shadow boxing – could only be understood within the history of the different ideologies propagated by the factions constituting the Likud.

PROLOGUE

HALF-FORGOTTEN MEMORIES

The Traumatic Upheaval

On 17 May 1977, the citizens of Israel chose Menachem Begin and his Likud union of liberal and nationalist parties to lead them into their fourth decade as a sovereign nation-state. The Ma'arach, the Labour Alignment of socialist parties which had essentially governed the country since independence in 1948, was put out to political pasture after a disastrous decade in government. The election for the ninth Knesset produced 43 seats for Likud and only 32 for Labour. Nearly half of the Alignment vote had disappeared since the previous election in 1973. One half of the electorate had changed their political allegiance. Moreover, in 1977 a new party, the reformist Democratic Movement for Change, had been established. It competed with the Labour Party for the mainly Ashkenazi vote of the higher waged and the better educated. It had capitalized on public disillusionment with the Ma'arach, taking a record 15 seats and effectively fragmenting the vote for the Labour Alignment. Thus, for the first time, Israeli voters were given a real choice. No longer was the outcome a forgone conclusion – the victory of the Israeli Labour Party; there were now three options – the Labour Alignment, the Democratic Movement for Change, and Menachem Begin's Likud.

Nevertheless, the outcome was unexpected. Usually reliable opinion pollsters such as Pori and Dahaf had predicted an Alignment victory. The Hanoch Smith poll in *Ma'ariv*[1] on the eve of the election indicated 30 per cent for the Alignment, 25 per cent for the Likud, and only 11 per cent for the Democratic Movement for Change. The daily *Yediot Aharonot* showed the Alignment and the Likud neck and neck at 38–39 seats each. This confirmed the findings of a survey commissioned by the Ma'arach themselves. Even the most favourable

Modi'in Ezrachi poll gave the Likud only a possible three-seat advantage. The magnitude of the electoral victory for the Likud had thus been neither expected nor predicted. The Labour Party had anticipated an Alignment-led coalition with possibly the Democratic Movement for Change as its major partner. Yet it was rumoured in the Israeli press, some months before the election, in mid-April 1977 that Shimon Peres, the Ma'arach's leader, had floated the possibility of a worst-case-scenario coalition with the Likud at a closed party meeting in Tel Aviv. As in the British election of 1992, few opinion-poll analysts had taken due account of the large number of undecided voters, an estimated 20–25 per cent. This factor, together with a strong movement towards the Likud in the closing days of the campaign, upset all predictions and calculations.[2]

The election of Menachem Begin at the age of 64, in his ninth term as head of Herut, one of the constituent parties within the Likud, was both a psychological and a political watershed for many Israelis and Jewish supporters of Israel abroad. He was, for many, an irascible, uncontrollable hate-figure whose controversial exploits over four decades had tarnished and retarded the best endeavours of the great Zionist experiment. The shape of things to come was not a happy prospect for many sections of Israeli society. Shulamit Aloni, whose Civil Rights Movement had been all but decimated in the election, expressed the view of the secular Zionist left. She believed that 'the nation has become less rational, more nationalistic, more mystical, less governed by common sense and more influenced by money'.[3] The genie had been let out of the bottle and, given his past record, would do great damage.

Outside Israel, Western governments, of both left and right, privately reacted with abject horror at the prospect of a Begin administration. President Jimmy Carter believed that Begin laid claim not only to the West Bank, but also to the East Bank – the Hashemite Kingdom of Jordan.[4] Treading the path to peace with the participants in the Middle East conflict was never easy at the best of times. Now it appeared to many observers that Begin would lead the people of Israel into a hard-line ideological wilderness with no prospect of the promised land of peace negotiations at the end of it.

Diaspora Jews were similarly aghast. They had been weaned on the Zionist ideals of Ben-Gurion and Weizmann: the struggle for independence, the kibbutz and the blooming of the desert – the image of Israel as a brave socialist experiment and truly 'a light unto the nations'. The Board of Deputies of British Jews was described as 'tight-lipped' when asked for an opinion on the outcome of the election.[5] How could they suggest to the British public and the British government that the former commander of the Irgun Zva'i Leumi, who was associated with the blowing up of the King David Hotel, the hanging of British Army sergeants, and the massacre at Deir Yassin, was cast in the mould of his predecessors? Indeed, only a few years before, they had to contend with a demonstration of left-wing Jews – 'Zionists against Begin' – on their very doorstep when the Likud leader paid his first visit to Britain. Their decision to send Begin a congratulatory telegram became a long-drawn-out, agonising process. They saw him 'as a source of shame and embarrassment'.[6] The BBC gently referred to Begin as 'the former guerilla leader'. Others, however, were not afraid to label him 'a terrorist chieftain'. The memories of Mandatory Palestine had clearly not dimmed.

Israeli career diplomats who were well versed in the culture of Labour Zionism now had to prepare themselves to say the exact opposite of what they had said before, and to do so with equal conviction. For more than thirty years, there had existed within Labour Zionism a sense that the party possessed an inalienable right to govern, embellished by an almost divine sense of purpose in constructing a new civilization in its own image. Political adversaries had to be opposed and contained if the new Jerusalem was to be built on the foundations of the old. Genuine religious fervour – based on faith in Judaism – had to be controlled, managed and marginalized. The dark forces of Revisionist Zionism were thus regarded as both subversive and satanic. To lose power to the right, with its belief in a nationalistic mythology and its worship of military symbols, was therefore both unthinkable and unimaginable. A victory by the right would represent a posthumous triumph, they argued, for the followers of those reactionary forces which had plagued Europe during the inter-war years and initiated the world into a new age of unprecedented barbarity. Such an absolutist mind-set dominated the thoughts of tens of thousands of life-long Labour people. The victory of 1977 was thus a blow of unique proportions.

In his diaries, Ben-Gurion records a discussion between Yigal Allon and an Israeli diplomat in 1948:

'What would happen' Allon asked, 'if Menachem Begin became Prime Minister?'
He was clearly taken aback.

Finally, he replied 'If Begin seized power, I would not serve him; if he were elected, then that would be different'.

Allon told him that he would never accept Begin as Prime Minister.[7]

This conversation took place two months after the *Altalena* controversy, where an Irgun gunship had been destroyed on the orders of Ben-Gurion and when the whiff of a coup d'état and the prospect of civil war were still in the air. Now, it had come to pass: Begin had indeed been elected by the people, and ironically Yigal Allon was number two on the defeated Ma'arach list and the outgoing Foreign Minister.

The deep emotions which the figure of Menachem Begin evoked – even before he had taken office – were therefore symptomatic of the great divide that separated the Revisionists and the Labour movement. Yet while there existed very clear political differences, the personal bitterness and the decades-long megaphone war between the two camps had imbued the ideological schism with a medieval righteousness. In part, both camps were products of an age of ideology which by 1977 already possessed a jaded, passé feeling of belonging to another time. The derision which each side heaped on the other seemed to defy scientific analysis and could not simply be explained away in purely political terms. One writer commented that,

> while it would be misleading to argue that Mapai [the forerunner of the Israeli Labour Party and the Ma'arach] and the Revisionists were ideologically close, the differences in ideology cannot by themselves explain the psychological rivalry between them. The two movements created different political sub-cultures which accelerated the inter-party rivalry. They competed for the same resources through different organizational bodies and it was this inter-organizational competition which was translated into a deep political rift. Both parties tried to justify their rivalry and hostility by sharpening the ideological gaps; thus contributing to the conventional wisdom which explains inter-party relations as an expression of deep ideological controversy.[8]

In effect, this deep rivalry sustained the conviction of both sides in the political correctness of their positions throughout the decades of Labour rule. It also led to competing versions and different interpretations of history being constructed and promulgated. It was often more convenient to obfuscate the minutiae of events or omit them altogether.

In his introduction, written in March 1951, to the first edition of Begin's account of the Irgun's campaign against the British, *The Revolt*,

Ivan M. Greenberg, a former editor of the London *Jewish Chronicle*, wrote that 'a conspiracy of silence, inspired by diverse and often irrelevant motives, barred all effective publication in the United Kingdom of the case of the Jewish "rebels".' Greenberg clearly was referring not only to the patriotic British media but also to knowledgeable British Jews who acquiesced in propagating the official line.[9]

Thus, although Herut became the second largest party in 1955 and continued to build on that base through the formation of Gahal in 1965 and the Likud in 1973, the policy of ignoring them and reducing knowledge of their history and that of the Irgun Zva'i Leumi to the absolute minimum had actually contributed to the creation of an informational vacuum. This was only filled by Herut's own laudatory propaganda which deified Revisionism's founder Vladimir Jabotinsky and beatified Begin. By 1977, few people outside Israel had any clear idea of what the Likud actually stood for and how indeed it had managed to come to power. The demonization of Begin – as terrorist and demagogue – substituted for understanding and analysis. Even in Israel, many were unaware of the Likud's true position on many issues.

The maxim that observes that governments lose elections rather than oppositions winning them undeniably held true in the political circumstances of 1977: the electorate voted against the Labour Alignment rather than for the Likud. So great was the disillusionment with the Ma'arach that some 30 per cent of the Likud vote came from former Labour Alignment voters. The political upheaval of 1977 represented such a severe psychological dislocation that in the aftershock many sought a more convincing explanation for the ascendency of the Likud than that of simple vote splitting by the Democratic Movement for Change combined with the incompetence and bad luck of the Rabin government.

Shortly after the election result was announced, Yigal Hurvitz, a leader of the La'am faction of the Likud, suggested that the outcome was indirectly a result of the ideological deviation and moral decline of Mapai – a party to which he and other members of Likud had formerly belonged. Significantly, he remarked that the electorate had endorsed 'the covenant between the disciples of Ben-Gurion and Jabotinsky'. Begin as the leader of Herut – the self-proclaimed heir of the Revisionist movement – understood the election result in much more specific terms: it was not a blanket victory for the realignment of hitherto hostile opponents who had found a commonality of interests and language through the Likud confederation of anti-Labour parties, but a victory for Revisionism *per se*. Begin viewed his victory as the culmination of the long and bitter struggle between the Revisionists and the Labour movement to win the hearts and minds of the supporters of Zionism. Labour Zionism had finally been defeated by the disciples of Jabotinsky. Its long rule was over. In his acceptance speech, shortly after computer predictions of a Likud victory, Begin made a pertinent reference to 'the titanic struggle of ideas stretching back to 1931'. This somewhat obscure comment floated over the heads of the majority of the audience. Yet Begin was very much a man who carried the past with him. He had never forgotten 1931, the year of the 17th Zionist Congress when Chaim Weizmann had tendered his resignation as president of the World Zionist Organization. At his moment of triumph, then, Begin recalled the year in which the Revisionists had for the first time challenged the Labour-dominated leadership. The occasion had marked the arrival of Revisionist Zionism as a powerful and militant force in Zionist politics, with its own world-view and idea of the shape of things to come. The Zionist movement would never be the same again.

CHAPTER ONE

THE LONG AND
WINDING ROAD

1931 and All That

Zionist policy under Chaim Weizmann had seemingly repudiated the very idea of a Jewish state – or even a Jewish majority in Palestine – in favour of an autonomous community. Indeed, the Balfour Declaration of 1917 spoke only about a Jewish homeland in Palestine. Weizmann, like many other figures of the period, was for tactical reasons deliberately vague about the objective of Zionist aspirations in his dealings with both the British and the Arabs. By 1931, this softly-softly approach had achieved little and was under fire from critics within the Zionist movement.

'A majority does not guarantee security, neither is it necessary for the development of Jewish civilization and culture', Weizmann remarked in an interview with the Jewish Telegraphic Agency during the 17th Zionist Congress. His cautious comments reflected his fear that any call for a Jewish state at that time would be interpreted as a call to expel the Arabs. This typified the mainstream, piecemeal approach of the Zionist leadership, based upon an accommodation with the British and directed towards the final goal of statehood. It contrasted sharply with the militant declarations and instantaneous solutions of the newly formed Revisionist Zionists, who believed that a state could be established solely through the iron will of the Jewish people. Weizmann's political passivity, apparent meekness and perceived compromise on fundamental principles were seen as a provocation. His aristocratic demeanour and belief in practical and realistic diplomacy were regarded as of secondary importance, although they were considered nevertheless to be a sign of weakness. The Jewish state was the unclouded immediate goal of the Revisionists.

The founder of the Revisionist Movement, Ze'ev Vladimir

7

Jabotinsky, brilliantly and eloquently attacked Weizmann at the Congress – for his 'Fabian tactics', for his minimalist stand, and for his assertion that the call for a Jewish state was 'extremism'. Weizmann's *faux pas* in explicitly going against the broadly shared sentiments of the Congress delegates at a time of ebbing fortunes for the Zionist movement played straight into Jabotinsky's hands. For the first time, the supremacy of the Zionist establishment was challenged. The World Zionist Organization elections revealed that the Revisionists had garnered 21 per cent of the vote, compared to 29 per cent for Ben-Gurion's Mapai. This was a tremendous advance for a movement which had been established only six years before. Although the Revisionists' resolution defining the Zionist goal as a Jewish majority in Palestine was defeated, Weizmann resigned and reputedly suggested that Jabotinsky should take over as president of the WZO.[1] Instead, Nahum Sokolov emerged as the new leader.

Weizmann's resignation represented not only the defeat of the Zionist establishment and the price of compromising fundamental principles; it also pointed to the distinct possibility of a Revisionist alternative. The strength of the Revisionists' emergence as a political force and their ingrained disdain for the policies of the leadership certainly made their mark. Their aggressive triumphalism contrasted sharply with the 'fair play' approach of the anglicized Weizmann. Years later, Weizmann recalled his treatment at the hands of the Revisionists – their barracking and 'utter lack of realism':

> Palestine can only be built up the hard way, by meticulous attention to every object … snatching at occasions as they presented themselves, and believing that these accidental smiles of fortune constitute a real way of life.… My guiding principle was the famous saying of Goethe: 'Was du ererbst von deinen Vatern / Erwirb es, um es zu besitzen' [What you inherit from your ancestors / Earn it so that you may truly own it]. The others believed in the Erbe [inheritance], and therefore were always claiming their rights; they wanted the easy road, the road paved with the promises of others. I believed in the path trodden out by our own feet, however wounded the feet might be.[2]

The pragmatic mainstream had no time for myopic militancy and romantic melodrama as acted out by the passionate Jabotinsky. Empty posturing, they argued, could not overcome Jewish powerlessness. Weizmann was wounded by the attacks of the Revisionists and their supporters. He regarded the Congress as animated by 'hatred, vendettas, trickery and treachery'.[3] In a private letter to Baron Edmond de Rothschild, Weizmann blamed his fate on 'a group of reactionary obscurantists – people like the pseudo-religious politicians of the Mizrachi – in happy combination with Jewish fascism as represented by the Americans'.[4] He labelled the Revisionists 'the big noise on the Jewish street – Hitlerism all over in its worst possible form'.[5]

The Congress of 1931 pitted the left against the right in a bitter confrontation. Both political tendencies had by this time coalesced into structured ideological movements. In 1930, Mapai – the Israel Workers' Party – was established through the merger of Achdut Ha'avoda and Hapoel Hatzair under the leadership of Ben-Gurion. The following year, 1931, Jabotinsky at the age of 50 became head of the Revisionists' youth group Betar. The political ardour of young activists on both sides of the divide manifested itself during the Congress. It grew into an uncompromising antagonism which was not without violent expression. Jabotinsky, although influenced by Marxism, did not regard socialism as the answer to social injustice. He even rejected any connection between socialism and the Hebrew Bible. Instead, he put forward solutions based on the Biblical jubilee-year principle, whereby once every 50 years debts were abolished and slaves were able to regain their freedom.[6] In his 'Ideology of Betar', Jabotinsky wrote that 'there is one great flaw in such a [socialist] system; man would cease to strive, to fight, to seek for something better. Everybody's position would be automatically regulated; nothing could be changed; dreams would be dispensed with, the mind would not be "exerted" and there would vanish every individual's constructive impulse.'[7]

Jabotinsky was, in part, influenced by members of the Jewish middle class who emigrated to Palestine from Poland during the fourth *aliyah* (immigration), 1924–28. They urged Jabotinsky to fight for their interests. Jabotinsky argued that an injection of capitalism was necessary to create the conditions for large-scale settlement in Palestine and the formation of a Jewish state thereafter. Class conflict between worker and employer in Palestine, he believed, would therefore undermine the very essence of Zionism by deterring prospective investors. Thus, 'both strikes and lockouts should be declared treasonable to the interests of Zionism'.[8] Industrial disputes could be settled through a neutral, yet compulsory, system of 'national arbitration'. During this time, no strike by the workers would be permitted, but neither would the employer be allowed to dismiss any worker. An arbitration commission would examine the books of the employer and make a unilateral decision as to whether to award the workers an increase. This decision would be binding on both sides. In one famous article,

entitled 'Yes, break it', in 1932, which outraged the Labour movement, Jabotinsky proposed the creation of a new *histadrut*, or workers'
union, which would not organize workers to strike or promote class
war during the period of national solidarity needed to build the Jewish
state. He attacked the Mapai-controlled official Histadrut for organiz-
ing Arab labour and assisting them to go on strike in Jewish factories.
The *lishkat avoda*, the exchange which provided labour for employers,
should be taken out of the hands of the Histadrut and placed under
neutral auspices. Jabotinsky wrote that, if a Jew came to settle, he was
'no longer a labourer, no longer a member of the proletariat, but a
volunteer'. He should suffer with dignity all the difficulties arising
from his status as a worker. He advised those socialists who came to
build Zion but did not care for the idea of capitalism to remain in
their own countries and to fight for the proletariat there. He requested
an increase in Jewish policemen, particularly in mixed Jewish–Arab
neighbourhoods, since non-unionized labour could only seek protection from mainly English and Arab police.

In the article, Jabotinsky further developed the argument that the
situation in which the Jews found themselves during this period before
the establishment of the Jewish state was an abnormal one. Full
democracy, he argued, with all its weaknesses, could impair the
national effort since it possessed inherent flaws. What would happen,
Jabotinsky asked – with prophetic insight – if Hitler were to be
elected in the next German election: would the Jews have to accept
the result of that democratic process? It followed from this argument
that democracy and even the idea of a Jewish parliament could be
placed in abeyance until all the Jews had returned to Zion.

All these challenges to the prevailing Labour orthodoxy led to
deep rifts. Matters were brought to a head by the unexplained murder
of the brilliant Labour theoretician Chaim Arlosoroff in June 1933.
The killing was attributed by most members of the Labour movement to Revisionist assassins.[9] Yet the murder also impelled both Ben-
Gurion and Jabotinsky to attempt a reconciliation in order to limit
internecine violence.

Jabotinsky: A Man of His Time

Jabotinsky's passionate arguments at the 1931 Congress for a Jewish
majority and a Jewish state, in contrast to Weizmann's aloofness, must
have deeply impressed the then eighteen-year-old Menachem Begin,
who had already been a member of the Revisionist youth group

Betar for some three years. Jabotinsky's demand for a clear Zionist vision, an end to fudging Jewish demands, and advocacy of a more radical, more militant stand excited many young Jews. In his assault on Weizmann, Jabotinsky pointedly disregarded the British division of Mandatory Palestine in 1922 and stated that the Revisionist definition of the aim of Zionism was the creation of *malchut Israel* (the kingdom of Israel) with a Jewish majority on both sides of the River Jordan. Begin imbibed from Jabotinsky's approach the idea that the Zionist movement had lost its way. It had readily acquiesced in the British proposal to surrender the East Bank to the Emir Abdullah to form the Hashemite Kingdom of Jordan. It had retreated from the original understanding of Zionism, and now it had even faltered over the very mention of 'a Jewish majority' in Palestine.

On establishing the Revisionist movement, Jabotinsky had at the outset questioned the tactics of mainstream Zionism:

> What is the practical objective of Zionism? To say: 'We want to create a national home', is not enough, as the term 'national home' has no fixed meaning and can therefore be 'interpreted' by interested persons to mean nothing – to mean the equivalent of a new ghetto. The only precise way of describing our objective is this: We want to create in Palestine a Jewish majority. This does not mean that we intend to 'rule' over our neighbours; but we want Zion to become a country where the Jew can no longer be 'overruled'.[10]

Jabotinsky propagated the belief that the Zionist movement had forgotten its Herzlian origins and surrendered its heritage to the philanthropists and the petty bureaucrats. It had sold out to the diplomats and the political operators. Over thirty years later, Begin wrote:

> Above all, Ze'ev Jabotinsky was the bearer of the vision of the State in our generation. After Herzl, there was none but him to carry on high the vision of redemption – even in the face of renegades. This is the truth. There is no need to elaborate.[11]

The year 1931 also signalled to Begin the importance of building a self-contained opposition to the ruling elite, which was then dominated by the Labour movement – even if the price was a schism within his own movement. Even before the 17th Zionist Congress, Jabotinsky had indicated to his colleagues that he felt that the Revisionist movement should operate outside and independently of the World Zionist Organization. Although he was in a minority on his own executive, Jabotinsky argued that, there was little chance of 'conquering' the World Zionist Organization because Revisionism is in essence not only a political party and a *weltanschauung* but above all a 'psychological race', a definite inborn mentality which can hardly be communicated to those who do not possess it inherently. The mission of the Revisionist Movement is therefore to look for people of its own 'race', to organize them for constructive achievements and not to waste its energies in attempts to 'conquer' a Zionist crowd with a different outlook.[12]

The year 1931 also saw the co-option of Betar, the movement's youth group, onto the executive of the Revisionist Party. It is no exaggeration to say that the group showed enormous loyalty to the figure of Jabotinsky – who in return demanded total allegiance. His recruitment of Jewish youth took the form of stirring addresses in towns and villages across the length and breadth of pre-war Poland and other countries of Eastern Europe. His main means of communication with the mass of Jewish youth was through the medium of an impassioned rhetoric – and particularly a rich command of Yiddish which he studied and perfected. Through his personal magnetism, great charm and mesmerizing eloquence, Jabotinsky attracted thousands of young, often impoverished, Jews across Eastern Europe with the intoxicating dream of building a renewed Jewish commonwealth. He exalted beauty over ugliness, dignity over denigration, hope over despair. He infused the multitudes that came to hear him speak with a sense of self-respect and an assertive self-image. His followers – and, in hindsight, many opponents – regarded him as 'the single most charismatic figure after Herzl in Zionist history'.[13] His clear-cut views – action rather than talk – appealed to his youthful audience. Shortly after the founding of the Revisionist movement, Jabotinsky called for the immigration of a million Jews over the next quarter of a century. Unlike Ben-Gurion, he regarded Arab opposition to Zionism as inevitable and he believed that efforts aimed at reconciliation were pointless and doomed to failure. Jabotinsky believed in *barzel* – iron. The Iron Wall of Jewish military endeavour would protect Israel against Arab hostility.

Shortly after resigning from the Zionist Executive in 1923, Jabotinsky expounded his views concerning the Arabs of Palestine.

There can be no voluntary agreement between ourselves and the Palestine Arabs. Not now, nor in the prospective future. I say this with such conviction, not because I want to hurt the moderate Zionists. I do not believe that they will be hurt. Except for those who were born blind, they realised long ago that it is utterly impossible to obtain the voluntary consent of the

Palestine Arabs for converting 'Palestine' from an Arab country into a country with a Jewish majority.[14]

The Arabs, he argued, would eventually accept the distant reality of a Jewish state through Jewish economic and military power in the future and not through voluntary agreement in the uncertain present. This contrasted with Ben-Gurion's belief in an alliance between Jewish and Arab workers against their British rulers. Indeed, at the 17th Zionist Congress in 1931, Ben-Gurion had accused Jabotinsky and the Revisionists of 'Hottentot morals which refuse to others what they claim for themselves. Just as we reject Arab rule over us, we also reject our rule over the Arabs even when the proportion of population in the country will shift in our favour.' This approach changed as the intractable nature of the conflict became more apparent. As Arab nationalism was in the ascendant, Ben-Gurion believed that the partition of Eretz Israel, the Land of Israel, into two autonomous states, linked in a federation, was the only way forward.

Jabotinsky, for his part, believed that Ben-Gurion's attempts at dialogue and conciliation with the Palestinian Arabs were misplaced and futile. He believed that nationalism was the higher sentiment in the Arab world and they too would struggle for the whole of Eretz Israel. Thus, in Jabotinsky's eyes, partition was not acceptable from either the Arab or the Jewish point of view. He ridiculed the Jewish left for their naivity in attempting to accommodate Arab political demands:

> Our peace-mongers are trying to persuade us that the Arabs are either fools whom we can deceive by masking our real aims, or that they are corrupt and can be bribed to abandon to us their claim to priority in Palestine in return for cultural and economic advantages. I repudiate this conception of the Palestinian Arabs.... We may tell them whatever we like about the innocence of our aims, watering them down and sweetening them with honeyed words to make them palatable, but they know what we want as well as we know what they do not want. They feel at least the same instinctive jealous love of Palestine as the old Aztecs felt for ancient Mexico and the Sioux for their rolling prairies.[15]

Jabotinsky's views were based on his interpretation of political reality in the Middle East after World War I when the British ruled Palestine. Jabotinsky viewed the epoch as one which demanded a total commitment by all Jews to achieve the goal of statehood. The final breakthrough, he maintained, could not be attained through dilution or obfuscation. 'Either Zionism is moral and just or it is immoral and unjust. But that is a question that we should have settled before we became Zionists.'[16] He argued strongly against the right of the Palestinian Arabs to national self-determination simply because they were in the majority at that time. While accepting that democracy and self-determination were 'sacred principles', he contended that the principle of self-determination

> does not mean that if someone has seized a stretch of land it must remain in his possession for all time and that he who was forcibly ejected from his land must always remain homeless. Self-determination means revision – such a revision of the distribution of the earth among the nations that those nations who have too much should have to give up some of it to those nations who have not enough or who have none ... the democracy of Palestine consists of two national groups, the local group and those who were driven out, and the second group is the larger.[17]

Following his imprisonment by the British in the fortress of Acre for incitement, Jabotinsky was seen as the leading advocate for a militant Zionism. His refusal to compromise avoided the acknowledgement of private doubt and the dilution of fundamental truths. No 'ideological sha'atnez'[18] – no mixing of ideologies such as socialism and Zionism – could be permitted, as this would serve to weaken the national struggle. Future generations, nevertheless, would enjoy the Land as 'a national laboratory' for social and economic experimentation.

The complexities of a difficult situation and the necessary falseness of the diplomatic process contrasted starkly with Jabotinsky's emphasis on idealism and self-reliance. His anti-establishmentarianism, an ongoing defiance of the Zionist leadership, a proud nationalism and a celebration of military prowess – all vividly illustrated by his spellbinding oratory – were a great attraction to Jewish youth in the 1930s. Discriminated against by host nationalist governments and unable to relate to Stalin's Russia, Jabotinsky's Revisionist brand of Zionism was the utopian lodestar to which their heads were turned. 'Brit Trumpeldor [Betar]', Jabotinsky wrote, 'seeks to do away with the "sha'atnez of the soul".'[19]

Jabotinsky believed that only concerted pressure for a Jewish state would force the British to accede. This would be the task in part of a strong, committed Jewish youth movement. Jabotinsky believed that the studied lack of urgency and a 'shallow conception of Zionism' had a debilitating effect on Jewish youth. He complained that the youth were being spoon-fed 'a grotesque Ahad Ha'amism' and that liberal figures such as Martin Buber were causing considerable damage.

Ahad Ha'am himself complained bitterly to me and to others that his teachings had been distorted, for he had always favoured the creation of a Jewish majority in Palestine.... To them is babbled the doctrine of Martin Buber, a typical provincial in outlook, a third-rate would-be thinker, with nine parts twisted phrases to one part ideas, and these neither his own nor of value. The youth is taught to regard Zionism as a dream and that it is desirable for it to remain a dream, never to become a reality.[20]

The pupils learned the lesson well, for his young acolytes proved far more radical than Jabotinsky himself. Despite himself, their mentor was the archetypal *fin de siècle* Jewish intellectual: cosmopolitan where they were often insular; assimilationist in inclination where they were often children of the *shtetl* (small village); a relativist where they were dogmatists; a secularist who approached Judaism like music – a matter of taste rather than belief; a writer who felt as much at home with the delights of Italian culture as with the world of Yiddish homilies; a nineteenth-century liberal democrat whose thought had been fashioned by the plight of East European Jewry and the carnage of the First World War.[21] Jabotinsky's elevation of individualism and the hint of anarchist philosophy in his political thought coloured the outlook of his young followers. The words of the rousing Betar anthem – '*ivri gum b'oni – ben sur*' – promoted the idea that even the poorest Jew was a prince, the bearer of the crown of King David.

As the head of Betar, Jabotinsky was viewed as the embodiment of the national ideal rather than the representative of the consensual wishes of the membership – the triumph of military discipline over democratic argument. Ritual and ceremony were thus an integral part of Betar's public image – an attraction which remained for Begin and many of his contemporaries. At the Third World Conference of Betar in Warsaw in September 1938, Jabotinsky told his audience that 'ritual demonstrates man's superiority over beast. What is the difference between a civilized man and a wild man? Ceremony. Everything in the world is ritual. A court trial – ceremony. How else is a case conducted in court?'[22]

The authoritarian tendencies which Jabotinsky absorbed from the growth of the far right in Europe were transmitted to and enthusiastically received in Betar. Even if the movement's members ultimately disagreed with Jabotinsky, they generally submitted to his will. Moreover, Betar's radical posture provided Jabotinsky with a political counterweight to the more traditional approach of the executive of the Revisionist movement. Yet Jabotinsky's inability to create a structured, hierarchical movement ruled out any centralized control of

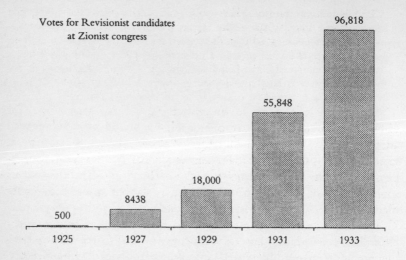

Figure 1.1   The growth of the Revisionist movement

Betar and thereby allowed those within the group a considerable degree of autonomy. In effect, they were responsible to no one except Jabotinsky himself.

At the Fifth Revisionist Zionist Conference in 1932, nevertheless, Betar unprecedentedly attacked Jabotinsky for being insufficiently assertive in refusing to secede from the World Zionist Organization. His reticence, in part, was due to the growing number of people who were voting for Revisionist candidates at Zionist Congresses.[23]

Still other Revisionists wished Jabotinsky to imbue his growing movement with a dictatorial structure on the European pattern. In a contribution to a Revisionist publication, however, he distanced himself from the aspirations of some of his youthful admirers:

> In the world of today, in particular among the younger generation, the dream of a dictator has become epidemic. I use this opportunity to state once more that I am an implacable enemy of this dream. I believe in the ideological patrimony of the nineteenth century, the century of Garibaldi and Lincoln, Gladstone and Hugo.[24]

Jabotinsky regarded Fascism as 'wholly and organically inapplicable to any aspect of Jewish life'.[25] On founding the Revisionist movement in 1925, Jabotinsky wrote scathingly about Italian Fascism:

There is today a country where 'programmes' have been replaced by the word of one man. Whatever he says is the programme. Popular vote is scorned. That country is Italy; the system is called Fascism; to give their prophet a title, they had to coin a new term – 'Duce' – which is a translation of that most absurd of all English words – 'leader'. Buffaloes follow a leader. Civilized men have no 'leaders'.[26]

Although a few of his followers expressed an 'understanding' for Hitler, Jabotinsky, for his part, bemoaned the fact that the Nazis had adopted the youth movement's brown attire. Yet on the surface, at least, in the eyes of the socialist Zionists, there was a sinister resemblance between the Revisionists and European Fascism. Jabotinsky's sophisticated arguments and his plethora of writings and speeches made no difference: the imagery remained.

The left also resented Betar's embrace of Jewish tradition under Jabotinsky's direction. Jabotinsky believed that it fortified Jewish identity and enhanced identification with the national struggle through an understanding of Jewish history and religious culture. Ironically, Jabotinsky privately expressed reservations similar to those of his socialist opponents on aspects of contemporary Judaism such as the role of women in Jewish religious life. Jabotinsky argued that Judaism died when the Land was lost two thousand years ago. The geographical isolation of the Jews had been replaced by a religious isolation which allowed them to survive as a people on the margins. Yet he argued that Judaism had not progressed in those two thousand years, and that the inner meaning of this religious encasement had been forgotten.

> If the people voluntarily encased their religious consciousness within an iron frame, dried it out to the point of fossilization, and turned a living religion into something like a mummified corpse of religion – it is clear that the holy treasure is not the religion, but something else, something for which this mummified corpse was supposed to serve as shell and protection.[27]

The ambivalence of Jabotinsky's position was evident in the contrast between his encouragement of the radicalization of his youthful followers and the actual results of that process. Whereas Jabotinsky could set himself limits or make a pragmatic decision to change course, the members of Betar were unable to see shades of grey. Interestingly enough, the Revisionist movement was relatively weak in Palestine itself. Even so, Jabotinsky attracted the support of a number of youthful intellectuals such as Abba Achimeir, Uri Zvi Greenberg and Avraham Stern. Quite a few of them had started off as committed and often doctrinaire socialists. Menachem Begin himself had been a one-time member of Hashomer Hatzair in Poland, the Marxist–Zionist youth group, while Uri Zvi Greenberg had belonged to Achdut Ha'avoda. The figure of Lenin was a focus of fascination and respect for them, as indeed it was for many young Zionists. This was due not to his brand of communism but, rather, to the fact that he alone had shown how to translate theory into practice – how to be a man of action and not just of words. Even Ben-Gurion saw Lenin as the leader to be imitated:

> Here is a man who is the quintessence of revolution, single-minded, disdaining all obstacles, faithful to his purpose, knowing neither surrender nor concession, a radical of radicals who knows how to crawl on his stomach through deepest mire to gain his end; an iron-willed man who spares neither the lives of grown men nor the blood of innocent children in order to further the revolutionary cause; the tactical genius who knows how to retreat from battle in order to gather forces for a new assault; who is not afraid to deny today what he supported yesterday, and to support tomorrow what he denied today; who does not permit webs of phrases to entrap his thought and refuses to be entangled either by formula or doctrine. For this sharp and clear vision sees only naked reality, the brutal truth, and the actual balance of forces.[28]

Ben-Gurion committed that appraisal of Lenin to his diary in 1923. The Leninist model of revolutionary determination was clearly interpreted differently by his far-right opponents. Yet the influence of the amoral teachings of Sergei Nechaev in Leninism doubtlessly provided an antecedent for the far right in their legitimization of revolutionary fanaticism and the extolling of expediency as a political virtue.

Jabotinsky was unimpressed by the exhortations of some of his youthful followers and publicly disagreed with groups such as Brit Ha'Biryonim in Palestine which synthesized a mixture of admiration for contemporary Fascism – and occasionally National Socialism – and a respect for the first-century Sicarii, who had proven adept at murdering a series of Jewish notables when they advocated a pragmatic approach toward Roman hegemony.

The crisis in the Revisionist movement came to a head at a meeting of the world council in Katowice early in 1933. The movement fragmented, with the liberal wing defecting to form the Jewish State Party in 1934. Jabotinsky lost his executive but retained the radicals within the movement and, of course, Betar. The New Zionist Organization, which was formed by Jabotinsky in 1935, thereby gained the adherence of the far right of the Zionist movement and operated independently of the World Zionist Organization. With the departure of the more traditional Revisionists, it became a far more authoritarian, militant grouping, shorn of any bourgeois trappings. This proved to be an advantage in terms of recruitment.

The increasingly dire situation in Europe now drew large numbers of Jews into Jabotinsky's orbit. Indeed, at its first congress the New Zionist Organization boasted more voters than at the World Zionist Organization's parallel congress. Yet it also meant that Jabotinsky's ability to adopt a centrist position between factions had been severely curtailed. As persecution increased in Europe and no progress was made towards the establishment of a Jewish state, the frustrations of Jabotinsky's youthful supporters increased – frustrations which could not be quenched by the most powerful grandiloquence. The components of far-right Zionism, Betar and the Irgun Zva'i Leumi (National Military Organization), were only connected through the person of Jabotinsky himself, and not through the machinery of a party bureaucracy. The tensions created through the organizations' different functions and self-perception of their destinies grew dramatically between 1935 and the outbreak of the Second World War. Thus Jabotinsky found it increasingly difficult to maintain his authority over Betar and the Irgun. The Arab Revolt of 1936 and the White Paper of 1939, which limited Jewish immigration to Palestine, severely weakened the strong control he had hitherto exerted. This was the political world into which Menachem Begin entered in the mid-1930s.

CHAPTER TWO

THE ADVOCATES OF REVOLT

The Rise of Betar

The World Conference of Betar in Cracow in 1935 was a seminal moment for the development of the Revisionist movement. It made such an impression that an observer could vividly describe it nearly fifty years afterwards:

> Jabotinsky had announced at an earlier conference that at the next one only Hebrew would be spoken [which in 1935 would have excluded a great many of those willing and anxious to speak]. A young man of pale complexion and with a black shock of hair mounted the rostrum and addressed the audience in the purest Hebrew [not a common accomplishment in those days]. The speech was enthralling, in form and content. It was constructed around the 'Hymn of Betar', written by Jabotinsky, which, in contrast to the insipid Hatikvah [Israel's national anthem], speaks of pride and defiance, torches and flames, and a whole noble and pitiless race of princes, and of conquering the summit or dying in the attempt – rousing, heady stuff. The audience was stirred, Jabotinsky was enchanted. He embraced the speaker: 'Such young men', he said, 'grow up all around me and I don't even know their names'....
>
> It was Begin. After all those years the recollection of that moment still lingers in the memory.[1]

Begin emerged as a charismatic leader of the maximalists within Betar, an advocate of military action. He strongly supported the idea of a military revolt against the British. Jabotinsky, on the other hand, had modified his views since the early 1930s; the ominous rise of Nazism persuaded him to move towards a more cautious position regarding the Zionist leadership. Begin strongly opposed an agreement between Ben-Gurion and Jabotinsky in 1934 – a *rapprochement* which in any event could not ultimately be sold to either camp.

By 1938, Jabotinsky's main concern was to avert a second partition of the Land of Israel, as advocated by the Peel Commission the previous year. Ben-Gurion had accepted the Commission's proposal for a Jewish state, an Arab state united with Trans-Jordan, and a British enclave. Jabotinsky formulated a ten-year plan to bring all the Jews of Eastern Europe to Palestine, not only as a means to escape persecution but also as the basis for retaining the East Bank – Trans-Jordan – which had been ceded to Abdullah 15 years before. Jabotinsky argued that millions of Jewish settlers would require the space on both sides of the River Jordan.

Begin had proposed civil disobedience as a course of action in Palestine at the time of the Katowice conference. Five years later, at the Third World Conference of Betar in Warsaw in 1938, he argued the case for military Zionism, much to the public irritation of Jabotinsky. Begin dismissed appeals to the 'world's conscience' and cited the armed struggles of Garibaldi and the Irish as examples to be respected. Jabotinsky's response was to tell Begin that there were three noises he hated: the clatter of cartwheels, the sound of railway carriages and, worst of all, the creaking of a door whose hinges required a good dose of oil. Begin's rhetoric, he told the audience, reminded him of the latter. Although Jabotinsky was respectfully heard out, his political influence over the young radicals had waned dramatically. They no longer obeyed the every word of their mentor, but carried out independent actions. Significantly, the clash at the conference was not reported in the Revisionist press.

The Irgun's spasmodic campaign was assisted by the short-sighted policies of the British High Commissioner, Sir Harold McMichael, whose belief in suppression through the short-sharp-shock school of thought simply fuelled the fire. His refusal to commute the death sentence on the youthful Shlomo Ben-Yosef, who had shot up a number of cars belonging to Arabs, gave the Irgun their first martyr. Moreover, Jabotinsky had become increasingly isolated from the Irgun's military aims.[2] He knew little about the Irgun's cooperation with the Polish military and their plan to bring 5000 armed and trained members of Betar to Palestine to form the nucleus of an uprising against the British. By the eve of World War II, Betar had become a law unto itself and was cooperating closely with the Irgun, which carried out attacks on both the British and the Arabs – much to the private anguish of Jabotinsky.

Although Jabotinsky humoured his youthful opponents with talk of an uprising, at the outbreak of war he placed his faith in diplomacy and Britain – and instructed his followers similarly to follow an anti-Nazi course. This new pro-British orientation provoked an internal debate within the Irgun. Avraham Stern, a leading Irgun militant, argued that the era of Zionist diplomacy had come to an end. There was no Jewish state, and the only way forward was armed struggle against the British. The Allied powers' war against Nazism was of no concern to them – 'a conflict between Gog and Magog'.[3] Stern made no distinction between 'Nazi-Fascist' states and the Western democracies, or between communists and social democrats. Stern and his supporters distanced themselves from Jabotinsky's support for Churchill and indeed rejected the Balfour Declaration as pro-British. He argued that 'no difference existed between Hitler and Chamberlain, between Dachau or Buchenwald and sealing the gates of Eretz Israel'.[4] Jabotinsky was disparagingly referred to as 'Hindenberg' or 'Petain' to indicate his ideological staleness as yesterday's man. By the time of Jabotinsky's death in the United States in 1940, a group around Avraham Stern had effectively broken with the founder of Revisionism.

There had been great resentment over the 1939 White Paper, where a quota of 10,000 immigrants a year for five years had been proposed. Jews, the White Paper stipulated, could become one-third of the total population, but then Arab consent would be required for further immigration. By early 1940, Jews were prohibited from buying land in Judea, Samaria, Western Galilee and the Northern Negev. This policy was backed up by a decision to turn back refugee ships that brought immigrants to Palestine. Despite the anger against British policy under which Jews were being trapped in Nazi-occupied Europe, Avraham Stern failed to persuade a majority of the Irgun to support him and eventually went his own way with his faction, the Irgun Zva'i Leumi b'Israel (Irgun Zva'i Leumi in Israel), known popularly as the Stern Group.

Avraham Stern's models for armed struggle were as diverse as the Jewish revolt against the Romans, the activities of the Narodnaya Volya (the Russian anarchists) and the Easter Rising in Dublin in 1916. Significantly, Stern came of political age at a time when the example of Lenin and the Bolsheviks indicated to many would-be revolutionaries that struggle could succeed if the right tactics were employed. He admired Boris Savinkov, the Russian Social Revolutionary who later became a member of Kerensky's government and a key player in the 'White' anti-Bolshevik forces that tried to defeat Lenin. Stern's *nom de guerre* was 'Yair' after Elazar Ben-Yair, who had committed suicide at Masada rather than fall into the hands of the Romans. Like other Revisionists, he took a great interest in the Irish struggle against the British and saw a parallel there – inasmuch as it showed that a small determined group could awaken the slumbering masses. He was particularly taken by the heroism of the Irishmen who occupied the General Post Office in Dublin on Easter Monday 1916. The example of Padraig Pearse's proclamation of the establishment of a Provisional Government of the Republic of Ireland 'to a bemused crowd of Dubliners' had a particular resonance:

> Irishmen and Irish women: in the name of God and of the dead generations from which she receives her old tradition of nationhood, Ireland through us summons her children to her flag and strikes for her freedom.... We declare the right of the people of Ireland to the ownership of Ireland and to the unfettered control of Irish destinies, to be sovereign and indefeasible. The long usurpation of that right by a foreign people and government has not extinguished the right, nor can it ever be extinguished except by the destruction of the Irish people.[5]

James Connolly, the commandant-general of the Uprising, spoke about the flag of free Ireland flying over Dublin for the first time in 700 years. The example of a small group of patriots willing to fight the might of the British Army with few weapons and to sacrifice their lives for their cause impressed Stern. He understood that the execution of the signatories to the proclamation at Kilmainham prison a few days later had awakened the Irish people to their struggle. As martyrs for the cause, their political influence was far more powerful in death than it had ever been in life.

Although the Stern Group never amounted to more than a couple of hundred adherents, its obsession with initiating a military struggle against the British in Palestine outweighed all other considerations. At a time when Britain stood alone against the conquering armies of Nazism, Stern saw the British as the central enemy of the Jewish people because they had so far reneged on their promise to establish a national home for the Jews. Whilst both mainstream Zionism and the adherents of official Revisionism cooperated militarily with the British against Hitler, Stern overlooked the anti-Semitism of the Axis powers. He looked for ways and means to utilize their common opposition to the British to secure a sovereign Jewish state. Yet he found few domestic allies; his doctrine 'the enemy of my enemy is my friend' distanced him from even the radical right in Palestine.

After a suspension from the Hebrew University for disruptive activities, Stern studied in Florence, Italy, in the early 1930s. He was greatly impressed and influenced by Mussolini's regime, which did not enact discriminatory legislation against Italian Jews until 1938 – and then only under pressure from Hitler. Unlike the Germans, the Italians did not exhibit racist paranoia. Jews had been amongst the founders of the Italian Fascist Movement and a not inconsequential number voted for Mussolini. The Duce's influential mistress, Margherita Sarfatti, was Jewish, and so was Guido Jung, a finance minister in the early 1930s. The Duce himself regarded Jabotinsky as a 'Jewish Fascist' and there was a healthy respect for Mussolini in far-right circles in Palestine.

Although he had opposed Italian Fascism and Mussolini, Jabotinsky also recognized that Jews in Italy did not suffer from anti-Semitic persecution.

> Whatever we may think of Fascism's other points, there is no doubt that the Italian brand of Fascist ideology is, at least, an ideology of racial equality. Let us not be so humble as to pretend that this does not matter – that racial equality is too insignificant an idea to outbalance the absence of civic freedom. For it is not true. I am a journalist who would choke without freedom of the press, but I affirm it is simply blasphemous to say that, in the scale of civic rights, even the freedom of speech comes before the equality of men. Equality comes first, super-first; and Jews should be the first to remember it, and to hold that a regime maintaining that principle in a world turning cannibal does partly but considerably atone for its other shortcomings.[6]

There was, then, a measure of 'understanding' for Mussolini in Revisionist circles. This provided the bridge for Stern to establish contact with the Italian Consulate in Jerusalem at the end of the 1930s – despite the newly introduced anti-Jewish laws. The Italian advance in the Middle East and the bombing of Tel Aviv and Haifa further encouraged Stern. He submitted a plan which elucidated how the Italians would assist the Stern Group in expelling the British from Palestine. In return, the new Jewish homeland would become a corporate state and a satellite of the Axis powers. Jerusalem, with the exception of the Jewish holy places, would be handed over to the control of the Vatican.

When Italy had been easily repulsed by the Allies and its forces were in retreat, Stern turned his attention to securing the assistance of Nazi Germany to drive out the British. Working with the Nazis was not an uncommon occurrence in other Third World countries where nationalists were trying to rid themselves of the colonial order. For Jews to work with anti-Semites seemed bizarre, yet Stern saw precedents in the work of Herzl and Jabotinsky. Herzl had met the tsarist Minister of the Interior, Plehve, shortly after the Kishinev pogrom in 1903. Jabotinsky, for his part, had negotiated with the representative of Semion Petliura a few years after his forces had butchered Jews in massacres in the Ukraine. Both Herzl and Jabotinsky rationalized their behaviour with the claim that such encounters were in the Jewish interest regardless of the personal attitudes and past behaviour of the protagonists.[7] Jabotinsky had accepted Max Nordau's dismissal of the notion of 'the anti-Semitism of men' in favour of 'the anti-Semitism of things' – 'the inherent xenophobia of the body social or the body economic under which we suffer'.[8]

The difference, however, was that Stern saw the saving and protection of Jewish lives as a secondary matter. His main concern was to secure a Jewish state – all other questions were relegated to a lesser status. Stern perceived Hitler as the latest in a long line of anti-Semites who could be won over if the common interest was identified. In Palestine at that time, Stern was not alone in regarding Hitler as a persecutor and not an exterminator. The dream of attaining a Jewish state dominated Zionist thinking and the very idea of the Final Solution was unthinkable in 1940. Thus, in December 1940, Stern sent an emissary to meet a representative of the German Foreign Office in Beirut. Stern believed that Hitler wanted Germany to be *judenrein* through emigration. Stern proposed a '*volkischnationalen Hebraertum*' allied to the German Reich and requested the recruitment of 40,000 Jews from occupied Europe for a proposed invasion of Palestine to oust the British. He even quoted one of the Führer's recent speeches to this effect to support his case.

The Germans did not take the proposal seriously. The ideological issue aside, the Germans did not wish to antagonize friendly Arab nationalists in both Palestine and the Arab world. But even Stern's mentors on the far right were astounded by a logic which did not view the Nazis as the central enemy of the Jewish people. Even when there was imminent danger of invasion by the German armies, Stern opposed the conscription of young Jews and military cooperation with the British. He argued that as long as the British refused to allow the establishment of a Jewish army, the duty of the Jews of Palestine was to fight 'the local anti-Semitic administration'. According to Stern, those Jews who did volunteer for the 'Palestinian' units of the British Army were not even allowed to use the washrooms reserved for European soldiers.

Stern saw his approach to the Germans as part of the same progression of contacts with the Polish military and the Italians. Yet the ideological contortions of Stern and their consequences bewildered the majority in the Irgun Zva'i Leumi. They had a more realistic view of the Nazi threat. After the Reichstag speech of Hitler in April 1939, David Raziel, the Irgun commander, asked Reuben Hecht to go to Europe to investigate the possibilities of attacking Nazi Germany with chemical weapons.[9] Raziel also wanted cooperation with the British to ward off Arab hostility, and agreed to go to Baghdad where pro-Nazi Arab nationalist forces under the Mufti of Jerusalem and Rashid Ali were all-powerful.[10] Raziel's agreement to undertake this mission for the British was conditional upon their willingness to allow him to apprehend the Mufti of Jerusalem. Instead Raziel lost his life in a bombing raid. The Revisionist movement had lost both Jabotinsky and the commander of the Irgun within a short period.

Stern's political dissent and military activities added considerably to the Irgun's lack of direction and general confusion at this time. Jabotinsky's son, Eri, described Stern as an unselfish patriot and fierce opponent who nevertheless had done 'more to harm our movement in Palestine than the whole Zionist Organization put together'.[11] In a letter to Hillel Kook, Raziel himself described Stern 'as a counter-feiter ... where no borders of reality exist for him and a double demagogue times eight'.[12]

In a private letter, Raziel's successor as commander of the Irgun, Ya'akov Meridor, confided that Stern and his people were

> ravenous for power, only for power, and hope to achieve it by all means and all ways. Yair [Stern] clearly hopes that when the Germans get here he will be Deputy-Governor of the Jews by virtue of his conspiracy, but he forgets one thing: just how little the promises of the Germans can be relied on at all. Meanwhile, Radio Berlin has already announced that the Jews in this country have already surrendered to the Germans ... I am looking for the logic in all this, but I cannot find it ... [Arab] riots are only started under the influence of German money and arms. If the IZL in Israel [Stern Group] is also linked to the Axis, then they must also be linked to the Mufti and his gang! Logic can find no other solution. We always con-demned the defeatists and the supporters of the idea of an Arab federation with the Jewish state in the middle. And here a new axis is developing in the Near East: the Mufti, Yair and Rashid Ali in Iraq. I am still walking about in a dream and I cannot believe my eyes.[13]

Tensions in the Stern Group almost led to a split at the end of 1941. Unlike the participants in the Easter Uprising in Ireland, the group had so far failed to fire the imagination of the public at large. The contacts with the Poles, Italians and Germans had come to nothing. Even the bank robberies the Group carried out began to antagonize when Jewish passers-by were killed. An attempt to assassinate two leading British detectives by means of booby-trapped explosives led, through misidentification, to the killing of two well-liked Jewish policemen, Schiff and Goldman. This was condemned not only by the ordinary man and woman in the street but also by the official Revisionists, who published 'wanted' photographs of the Stern Group in their newspaper.

Eventually, the leadership of the group was eliminated through killing and imprisonment. Stern acted out his self-assigned role to the end, refusing to take refuge from his political opponents. On 12 February 1942, Avraham Stern was shot and killed by the British. This was shortly before Menachem Begin's release from Soviet imprisonment and his arrival in Palestine with General Anders' army. When Begin announced the beginning of 'The Revolt' against the British as the new Irgun commander in 1944, he made no mention of Avraham Stern, who was in reality the originator of the military struggle against the British presence in Palestine. Jabotinsky, who had actually opposed military action, was instead proclaimed the symbolic 'father' of the revolt. In turn, the newly resurrected Lehi (Fighters for the Freedom of Israel), which had grown out of the original Stern Group, mythologized its founder, later glossing over any reference to the now embarrassing Nazi–Fascist connections. Yet as the precise details of Stern's ideological direction began to fade in the public memory, his activities came to be viewed by growing numbers as the spark of activism which ignited a national liberation struggle against the British, standing in stark contrast to the bland inactivity of the mainstream Zionists and the official Revisionists. Avraham Stern passed into history as a martyr for the cause, and the manner of his death an example to those who came after him.

Ben-Gurion, the Irgun and Lehi

Within a few days of becoming Prime Minister in 1977, Begin commented that his rise to the premiership 'paled in comparison' with the heights reached as commander of the Irgun Zva'i Leumi. In a new introduction to The Revolt, Begin wrote in October 1977 that 'it was a higher task to lead the fighting patriots in that unequal struggle under the heaviest odds possible, of the few against the many.' The Churchillian tone indicates more than mere nostalgia. Begin's recollection of those exciting, dangerous times reflected a certain romantic escapism – a marked characteristic of his strand of Revisionism and one which created a lifelong sense of solidarity within the movement while causing great irritation to its opponents. There existed a strong sense that the time had come to recognize the role of the 'dissidents' – the *porshim* – and to reclaim history. Indeed, it was not by chance that at the ceremony to commemorate the anniversary of Jabotinsky's death – only a few weeks after the Likud's victory – the new Prime Minister, Menachem Begin, was introduced as the commander of the Irgun, while his eventual successor, then speaker of the Knesset, Yitzhak Shamir, was presented as 'a member of Lehi'.

Begin's declaration of the Irgun's military revolt against the British signalled the end of the 'armistice' which his two predecessors, David Raziel and Yaakov Meridor, had both observed despite the activities of Avraham Stern and Lehi. Although the Irgun effectively joined Lehi in the armed struggle, the former regarded themselves as the military reflection of a political philosophy which viewed armed rebellion against the occupying regime as both inevitable and necessary in order to establish a Jewish state.

Throughout his life, Begin distanced himself from the charge of terrorism. 'We were not a "terrorist" group – neither in the structure of our organization, in our methods of warfare, nor in spirit.'[14] Begin considered the Irgun to be a legitimate underground army engaged in warfare with another legitimate military force. Begin justified incidents such as the hanging of the British Army sergeants in the orange grove as an equal retaliation for the execution of his own men engaged in the normal course of warfare. The act was also a psychological weapon aimed at an empire unused to considering military rebellions in the colonies in the same way that it viewed conflict between European sovereign states.

Unlike Raziel or even Jabotinsky, Begin felt no particular warmth towards Britain. When a young member of the Irgun was flogged in Jerusalem at the end of 1946, Begin threatened the British in the Irgun's underground publication, *Herut*.

For hundreds of years, you have been whipping 'natives' in your colonies – without retaliation. In your foolish pride you regard the Jews in Eretz Israel as natives too. You are mistaken. Zion is not exile. Jews are not Zulus. You will not whip Jews in their Homeland. And if the British Authorities whip them – British officers will be whipped publicly in return.[15]

If the deaths of innocents were incurred during the course of the rebellion, Begin reasoned that such things inevitably happened during the course of a bloody confrontation between two armies; events did not always go according to plan, despite the best of intentions to operate only against the defined enemy. The destruction of the King David Hotel and the killings of Arabs in the village of Deir Yassin,[16] for example, were excused in this fashion. This was no mere public-relations exercise to explain away bad news. It was a cardinal principle of the Revisionist faith that Judea would arise *b'dum v'esh* – 'in blood and fire'. There was also a sense that 'the conscience of the world' – as stimulated by the Irgun's fronts and friends abroad – would increase the pressure on the British to leave. The moral scruples of the British would sooner or later, it was argued, be provoked. The spectacle of British soldiers clubbing concentration-camp survivors and turning back the bedraggled passengers of the 'Exodus' ships would symbolize the moral dilemma of their position.

Lehi, for its part, was organized more along the lines of the nineteenth-century conspiratorial Russian anarchists, who considered the use of terror and assassination as valid political tools. Numbering no more than a few hundred, Lehi was run by a triumvirate of Natan Friedman-Yellin (Yellin-Mor), Yitzhak Yezernitsky (Shamir) and Israel Sheib (Eldad). The organization was an amorphous coalition of differing political tendencies with a preponderance of intellectuals and mystics as well as gunmen. Yellin-Mor wrote that Lehi's *raison d'être* was 'to break the foreign ruler's willpower and place the problem on the world agenda. Together with von Clausewitz, we believed war to be a continuation of diplomacy by other means, but we also believed political action to be the companion of war and its continuation.'[17]

Lehi denounced not only mainstream Zionism but also the New Zionist Organization – the official Revisionists – for relying on diplomacy: their 'unrealistic belief that petitions, speeches, meetings, pronouncements and coalitions will coerce the British occupier to surrender'. Weizmann and Jabotinsky were condemned for residing in London, 'the capital of the conqueror'. Jabotinsky was berated because he did not adopt 'sufficiently extreme methods'. The second issue of *He'Hazit*, the Lehi publication, asked if it was possible to achieve liberation through terrorism. 'The answer is no! If the question is, are terrorist activities useful for the progress of revolution and liberation, the answer is yes.'[18]

Avraham Stern's formative leadership had couched revolutionary violence in quasi-mystical terms based on the approach that 'the book and the sword came bound together from heaven' (*Midrash Vayikra Rabba* 35:8). His 'Eighteen Principles of National Renewal' proclaimed a Jewish state from 'the Great River of Egypt' to the Euphrates and the building of the Third Temple. Only Eldad, who was in charge of Lehi's ideology and education, truly remained loyal to this approach. The martyred Stern was now canonized. Five years after Stern's killing, Eldad wrote in the Lehi bulletin:

> Avraham Stern did not lose a lot. He lost his body, his life which long ago had been consecrated to the Homeland. But within Avraham Stern's body had lived Yair – an idea, a truth, a flame and these could not be destroyed by bullets. Here was the enemy's greatest mistake. Yair fell like a giant tree in a field covered with bushes. His blood permeated the ground, watered the seed of freedom and before long, new miraculous plants grew up.[19]

Ideologically, Lehi could not unite with the Irgun. It preferred to remain independent and not under Begin's control. Lehi's growing support for the USSR affirmed that Stern's line, 'the enemy of my enemy is my friend', was still a guiding principle. Stalin had simply replaced Hitler and Mussolini as the greatest threat to the British Empire. Begin questioned Lehi's policy of automatically supporting the latest adversary of the British. He argued that anti-British views did not automatically mean support for the Zionist struggle. In addition, Yellin-Mor's gradual movement to the left and growing sympathy for socialism did not impress Begin, who had suffered in the Gulag. Yellin-Mor pursued an anti-imperialist line which led him to advocate an alliance with Arab liberation movements in the Middle East who were struggling to throw off the colonial yoke.

Shamir, who was in control of operations, appeared to be the least ideologically innovative. He projected himself as taciturn and ruthless, dedicated to the armed struggle. Yet Shamir's *nom de guerre* in the subterranean, conspiratorial world of Lehi was 'Michael' – after Michael Collins, the progenitor of the IRA and the Irish struggle against the British. The Black and Tans' murderous conflict with the IRA, the torture and the hangings, the readiness for sacrifice and martyrdom, and the importance of anti-British propaganda – especially in America – provided a salutary model for both Lehi and the Irgun. The Irish struggle for independence was almost obligatory reading for Jabotinsky's disciples. They faced the same enemy and a similar colonial situation. Although other movements such as Garibaldi's campaign in Italy were noted, it was the Irish situation that most closely resembled the position in Palestine in both nature and time.

Begin quoted the Irish example in defence of 'military Zionism' against Jabotinsky at the Betar conference in Warsaw in 1938. David Raziel, the commander of the Irgun during its initial campaign against Arab targets in the late 1930s, had studied the Irish struggle in depth. Avraham Stern had translated *The Victory of Sinn Fein* by P.S. O'Hegarty, an ardent admirer of Michael Collins, into Hebrew in 1941.[20] Both Stern and Collins had died violent deaths as young men in their mid-30s. The example of the Irish struggle was also used by prisoners in the dock. Avshalom Haviv, a member of the Irgun, accused the British of 'drowning the Irish Uprising in rivers of blood ... yet free Ireland rose in spite of you'. Quoting George Bernard Shaw's denunciation of British treatment of the leadership of the Easter Rebellion, Haviv told the court:

> if you were wise, British tyrants, and would learn from history, the example of Ireland and America would be enough to convince you that you ought to hurry out of our country which is enveloped in the flames of holy revolt, flames which are not extinguished but only flare up the more with every drop of blood shed by you or in the fight against you.[21]

Haviv went to the gallows at Acre prison in July 1947. The following day, the Irgun hanged Sergeants Cliff Martin and Mervyn Paice.

Thus, Begin propagated the idea of an 'open underground', a notion that distanced the Irgun from the closed world of Lehi, whose members remained armed at all times. Begin's attempts at a reunification between the Irgun and Lehi failed in 1944. Although there was liaison between the groups, Begin was not forewarned about the assassination of Lord Moyne and only learned about it from the radio.

The killing of a British minister who was Churchill's friend persuaded Ben-Gurion to move against both the Irgun and Lehi. He clearly could ill afford to allow control to slip from his hands. In an address to the Histadrut Conference in November 1944, he condemned the perpetrators of 'murder and robbery, blackmail and theft'. Ben-Gurion understood the Irgun and Lehi as the offspring of the European far right, which in its pre-war existence had not only utilized the democracy of the ballot box as a route to power but had also upheld the validity of a *coup d'état*. The course of the Irish struggle has also led to schism and internecine violence. This, too, had been Michael Collins's legacy.

> There is no compromise, no equivocation. The way of terror or the way of Zionism, gangsterism or an organized Yishuv; murder from ambush and banditry in darkness or the voluntary self-discipline of youth movements,

of farmers and industrialists, a union of freedom and cooperation in
argument, decision and act.

Whenever and wherever there is a self-governing community of free
men, gangsters find no place. If gangsters rule – free men are homeless.
Take your choice – violence and repression, or constitutional liberties ...
let us rise up against terror and its agencies, and smite them. The time for
words is past.[22]

Ben-Gurion went on to call for the expulsion of anyone found
assisting the dissidents, whether from the factory or kibbutz, from
school or college. 'Every organized group must spew them out ...
refuge and shelter must be stringently denied these wild men.... It is
our hearts – not the heart of Britain – that the terrorist iron has
entered. Our hands then, no others, must pluck it out.'

Throughout the winter and spring of 1944/5, the Haganah – often
in cooperation with the British – hunted down members of the Irgun
in the spirit of Ben-Gurion's address. Significantly, the Lehi, whose
killing of Lord Moyne had sparked off this entire campaign, were
hardly touched. Ben-Gurion clearly utilized the incident to crack
down on his main rival, the Irgun, which ironically had no part in
the assassination. The Irgun's activities were thus considerably curtailed.
Begin's approach was rooted in the belief that 'the proper balance of
official condemnation and public toleration would permit the Irgun
to function. The longer the revolt lasted, the more obvious it would
be that the original fears of the Yishuv concerning such provocation
were groundless, and the more difficult for the authorized agencies
to act against the Irgun with rigour.'[23]

Partly for this reason, Begin ensured that the Irgun did not retaliate – not that they were in any real position to do so. He was also
mindful of the easy temptation to wage civil war which had afflicted
so many other liberation movements. Jewish tradition had preserved
– as almost a prohibition – the memory of the killings and the anarchy
within a Jerusalem besieged by Roman armies during the first Jewish
Revolt. The killing of one Jew by another was undoubtedly deeply
abhorrent to Begin – although the Irgun did kill several Jews who
were in the service of British Intelligence. His emotional broadcast
shortly after Ben-Gurion had ordered the shelling of the Irgun arms
ship, the *Altalena*, later in 1948, when several members of the Irgun
were killed, was another indication of Begin's extreme sensitivity in
this area. Even so, Ben-Gurion's ruthless pragmatism and the depth
of his determination to retain political control were an unknown
factor for the Irgun.

The day after Lord Moyne's assassination, Weizmann wrote to Churchill to express his 'deep moral indignation and horror'. He feared that it would weaken his good relations with the British. The world of sedate and patient diplomacy was at a total remove from that inhabited by the Lehi gunmen and the Irgun bomb-makers. Ben-Gurion was also less sensitive. He had already moved away from es-pousing the principle of a Jewish homeland towards demanding the establishment of a Jewish state. Yet there was still a hesitation within the Zionist leadership about demanding statehood. Unlike Weizmann, Ben-Gurion was ready to act against the British if necessary. Ben-Gurion's keen grasp of the tactical realities led him to utilize all the options available to achieve the ultimate goal of a Jewish state. Dip-lomacy and extensive public relations in America and Britain were certainly important, but so was military pressure. In one sense, there-fore, the activities of the Irgun and Lehi provided Ben-Gurion with more political cards to play. The publicized horror arising from their actions, combined with official Zionist condemnation, hastened the process of British decision-making. From Ben-Gurion's standpoint, as long as the 'dissidents' directed their efforts along ultimately productive paths, then their efforts were constructive in the overall strategy. If, however, their unpredictability or military incompetence – as in the case of the bombing of the King David Hotel – exceeded a critical threshold such that they came to be perceived as a political liability, then the mainstream would turn against them to exert control. As real power passed from Weizmann to Ben-Gurion, the latter increasingly inhabited the hard world of choices and options – in stark contrast to the impassioned declarations of Begin in the underground.

Both Ben-Gurion and Weizmann had greeted the election of a Labour government in Britain with great enthusiasm. They truly believed that the Attlee government would deliver on their long-standing support for Labour Zionist demands. There had been no change in Labour policy throughout the period of wartime coalition. By 1944, Labour Party Conference resolutions in support of a Jewish homeland had become more vociferous as the news of the extermi-nation of European Jewry began to reach Britain. Only a few weeks before taking power, Hugh Dalton told the Labour Party Conference that 'we consider Jewish immigration into Palestine should be per-mitted without the present limitations which obstruct it ... and in consultation with the Soviet and American governments, [we should] see whether we cannot get that common support for a policy which will give us a happy, free and prosperous Jewish State in Palestine.'

Yet a few months after the 1945 election, a volte-face by the new Labour government offered only a new Commission of Inquiry, a promise of 1500 immigrants a month, and the suggestion that the surviving remnant of European Jewry should remain in the countries of their extermination. The British Foreign Office preferred the establishment of an Arab state under effective British suzerainty where the Jews would be guaranteed minority rights. The new Foreign Minister, Ernest Bevin, viewed the Jews essentially in religious terms. He was unsympathetic to the Zionist cause and otherwise brusque towards Jewish sensitivities in general. Attlee, for his part, although more diplomatic in his approach, shared this tunnel vision. A member of the Commission, Richard Crossman recalled years later:

> On the first occasion that I spoke to Mr Attlee, after he had rejected our Report, he greeted me with the words, 'I'm disappointed in you, Dick. The Report you have produced is grossly unfair.'
> I was genuinely puzzled and said, 'Unfair to the Jews or to the Arabs?'
> To this, he replied crossly, 'No, unfair to Britain, of course. You've let us down by giving way to the Jews and the Americans.'[24]

In his incisive book on the Anglo-American Commission of Inquiry, Crossman touched on the changed attitudes towards the Palestine question:

> Was it that we were all on the lookout in 1939 for *appeasement* and saw the Arabs as a Fascist force to which Jewish liberty was being sacrificed? Partly, perhaps. But I suspect that six years of this war have fundamentally changed our *emotions*. We were pro-Jew emotionally in 1939 as part of 'anti-fascism'. We were not looking at the actual problems of Palestine, but instinctively standing up for the Jews, whenever there was a chance to do so. Now, most of us are not *emotionally* pro-Jew, but only rationally 'anti-antisemitic' which is a very different thing.[25]

When the fact of the volte-face had sunk in, Ben-Gurion moved from hunting down the Irgun to working with them. The faith which Weizmann had placed in the British had seemingly proved groundless. Conversely, the validity of the Revisionist slogan 'Rak Kak' (Only Thus), and the teachings of Jabotinsky which embellished it, took on the mantle of revelation. For the Revisionists, the military struggle against the British was a matter of good judgement and original truth. For Ben-Gurion and the Labour movement, it was a question of timing and the exploration of diverse options.

In November 1945, an agreement was signed by the three military groups to establish the Tenuat Ha'Meri Ha'Ivri – the United Resistance

Movement. The military offensive for the first time now involved the Haganah, which dwarfed the Irgun in numbers thirtyfold. Despite the cooperation, there was still a tension between the three groups which sometimes led to military mistakes. Begin, while feeling vindicated about his military initiative, refused to integrate the Irgun with the Haganah. There were those on the other side who felt strongly that the actions of the Irgun and Lehi were now blurring the professionalism and good name of the Zionist endeavour. Such reticence showed itself in the relatively few operations carried out by the Haganah and Palmach compared to the increasing proportion on the part of the Irgun and Lehi. The political repercussions emanating from the botched destruction of the King David Hotel and the deaths of many innocent people – British, Jews and Arabs – finally terminated the agreement. In August 1946, the Haganah ceased its military campaign against the British. Ben-Gurion called the Irgun 'the enemy of the Jewish People'. Yet, together with Lehi, they continued their military campaign, increasing the number of their operations almost tenfold.[26]

CHAPTER THREE

A JEWISH STATE
IN THE LAND OF ISRAEL

The Birth of Herut

The State of Israel has arisen. And it has arisen 'Only Thus'. Through blood, through fire, with an outstretched hand and a mighty arm, with suffering and with sacrifice.

So spoke Menachem Begin on 15 May 1948, the day the State of Israel was established. Yet Begin's military campaign had not simply been directed against the British. The fight against the colonial power subsumed the equally important objective of the attainment of the entire Land of Israel, Eretz Israel. The British, in Revisionist eyes, had gone back on their word to the Jews. They had partitioned the Land in 1922 — with the acquiescence of the leadership of the Zionist movement — and given Eastern Eretz Israel to the Emir Abdullah to create his own kingdom of Trans-Jordan. On 29 November 1947 the United Nations General Assembly divided the Land a second time. Western Eretz Israel was partitioned into two states, one Jewish, the other Arab. In the face of Revisionist, left-wing and, indeed, religious opposition, Ben-Gurion, Weizmann and the mainstream leadership accepted the principle of partition yet again. They were prepared to build on whatever they were given. Begin, like Jabotinsky before him, regarded the pragmatism of Mapai as a capitulation of the highest order. Whereas Ben-Gurion implicitly left the recovery of the whole land to future generations, Begin demanded it immediately.

On 15 May 1948, Begin surfaced from the underground to broadcast on Irgun Radio. Here he articulated the idea that the War of Independence had not in fact ended, but was, in essence, ongoing:

The foundation has indeed been laid, but only the foundation, for true independence. One phase of our battle for freedom, for the return of all the people of Israel to its homeland, for the restoration of the entire Land of Israel to a People who have made a covenant with God – has now come to an end.[1]

Thus at the very birth of the State of Israel, Begin bitterly attacked the division of Mandatory Palestine – and those Jews who willingly accepted that division – as 'a crime, a blasphemy, an abortion'. He did not permit the siege mentality then prevailing to restrict his options, but instead insisted on the borders promised by the British. Begin told his audience that 'whoever does not recognize our natural right to our entire homeland, does not recognize our right to any part of it.... The soldiers of Israel will yet unfurl our flag over David's Tower and our ploughshares will yet cleave the fields of Gilead.' David's Tower was then situated in Arab Jerusalem, while the fields of Gilead were on the East Bank of the Jordan, an integral part of King Abdullah's territory. Begin continued: 'We shall continue to bear the vision of full independence. And we shall bring it about. For it is an iron rule of life: that which comes between the people's state and the people's homeland must disappear. The state will cover the homeland. The homeland will be the state.'

Thus, although Begin advocated a continuing war of independence, he was nevertheless astute enough to locate his demands within a political context rather than a military one. In his address to 'the citizens of the Hebrew homeland' on that Saturday night in May 1948, Begin proclaimed the end of the underground and the emergence of Tenuat Ha'Herut – the Freedom Movement. 'The Herut [Freedom] Movement will arise out of the depths of the Hebrew Underground and will be created by our great fighting family, composed of all classes of people from all over the world, of all classes and tendencies who rallied to the banner of the Irgun Zva'i Leumi.'[2]

Herut thus came into existence at the precise moment that the Irgun Zva'i Leumi ceased to operate as an independent force. Unlike the leadership of Lehi, Begin made a determined effort – albeit with difficulty – to adapt to the reality of statehood. The débâcle of the *Altalena*, the Irgun arms ship, was a sharp lesson that he – and the Irgun in general – could no longer behave as they had in the recent past. They were constrained by the legal parameters of statehood.

The *Altalena* episode, in which several members of the Irgun were killed, crystallized all of Begin's vehemence against the Mapai establishment. An unrepentant Ben-Gurion spoke of the 'holy cannon' which had carried out the act. Yet in Begin's eyes, at Ben-Gurion's behest

Jews had killed Jews – and this was a bridge he was not willing to cross. Writing a few days after the incident, Begin exclaimed:

> now when we have to endure the 'Emergency Regulations' drawn up by the British oppressor and now applied in the State of Israel, in these days when a definite step towards bloody tyranny has been taken by the government of Israel, there is an added significance in that word 'herut' [freedom] which is engraved upon our banner and our hearts. It is plain and obvious and needs no explanation.

He then issued a dire warning to the new administration:

> We will be ruled neither by whip nor by sten-gun.... Those who attempt thus to rule us will fail as surely as did the British ... perhaps not immediately, but surely in the very near future. That is an unalterable law, a law of iron. Tyranny in Israel cannot endure.[3]

This vitriol did not appear as an article, but in an unsigned introduction to the principles and programme of the new Herut movement. While Begin resisted the call to insurrection from old comrades such as Israel Eldad, his strident call to opposition characterized the Herut movement from its very beginning. As such, it was symptomatic of Begin's difficulty – in spite of himself – in making the transition towards conventional parliamentary norms.

In a speech in the Old City of Jerusalem at the beginning of August 1948, Begin accused the mainstream leadership of being gutless and blinded by the belief that there would be no war with the Arabs. Ben-Gurion and his followers, he told his audience, were unprepared for war. Israeli soldiers carried inferior arms and had paid for the fact with their lives. He further accused the leadership of having missed opportunities in not exploiting the ceasefires in June and July 1948. Israel had thus attained only a pyrrhic victory. Looking down upon a crowd from a high balcony, Begin said 'We had an opportunity to reach the [River] Jordan – and beyond – because in front of us were *analphabetim* [illiterates] who did not know why they were fighting.'[4]

Such language coloured the principles and programme of the new Herut movement. It echoed the nationalist ethos in Eastern Europe – and particularly Pilsudski's Poland – during the inter-war years. Yet, all this was now a discredited force. In its worst incarnation, it had brought death and destruction to millions in a fashion unimaginable in the 1930s. The year 1945 had borne witness to an ideological victory as well as to a military one. Those nationalist regimes which had survived the conflagration through a policy of wily non-intervention, such as those of Franco and Salazar in the Iberian peninsula, were treated as pariah states. Like nationalists in other struggles during the post-war period, Begin had to respond to the spirit of the times despite the Irgun's – and, by extension, the Revisionists' – flirtation with the European far right. The adjustment to normal political life was not easy. On emerging from the underground, Begin promised to obey the laws – 'for they are our laws' – and to respect the government – 'for it is our government' – but he also warned the Provisional Government that it should not 'through appeasement and tyranny, create a new underground'.

The *Altalena* affair and Begin's antagonistic style went far beyond the bounds of normal political opposition as far as the left was concerned. They viewed Begin solely as a representative of an authoritarian nationalism which had wreaked havoc in the inter-war years – and caused many ultimately to suffer under Nazi hegemony. The lesson of the recent past was that such figures should be stopped before their political bandwagons began to gather speed. The left perceived it as a question of physical and political survival. In a debate on the *Altalena* affair in the Provisional Council, a Mapam representative rejected benevolent pleas from religious parties to paper over the cracks.

> We all feel that for at least one generation, we must preserve our internal unity in order to fulfil the important tasks of defeating the enemy and building our state. [But] how can we tolerate this hostile internal force in our midst which always carries a sword and brandishes it at us? We are at its mercy, for its commander may at any moment give the order to kill or tell his soldiers 'Do not murder, the time has not yet come.'[5]

Several members of the Provisional Council believed that Begin's inflammatory language following the sinking of the *Altalena* was an incitement to civil war and lent credence to the possibility of a Herut putsch.

Ben-Gurion publicly defended his action as one that stemmed the tide of potential chaos and erected a bulwark against the prospect of a plethora of private armies with accompanying warlords. Ben-Gurion rarely tried to rationalize his policies in the face of Herut anger. He had nothing but contempt for Begin. And in the specific case of the *Altalena* affair, Ben-Gurion had no intention of renouncing his action or diminishing his authority.

Mr Pinkas asked many questions in Begin's name. The Irgun Zva'i Leumi's 'leader' may be a very important person, an ardent patriot, a great fighter and a brilliant commander, and it may be a great honour to speak in his name, but I do not owe him any answers, even if the questions are asked by surrogates.[6]

Despite a concerted attempt by the movement to purge itself of counterproductive tendencies, such an exercise could not be conducted overnight. What is more, Mapai and its supporters were doubly keen for political reasons that Herut should be tarred with the fascist brush. Thus, when Begin made his first visit to the United States at the end of 1948, there was considerable opposition and general animosity to the presence of the Irgun commander. In a letter to the *New York Times*, Albert Einstein and several other prominent American Jews condemned Herut's activities in the United States as 'a mixture of ultra-nationalism, religious mysticism and racial superiority'. They commented that,

it is unbelievable that anyone who opposes fascism, wherever it may be, should find himself able to support the movement represented by Mr Begin, if he has been accurately informed about Mr Begin's political record and his intentions for the future.... He speaks today of freedom, democracy and anti-imperialism, while not so long ago he was openly preaching the doctrine of a fascist state.[7]

Begin retaliated in a speech at the Carnegie Hall. Acknowledging the eminence of the formulator of the theory of relativity, Begin commented:

I now know that the political judgement and indeed knowledge of a great scientist is very relative indeed ... I must say that if there is any meaning in the word 'anti-fascist' – we are the anti-fascists. For five years and more we fought not in words but in deeds; not by mouth but with the blood of our hearts against the most fascist and indeed Nazi regime in the Middle East and we succeeded in overthrowing it. At that time, those groups who call themselves left wing were absolutely legal and recognized by that fascist rule, lived in peace with it and even enjoyed certain privileges from the British tyrants.[8]

Begin's attempt to transform the Provisional Government into 'Nazi collaborators' was in part an attempt to deflect the demonizing rhetoric deployed by his political opponents, but also a means of weakening the total hegemony of Ben-Gurion and Mapai in Israeli society. Thus, Begin was quick to distance himself from the assassination of Count Bernadotte by a Lehi front, Hazit Ha'Moledet (the Fatherland Front) in September 1948, especially as he believed that Mapai had instigated rumours that former members of the Irgun had been responsible for the act. Yet he was also quick to assign 'indirect responsibility' for the assassination 'with the mistaken policy of the Provisional government of Israel'.[9]

In response to Ben-Gurion's crackdown on former Irgun members and Lehi, Begin once more warned the Provisional Government not to create a new underground by its actions. At a public meeting at Rishon L'Zion, he warned that 'fascist characteristics which are becoming evident already in government circles are exceedingly dangerous. We shall not agree to any rule that is based on fear like the rule of the Fascists.'[10] Thus, although Begin condemned the use of such epithets as inaccurate and a distortion, he was not averse to using them himself against Mapai and its supporters.

Despite its own use of such highly charged language in the cause of inter-party warfare, Herut's development – its expansion first into Gahal in 1965 and then into the Likud in 1973 – was ideologically coloured by its far-right associations and especially by the legacy of Polish nationalism. In the early 1950s, there was clearly a role for opposition to Mapai's political saturation of Israeli society and Ben-Gurion's increasingly autocratic style. Given the history of bitter rivalry – the Labour Zionists and the Revisionists could not even agree to fight together in the Warsaw Ghetto – Begin was able to occupy the post of leader of the Opposition to full effect.

From the outset, Begin propagated the image of the Opposition leader as the embodiment of the national ideal – a humble and honourable man, wedded to his people and their struggle to survive. He was vociferous in advocating his beliefs and uncompromising in his attitude to his country's enemies, and yet at once approachable and accessible to its ordinary citizens. Despite Jabotinsky's private antagonism toward 'the treasure of Judaism', Begin exuded religious piety and was true to the faith of millennia. He appeared willing to make any personal sacrifice for the cause of Israel. Yet many who knew Begin in Poland described all this as merely a mimicry of the Polish nationalist mentality. Such personality traits and positive attributes of character may indeed have described the private Menachem Begin. Their public, political expression, however, gave rise to a popular mythology which the Herut leader was to cultivate and offer as almost an ideological religiosity to many utopian seekers after truth.

The First Elections and the First Knesset

When Herut held its founding conference at Tel Aviv's Ohel Shem synagogue in October 1948, Begin entered the crowded hall on the arm of Jabotinsky's sister to the tumultuous applause of the audience. Surrounded by portraits of Jabotinsky, Raziel and Herzl, he dedicated his speech to them – and to Avraham Stern. Begin projected himself as the heir to all the great thinkers and fighters of the Revisionist movement. The realities of history proved awkward, however. The official Revisionist Party still existed and was actually negotiating with Herut in the hope of presenting a joint list of candidates for election to the National Assembly – the first Knesset. Indeed, the official Revisionist Conference had already taken place a month earlier. Aryeh Altman's opening speech even reiterated the point that the Irgun had been founded by Jabotinsky at the instigation of the Revisionists many years before. Very clearly, there was considerable opposition to Begin and many regarded him as a usurper of the Revisionist faith. When a majority of delegates favoured a merger with Herut, the Revisionist old guard walked out.

Begin's dedication of his speech to the heroes of yesterday served to cover up some fundamental differences. Jabotinsky himself had fervently opposed Begin's concept of 'military Zionism', and instead advocated cooperation with the British in the war against Hitler. Begin, who had been incarcerated in the Soviet Gulag, was luke-warm about the 'armistice' with the British while hating the Germans even more. David Raziel, the original commander of the Irgun, had died in their service. Avraham Stern, for his part, actually turned his back on the philosophy and diplomacy of Jabotinsky and split the Irgun by deciding to fight the British. Indeed, the fact that the Stern Group saw themselves as post-Jabotinskyian prevented a union with the Irgun during the Revolt. Yet Begin's task – even at this early stage – was to cement a coalition of all nationalist forces. For only a united movement could pose a threat to Ben-Gurion and the socialist Zionists.

In his speech to the Herut Conference, Begin attacked the foreign policy of the Provisional Government and publicly stated his refusal to accept any position in a future Israeli government that bore even the slightest resemblance to the current one. He would instead form a government centred on Herut in coalition with other parties. This government would annul the partition agreement. The National Council 'had no right to agree to a reduction of the size or degree of sovereignty ... such an agreement will not be binding on any elected government which may succeed the Provisional – unelected – government'. In his demand to recover the whole of Eretz Israel, Begin condemned the willingness of the Provisional Government to accept the wishes of the United Nations. They 'slavishly accept the dictates of Bevin and his collaborators in the US State Department'. Resolutions at the convention mirrored Begin's militancy. One called for an immediate declaration of war against the Arab states.[11]

But Begin had been the commander of an Irgun Zva'i Leumi which had fought the British not only militarily but in the publicity stakes as well. The high public profile of the mysterious Irgun commander was also a factor which served him well. Begin portrayed the Irgun's activities as being crucial to the struggle for independence and a central factor in inducing the British to depart.[12] Heightened public awareness of the Irgun's activities was exploited and put to good political use. 'The British Enslavement was flung off by sacrifice of blood and tears, by war and affliction, by fire and battle. "Only Thus!" was it done.' Begin reiterated this theme time and again in the immediate post-independence period. Herut's foreign-policy statements in its manifesto for the elections to the first Knesset stressed the centrality of its belief that the Jews had gained their independence primarily through the efforts of the Irgun. This was further expressed in its fears that the British would return through their surrogate, Abdullah of Jordan, since Judea and Samaria had now been occupied by the king.

In Herut's manifesto, Begin accused the British of waging a war of attrition 'to force us to reach an agreement with their chief hireling, "King" Abdullah' – in order to allow British forces to remain in Western Eretz Israel. Although the Irgun had been dissolved, Begin tantalizingly entertained the prospect of war against Abdullah in order to recover both the East and West Banks. 'Only the removal of the conquering armies will bring about a stable peace.... No one doubts that we have the power to remove the hired invader.'[13] The secret negotiations and ongoing contact between Abdullah and the Israelis,[14] which eventually resulted in the acceptance of the disappearance of an Arab Palestine and its annexation by Trans-Jordan to form the Hashemite Kingdom of Jordan, angered Herut. The mutual interest of Ben-Gurion and Abdullah was that the British should not use the Palestinian state for their own imperialist purposes to the detriment of their neighbours.

Herut, however, opposed a 'political–territorial compromise' with

Abdullah, a prospect it regarded as an Israeli equivalent of the Munich Agreement.[15] During the election campaign, Begin also exploited a public mood which exhibited strong reservations about any possible agreement with Jordan. After all, 6000 people – a large proportion of Israel's small population – had been killed in a war against its neighbours, which included Abdullah's Jordan. Begin had not forgotten Jabotinsky's proclamation that 'the Jordan has two banks, one is ours – so is the other'. Indeed, Ben-Gurion feared that the arms carried on the *Altalena* were to be used by the Irgun in areas outside the boundaries of the new state. Capitalizing on the public's security anxieties, Begin emphasized the inadequacy of the 'statelet' of Israel that had been established during the previous year. He argued that obtaining the entire Land of Israel, 'not a strip along its coast', was not simply an ideological issue, but one with fundamental security implications.

> The tiny partition area cannot secure freedom even for the few who inhabit it – let alone for the millions who remain outside. If we do not expand, we shall be thrown into the sea – not at once, but in a short time or with the next international upheaval. That is why phrases about the Hebrew *irredenta* is foolish, empty talk. There is no irredenta. There is a minimum necessity for our national existence – and if we choose to live, then we are compelled to demand this minimum.[16]

Herut's blanket opposition to any concession to an external enemy, and its promotion and glorification of the Irgun's military campaign, paid political dividends. Herut was returned as the largest non-socialist party, with 14 seats and 11 per cent of the vote. The official Revisionists were routed, failing to gain even one seat. The result effectively legitimized Begin as the heir to the Revisionist heritage and essentially the leader of the right-wing nationalist opposition.

Defining the Opposition

From the beginning of the first Knesset, Begin shaped a distinctive opposition to the Mapai government of Ben-Gurion. He objected to the oath that Weizmann was asked to take as first president. Begin argued that Weizmann should swear allegiance not only to the State of Israel but also to the people of Israel. Mapai saw in this the implication that Weizmann should be president only of the Jews, and not of the Arab citizens of the state as well. Weizmann opened the proceedings of the Constituent Assembly by reading a roll call of Zionist heroes from Herzl and Ahad Ha'am onwards. Jabotinsky's name was missing from this pantheon, as Begin vociferously reminded the new president. To complete Weizmann's embarrassment, Begin recalled the president's aversion to espousing openly the goal of a Jewish state at the 17th Zionist Congress in 1931, when Jabotinsky effectively forced his resignation. 'And still the state arose', he taunted Weizmann. Begin was determined that the Revisionist contribution should be neither omitted nor forgotten.

> No one can prevent us from participating in the great deeds which need to be done, now that the main stage of attaining our independence has been achieved. No one is entitled to judge who is a constructive force in the Jewish nation and who is not.[17]

In the first Knesset, Begin continued to condemn the partition of 1947, and criticized Ben-Gurion's acceptance of it. He believed that 'the eastern part of the western Land of Israel' – the West Bank – was under indirect British control through Abdullah's rule. Reconstruction of the Jewish state could not begin, he argued, until 'our country is completely cleansed of invading armies. That is the prime task of our foreign policy.'[18] The ultra-nationalist intellectual and poet Uri Zvi Greenberg, now a Herut member of the Knesset, similarly attacked the government for their lack of will to reclaim the whole of the Land – not only Trans-Jordan, but also 'the slopes of Lebanon and the approaches to the Nile'. He told the Knesset that the Israel Defence Force (IDF) 'stands like a beggar at the door before the bedouin tribe from Trans-Jordan ... there is no Trans-Jordanian people, there are desert tribes and an impoverished, hired king.'[19]

When an orchestrated lobby of pro-Jordanian Palestinians in Jericho asked Abdullah to integrate the West Bank into his kingdom, Begin attacked the government for their acquiescence in the annexation of this part of the Land of Israel. 'Who gave the government the right to hand over the cave of Machpela, Rachel's tomb ... Gilead and Bashan to a foreigner, an enemy, an oppressor'? – sites which had been 'historically hallowed for 120 generations.' Begin strongly opposed any idea of the internationalization of Jerusalem. And even though Abdullah controlled the Old City with its religious and historic sites, Jerusalem was still 'the undivided capital of Israel'. He condemned the Armistice Agreement with Trans-Jordan of April 1949 as 'an enslaving agreement with Britain's vassal', and Ben-Gurion's willingness to take back thousands of Arab refugees as the means of creating a fifth column.

A year later, a new Jordanian parliament which was partly elected from both banks confirmed the annexation of the West Bank. The Israeli government regarded this as 'a unilateral step which is not binding on Israel'. Begin, however, regarded it as virtual recognition of the partition of Eretz Israel. His suspicions deepened when Britain recognized the new situation three days after the vote in the Jordanian parliament, and British bases were established in Abdullah's expanded kingdom. In a speech in the Knesset on 3 May 1950, Begin referred to the 'vassal-state that exists on our homeland', and in a Biblical analogy labelled Abdullah 'the Ammonite slave'. He pleaded with Foreign Minister Sharett not to agree that 'Allah's slave will rule 80 per cent of our homeland'. Thus, from the very beginning, Begin opposed 'the freezing of artificial borders' and the Mapai government's tacit acceptance of the status quo. 'Our regime aims at forgetting and making us forget', he told the first sitting of the first Knesset. Instead, he suggested that the government should educate people about the lost territories just as 'France has never forgotten Alsace-Lorraine and Lithuania has never forgotten Vilna'. Even Lenin was invoked when Begin recalled that Brest-Litovsk had been signed away by the Bolsheviks to the Germans only to be recovered later.

Yet this passionate start to Herut's political odyssey was marred by Begin's inability to devolve power within the movement. As the glory days of the Irgun began to fade, the Revisionist collective inheritance as manifested in the Herut movement began to dissipate very quickly. Begin relied on Irgun loyalists to the exclusion of other sections of the Revisionist movement. Independent-minded people began to leave the party, as did many intellectuals and professionals. They began to make a distinction between the cosmopolitan Jabotinsky and Begin, 'the provincial boy from Briisk'. Clearly, their expectations of the latter did not match their memory of the former. This exodus left the party in the control of a few loyalists 'lacking in administrative and leadership ability', which allowed Begin to consolidate his hold on the party through the absence of real opposition within Herut.[20]

The departure of those intellectuals who – by definition – asked questions and expected internal debate produced a party far removed from that bequeathed by Jabotinsky. None of those who remained could or wished to challenge the partial rewriting of recent history which Begin propagated. Documentation, policy statements and electoral platforms were all drawn up by Begin, as was the list of candidates to the first Knesset in 1949. Hillel Kook and Jabotinsky's son Eri eventually broke away to form an independent, right-wing grouping,

Lamerhav, initially within Herut and then outside it. Their dissent initially arose in reaction to Begin's orthodox rhetoric and his broad support for religious views and legislation, but it subsequently developed into a more thoroughgoing opposition. A workers' organization, the National Workers Federation, which had been created by Jabotinsky in the early 1930s to confront the Histadrut, similarly became a locus of festering opposition to Begin's approach. Yet, throughout the long years in the political wilderness, challenges to Begin's leadership from frustrated Herut activists[21] were overcome, sometimes through the use of dubious tactics, but always with the loyal support of the Irgun faithful.

The need to believe in a national leader and to be comforted by his wisdom, or to worship certain fundamental hallowed beliefs, characterized sections of Herut throughout Begin's leadership until his resignation in 1983. One recent academic researcher, Yonathon Shapiro, has commented:

> [Such] myths are based on an interpretation of historical events and concrete events that is not necessarily consonant with reality. To argue that the boundaries of Mandate Palestine (with or without Jordan) were the borders of the historic Land of Israel was devoid of factual historical basis. But Herut, like Betar and like the Revisionist Party, which also embraced this principle, never bothered to examine the subject. I found no one among them who refuted this notion, although this camp contained scholars and researchers who knew it lacked historical foundation. Correlation between myth and reality was unnecessary.

And on the question of the Revolt, Shapiro writes:

> But to this day, the wealth of research documenting these historical facts have not shaken the faith of Betar and Irgun veterans that their role was crucial, nor that of the disappointed Betar intelligentsia who eventually found themselves outside the Herut movement.[22]

Begin's need to project himself as an authentic leader of the people and the fount of national wisdom, the approved successor of Jabotinsky – a projection coloured by an autocratic persona – appealed strongly to those still emotionally tied to membership of such a 1930s-style popular movement. A reliance on dramatic gestures and impassioned speeches to the masses – direct contact with 'my people' – often stood in for serious decision-making, and was in this sense the antithesis of a rigid party bureaucracy – the hallmark of the leaden Mapai. The desire for a benevolent and wise father-figure, and that figure's desire for unqualified adulation, fall outside the realm of politics proper; nevertheless the existence of this dimension in a political context undoubtedly made Begin's position within the party virtually unassailable.

All problems and difficulties were laid at the feet of Ben-Gurion and the Mapai establishment. Indeed, from the very beginning, Begin poured scorn upon them; they were 'stubbornly blind', 'phoney realists', 'muddle-headed pacifists', 'MayDayniks'.[23] They were the source of all mistakes, past and present. If there existed feared external enemies in a generally hostile world, Mapai was the internal enemy which continually undermined the national endeavour with its flawed thinking. Begin dwelt on the psychological traumas and historical sense of injustice of a persecuted people. The demonizing of both external foes and internal enemies was, in political terms, a fruitful policy which would eventually pay dividends, given the extreme pressures that the young State of Israel lived with between 1948 and 1967.

CHAPTER FOUR

LOOKING FOR PARTNERS: REVISIONISM IN TRANSITION

No Concessions to the Germans

Begin came very badly unstuck right at the beginning of his parliamentary career. The elections to the second Knesset resulted in the loss of almost half of Herut's seats. It became clear that a large number of voters had deserted Herut for the General Zionists, who trebled their number of seats. There also existed strong disillusionment with Begin, who continually dwelled on past triumphs rather than planning future policies. After the election he disappeared from the political scene and did not attend the Knesset during the second half of 1951. His political comeback was manifested through his opposition to the German reparations agreement. Begin called this move 'the abomination of abominations in Israel'. He continued: 'There are things in life more precious than life itself; there are things more terrible than death itself ... and this is one of these things – there will be no negotiations with Germany.' He likened Adenauer's Federal Germany to a modern-day Amalek – the Biblical enemy of the Jews. 'The Lord will be at war with Amalek throughout the ages' (Exodus 17:16). Begin asked 'How can you take money from Amalek?'[1]

Yet Begin himself, together with Chaim Landau, had originally been in favour of securing funds from Germany for the survivors of the Holocaust via the four wartime allies, and berated the government for not doing enough. When such negotiations had been mooted in 1951, there was qualified support from Herut. However, at a time when he was at a very low ebb, psychologically and politically – and, indeed, was contemplating resigning and leaving politics – Begin was advised by Yochanan Bader to change his position on the issue and challenge the government.[2] Partly through gut conviction and partly through political opportunism, Begin was able to arouse the deepest anti-German emotions in Israel – especially from Holocaust survivors – to mobilize within and beyond Herut to outmanoeuvre his opponents in the party and to attack the pragmatism of Mapai on this, the most sensitive of issues. His opponents saw him as a possessed rabble-rouser who had encouraged the crowd to march on the Knesset during the debate. Begin viewed the episode differently, as he told the Knesset:

> In Zion Square, before the 15,000 Jews who gathered there outraged, in the rain and cold, I said 'Go, stand around the Knesset. Do not disturb the proceedings.'
> All those lies, as though we intended to disrupt the debate – rubbish. I said 'Go! Surround the Knesset as in the days of Rome when a Roman governor wanted to put a statue in the Temple. The Jews were alerted from all over the country and they surrounded the Temple and said: Over our dead bodies, shall you pass.'
> I said 'let your silence scream out for there shall be no negotiations with Germany'.
> They [the police] attacked them with gas bombs made in Germany and that is when it [the stoning of the Knesset] occurred.
> I warn but I do not threaten. Whom should I threaten? I know that you will drag us away to a concentration camp. Today you arrested hundreds. Perhaps you will arrest thousands. It is nothing. They will go along, they will sit there and we will sit with them. If necessary, we will be killed together with them. But there will be no reparations from Germany.[3]

The intense dislike – indeed, hatred – of the notion of having any truck with the successor regimes of Nazi Germany was undoubtedly a gut issue for Begin. Yet it was also an issue which bore abundant political fruit, and Begin was acutely aware of this. He believed that the Federal Republic of West Germany did not have clean hands. The bureaucrats and functionaries who had processed mass murder had found good jobs in the new German republic. He made no concessions, would entertain no change of heart or any display of reconciliation. In his pre-election speech to the Fifth National Conference of Herut in November 1958, Begin told the delegates that a National Liberal government, headed by Herut, would neither permit 'a German Ambassador to reside in the State of Israel' nor 'an Israeli Ambassador to officiate in Germany'.[4]

In the debate on the establishment of diplomatic relations with West Germany in early 1965, he told the members of the Knesset that the new German Ambassador would also represent the millions who had voted for the National Socialists in 1933. He asked what had happened to the 11 million members of the Nazi Party in 1945. He recalled that the West German Foreign Minister, Schroeder, and two other ministers had been members of the SS. The current Minister of Justice had praised Hitler in the past, while 27 presidents of West German regional courts were former Nazis. Even the misdemeanours of West Germany's most celebrated soldier, Marshall Milstein, were quoted: 'The German soldier must show understanding for the need to take severe vengeance on the Jews.'

Begin also condemned those who had simply acquiesced in the ascendancy of Nazism. This included the opposition – many of whom had in fact escaped or been tortured and imprisoned. He asked what had happened to the 12 million socialists and communists who had voted against Hitler in May 1933. Where had they disappeared to? 'Not in Auschwitz, not in the gas chambers and not in the pits. They disappeared into the German nation acclaiming Hitler.' The many captains of German industry who fuelled the war machine and then effortlessly returned to their posts shortly after the war to rebuild the new Germany were particularly detested by Begin.

> The ancient firm of Topf and Sons supplied the ovens and furnaces. When Auschwitz was liberated, a letter was found there from Mr Topf and his sons saying: 'We hereby supply a useful instrument for filling the furnace with coal and a metal fork for putting the bodies into the ovens.' Hoess [the commandant] was hanged at Auschwitz by the Poles, but the firm of Topf and Sons still exists. The secretary who wrote that letter is still alive. The engineer who drew up the plan is still alive. The workers who cast those furnaces are still alive. The German Ambassador will also represent them in the Jewish State.[5]

The German scientists who were working in Egypt to help build Nasser's military machine provided the focus for a passionate Herut campaign beginning at the end of 1962. It provided Begin with the political stick to beat Ben-Gurion and his governments for their decision slowly to 'normalize' relations between Israel and West Germany. In a Knesset debate in March 1963, an infuriated Begin mounted a scathing attack on government policy:

> For ten years, since Germany began to pay a fraction of what it stole, you have endeavoured to endear yourselves to it and abase yourself before it. It is a paradox. You invite German experts on education and Germany sends Nasser experts on death. You sew uniforms for the German Army and Germany sends knowhow about gases to be used against the Jewish people. You send our 'uzis' [machine guns] to Germany and the Germans give our

enemies bacteria. Please at least now, weigh matters up. How long will you continue to grovel, abase yourself and seek their friendship?[6]

Growth through Coalition

How, then, did Begin make the transition from tainted demagogue to Prime Minister; from inciting a crowd to march on the Knesset in 1952 over the issue of German war reparations to winning the Nobel Peace Prize in the company of Egypt's President Sadat a quarter of a century later? Clearly, demographic change and the political implosion of the Labour Party were essential factors; yet Begin also benefited from a strategy which, together with good fortune and the mistakes of others, allowed him to build a viable alternative to the Labour Alignment. He was also fortunate that both the war of 1967 and that of 1973 worked to the detriment of the ruling party, Mapai.

In fact, Herut's representation in the 120-seat Knesset remained small and relatively constant between 1949 (14 seats) and 1977 (20 seats), the year of victory (see Figure 4.1). Begin did not, therefore, expand Herut as such; nevertheless, he was able to build the Likud alternative through a series of agreements with other anti-Labour groups.

The disadvantage of Begin's displays of impassioned rhetoric was that although they strengthened his own position in the nationalist camp, which was entranced by these spectacles, they served to distance other parties – possible political partners and allies – from Herut. Begin began to understand that Herut by itself would never become an alternative to Mapai. The only way to achieve power and a total humiliation of the ruling elite would be through the construction of an anti-Mapai bloc which Herut would effectively dominate. Herut had to change its image from 'a revolutionary, irrational and belliger-ent faction'[7] with Begin as its vitriolic mouthpiece. The natural part-ners in such coalition-building were the General Zionists – a party of the entrepreneurial middle class and a far cry from the Irgun's embrace of blood and fire. In 1951, they became the largest non-socialist party. At that time, Begin refused to contemplate negotia-tions with the larger General Zionists because he would therefore have had to assume a minor role in any subsequent coalition. By 1955, the position had been reversed: Herut had returned to its 1949 level of representation in the Knesset, while the vote for the General Zionists had fallen dramatically. Begin was now ready to initiate ne-gotiations with the disheartened General Zionists.

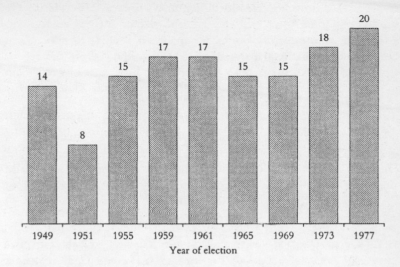

Figure 4.1 The relative stability of Herut's representation in the first nine Knessets (no. of seats)

Publicly, there was great animosity between Ben-Gurion and Begin The former even refused to acknowledge the latter's presence in Knesset debates. Yet there were at least three occasions – 1952, 1955 and 1961 – when Mapai approached Herut to join the ruling coalition.[8] Significantly, each time, Begin rejected the political overture from Mapai. He believed – with good reason – that the approaches were designed to divide him from his followers and to sow dissension in Revisionist ranks. While the organizations displayed clear ideological differences and modes of behaviour, one important bone of contention lay in the not-too-distant past:

> The acceptance Herut sought from Mapai was *ex post facto* approval of its political behaviour during the period of the Yishuv. This was not a matter of getting Mapai to forget, condone or forgive what had taken place before the establishment of the state, for all these would have implied that the Etzel [Irgun Zva'i Leumi] was in the wrong. What Herut wanted, even if only symbolically, was no less than an admission by Mapai that it had erred in its policies towards the underground and in its condemnation of its members as separatists and terrorists. In short, this was no less than retroactive justification and acceptance of the Etzel and its complete political rehabilitation.[9]

Ben-Gurion, however, remained implacably opposed to Herut. He studiedly ignored them and attempted to reduce their endeavours to a footnote in the history books. He made no attempt to grant them even grudging national recognition. He refused to allow the return and burial of Jabotinsky's body in Israel. The disabled who had served in the Irgun received lesser rights than those who fought in the Haganah and the Palmach.

Begin represented the nationalist Antichrist in Labour Zionist mythology. Moreover, he was an observant Jew in a secular age – 'a believing Jew, the son of a believer', he told the reparations debate. He was a fervent premature anti-Communist at a time when socialist Israel was still struggling to come to terms with the revelations of Stalinism. In a debate on the Slansky trial in 1952, he drew upon his experience as a Polish prisoner in the Gulag.

> I saw them [members of the Communist Party] in their exhilaration and in their brokenness, at the peak of happiness and in the depths of despair. I have never seen, nor do I think that anyone else has ever seen, greater exhilaration or blacker despair. Indeed there is nothing comparable to their tragedy in the history of human aspiration and remorse.[10]

All this cut no ice with the Mapai elite; nonetheless, their moral diffidence stoked up the fires of resentment. The sense of burning indignation which fired the Irgun veterans strengthened Begin's hold over Herut. It also suited Begin's sense of grievance over past injustices and his inability to let bygones be bygones. In 1935 Begin had rebuked Jabotinsky for desiring a reconciliation between Labour Zionism and Revisionism. 'You may forget, sir, that Ben-Gurion called you Vladimir Hitler, but our memories are better.'[11] That bitterness continued to guide Begin in his dealings with, and opposition to, the ruling Mapai elite.

In the decade between 1955 and 1965, Begin strenuously attempted to forge an alliance with the General Zionists. In its election manifesto for the fourth Knesset, Herut pointedly chided the General Zionists for having joined the government in 1951:

> In 1951, the General Zionists came out with the slogan 'Enough of Mapai rule' in the hope of winning the confidence of the people. But in the same year, a short time after the elections, they betrayed the trust of those who had voted for them and joined the Mapai government, thereby enabling Mapai to consolidate its rule and cover up the enriching of its own enterprises, the oppression of the worker and the pauperization of the Middle Class.[12]

The language of the 1959 election manifesto plainly spelled out Begin's intentions and these were directed solely at Mapai and the General Zionists. The manifesto's main title was 'Programme for a National Liberal Government Headed by Tenuat Ha'Herut'. The introduction began: 'The Elections to the Third Knesset which took place in July 1955 marked the beginning of the decline of Mapai and a decisive step towards its removal from power.' A significant part of the manifesto dealt with economic policy, labour and taxation – areas which had been of relatively little concern to Herut until the mid-1950s. It specifically attacked the dual role of the Histadrut and proposed 'the separation by law between the trades union of workers and ownership of enterprises whilst safeguarding the rights of employees'. It demanded the encouragement of private enterprise, the restoration of investors' confidence, the freeing of settlements and agricultural cooperatives from party control – and a reduction in income tax of 25 per cent. This was intended to win over those who had previously voted for the General Zionists, but was also a political flirtation with the party itself.

Whereas a few years before, Begin had hinted about the possibility of taking both the East and West Banks by military force, the programme sedately commented that 'the right of the Jewish People to Eretz Israel in its historic entirety is an eternal and inalienable right'. Yet the issue of the Territories remained a central stumbling block in any potential realignment. The General Zionists were opposed to Herut's maximalism, despite Begin's attempts to soften his strident demands. Herut's foreign policy stand was minimal and contained, but still illiberal enough to be any sort of commendation to the General Zionists. Its policies were coldly predicated on Israel's short-term national interests.

Sinai and After

Ben-Gurion's illusions about the progressive nature of the new leadership of Egypt had been dispelled after a reading of Nasser's book, *The Philosophy of the Revolution*. Begin had entertained no such feeling. He viewed the new Egypt as a 'Titoistic Republic' through which Communism would be introduced to the Middle East. In an address to French parliamentarians in September 1956, he suggested that it was in France's political interest to help Israel contain Nasser's influence in the Arab world. He thereby touched on the sensitive issue of 'Algérie Française':

Algeria is a problem for France and for France alone to solve. But if a possibility would arise that Nasser became the real ruler of Algeria, then it would be of paramount interest to Israel.... Allow me to express the hope of all Israeli patriots that no vacuum is going to be created in Algeria into which a foreign dictator's agents will pour immediately for his own designs.[13]

The approach to the French in Algeria was echoed in attitudes to South Africa. Herut also regarded Verwoerd's Nationalists as friends of Israel and condemned Ben-Gurion's support for the imposition of sanctions on the apartheid regime. In a Knesset debate, Aryeh Ben-Eliezer called it 'the nearest thing to declaring war on a country'. Yet this did not mean that Herut condoned apartheid. Ben-Eliezer also stated that 'our world-view leads us to reject unconditionally any regime or policy which represses nations or discriminates against races, religions and beliefs'.[14] Herut viewed their stand as an act of political expediency in support of the Jewish state which superseded any universal moral principle.

Herut and the General Zionists achieved a measure of common ground when they immediately advocated a military offensive against Nasser when the Czech arms deal with the Egyptians was announced.[15] If the Suez crisis confirmed the General Zionists' belief that Israel had to take the initiative to preserve its existence, it also became clear that Begin, while in total agreement with this position, had not renounced his basic views on the exact location of the borders of the state. Before the Israeli advance in Sinai, Begin urged a strong response, leading to 'our liberation of Hebron and Bethlehem'. Following the capture of the Gaza Strip from the Egyptians, Begin told his fellow members of Knesset that,

no longer will it be said in Israel when we demand a campaign to liberate the Land of our forefathers that it is 'aggression', 'expansion', or that 'the permanent border has been determined in the Rhodes Agreements and will remain where it is'. Let the whole nation draw the conclusion from the liberation of the conquered area in the South. Part of the homeland which is under foreign rule does not cease to be part of the homeland. Alien conquest does not annul our eternal right to the land of our forefathers and of our sons.[16]

Begin's demand for war was predicated on the perceived weakness of Ben-Gurion and his government. As early as April 1956, he condemned the 'phony war' before the Sinai campaign and the efforts to resolve the matter by diplomatic means. In an address to the 24th Zionist Congress, he said:

In 1938, Neville Chamberlain returned from Rhodes – sorry from Godesburg – and on arriving home, he waved a scrap of paper, declaring: 'Peace in our time, peace with honour.' And less than a year later, this same Chamberlain, grand-master of self-delusion, was forced to bring his people to the brink of the abyss, to a bloody war more terrible than any war had been before.[17]

The acceptance of the 1949 boundaries at Rhodes was portrayed as an Israeli 'Munich', and Ben-Gurion its 'Chamberlain'. Mapai, in Begin's eyes, continually played the role of the appeaser of Arab states, forfeiting territory and relegating the British Mandate borders of Eretz Israel to history. When Ben-Gurion under American pressure announced an Israeli withdrawal from Gaza, Begin viewed this as a totally pusillanimous act of betrayal. He told the Knesset that if Herut had been in power, they would have declared to the nations of the world that 'we will not retreat, we will not move, we will stand firm and we will succeed.'[18]

The issue of 'the lost territories' may gradually have become submerged with the passing of time, but it was never forgotten. The hope remained that the territories would one day pass to Israel. At the Fifth National Conference of the Herut movement at the end of 1958, Begin, although he did not refer directly to the East Bank, spoke nevertheless about *shlemut historit* – the 'historic completeness' of Eretz Israel – and pointed out that there were at least three other political parties who did not recognize the Green Line with the West Bank as the final border of Israel. Even as late as 1960, Herut leaders such as Yaakov Meridor publicly still sought both sides of the River Jordan: 'The primary goal of foreign policy is to re-create historic Israel – by liberating TransJordan. Israel can never rest until this is accomplished.'[19]

Although Begin was unable to concede such fundamental points with regard to the Territories, he was more sympathetic to the General Zionists' demand for representation in the Histadrut. This, however, posed a problem in that Revisionism had strenuously opposed the idea of a Histadrut hegemony under the control of Mapai. Indeed, Jabotinsky advocated breaking the control of the Histadrut and to this end had formed the rival National Labour Federation during the early 1930s. The National Labour Federation, however, was one of the few groups that was well organized and independent-minded, yet had not left Herut – and they strongly opposed Begin. After a protracted fight, Begin finally pushed the issue of joining the Histadrut through the Herut Conference in 1963 by a margin of 324 votes to

257 after several years of struggle. This came at a time when Mapai was beginning to show signs of fraying around the political edges, with Ben-Gurion's resignation and open discussion of the profound differences within the ruling elite. The General Zionists in the meantime had reunited with their former liberal wing, the Progressives, to fight the 1961 elections as the Liberals. Ben-Gurion had been prepared to include the Liberals in the ruling coalition, but this had been opposed by Eshkol, who favoured a realignment of the numerous socialist parties. The Liberals, who won 17 seats in 1961, were on this occasion left out in the political wilderness and were thus susceptible to Begin's blandishments.

The approach to the General Zionists had been made on the assumption that an anti-socialist coalition could be built which would attract an essentially middle-class electorate. The workers, it was reasoned, would be permanently affiliated to Mapai and other socialist parties. However, a new proletariat arrived in the 1950s in the emigration from Morocco and other parts of the Magreb. The communal leadership and mainly secular intelligentsia had left for France despite Ben-Gurion's best efforts to attract them to Israel. It was clear from Golda Meir's comment that 'we shall bring them here and make them *b'nei adam*' – 'worthy people and good citizens' – that the Mapai apparatchiks had little idea how to value often deeply religious people who were far removed from the European Jewish experience.

Begin cultivated these new arrivals, who soon felt alienated from the secular Zionist ethos of Mapai and quickly began to resent their European socialist instructors. Begin's religiosity, populism and patriotism appealed to them. Indeed, during one election campaign, a leaflet was distributed which insisted that Begin had in fact been born in Morocco and sent to study in a *yeshiva* (religious seminary) in Poland.[20] The Sephardim warmed to the patriarchal images and nationalist rhetoric which Begin used in his appeal to them. 'Begin – King of Israel' was more than a populist slogan; it mobilized a psychology which was far removed from scientific socialist Zionism. Too many Mapai functionaries wanted to make the new immigrants into stereotypical Israelis. Begin was content to allow them to remain Jews. It followed, then, that in their manifesto for the 1959 elections, Herut promised tax reductions for large families, full employment, national unemployment insurance and a minimum-wages law.

The first indication of workers' support for Herut came in the 1965 Histadrut election when 100,000 people voted for a joint Herut–

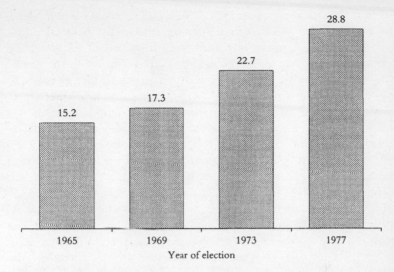

Figure 4.2 Workers' vote for a right-wing bloc in Histadrut elections (%)

Liberal bloc. Indeed, for the first time, workers had the choice to vote for a right-wing alternative in a Histadrut election. This vote increased dramatically in subsequent elections (see Figure 4.2).

Having achieved meaningful representation in the Histadrut, Herut – and subsequently Gahal – had to respond adequately to the social needs of its working-class supporters. Up to now, this issue had been glossed over. For example, in 1961 the Herut Central Committee had issued an internal guide to its economic programme during the election campaign. Significantly, only one of thirteen points dealt with the rights of workers. The economic programme was clearly aimed at the Liberal middle-class voter. The theoretical approach to working people was classically Jabotinskyian:

> [Some] openly express their opinion that it is possible to expedite economic development by curtailing the rights of the worker through freezing wages and lowering standards of living – these opinions originated during the period of exploitation of the working class and low productivity and so they exclude *a priori* cooperation between the employer and employee.[21]

During the early 1960s, Begin tried earnestly to mollify the public perception of Herut and to project a more responsible image with less emphasis on the 'fighting family' subculture of the Irgun. His attempt to woo the Liberals was helped by their increasing frustration

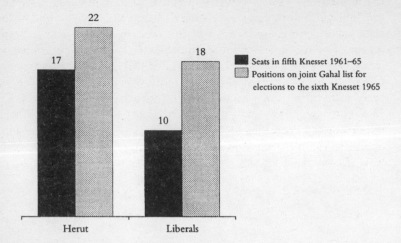

Figure 4.3 A comparison between the seats obtained by Herut and the Liberals separately in the 1961 election and the proposed distribution of seats in a joint Gahal list for the 1965 election

after more than a decade in the political wilderness. Their recombination with the Progressives in 1961 had only increased their total number of seats by three. Consequently, many in the Liberal Party began to look more favourably on the prospect of an alliance with Herut. At the beginning of the election year, 1965, Begin offered some generous concessions. The Liberals, he proposed, would have disproportionate representation on any joint list.

The Liberals felt unable to refuse what seemed to be an electorally profitable and politically magnanimous gesture. The Liberals thereby gained a secure political base, whilst Herut gained respectability and access to the middle class. Together they formed Gush Herut Liberalim – the Herut–Liberal Bloc or Gahal. Although Herut played down its maximalist territorial policies and Revisionist iconology, each party maintained its separate programme. After 1965 – over 40 years after the British gave Eastern Eretz Israel to Abdullah – Herut rarely publicly mentioned its belief in the Jewish right to the East Bank. The realities of coalition-building took precedence over the historical Revisionist opposition to the exclusion of Trans-Jordan from the borders of Mandatory Palestine.

In its agreement with the Liberals, Herut reserved its right to articulate the principle of *shlemut ha'moledet* – the 'completeness' of the homeland. Despite Herut's willingness to tone down its approach, the Liberals' hunger for power caused them to overlook the fact that such a cosmetic exercise was not the same as a fundamental policy change. For the liberal wing of the Liberal Party, which comprised many former members of the Progressive Party, such an arrangement proved to be an ideological burden too heavy to carry. They left the party to fight the 1965 election as the Independent Liberal Party. The ease with which all this happened belied a degree of profound opportunism in the Liberal Party. To form 'an alliance with the most dovish to the most hardline elements in the Israeli polity suggested a lack of conviction among the General Zionists on the issues deemed central by Herut'.[22]

CHAPTER FIVE

THE END OF THE
SOCIALIST ZIONIST DREAM

The Fragmentation of Labour

The Gahal list achieved only 26 seats in the 1965 election – one fewer than the combined Herut and Liberal representation in the previous Knesset. Ironically, this was exactly the same combined total achieved by Herut, the Liberals and the Progressives in the very first elections in 1949. While some blame could be attached to a desertion of voters to the Independent Liberals and Rafi, Ben-Gurion's new party, it was still a poor performance. In the 1969 elections, although Gahal was legitimized as a bona fide political force through its membership of the government during the crisis of the Six Day War, its weak showing was repeated when the joint list once again picked up 26 seats. How, then, did Herut dramatically reverse this static situation and take power as Likud eight years later in 1977? There were several reasons for this breakthrough, yet the real possibility of an alternative to the ruling Labour hierarchy only emerged during the 1969 election when the components of a future right-wing bloc became politically visible. The reawakened ideological controversy over the Territories after the Six Day War produced an eventual coalescence around a nationalist anti-Mapai nucleus. Yet this political crystallization grew around a locus of fierce dissent within Mapai itself which had existed for many years.

Ben-Gurion's last years in the political arena were not glorious ones. The reopening of the Lavon affair,[1] the prospect of a Labour alignment of socialist parties, his inability to circumvent the stultifying party bureaucracy and promote younger people – all became crucial issues for the ageing Ben-Gurion. Following his eventual resignation, he also proved unable to control his successor, Levi Eshkol, whom he perceived to be leading the party leftwards. Ben-Gurion's observation

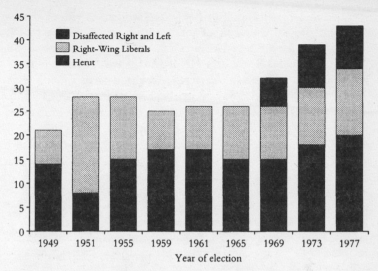

Figure 5.1 The growth of the potential right-wing coalition, in terms of the number of seats held during the first nine Knessets

that 'there is no egalitarianism, there will be no egalitarianism, there is no need for egalitarianism' did not please the party hierarchy. His desire to remove the health service from the control of the Labour movement and place it under the jurisdiction of the state was attacked by those who fervently believed in the party's socialist mission. Thus, at nearly 80, Ben-Gurion stood for the kind of flexible change that the succeeding generation, Dayan and Peres, espoused – a break with the sense of divinity of the party. Eshkol, for his part, tried to distance himself from Ben-Gurion by attempting to normalize the antagonistic relationship between Mapai and Herut.

Ben-Gurion, however, had not forgotten. He still harboured a deep antipathy to Begin personally and abhorred the Revisionist philosophy. In a private letter to the writer Chaim Guri, Ben-Gurion reiterated his conviction that Begin was 'a Hitler type' and a bigoted racist as far as Arabs were concerned. Ben-Gurion wrote that Begin would institute a 1930s-style fascist regime, built on jackbooted thuggery, if he ever attained power. In what seemed like a symbolic act of defiance, Eshkol showed his independence by permitting the return of Jabotinsky's body for burial in Israel in accordance with the last wishes of the Revisionist leader. There was thus a softening of political attitudes towards Herut. Unlike Ben-Gurion, Eshkol attempted to maintain civilized relations with Begin and worked to reduce tension.[2] He did not project the kind of public animosity to Herut that had been the hallmark of Ben-Gurion's tenure in office. All this served further to legitimize Begin and Herut in the eyes of the public.

Ben-Gurion's strength of character and vision were a guiding force for large numbers of socialists. Many believed that he alone had been responsible for the establishment of the state. The loyalty of decades – and through such momentous times – was not easily overturned, even by the most vociferous of critics. Yet there were some, like the more liberal Moshe Sharett – effectively ousted as Prime Minister through Ben-Gurion's endeavours – who nevertheless possessed the motivation to analyse and publicize his flaws:

> Ben-Gurion's egocentrism is threefold. As a man, he is completely pre-occupied with himself, his thoughts, deeds and emotions. The evidence is his loneliness, his apartness, for Ben-Gurion is a solitary figure without close friends. His constant stress on the uniqueness of the Jewish people is another aspect of his egocentrism – cultural egocentrism. The third aspect is his assumption of a messianic mission vis-à-vis Israel and Jewry.[3]

While Mapai had indulged in internecine warfare and consequently suffered internal fragmentation, Herut had engaged in coalition-building. Ben-Gurion was not blind to the potential openings to the right and he may have believed that the establishment of a new party, a substitute for the disintegrating Mapai, was the last opportunity to forestall such an eventuality. Indeed, at the beginning of 1963, he wrote to Sharret that he had 'no doubt that a Begin regime would lead to the destruction of the State or, at the very least, his regime would turn Israel into a monster'.

Ben-Gurion strongly opposed the idea of a joint list with Achdut Ha'avoda in the 1965 elections. There existed deep ideological differences with its leader Yitzhak Tabenkin stretching back over forty years. Achdut Ha'avoda was further to the left than the more pragmatic Mapai. But it also espoused a maximalist approach to the Territories – and, like Begin, mourned the declaration of a 'statelet' in 1948. Ben-Gurion argued that since Achdut only held 8 seats compared to Mapai's 42, too much power would be unnecessarily ceded to the smaller party. What is more, an alignment with another socialist party would limit Mapai's flexibility to build coalitions with other parties. More importantly, Ben-Gurion predicted, a leftist bloc could catalyse the construction of a right–centre bloc in reaction.

Meanwhile, Ben-Gurion was uncompromising, indeed obsessive,

in his demand for a judicial inquiry into the Lavon affair. In his memoirs, Shimon Peres recalled that 'often Ben-Gurion consulted no one and took decisions which all of us thought were ill-advised ... as the Affair progressed, he grew more and more lonely, isolated from his longtime party comrades and solitary in his decision making. He began to like this loneliness and seemed, in a strange way, to enjoy it.'4 In an interview in 1964, Ben-Gurion commented: 'if I am confronted with the choice of closing my eyes to justice but thereby gaining the seat of power, or crying out against injustice and being driven into the political wilderness, I choose the wilderness.'5

Ben-Gurion's zeal as a political backseat driver to push through his views split the party in June 1965. A majority preferred party unity and cohesion over Ben-Gurion's charisma and dynamism. They preferred the dull party bureaucrat to the ageing hero of yesterday. Ben-Gurion left Mapai to form the right-of-centre Rafi – Reshimat Poalei Israel – the Israel Workers' List. Rafi was significantly a 'list' and not a 'party', and thereby held open the possibility of a return when political conditions seemed more favourable. Although Shimon Peres, Moshe Dayan, Chaim Herzog and Teddy Kollek all went with Ben-Gurion, Rafi obtained only 10 seats in the 1965 elections, compared to Mapai's 45. Yet Rafi was the first 'Israeli' party to make even this limited breakthrough. Most political parties had their roots in the pre-state era. To win as many as 10 seats before the institutionalization of party financing was a measure of the decay within Mapai.

The emergency of the Six Day War forced Mapai's leader Eshkol to establish a National Unity government. This outcome was also in part the result of an orchestrated campaign by Gahal and Rafi to discredit the quiet Eshkol and to erode his authority. The deep anxiety of the Israeli public in the lead-up to the outbreak of war was exploited by Mapai's political opponents. Following contacts between Peres and Begin, both Gahal and Rafi had worked together in the weeks preceding the war on the idea of a coalition – probably led by Ben-Gurion – which would displace Eshkol and effectively challenge the dominance of Mapai as the leading political force in the country. The Independent Liberals and the National Religious Party added their political weight in favour of change. Eshkol, however, was not displaced and Mapai retained its position as the leading political force in government. Instead, Eshkol was forced to capitulate to the external pressure and to integrate his critics in a government of national unity due to the nervousness of certain

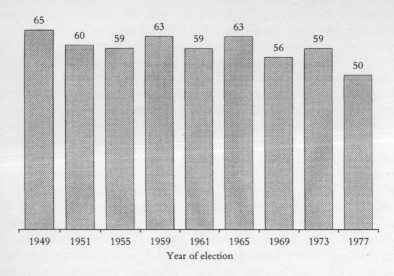

Figure 5.2   The centre-left during the first nine Knessets

elements within Mapai. Ben-Gurion excluded himself, but Rafi's Moshe Dayan became Minister of Defence and Gahal's Menachem Begin and Yosef Sapir became Ministers without portfolio. The 'young Turks' of Rafi had returned to positions of power in Mapai, but they had brought Menachem Begin and Gahal in their train into the Cabinet. This marked a crucial stage in the movement to the right which resulted in the election of Begin some ten years later. It also laid the psychological basis for Rafi to return and form a coalition with Mapai and Achdut Ha'avoda: the result, the Israeli Labour Party, was founded in 1968. Rafi was said to be a party consisting of only 'princes' – those ex-Mapai members who aspired to high office. They could see no real future in following Ben-Gurion, who opposed a return while Eshkol remained in office. The 40:60 split in Rafi left a sizeable minority who continued to profess allegiance to the 83-year-old Ben-Gurion. In 1959, Mapai had coined the election slogan 'Say Yes to the Old Man'. Those who stood by the slogan ten years later formed the State List and were reduced to four seats in the 1969 elections. The Labour Party meanwhile formed the Ma'arach – the Labour Alignment with the left-wing Mapam. The Labour Alignment of four socialist parties won 56 seats, compared with Gahal's 26, in the 1969 elections (see Figure 5.2 for comparative data on the centre-left's representation in the Knesset 1949–77).

The centre-left – Mapai and other socialist parties plus their leftist allies – always hovered near the 61-seat blocking majority in the 120-seat Knesset.[6] Thus any disagreements which resulted in the defection of even a few seats could politically destabilize a Labour-led government. After 1967, the centre-left's position therefore became precarious because the Rafi split and the defection of members of the centre-left to the centre-right over the future of the Territories effectively tipped the balance and thereby denied Labour its automatic right to govern. This persuaded the religious parties and non-socialist parties, which were already moving towards the right after the Six Day War, to look for rival blocs to join and thereby improve their bargaining power.

Although Eshkol had succeeded in uniting the numerous socialist parties electorally into the Labour Alignment, he had not brought them closer ideologically. The creature which emerged in 1969 was a quarrelsome organism with diverse political philosophies. Some components, like Mapam, espoused dovish policies, whilst Achdut Ha'avoda wanted to retain the Territories captured in 1967. Just before his untimely death, Eshkol had floated the idea of negotiating with Arafat's Fatah. The candidates to succeed him, Yigal Allon and Moshe Dayan, had, however, advocated maximalist solutions involving Jordan rather than the Palestinians. Yet both were passed over by the newly formed Labour Party, which feared both handing over power to a new generation and the schism that would be caused if a non-Mapai leader – such as Allon or Dayan – was selected. Rather than risk splitting the party, a compromise candidate, Golda Meir, was chosen. Her inflexibility was to lay the psychological foundations for Begin and the Likud. Indeed, in hindsight, many have referred to her as the first Likudnik. Meir's genial hawkishness prevented Rafi from seceding once more and forming a pact with Gahal and the National Religious Party – which had dramatically turned to the right after 1967 and distanced itself from its long-time partner, Mapai. Whereas Dayan and Allon recognized that the Palestinians had rights, both Begin and Meir, who had been brought up in the Diaspora, would have liked to have wished away their very existence. Dayan once remarked that the difference between Golda Meir and himself was that she loved the Jewish people whereas he loved the Land of Israel – Palestinian inhabitants included.

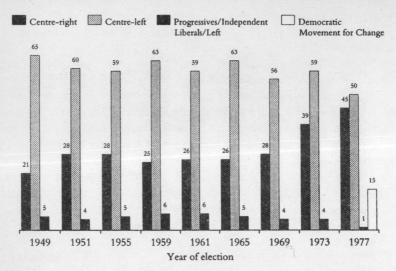

Figure 5.3   The centre-right/centre-left division of seats in the first nine Knessets

The Formation of Likud

While the slow fragmentation – both internal and external – of the Labour Party proceeded apace, the opposite process took place on the right. Begin took advantage of this shifting political terrain, including the ideological realignment that had taken place in the Labour movement after the Six Day War, to establish an alternative right-wing bloc from his base in Gahal. Nevertheless, Herut won only 15 seats out of Gahal's total of 26 in the 1969 elections – the same low total as 1965 (see Figure 5.3 for the centre-right/centre-left division of seats in the first nine Knessets). Yet a number of factors had clearly changed during that period. Through his association with Rafi, Begin had assumed the mantle of respected elder statesman because of his 'responsible' attitude during the Six Day War. He had supported a Mapai-led government and served in it as Minister without portfolio. The Israeli public had enthusiastically rallied to a National Unity government which included both Herut's Begin and Rafi's Dayan; Mapai's Eshkol, on the other hand, had been perceived as slow and dithering, and the leader of a narrow coalition. Even Ben-Gurion seemed to have changed his mind about Begin.

At the beginning of 1967, Ben-Gurion commented that *shlemut*

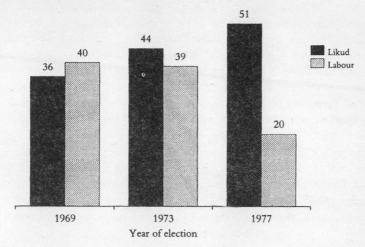

Figure 5.4   Distribution of the vote of those aged 24 and below (%)

ha'moledet – the 'completeness' of the homeland – had assumed a secondary importance for Herut. A few months later, Begin called upon Ben-Gurion to head a National Unity government as the crisis which led to the Six Day War deepened. In addition, a new post-independence generation had come of age and was eligible to vote for the first time in the 1969 election. The quarrels between Begin and Ben-Gurion, the bitterness between Mapai and the Revisionists, were to some extent things of the past. The finer points of political argument – so important at the time – now seemed distant and less relevant. Begin had assumed the public persona of a well-known figure in the fight for independence. Moreover, this was no longer the age of the struggling pioneer and of ideological debates about the finer points of socialist Zionism. As the Labour Alignment showed itself unable to inspire and lead the country, more and more young people demanded an alternative – and for many it resided in the formation of an anti-Mapai coalition (see Figure 5.4).

The coalition building around Herut was ultimately successful because Begin himself had more than his fair share of political luck. Following the lack of any breakthrough in the 1965 elections, Gahal was for some considerable period on the verge of disintegration. In both the Liberal Party and Herut, Begin was perceived as an obstacle to progress. In 1966, the Herut leader fought off a determined attempt to unseat him by Shmuel Tamir and other disaffected party members. By early 1967, the rumblings in the Liberal Party reached a dangerous level for the stability of the Gahal alliance. Some Liberal leaders argued that there could have been a realignment with Rafi if it were not for the figure of Menachem Begin. Indeed, discussions were held between Shimon Peres and the Liberals, and it became clear that there was considerable common ground between the right wing of the Labour movement and the liberal wing of Gahal.[7] The political crisis which led to the Six Day War a few weeks later effectively saved Begin. The Herut leader's inclusion in the Cabinet – and his insistence that Rafi's Moshe Dayan also be co-opted – further erased any political stigma from the public's perception of Begin. Such statesman-like behaviour was propagated for public consumption as well, of course. Gahal's platform for the 1969 election stated:

> In the days of siege and anxiety, Gahal took the initiative in forming a National Unity government which would put an end to the stance of passive waiting which could only end in disaster, and would decide to exercise the right of self-defence in order to repel the aggressors. We for our part let no memories of the past or other considerations stand in the way. The nation was in danger and time was short. We did not insist on due representation in the government according to the accepted rules. But we rejected the proposal that Gahal should join the government alone without Rafi of that time. We insisted on a wall-to-wall coalition. On the first of June, the National Unity government came into being. The enemy was confronted with a united nation. Confusion, despondence and indecision were at an end. The government decided, the army overcame, the nation was saved.[8]

This introduction, probably written by Begin himself, projected Gahal as selfless patriots and saviours of the nation. After the war, such retelling of history influenced many inside Gahal and beyond it. The Liberals certainly looked at Begin in a new light. They now genuinely regarded him as the leader of their combined movement. The occupation of the Territories in 1967 persuaded some Liberals – and many others too – that perhaps Herut had been right all along. After 1967, they too increasingly subscribed to the idea of a Greater Israel. In Gahal's platform for the 1969 election, the Liberals agreed with Herut that 'no plan or proposal which would result in another partition of the Western part of the Land of Israel shall be acceptable ... Jewish urban as well as agricultural settlement on a wide scale in the regions of Judea, Samaria, Gaza, the Golan Heights and Sinai is a national effort of overriding importance, and must be accorded priority within the development plans of the State.'[9]

Gahal was awarded six ministries following the 1969 election. This was a long way from the Mapai secretariat's vote against the co-option of Gahal and Rafi to form a National Unity government on the eve of the Six Day War. Their continuing presence in the government ensured a growing legitimacy for the right and they were able to nullify any peace initiatives after 1967 which hinted at withdrawal from the Territories. When Begin and his Gahal colleagues finally left the government in 1970 over the Rogers Plan, it was the possibility of withdrawal on the basis of UN Resolution 242 which finally caused the rift. Moreover, the status quo between 1967 and 1973 was the retention of the Territories in the absence of peace. Begin, in his advocacy of a Greater Israel, thus became the agent of stability and security. The doves in the Labour Party and the left, in contrast, became the patrons of change and advocates of a step into the political and military unknown.

The return of Rafi to the Labour Party by a narrow vote was primarily a question of tactics. The State List, the Rafi rump which remained outside, remained in close contact with their former colleagues inside Labour – even though Ben-Gurion had formally bowed out of politics in 1970. The ascendency of Dayan and Peres in the Labour Alignment, headed by the hawkish Golda Meir, characterized the general direction of Israeli politics after 1967. Although the split with Mapai in 1965 had not been over matters of foreign policy, Rafi after the Six Day War was decidedly hawkish and there was a general feeling that the territorial gains of 1967 should not be squandered. Dayan, for example, remained in contact with the Ein Vered Group, which advocated retaining the Territories. Although Golda Meir was never happy about the return of Rafi and despite the fact that her relationship with Ben-Gurion's young Turks was less than straightforward, they strengthened her right-wing political stance in the new Labour Party. Thus, Peres and Dayan, the advocates of 'functional compromise' rather than territorial partition, found common cause with Golda Meir, Israel Galili and the hawkish old guard in the party.

Some maximalist Rafi members were active in the Land of Israel movement. The victory of 1967 and the desire to retain the Territories produced a common platform with former enemies in the Revisionist camp. The decline of Mapai under the rule of Golda Meir initiated a coalescence of these groups in a broad coalition with Gahal. Other Labour Alignment defectors, such as Moshe Shamir, Zvi Shiloah and Avraham Yoffe, grouped in the Land of Israel Movement, promoted the slogan 'The Land of Israel for the People of Israel'.

Despite the inhibitions of Begin, right-wing military figures such as the Liberals' Arik Sharon and Herut's Ezer Weizmann began to push for a broader alliance of anti-Labour parties. The State List's Zalman Shoval, who took over Ben-Gurion's Knesset seat in 1970, advocated a wide coalition of Gahal, the State List, the Free Centre and even Dayan and his followers in the Labour Party. Shoval sent Ben-Gurion a detailed document outlining his proposals. Ben-Gurion replied that he had left political life and suggested that Shoval and his friends should do as they wished. The implication was that he neither supported the formation of the Likud nor opposed it.[10]

Such efforts bore fruit in the formation of the Likud in September 1973. This consisted of the Herut–Liberal bloc; the Rafi fragment, the State List; the Land of Israel Movement; and Shmuel Tamir's Free Centre. As if to emphasize the Labour component of this new alliance, the Labour Movement for the Land of Israel was established a few days later and resolved to fight the 1973 election as part of the Likud. Moreover, the new Likud was vastly different from the old-style Gahal, since its ex-Labour components brought with it strong support from the Moshav movement of smallholders. The common interest of the new grouping was to safeguard the security gains of the Six Day War and to negotiate at some point in the future. The interpretation of policy was, however, left vague since there were clear differences between the approach of Herut and that of the other components of the Likud.

The Likud Statement of Principles spoke of 'a social order based on freedom and justice; elimination of poverty and want; the development of an economy that will ensure a decent standard of living for all; the improvement of the environment and the quality of life'. It also spoke of 'working together for the territorial integrity of Eretz Israel'. The Liberal executive met in November 1973 to consider their contribution to the Likud election manifesto. They recommended concessions in Sinai and the Golan but not in Gaza. They asserted that the best solution was to declare Jordan the Palestinian state. They disagreed with Herut on the territorial question – 'security frontiers were more important than historic rights' – and significantly condemned Labour's assertion that Gahal's line was that 'not one inch' of territory should be returned. Yet the Liberals were in no real position to argue for more moderate policies: Herut was the leading party with Menachem Begin as its leader.

Begin was not ready to water down his lifelong convictions. At a meeting in early December 1973, he told a Likud election gathering that he objected to UN Resolution 242 since it meant the redivision of the Land of Israel.[11] Although Golda Meir had in 1970 asked 'who are the Palestinians?', many other Labour Party members had taken a firmer grip on reality in recognizing the Palestinians as a people. Begin exploited this difference within Labour and utilized it to delegitimize the Palestinians as a national entity.

> Another sign of confusion, one which magnifies the danger. Palestinians? If that's who the Israeli Arabs in Hebron are, or those in Jericho, Bethlehem or Shchem. Then who are the Arabs in Nazareth or Acre? ... With iniquitous irresponsibility the Ma'arach talks of the need to consider the desires of those they call by the worthy name of Palestinians – don't they know what these people are?[12]

For Begin – as for the old guard of Mapai – 'Palestinians' meant 'Palestinian Jews' as understood in the pre-state days. If the Mapai elders wore blinkers, Begin additionally could not recognize the concept of a Palestinian people since it would imply their right to national sovereignty in the areas where they lived. A recognition of another claim to the Land of Israel could lead to new negotiations and a legitimation of partition which would reverse the conquests of 1967.

The name of the Likud became instantly known to the discerning Israeli voter as soon as it was formed. The Histadrut elections which took place on the same day as the establishment of the Likud showed no change of allegiance despite a deepening criticism of the Ma'arach. The combined vote of Gahal, the State List and the Free Centre in the Histadrut elections in 1969 was 22.71 per cent. When these parties stood as the Likud in the Histadrut elections four years later, they polled virtually the same figure, 22.69 per cent. This further implied that there had been virtually no movement in the Gahal vote in the Histadrut since it first stood in 1965. Yet three months later, under the Likud, the centre-right increased its total Knesset representation from the 28 seats won in 1969 to 39 seats.

Shortly after the formation of the Likud, the Egyptians launched a surprise attack which caught Israel very poorly prepared and not mobilized. The Yom Kippur War forced the postponement of the national elections. The resulting military débâcle was deemed by the

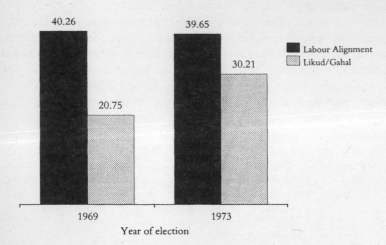

Figure 5.5   Votes for Labour and the Likud in the 1969 and 1973 elections (%)

Israeli public to be the responsibility of the Labour government. It proved to be the catalyst which brought criticism of policy, style and ethos to a head. Most importantly, the war persuaded many Sephardim to desert Labour. The Sephardi vote for the Alignment in 1973 plummeted by 20 per cent, from one half of all Sephardi votes to a third. Begin's cultivation of the development towns began to pay political dividends. In 1969, Moshe Katzav had been elected the first Gahal mayor of a development town, Kiryat Malachi, at the age of 24. The new generation of Israeli-born Sephardim deserted Labour in droves. A survey by the Israel Institute of Applied Research showed that 62 per cent of Israelis born in Asia and Africa were prepared to support the Labour Alignment in September 1973. The Institute found that, after the Yom Kippur War, in December 1973, only 43 per cent of Israelis from that background were willing to endorse the policies of the Alignment. A similar drop in support was mirrored in the native-born population. Israeli voters between the ages of 25 and 39, in particular, turned their backs on Labour.[13] The massive shift in the Sephardi vote away from Labour permitted Likud to increase massively the percentage of its vote compared to past elections (see Figure 5.5).

On the eve of the election, opinion polls showed that huge sections of the electorate, ranging from 20 to 40 per cent, were undecided as to which party to support. This was unprecedented, given the political conservatism of the Israeli voter. Herut had been supported by a minority of Sephardim – and the poorer elements at that – since the 1950s. The sense of discrimination experienced by the Sephardi proletariat finally boiled over in the 1973 elections. It thereby assisted in producing the breakthrough which Begin had been searching for ever since the establishment of the state. As in 1967, Begin had been lucky: the advent of war had prevented a disintegration of his very fragile coalition of anti-Labour parties. Gahal's departure from the National Unity government in 1970, which had caused so much anguish to the Liberals, fortunately meant that the Likud could distance itself from the Labour Alignment's conduct of the Yom Kippur War.

Perhaps the Likud would have edged forward by a few percentage points due to Gahal's acquisition of the State List, the Free Centre and the Land of Israel Movement. The new coalition would have made modest progress compared to the static results of 1965 and 1969, but the Yom Kippur War proved to be the straw which broke the camel's back. Public patience with an ossified, vacuous Labour movement had run its course. The decline of Labour manifested itself in the rise of the Likud. The election of 1973 proved to be a watershed: the Likud came to be regarded in the eyes of ordinary Israelis as a genuine alternative to the ruling Labour elite.

Labour's Last Breath

Begin pressed home his advantage by asking why the reserves were not mobilized prior to Yom Kippur and called for the resignation of Golda Meir. He further called upon Labour to form a National Unity government for the duration of the war. The Likud portrayed Labour as a decaying party, one that could not be trusted with the nation's security. Labour's claims to be strong, vigilant and peace-seeking were mocked. One Likud election advertisement, which asked 'Which is the Peace Party?', stated: 'If we took a leaf from the Ma'arach's book, we would have to call them "The Party of Wars and Permanent Bloodshed".'[14] Labour, however, made much of the Likud's internal divisions. In seeking to expose the differences between Begin's hard-line Herut and the more moderate policies of the other components, Labour advertisements asked whether the Likud was ready for territorial compromise with Jordan and whether they supported UN Resolutions 242 and 338 and were ready to attend the Geneva peace conference.

The Likud was further bolstered by the messianic colouring and territorial aspirations of the National Religious Party and other groups who were intent on settling the Territories – Judea and Samaria – which they regarded as a religious duty. The Likud message was clear and was predicated on public shock and sensitivity to the suddenness of the Yom Kippur War: 'For peace, not surrender, vote Likud'. Labour could not project such a focused approach. It had to explain away its mistakes in the war and to account for its inability both to reform itself and to relate to a proletariat which should have constituted a natural source of support. It also had no clear approach on the future of the Territories despite the much promulgated Allon Plan. In 1973, the Israeli voter was unsure whether a vote for Labour meant restricted settlement and economic integration of the Territories or withdrawal as illustrated by the 'Land for Peace' formulation.

At the beginning of December 1973, just a few weeks before the election, an acrimonious debate took place in the Labour Central Committee, where Pinchas Sapir, the Minister of Finance and party strongman, attacked the hawkish policies of Moshe Dayan and Israel Galili. In November 1968, Sapir had strongly opposed the economic integration of the Territories and criticized Dayan's plans for establishing settlements. The Yom Kippur War had brought matters to a head. A party split was only narrowly averted by a compromise – and therefore meaningless – formulation. The party's lack of direction was summed up by an apologetic Labour advertisement that appeared one day before the election: 'Even a responsible government can err, but to elect an irresponsible government would be a grave error.'

Golda Meir's approach was instinctively hawkish, but she also sought to be consensual. This, in effect, meant giving no clear lead on the question of the Territories. By 1974, this policy of management through the evasion of fundamental differences led, not to a closing of ranks behind Meir, but to a schism of serious proportions. Her appeals for a return to traditional Labour Zionist values fell on deaf ears. The Agranat Commission on the Yom Kippur War, which amounted to an indictment of the political and military elite, subsequently led to the exit of both Golda Meir and Dayan. Sapir, who could have succeeded Meir, declined to serve and thereby ended the lineage of Mapai, and the hegemony of the old guard. Yitzhak Rabin, the hero of the 1967 war and a former ambassador to the United States, was brought in as a relatively non-factional outsider to prove to the party and to the country that Labour was still the natural party of government. Rabin's victory over the other contestant,

Shimon Peres, was won by only the narrow margin of 298 votes to 254. This, in itself, gave the clearest evidence to the Israeli public that Labour was divided – and that was without taking into consideration the bitter personal rivalry and important differences between the two men.

The contest nevertheless revealed a new face of Labour: the party was attempting to show that decisions were not being made behind closed doors and that it wanted to distance itself from past undemocratic behaviour where lack of consultation and unilateral decisions were deemed acceptable. The Labour Party now rested in the hands of three men: Rabin, Peres and Allon. None owed his allegiance to Mapai. Allon was from Achdut Ha'avoda, Peres from Rafi, and Rabin – although nominally from Achdut Ha'avoda – did not align himself with any faction. As the Rabin–Peres feud developed during the next twenty years, ideological positions developed often as a result of expediency. Peres was perceived as a hawk in the 1970s, but as a dove in the 1980s. For Rabin, the reverse process occurred. The Labour Alignment – the Ma'arach – was less than the sum of its different diverse ideological parts. Where once Ben-Gurion's Mapai had given a strong consistent lead, the Labour Party line was unfocused and confusing.

Rabin's great misfortune was to take over the reins of government at a historical low tide for Labour Zionism. He was also untried and inexperienced in dealing with politicians and political issues. Moreover, the public sense that Labour was a party grown fat and indolent after nearly three decades in power began to manifest itself in a series of scandals. Misdemeanours by leading officials in the Israel–British Bank and the Israel Corporation earned them heavy prison sentences. These and other crimes had taken place at the outset of Rabin's premiership, but the election year of 1977 began with the suicide of Avraham Ofer, the former head of Shikun Ovdim, the Histadrut Housing Corporation. He had been under investigation for embezzling public funds.

Rabin and his Justice Minister, Chaim Zadok, had formally broken with the past, when the practice of covering up for people in public life was common. Moreover, as a result of the news blackout on Egyptian manoeuvres prior to the Yom Kippur War, a new breed of investigative journalist had arisen that was not content to accept the official version of events. Thus *Ha'olam Hazeh*'s Yigal Laviv claimed that Shikun Ovdim officials had moved millions from the Corporation into Labour Party election coffers in 1973. A month later, Asher

Yadlin, the suspended head of Kupat Holim and the Cabinet nominee for Governor of the Bank of Israel, who was on trial for taking bribes, claimed in court to have moved large sums through secret funds into Labour Party accounts. Although this allegation was discounted by the judge in her summing up, the Yadlin affair seemed to confirm the cancerous corruption within Labour. The Likud, too, had its whiff of scandal when the Tel Hai fund became so depleted of cash that it was besieged by debtors. Nevertheless, the mud seemed to stick only to Labour.

> The sight of key figures in that party [Labour] vying among themselves for having heard nothing, seen nothing and known nothing is totally degrading. The party should clean its own house before the police, the State Comptroller and perhaps a Commission of Inquiry step in. It will therefore set an example to other political parties whose account books are similarly fixed. The social rot that has permeated our society can and must be eradicated even if it is a painful and undignified process both in our own eyes and in the eyes of others.[15]

Rabin's policy of openness had uncovered the malfeasance of his predecessors and clearly demonstrated the old way of operating. Yet the public perception of Labour was that it was still the same party albeit under a different leadership. Rabin, despite his good intentions, was tarred by the party's past misdemeanours.

The new Carter administration in the USA also signalled that the times were changing for Israel. Carter's emphasis on human-rights issues led, by extension, to a natural consideration of the Palestinian problem. Unlike previous administrations, it did not adopt an indifferent approach to the question of the Territories and the Middle East conflict in general. For example, it refused to sell cluster bombs to Israel. Yet it was not a cooling of US–Israeli friendship which forced Yitzhak Rabin to the point of resignation. During an eve-of-election visit to Washington, several Israeli Embassy employees heard gossip that Leah Rabin, the Prime Minister's wife, had carried out transactions at the Dupont Circle branch of the National Bank. An Israeli journalist, Dan Margalit, confirmed the existence of the account, no. 4698553, by depositing $50. It was illegal for an Israeli to hold a foreign-currency account abroad without prior authorization by the foreign-currency division of the Treasury; the punishment for violation of the law was up to three years' imprisonment and/or a fine of three times the amount illegally held. Margalit's incriminating article appeared in *Ha'aretz* on 15 March – the Ides of

March. Although Treasury officials decided upon an administrative fine, this was opposed by the Attorney General. Rabin's open admission on Israel Radio that it was a joint account led to his resignation. He made no attempt to invoke parliamentary immunity. The luckless Rabin was succeeded by his arch-rival Shimon Peres. Yet, as the findings of the Israel Institute of Applied Social Research at the time showed, Labour's chances were minimal regardless of who was the leader.

A Hanoch Smith poll for the American Jewish Committee showed that 'corruption' occupied the fifteenth position in matters of concern and importance for Israelis in 1973; by 1977, it had moved up to fourth position. Another Smith poll for *Ma'ariv* in May 1977 showed that 35 per cent thought the issue of corruption in public life would influence the outcome of the election. This represented a 10 per cent increase from March when the Leah Rabin scandal broke.

The annual report of the State Comptroller added fuel to the fire. It criticized the army for wasting financial resources and cited the use of planes for private use. It condemned large-scale expenditure that was not subject to parliamentary control. It blamed the big banks for taking advantage of an unaccountable subsidy system. It considered the telephone system to be in a state of total chaos – only half the number of public telephones planned for 1976 were installed. The report condemned the Ministry of Commerce and Industry's lack of control over allocations to approved investors who purchased rather than imported local products. Vague terms of reference and a lack of accountability led to the number of applications trebling between 1972 and 1975. The Ministry of Absorption was similarly shown to have been incompetent in permitting the abuse of kibbutz aid to new immigrants. Similarly, the Ministry of the Interior was held to be lax in supervising municipal expenditure.

In 1976, the Ministry of Religious Affairs allocated 109 million Israeli pounds to *yeshivot* (seminaries), *kollelim* (advanced studies for married students), schools and institutes of higher education. The Comptroller found that the Ministry kept inadequate records as to the number of students enrolled. There was no clear definition of what was meant by 'Torah Research Institutions'. Inadequate records of foreign contributions to *yeshivot* were maintained – an important issue, since the government matched such contributions with equal subsidies.

In the legal system, the State Comptroller found that court administrations had not collected hundreds of thousands of Israeli pounds in unpaid fines from some 10,000 companies between 1970 and 1975. Hundreds of cases between 1971 and 1975 were discovered where magistrates' courts in Tel Aviv, Haifa, Tiberias and Rechovot had not returned bail following either a trial or the dropping of charges. In cases where bonds had been accepted as sureties in place of bail, court secretaries more often than not had failed to investigate the financial position of the sureties. Fines, it was determined, were often not collected due to a lack of manpower and suitably qualified people.

The Broadcasting Authority also came in for scrutiny when it was discovered that 14 million Israeli pounds had been spent on replacing television equipment. Such decisions were made by unaccountable professionals rather than management. The State Comptroller highlighted the purchase of an electronic subtitling projector in June 1975 at a cost of 1.2 million Israeli pounds. It was discovered that the sum had not been included in the budget and, what is more, had forced the cancellation of more vital equipment such as fire detectors for the radio studios. Four employees made five trips abroad to purchase the machine, and when it finally arrived in Jerusalem in October 1975 it was deemed to be unsuitable. The State Comptroller's team found it gathering dust in a Broadcasting Authority storeroom in August 1976.

All these irregularities stirred up a great sense of resentment amongst ordinary hard-pressed Israelis. The Labour Party was perceived as having been sucked into a vortex of corruption which permeated its entire structure. The *askanim* – an impolite term for the party apparatchiks and bureaucrats – became hate-figures and symbols of the malaise affecting the entire country. In a letter to the press, a few weeks before the election, a new immigrant commented:

> This poor country is being wrecked by widespread law-breaking and corruption, by kickbacks, swindles and dishonest manipulations of the laws. In the circumstances, Mrs Rabin's illegal foreign currency account is not just a minor inadvertence of a naive little lady, but is a symptom of the sickness of the times.[16]

The new leadership, personified by Rabin and Peres, which was supposed to act as a new broom, was in effect overwhelmed by the degree of dirt accumulated over decades through saloon-bar politics where the cutting of corners was both expected and applauded. For example, secret ballots to elect candidates to a party list for the 1977 elections were then 'qualified' by a nominating committee whose

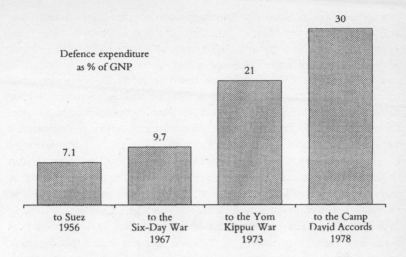

Figure 5.6 The increase in defence expenditure, 1950–78

responsibility was to ensure that all factions and vested interests were represented. Thus, although Yitzhak Navon gained 92.4 per cent support, he was placed eighth on the list; Yigal Allon, who secured 75 2 per cent, was placed second.

The age of ideology was rapidly fading and its instrument, the party of the masses, was regarded by many as having many dinosaur-like qualities. The post-1948 generation of Israelis had different expectations. Unlike their parents, they were not pioneers and builders: they wanted a decent life for themselves and their families and a government which governed fairly and rationally. These aspirations were set against a background of economic downturn and galloping inflation in the aftermath of the Yom Kippur War. When Pinchas Sapir presented his budget just a few weeks after the 1973 election, he announced that the cost of fuel oil had increased tenfold over the previous year. Increased oil prices and imports produced an annual rate of inflation of 30–40 per cent between the elections of 1973 and 1977. The surprise attack during the Yom Kippur War and strong Soviet backing for Israel's Arab opponents meant that nearly half the country's GNP went on defence in 1976 (see Figure 5.6 for the growth in defence expenditure 1950–78). A change in the growth rate of GNP was a clear sign of Israel's economic difficulties. Between 1970 and 1973, the increase was 9 per cent. In the following years up to the accession of the Begin government, the growth rate dropped to 2.6 per cent.

Between 1972 and 1974, Israel's arms import bill more than trebled. The percentage of Israel's defence spending was, proportionately, four times that of NATO.[17] By contrast, the share of funds spent on social welfare dropped from 54 per cent before the war to 36 per cent after it. The cost-of-living index trebled between 1969 and 1975. Yet the Labour Party did not exhibit the spirit of sacrifice that was expected from the citizenry. On 8 March 1977, the Governor of the Bank of Israel predicted that inflation would increase by 30 per cent in the coming year. On 28 March, the Labour Party announced that it would spend 10 million Israeli pounds on election propaganda. Some 68 million Israeli pounds had been allocated to all parties.

Although financial scandals hit both the Likud and the National Religious Party, they paled to insignificance compared to the perceived rottenness of the Labour Party. Thus, whether the issue was party democracy or runaway inflation, the future of the Territories or the honesty of party leaders, or simply the desire of a householder to install a telephone quickly, the Labour Party could offer nothing that the public wanted. The newly formed Democratic Movement for Change, however, could easily espouse the cause of democratization and fair play, while Simcha Erlich could claim that a Likud government would reduce the rate of inflation to a mere 15 per cent during its first year. In the television debate on the eve of the election, the newly elected Labour leader, Shimon Peres, looked decidedly ill at ease in trying to explain away Labour's fudged policies and its litany of failures. This was in stark contrast to his opponent, Menchem Begin, who, although recovering from a heart attack, was perceived as the panacea to the nation's ills, the elder statesman whose time had finally come.

CHAPTER SIX

THE FIRST BEGIN GOVERNMENT

Dayan's Defection

Four days after winning the election, Menachem Begin offered the Ministry of Foreign Affairs to Moshe Dayan, a member of the defeated Labour Party. Dayan had left office in disgrace together with Golda Meir in 1974, and effectively carried the public blame for the *mechdal* – the lack of preparedness before and during the Yom Kippur War. Golda Meir's successor, Yitzhak Rabin, distanced himself from the reputation of the previous government and significantly did not include the more hawkish Dayan in his Cabinet.[1] Although cleared of personal responsibility by the Agranat Commission, Dayan was not forgiven by the public, for whom the deaths of 2616 soldiers was a national disaster. Unlike Golda Meir, Dayan was seemingly never troubled by a sense of personal guilt, whether or not there was justification for such. He made short shrift of the army of critics who continually berated him. Among these critics, Motti Ashkenazi, the commanding officer of the only Israeli stronghold on the Suez Canal not to have fallen to the Egyptian onslaught, became the most prominent and vociferous of Dayan's public judges. Following a private meeting with Ashkenazi, Dayan wrote:

> In nothing Motti Ashkenazi said, did I find a spark of trust, of faith, of anything constructive. All was nihilistic. It was not by Motti Ashkenazi and people like him that Israel had been built, and not through them that Israel would grow and prosper. On the face of it, we had been sitting in the same room dealing with different things and living in two different worlds, separated by something far wider than the generation gap.[2]

This does more than provide evidence of Dayan's well-known disdain for intellectuals, philosophers and jejune protest movements. It also points to the widening gap between Dayan and the new, often articulate, political forces which were emerging in both Israeli and Palestinian national life. Despite his individualism, Dayan was a product of his age and felt more comfortable with the patriotism and Zionist declarations of the Ben-Gurion era.

Under Golda Meir's premiership, Dayan had endorsed a highly individualistic policy in the Territories. He rejected both the Allon Plan and the Jordanian option. He believed that no geographical line could be drawn which would satisfy Israeli security needs. He opposed the generally held view that the retention of the Jordan Valley was essential on security grounds since it could easily be isolated in a swift military advance. Dayan, unlike Golda Meir, believed that the Palestinians had to be involved in any negotiations, and consequently propagated the idea of a functional compromise rather than one based on territorial concessions. This could be interpreted in a variety of ways, he argued: a condominium, joint sovereignty, cantons, different approaches to autonomy.

In 1973, the division in the Labour Party was such that it was on the verge of splitting following Dayan's demand that Yamit in Sinai be developed as a deep-water harbour. His public pronouncements were seen to be increasingly at variance with other leading party members. Supported by Shimon Peres and Golda Meir, Dayan personified the right within the broad Labour movement. At that time, the party establishment greatly feared that Dayan, supported by the adherents of Rafi and the hawks within, would once more break away, but on this occasion join with the growing right-wing bloc – shortly to become the Likud. After all, Gahal and Rafi had joined forces on the eve of the Six Day War to install the National Unity government at the expense of Mapai. The party hierarchy papered over the cracks by issuing a hard-line compromise, the Galili document, in August 1973 on the eve of the Yom Kippur War.

Ironically, the hawkish leaders of the party were driven from office – not because of their policies, which were actually attuned to public opinion on the question of the Territories, but because of the débâcle of the war. Dayan's banishment to the margins of political life was accompanied by his growing perception of the Labour Party's movement away from the ethos of the Galili document. It was not religious messianism and the developing threat from the Likud which worried Dayan. His concern was, rather, that he perceived a more dovish approach from the Labour government of Rabin and Peres. While Labour was tentatively flirting with the notion of trading land for peace, Dayan was still advocating the right of any Jew to buy land beyond the 1967 borders. Significantly, he signed a Likud motion in October 1974 in support of retaining Judea and Samaria. Dayan once commented than he had more in common with Menachem Begin than with Meir Ya'ari, one of the ideological doyens of left socialist Zionism in Israel. Indeed, in a letter to Begin at this time, he told the Likud leader that he would be happy to serve in a government under his leadership.[3] Psychologically, therefore, it was not that big a step for him to join Begin. After all, although one part of Rafi had rejoined Mapai in 1968 to establish the Labour Party, the other part had eventually found a home in the new Likud union in 1973.

Dayan did not see any political future for himself in Rabin's Labour Party. At a press conference in London at the end of January 1977, Dayan made it clear that he would prefer Peres as Prime Minister. He was adamant that he had no plans to return to government and told the press that he planned to write a book about the Bible. Shortly afterwards, he was humiliated at Labour's conference when his stand against land for peace and his views on security settlements in the Jordan Valley were decisively rebuffed. As early as January, he had told his former Rafi colleague Shimon Peres and his hawkish allies Golda Meir and Israeli Galili that he could not stand as a candidate for a party which embraced territorial compromise.[4]

In late March 1977, Dayan entered into talks with Begin with a view to securing a position on the Likud list in the 1977 elections. Dayan's condition for making the break with Labour hinged on the Likud's willingness not to extend Israeli sovereignty to the Territories 'as long as' negotiations were in progress with the Arabs. Although Begin seemingly accepted the principle, he argued that he could not publicly declare it for fear of losing both Likud and far-right voters. This was also implicit in the strong wording of the Likud election manifesto:

> The right of the Jewish People to the Land of Israel is eternal, and is an integral part of its right to security and peace. Judea and Samaria shall therefore not be relinquished to foreign rule; between the sea and the Jordan, there will be Jewish sovereignty alone.
>
> Any plan that involves surrendering parts of Western Eretz Israel militates against our right to the Land, would inevitably lead to the establishment of a 'Palestinian State', threaten the security of the civilian population, endanger the existence of the State of Israel, and defeat all prospects of peace.[5]

Begin's public pronouncements stated the converse of his understanding with Dayan. Indeed, 48 hours after the election, in the synagogue of the settlement at Kaddum, he stated that 'you annex foreign land, not your own country'.

Dayan's terms for remaining with Labour was a pledge that the next government would consult the nation before territory was ceded. This was opposed by Rabin, but Dayan found support on the right of the Labour Party and particularly from Shimon Peres and Golda Meir. At the beginning of April, Dayan announced that he was still running with Labour. Two weeks later, he made a second approach to the Likud. The replacement of Yitzhak Rabin by Shimon Peres had not brought about Dayan's political rehabilitation or a return to former policies. Indeed, rumours surfaced in the Israeli press that Peres would offer Dayan the chairmanship of the Jewish Agency in order to marginalize him. While Peres headed the Labour list, Yigal Allon and Abba Eban occupied the next two positions. Both men were in favour of territorial compromise and were even more outspoken than Rabin.

Even though the Likud was still unable to accommodate Dayan's demands, the former Defence Minister clearly spoke for a hawkish constituency within the Labour Party and beyond. A month before the election, in a speech to the Tel Aviv Commercial and Industrial Club, Dayan told his audience that 'the Jewish affinity to Kiryat Arba, Beth-el and Shchem go far beyond security considerations'. The rationalization of positive sentiments towards the settlements beyond security considerations and use of the Hebrew name for Nablus – Shchem – made Dayan and the new Labour leadership seem strange bedfellows. In contrast, Allon was simultaneously telling the foreign press that he would refuse to contemplate a peace that did not include a homeland for the Palestinians.[6]

Dayan's open dissent from the leadership assisted in the public perception that the Labour Party was in the process of disintegration. His comments nevertheless made him more acceptable to the nationalist camp. Ariel Sharon, having been prevented from obtaining a position on the Likud list, proposed that Dayan join him in setting up a 'Front for Eretz Israel Loyalists'. This was an offer Dayan astutely declined since it was part of a wider strategy by Sharon to shore up the faltering campaign of his own party, Shlomzion. Sharon desperately wanted to join the Likud before the formal registration date for party lists. Although Begin warmed to the idea, both the Liberals and La'am were hostile to Sharon. Shlomzion stood alone in the elections, gained two seats and then swiftly merged with Herut at the earliest moment following Likud's victory.

When the first election results came through, Dayan commented that the Likud victory had been 'an expression of public feeling against giving concessions in Judea and Samaria'. Yet Dayan did not conform to the formal maximalist approach of the nationalists. He believed in an arrangement with the Palestinians, based on a coexistence where neither side would exercise or impose their sovereignty on the other. Begin agreed with Dayan that Israeli sovereignty would not be extended to the Territories 'while' there were peace negotiations with Arab states. This replaced Dayan's less specific and more open-ended 'as long as'. Begin also agreed that Israel should participate in the Geneva peace conference on the basis of UN Resolution 242. He even accepted Dayan's opinion that no Jewish religious services on the Temple Mount would be permitted, as such were viewed as a provocation by the Palestinians.

In making apparent concessions of interpretation to Dayan, Begin was able to give his administration a broader character than he had done with Herut in the years since 1948. Having secured victory in the election, any past agreements and promises made with old friends, whether from the Irgun or the Liberals, could now be transcended. For example, the Liberal candidate for Foreign Minister, Arye Dulzin, was simply passed over. For ultimate power was now in the hands of Begin – the disciple of Jabotinsky and the advocate of a Jewish state on both sides of the Jordan. The integration of Dayan into the nationalist bloc moved the centre of political consensus further away from Labour and towards the Likud. Begin half-heartedly tried to fragment Labour still further by offering Peres the Ministry of Defence and the deputy premiership in a government of National Unity. The utilization of Dayan as a national figure in Israel's recent history was conceived by Begin as a sign of continuity with the heroic past, a means of legitimizing the Likud through linkage with the epoch of Ben-Gurion. In addition, the presence of Dayan on the world stage as Foreign Minister would lend *gravitas* to an un-known government which was regarded in international circles as a collection of dangerous right-wing radicals and former terrorists. The unpopularity of Dayan within Israel, arising from the failures of 1973, had not touched the outside world. On the contrary, the potent image of the general with the eyepatch was seen as the very symbol of Israel's achievements and prowess.

Autonomy for the Palestinians

The celebrated visit of Anwar Sadat to Israel in November 1977 was a historic event. It cast Begin in the mould of statesman and peacemaker. Even the left, many of whom blamed Golda Meir for not having responded positively to a Sadat initiative shortly after Nasser's death, grudgingly acknowledged his achievement. At that time, Sadat, through the UN mediator Gunnar Jarring, had demanded the precondition of an Israeli withdrawal. The response, or rather the lack of one, had not been encouraging. The Yom Kippur War, the left argued, could have been avoided if the Labour Party had been more in touch with political reality. Thus, Sadat's historic visit to Jerusalem was also understood as a consequence of Labour's political staleness. In 1977, the coming to power of the hardline Likud paradoxically offered the prospect of change, and Sadat was advised by King Hassan of Morocco and Romania's Ceausescu that he could do business with Begin. However, the precondition of an Israeli withdrawal again proved a stumbling block. Sadat knew the revolutionary act of a visit to Jerusalem would break through the psychological barrier separating Jew from Arab. It would also avert the failure of a UN-sponsored Geneva conference, and effectively exclude the Soviets and their allies, plus the Europeans. The visit also reflected Sadat's realization that the other potential partners in the peace process – the Syrians, Jordanians and Palestinians – would be hesitant at best to follow him. Thus the seeds for a bilateral agreement between Israel and Egypt were sown from the beginning of Sadat's initiative.

Yet all this posed a major problem for Begin. After years of talking about peace and mooting vague solutions to the problem of the 'Arab inhabitants' of the Territories, he now had to confront the Palestinian issue head-on. While Sadat, in his historic speech to the Knesset, told his audience that 'the heart of the struggle is the Palestinian problem', Begin, in his reply, totally ignored the issue. However, by 1977, it was not possible simply to evade the question of the fate and future of the 'Arab inhabitants of Western Eretz Israel' with displays of fiery grandiloquence. Both domestic and international opinion expected a resolution of the Palestinian question.

Unlike Dayan, Begin knew few Arabs. Despite nearly four decades in Israel, he had only on rare occasions met Palestinian leaders from the Territories to discuss contentious issues. Begin studiedly avoided the issue of Palestinian nationalism which had arisen since 1948 and more specifically after Israel's taking over control of the Territories after 1967. He never spoke about a Palestinian nation. His definition of the Palestinians was couched in Jabotinskyian terms and focused on their status as a national minority. They were part of a wider Arab nation that had already secured national self-determination in a plethora of countries. The PLO, for its part, was deemed to be purely a terrorist organization. No distinction was made between the policies of its factions. There was no perceived difference between moderates and radicals. Any hint of their pursuing a political path was considered to be a deception, a ruse to force Israel to drop its guard. They were today's Nazis, and the PLO Covenant a Palestinian *Mein Kampf*. The Likud election manifesto made Begin's approach abundantly clear.

> The so-styled Palestine Liberation Organization is not a national liberation movement, but a murder organization which serves as a political tool and military arm of the Arab States and as an instrument of Soviet imperialism. The Likud government will take action to exterminate this organization.[7]

Although Begin paid lip-service to the far right, the Liberals and the defectors from Labour, he nevertheless remained a disciple of Jabotinsky. The growing problem of Palestinian nationalism after 1967 persuaded him, not to study the problem at first hand in the Territories and to engage in discussion with his adversaries, but instead to turn for guidance to Jabotinsky's early writings on national and cultural autonomy in Eastern Europe. In particular, Jabotinsky had been one of the architects of the Helsingfors Declaration in December 1906 which demanded that all minorities should be guaranteed cultural autonomy and civil rights in a liberal and democratic Russia. He challenged tsarist autocracy and argued that only in a free Russia could the Jewish masses be organized and educated in a Zionist spirit. Moreover, both he and Begin were familiar with the minefield of ethnic rights in Eastern and Central Europe during the inter-war years.

Thus, the Likud election manifesto stated that,

> those Arabs of Eretz Israel who will apply for citizenship of the country and declare their allegiance to it shall be granted citizenship. Equality of rights and duties shall be maintained for all citizens and residents without distinction of race, nationality, religion, sex or ethnic origin. Full autonomy of culture, religion and heritage, and complete economic integration, shall be assured to all parts of the population.[8]

Yet Begin believed that the 'historical right' of the Jews to Eretz Israel overrode all other claims. In this context of national autonomy, Begin did not differentiate between this historic right and a political claim to sovereignty. He effectively merged them and ignored inconvenient anomalies that were beginning to surface with the advent of Palestinian nationalism.

As the Likud came closer to achieving political office in the 1970s, the pressure increased on Begin to produce a coherent programme which would satisfy often contradictory goals. Conversely, Begin realized that it would not be politically prudent to trumpet publicly any genuine plan as this would create dissent and division in the relatively fragile Likud coalition of parties. They all knew what they were *against*, in that they opposed Labour and the left, but it was not always clear what it was specifically that they were *for*. The unifying centre was that sense of belonging which was cultivated through Begin's magnetism, charisma and general sense of direction. Begin's election partially freed him from the task of coalition-building and permitted him to test ideas and concepts which he believed to be profoundly Jabotinskyian, but which others would view as a sell-out. Just as Jabotinsky had an ambivalent relationship with his radicals – the members of Brit Ha'Biryonim, the Irgun, Betar and Begin himself – so did Begin some forty years later as Prime Minister of Israel. This signified the difference within the nationalist camp between the pragmatic ideologue and the true believer.

Begin's autonomy plan surfaced at the end of 1977. It called for the abolition of the Israeli military government in the Territories – which had been established after the victory of the Six Day War – and Palestinian elections to an Administrative Council. The Council would be responsible for education, religious affairs, finance, transportation, housing, health, industry, the administration of justice and the supervision of local police forces. Palestinians would be offered the choice of either Israeli or Jordanian citizenship. Israel would be responsible for public order and security. It would also control water and land rights. Jews could exercise their right to buy land, settle in the Territories and have the freedom to conduct their economic affairs. At the end of the 26-point document, Dayan's influence was quite apparent:

> Israel stands by its right and its claim of sovereignty to Judea, Samaria and the Gaza District. In the knowledge that other claims exist, it proposes for the sake of the agreement and the peace, that the question of sovereignty in these areas be left open.[9]

A New Kind of Friend

The new American president, Jimmy Carter, unlike his predecessors, had spoken positively about the national aspirations of the Palestinians. His national-security advisor, Zbigniew Brzezinski, had even endorsed the idea of a Palestinian state. Carter was very different from previous American presidents as far as the Middle East conflict was concerned. He was a man of high ideals which emanated from devout Christian beliefs and an involvement in civil rights. His Southern Baptist background projected an intense affinity with the course of Jewish history.

> The Judeo-Christian ethic and study of the Bible were bonds between Jews and Christians which had always been part of my life. I also believed very deeply that the Jews who had survived the Holocaust deserved their own nation and that they had a right to live in peace among their neighbours. I considered this homeland for the Jews to be compatible with the teachings of the Bible, hence ordained by God.[10]

Carter's Christianity also drove him immediately towards a genuine advocacy of global human rights, whether in Latin America or Eastern Europe. Therefore, if he strongly defended human-rights activists such as Sakharov and Orlov as well as Jewish refuseniks such as Shcharansky and Slepak in the Soviet Union, how could he ignore the plight of the Palestinians and their wretched lot in the Territories. His role as peacemaker in the Holy Land was thus beyond the normal pursuit of American interests. One Middle East expert who was involved in the Camp David process noted that Carter had 'an optimistic streak that led him to believe that problems could be resolved if leaders would simply reason together and listen to the aspirations of their people'.[11]

In meetings with the Americans, Begin and Dayan, while denying the rights of a 'foreign sovereign authority', omitted from discussion claims of Israeli sovereignty to the Territories. Dayan's open-ended approach allowed for the non-exercising of the Israeli claim. It did not 'disqualify Israeli sovereignty, but it was not our intention to apply it'.[12] It left the way open for an autonomy plan whereby the Palestinians would live harmoniously with new Israeli settlers.

Carter in Washington was dubious about the plan, while Sadat at the Ismalia summit was negative. It did not provide an adequate response to the demands of Palestinian nationalism and seemed to promote an expanding Israeli presence in the Territories without formal annexation. Clearly the Palestinians wanted separation from Israel, not integration. Moreover, an essential difference between the Israelis and the Americans was that the latter saw autonomy for the

Palestinians as a transient phase, directed towards a more definite arrangement. Despite this relatively lukewarm reception, Begin pressed ahead and the Knesset accepted the autonomy plan by 64 votes to 8 with 40 – mainly Labour – abstentions.

The next half year saw the proposals become submerged in the political mire. Begin had indeed produced a response to deal with the question of the Palestinians, but he had also attempted to maintain as ideologically watertight a stand as possible. The realization that Begin would not alter his stance on the future of the West Bank and Gaza, while maintaining a public readiness to negotiate at all times with Sadat, began to disturb sections of the Israeli public, who had begun to view the Prime Minister as an Israeli De Gaulle. The first indication of growing dismay came in the form of an open letter from 300 Israeli reservists, some 200 of them officers.

> A government which prefers settlements on the other side of the Green Line to the ending of this historic dispute and establishment of normal relations in our area, causes us to question the justice of this direction.
>
> A government policy which leads to the continuation of our rule over one million Arabs will damage the Jewish and democratic nature of our state and make it very difficult for us to identify with it.

This challenge catalysed the formation of the Peace Now movement in Israel and reinforced the minuscule peace movement in general.

On the far right, the very hint of negotiations and the possibility of ceding territory were seen as treasonous. Whereas it was initially believed that Begin would never compromise on his 'historic right' to Eretz Israel, this did not mean that all the territory under Israel's control was non-negotiable. Ben-Gurion had set the precedent when he had proclaimed the Third Kingdom of Israel following the invasion of Sinai in 1956. He had located a reference to an ancient Jewish kingdom in 'Yotvat' in Sinai which several geographers had identified as the island of Tiran.[13] Yet he subsequently ordered the Israeli withdrawal from Sinai several months later when confronted by the political realities of the situation. Some close associates knew that Begin had in the past privately acknowledged his willingness to return Sinai. Despite the fact that the Torah had traditionally been given to the Jews on Mount Sinai, the area clearly exuded little historical significance for Begin.

It was the fear that Begin might compromise that led to the establishment of a Circle of Herut Loyalists at the end of 1977. At the beginning of January 1978, Shmuel Katz resigned as Begin's information advisor. A founder of the Land of Israel Movement and a former high-ranking member of the Irgun, Katz had originally been appointed a Minister of Information in Begin's government. His attempts to propagate both a Revisionist interpretation of the previous thirty years and a hard-line version of contemporary events were consistently blocked by Dayan. Yet, in an internal election he received over 40 per cent of the vote from Herut's Central Committee against Begin's preferred candidate. In his speech, he attacked Begin for going too far in his autonomy proposals. Ariel Sharon also commented on 'the weakness of the government on settlements'. In an open letter to Begin, the former ideologue of Lehi, Israel Eldad, reminded Begin of Jabotinsky's eternal regret in accepting the partition of Eretz Israel in 1922 where the Emir Abdullah received the East Bank of the Jordan. Eldad told Begin that

> nobody is forcing you to sign. You want the government of Israel to sign a new White Paper and without the semantic fancy dress of 'self-rule' for the Arabs of Eretz Israel. What it means is a new partition of Western Eretz Israel.[14]

Throughout 1978, Begin found himself at odds with both the Americans and the Egyptians. Sadat and Carter found Begin exasperating. They quickly discovered that it was extremely difficult to decode his statements. Sadat closely observed Begin's emotional style of politics:

> I am bewildered when I think about Mr Begin's position. He is living in the past. He is of the old guard. Within him there is a bitterness and this is very unfortunate. I always try to live without bitterness. And it hasn't been easy. For many years I had no normal family life. I was in prison or in concentration camps. I was persecuted by the government. I never had any time to devote to my family, but I never became bitter.[15]

Carter believed Begin to be flexible when he met him for the first time in December 1977. In hindsight, he found that Begin's 'good words had multiple meanings which my advisors and I did not understand at the time.'[16]

Foreign condemnation of Begin actually fortified the right and persuaded some on the far right to give the Herut leader the benefit of the doubt for the time being. This static situation effectively permitted the numerous factions of the right to stay their political hand. Even so, informal meetings took place between the dissenters within Herut and those outside it, such as the Land of Israel Movement, the Labour-oriented Ein Vered Group and the religious settlers' movement, Gush Emunim. Many former Mapai members who had followed Ben-Gurion out of the Labour movement and who subsequently ended up in the same party as Menachem Begin now began to doubt whether the Likud was in fact the vehicle of their aspirations. They began to ask themselves if the right now too had betrayed them.

By the summer of 1978, it had become clear that Sadat's visit and the autonomy plan had effectively fragmented the façade of broad ideological unity that Begin had painstakingly constructed under the Likud umbrella. He had maintained the dominance of Herut over this plethora of right-wing groupings since the formation of Likud in 1973. By the end of 1977, Herut represented only a quarter of the total number of Knesset members who had pledged allegiance to the government. The realities of decision-making and forging of policy – particularly in the context of the peace initiative – showed that the Likud functioned primarily as a disparate anti-Labour coalition.

Jabotinsky, in his day, had disapproved of the activities of the far-right radicals who never acknowledged the powerlessness of the Jews. After 1948, Herut effectively absorbed these far-right elements. Those who preferred to remain outside were confined to the political wilderness – such as those who made up the minute readership of Israel Eldad's far-right journal *Sulam*. The far right as a political force subsequently re-emerged after the victory of 1967 and primarily through the Land of Israel Movement. Although Begin partially distanced himself from them, the only political home for many, in terms of practical politics, was in the Likud. They preferred to view Begin as the Betar radical of the 1930s rather than as the pragmatic politician of the 1970s. When the autonomy plan was published, some accused Begin of betraying the legacy of Jabotinsky. Begin retorted that he was in fact carrying out his mentor's approach to the letter.

Some certainly doubted Begin's sincerity in wishing to retain Judea and Samaria – the West Bank. Others – including leading figures like Yitzhak Shamir – believed that not one inch of territory should be returned, and were thus concerned at Begin's known lack of attachment to Sinai. Some, like Moshe Arens, were concerned with security and believed that the Territories provided the best buffer against future attack. Defence experts such as Yuval Ne'eman combined the security aspect with the territorial maximalism of Achdut Ha'avoda.[17] Others believed in the Biblical demarcation of Eretz Israel and knew that Begin tended to focus only on its boundaries in terms of the British Mandate. Some members of the Likud believed that ancient

Eretz Israel contained parts of Syria. Thus, even within the Biblical approach there was considerable room for interpretation. This evoked the ideological differences between the Irgun and Lehi, between Jabotinsky and Stern. In his 18 principles of national revival, Avraham Stern had quoted Genesis 15:18, which spoke about a Jewish home-land from 'the River of Egypt until the great river, the river Euphra-tes'. Some regarded 'the River of Egypt' as the Nile; others believed it to be the Wadi El Arish.[18] Yet by any interpretation, Begin com-promised and suggested a return of part of Eretz Israel in return for peace with Egypt.

For the Herut loyalists, the style and language of Menachem Begin, the legendary Irgun commander, Ha'mefaked, seemed to have under-gone a bizarre change. It was something they were unable to compre-hend or relate to. The unsettling alternative was to believe that Begin was following a politically correct path which was not apparent now, but would become apparent in time. Most Herut members were thus left with an appalling choice. They could either rationalize a volte-face or they could simply believe in Begin, the commander, as an all-wise, all-seeing leader who knew what he was doing. As Chaim Kaufman, the chairman of the Herut faction in the Knesset later remarked: 'It came down to one's faith in the Prime Minister and our party chairman. He is, after all, my mentor. It is a question of having confidence in his team.'[19]

CHAPTER SEVEN

THE COST OF CAMP DAVID

The Break with the Far Right

The far right's moratorium on criticizing Begin's approach was shattered by the Camp David discussions in September 1978. When Begin returned to Israel with a 'Framework for Peace in the Middle East', the schism was complete. The transition to autonomy for the West Bank and Gaza, as well as the return of Sinai and recognition of Egyptian sovereignty over it, seemed to confirm the deepest of suspicions. Even the language used was distinctly foreign for Revisionists. It appeared to be more in line with the approach of the Labour Party. The formal English translation read:

> The negotiations shall be based on all the provisions and principles of UN Security Council Resolution 242. The negotiations will resolve, among other matters, the location of the boundaries and the nature of the security arrangements.
> The solution from the negotiations must also recognize the legitimate rights of the Palestinian people and their just requirements. In this way, the Palestinians will participate in the determination of their own future...[1]

Begin, however, insisted that the Hebrew version referred to 'the Arabs of Eretz Israel' rather than to 'the Palestinians'. Nevertheless, although he continued to employ that phrase in general use and to label Sadat 'that peasant from the Nile' in private discussions with the far right,[2] he still proved unable to convince his radical opponents that he was not also going to return Judea and Samaria.

Begin's technique of procrastination at Camp David had averted any commitment on the issue of the West Bank. In his haste to achieve a successful outcome, Carter had not actually forced Begin to stop settlement activity on the West Bank and in Gaza. He believed that Begin had agreed to a long-term cessation of new settlements as long as across-the-board negotiations were taking place. Yet Begin told Israel Television on his return that this ban on settlement would only last three months while negotiations took place with Egypt and would apply only to 'certain places and not to all places'. Moreover, in an interview on US television, he said that it was conceivable that Israeli soldiers could remain in their positions in 'Judea and Samaria, for ten, fifteen or twenty years'.

Carter had, in fact, agreed to delete a clause on the settlements from the draft agreement in exchange for a letter from Begin. The US president had also dropped his demand that no further population expansion of existing settlements take place. Contrary to Carter's expectations, Begin's letter promised only a three-month freeze and – more important – linked it to the negotiations with the Egyptians rather than to the autonomy talks. Carter returned the letter and requested clarification of this 'misunderstanding'. Begin was able to show that the notes taken by the Israeli Attorney General at Camp David had only indicated his willingness 'to consider a freeze'.[3]

Begin entertained the possibility of an evacuation of the Sinai settlements only. Eventual withdrawal from the West Bank on a 'land for peace' basis and an end to settlement activity were not topics for negotiation. By agreeing to broader statements which in his mind only referred to withdrawal from Sinai and its settlements, Begin seemingly obscured discussion of possible concessions on this fundamental principle. Indeed, at the end of October 1978, Begin publicly announced that he had decided to expand the population of existing settlements. The American momentum to stop the settlements on the West Bank had therefore been lost, and no one – certainly not Carter – was willing to abrogate the peace treaty with Egypt because of this 'misinterpretation'. Moreover, the argument over Begin's 'multiple meanings' was taken no further, since within a short time Carter, Sadat, Dayan and Weizmann had all been removed from the political arena and the issue was effectively laid to rest.

The subtlety of Begin's approach had been based on the idea that the West Bank had always been part of Israel. In his eyes, the Six Day War had been a defensive war during which the West Bank had been purged of 'foreign aggressors'. Moreover, Begin always asserted that UN Resolution 242 did not apply to the final status of the West Bank. He did not consider that the West Bank had been 'occupied in the recent conflict'. In his view this clause applied only to Sinai.

Begin had been shrewd enough to avert linkage between a peace treaty with Egypt and the evacuation of Sinai with the future of the

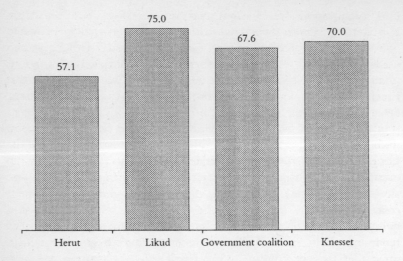

Figure 7.1 Vote in favour of the Camp David framework (%)

Palestinians and the West Bank. Sadat, for his part, primarily wanted Sinai returned and an end to hostilities with Israel. If a separate treaty with Egypt could be masked with a stillborn agreement on the West Bank and Gaza which neither the Palestinians nor Begin really wanted, then it was ultimately acceptable. Carter and Sadat were also persuaded by Begin to view the Camp David Accords as a process rather than as an end in itself. He hinted that those who would come after him might feel differently, and specifically told Cyrus Vance that he would no longer be Prime Minister at the end of the five-year transitional period leading to autonomy.[4] This accorded with the public knowledge that Begin wished to retire by his seventieth birthday in 1983. The motion in the Cabinet secured only two votes against the proposed framework – from La'am's hawkish 'State List' wing. The Minister without portfolio, Chaim Landau, who had been number two in the Irgun, abstained, while the Liberal Yitzhak Modai and the three National Religious Party ministers refused to cast their votes. The Knesset vote itself produced 84 in favour, 19 against and 17 abstentions. Yet this vote obscured the fact that only two-thirds of those belonging to government parties actually endorsed the Camp David framework. Begin in fact depended on the 36 Labour votes to secure a majority. (See Figure 7.1 for percentage breakdown of vote.)

The opposition to Camp David was most pronounced within Herut itself. Significantly, those who could not bring themselves to vote for the framework were from Herut and La'am. The latter, which had been formed from the Rafi remnant – the State List, a Herut remnant – the Free Centre, plus a member of the Labour Land of Israel Movement was far more strongly opposed than Herut itself. Seven of La'am's eight Knesset representatives did not vote in favour. (Only Eliezer Shostak, a founder of Herut with a long association with Begin, supported the framework.) Those who opposed the agreement were concerned about both the security aspects and the economic loss involved in returning Sinai to the Egyptians. Eventually, this led to the fragmentation of the coalition into its constituent components. Even the four-member Free Centre split – one part going to the Democratic Movement for Change and the other renaming itself the Independent Centre. Interestingly, those who opposed Camp David from within the ranks of Herut itself did no harm to their careers and, indeed, achieved high office under both Begin and Shamir in future Likud governments.[5] Begin was able by design – or by default – to avoid a binding commitment at Camp David on the return of Judea and Samaria – the West Bank. He allowed himself the freedom, by way of a strategic ambivalence, to reinterpret important points later on. This subtle deployment of politically ambiguous formulations outmanoeuvred the Americans and placed the first doubts in the minds of both Dayan and Weizmann as to the long-term plan of their Prime Minister.

Begin thus eliminated Egypt, Israel's most powerful military adversary, from the Middle East equation. Following Dayan's resignation in response to a policy of deliberate procrastination over the autonomy talks, Begin replaced him with Yosef Burg, the leader of the National Religious Party, which had no political or ideological interest in the talks succeeding or in antagonizing its supporters in the settlements in the Territories. The autonomy talks thus stalled, while settlement activity continued at a measured pace. The reality was that Begin had held on to Judea and Samaria in the face of tremendous pressure from different quarters to concede. Yet the far right did not perceive the course of events in this way. They simplistically concocted their own vision of Begin's betrayal, unable to perceive the brilliant deviousness of his approach. They believed that since Begin had negotiated the return of Sinai, this automatically implied that he would do the same with the West Bank and Gaza. In their eyes, Begin was implementing the foundations for a future Palestinian state.

The more subtle view of others on the far right was that, even if Begin was not going to return Judea and Samaria, autonomy was a concession, a compromise compared to outright annexation. Moreover, autonomy could become the basis for a later transformation into a Palestinian state by a future Labour government.

Begin, however, had even promised to settle in Northern Sinai himself when he finally stepped down from office. Interestingly, Dayan believed that Sadat would have permitted the Jewish settlements to remain for another 25 to 30 years if Israel had stressed their agricultural nature.[6] Yet Begin did not take this up. Jewish settlers under Egyptian rule in historic Eretz Israel, he may have reasoned, contained the seeds of complex political problems in the future.

Begin's failure at Camp David was that he was unable to avert a split in the nationalist camp. He had spent over two decades in constructing a diverse coalition of the right. Yet, despite all the political theatrics, he was unable to maintain the unity of this broad spectrum of political groupings, given the stresses and strains inherent in the Camp David framework. He admitted as much at the signing ceremony in Washington in March 1979:

> God gave me the strength to persevere, to survive the horrors of Nazism and a Stalinist concentration camp ... and some other dangers. To endure ... not to waver or to flinch from my duty. To accept abuse from foreigners and, what is more painful, from my own people and even my close friends. This effort, too, bore some fruit.[7]

The End of the Beginning

The thrust of Begin's government was to roll back or revise the Labour Zionist philosophy which had permeated the country since 1948. For example, in the media, Likud appointees were drafted into Israel Broadcasting such that the membership of the board of directors became noted for their nationalist views rather than their expertise. References in news items to 'expropriated land' at Karnei Shomron were regarded as subversive and thus cut. A revision of language was demanded: for 'administered territories', read 'Judea and Samaria'; for 'annexation', read 'incorporation'; for 'withdrawal', substitute 'returning the Territories'. Moreover, the oft-repeated phrase 'Israel's right to exist' was regarded as a condescending notion.

Television and radio employees were dismissed, or in some cases simply left because of the oppressive atmosphere. A group of 170 employees signed a letter which spoke of 'the erosion in the demo-

cratic character of the Israeli media'. This assault on the liberal conscience bothered many Israelis, particularly in the arts and academia.
The country's left-leaning professional and intellectual elite felt under
psychological and political attack. Although Begin spoke many
languages, he read very little outside his narrow political brief. His
swift reduction of the higher-education budget was believed by many
academics to have been made not simply in the cause of economic
expediency. Begin trumpeted the cause of the common man. He
preferred open expressions of populism. For example, he was happy
to meet the cast of the television soap *Dallas* when they visited Israel,
whilst ignoring the world-renowned physicist and Nobel prizewinner
Paul Dirac, who was there at the same time.[8]

Although the Labour Party had not shown much initiative, it had
not interfered in such matters. As one commentator wrote: 'The
struggle today is without a doubt over freedom of speech and
expression in television and radio. It is a bitter fight.'[9] The Likud and
their appointees often failed to distinguish between objective criticism
and notions of a 'leftist conspiracy'. The press were regarded as a
persistent threat – to the extent that the head of Herut's Knesset
faction suggested that the distribution of the daily press digest should
be discontinued.

The liberal conscience was further offended by the treatment of
Arabs. The new hardline Chief of Staff, Raphael 'Raful' Eitan, was
regarded by Begin as 'a soldier's soldier'. Moreover, he had told Israel
Television that the West Bank should be retained 'at all costs'. Eitan
chose to intervene when Danny Pinto, an officer from the Litani
operation in Lebanon, was found guilty by a military court of murdering four villagers. He summarily reduced Pinto's sentence from
eight to two years. It had earlier been reduced from twelve on appeal.
In an interview, Eitan made it clear that he took exception to the
court's findings. Avigdor Ben-Gal, the officer in charge on the Northern Front, likened the Arab population in the Galilee region to 'a
cancer in the body of Israel'. In the Knesset, Sharon used the term
zarim – foreigners or outsiders – to refer to Israeli Arabs. Other Likud
members suggested the use of the term *masigai gvul* – trespassers.

Such changes were nevertheless experienced as no more than an
irritation, and counted for little in electoral terms. For the ordinary
financially hard-pressed Israeli, all of this was irrelevant in the long
run. What was important was the ability to make ends meet. The
idealism of the past, where self-sacrifice was integral to the construction of the state, had effectively run its course. Ironically, in the

1970s, Israelis began to aspire to the standards of Jews outside the
Jewish state. Indeed, the economic deterioration under Rabin had
made daily struggle exceedingly hard. Begin came to power primarily
as a result of Labour's failure to manage the economy in the impossible years of huge oil-price increases. Nevertheless, despite public
acclamation of the Camp David Accords and the prestige this brought
Begin and the Likud, it did nothing to assuage growing domestic
dissatisfaction with the government's economic policies. Opinion polls
consistently indicated a higher Labour showing during the two-and-
a-half years preceding the 1981 election. A Modi'in Ezrachi Institute
poll in the summer of 1980 showed that the Likud under Begin
would obtain only 17 seats.

The Liberals in the Likud – the former General Zionists, whose
support resided in the middle classes and small business – embarked
on an economic strategy which was quite different from that of preceding Labour administrations. The philosophy of Milton Friedman
and Thatcherite economics were the model. In October 1977, the
Liberal leader, Simcha Ehrlich, told an audience of Tel Aviv business-
men that 'Israel [was] too small and too poor to be a welfare state'.[10]
The expansion of welfare services would be postponed for two years
and there would be no reduction to a five-day week. A week later,
the Central Bureau of Statistics announced that inflation was up by
20.6 per cent on the previous month. On 28 October 1977, Ehrlich
announced a new economic policy which marked a decisive break
with the past. Inflation, it was argued, would be curbed by budget
cuts and the abolition of government subsidies. The result was that
the cost of subsidized goods went up by an average of 15 per cent;
electricity and water costs increased by 25 per cent; telephone and
postal charges rose; the price of cigarettes went up 21 per cent and
that of instant coffee 26 per cent; the VAT rate was increased from 8
to 12 per cent. To compensate, welfare payments and child allowance
were increased by 12 per cent. Ehrlich also ended 38 years of currency
control and fixed exchange rate. Restrictions on foreign-currency
transactions were lifted and the Israeli pound was allowed to float.
Israelis could now have unlimited deposits of foreign currency in
their bank accounts. Israeli companies could open accounts abroad.
Customs duties were lowered and businesses encouraged to export.
Overall, this package amounted to a devaluation of over 40 per cent.

Ehrlich told the country that this economic therapy would permit
Israel 'to join the club of the affluent, comfortable and secure Western
nations'. In fact, just the opposite happened. The worst hit groups

were the working class and the lower middle class. In particular, the policy hit hard at Herut's lower-paid supporters and they increasingly protested against the government. In 1978, the cost of health care increased by 70 per cent. There was such a huge increase in house prices that young couples could no longer afford to buy. Cheap rental accommodation also vanished. The shift in favour of private enterprise also meant the abandonment of low-cost public projects. Indirect taxation seemed to be linked to an increase in crime, and it spawned a wave of strikes. The black market flourished. There was strong working-class resentment at the perceived enrichment of the Ashkenazi business community and the failure of the trickle-down economic philosophy. In addition, Israel's economic dependency on the Americans and foreign banks after Camp David became all the greater when the Begin government insisted on a loan policy rather than the obtaining of grants.

> The upper 20 per cent of the population receives twice its share of income. The lower 20 per cent, one fourth of its share. Even official figures which do not include distribution of black capital and property show that inequality has increased in Israeli society and this is in contrast to the tendency in all developed Western societies. Israel began as a more egalitarian society and became less so.[11]

Six per cent of the population were perceived to be below the poverty level and another 15 per cent on the borderline. The gap between the Sephardim and the Ashkenazim had grown wider. One factor was that Ashkenazi Holocaust survivors now had access to German funds following the lifting of controls. Government departments proved unable to contain their budgets within agreed limits. Investment in the settlements in the Territories and the funding of religious institutions, plus the unrestricted printing of money, all proved to be a drain on hard-currency reserves.

The terrible state of the economy finally forced Ehrlich's resignation after two years, but he was succeeded by the State List's Yigal Hurvitz, who had earlier resigned from the government after opposing the Camp David framework.[12] A Modi'in Ezrachi poll showed that two-thirds of the electorate was dissatisfied with the government. Hurwitz, despite his Labour origins, was a perfectly qualified hawk – as evidenced by his call for Ezer Weizmann's resignation because of his drift towards an accommodation with the Palestinians. One of his first acts was to send a message of support when the far-right Techiya party was founded. Hurwitz had earlier been involved in the formation of Techiya and been given the number two position on the party list before withdrawing. Hurvitz was equally a fundamentalist in economic terms, in the sense that he believed the remedy lay in the application of even more rigid monetarist policies.

Hurvitz's policy of cutting all government subsidies apart from bread and public transport, together with the imposition of a wage freeze on public-sector salaries, made no apparent difference, however. Three-figure inflation continued throughout 1980. His zeal to restrain public spending caused friction with fellow ministers. With unemployment almost doubling, the government only just managed to scrape home by three votes on a motion of no confidence in its economic policy. Significantly, both Dayan and Weizmann, who by then had both left Begin's administration, voted against. Within a few weeks, Hurvitz had resigned over the issue of pay rises for teachers, and the State List actually left the Likud. He had been Finance Minister for all of nine months.

Another increase in oil prices in 1979–80 plus the cost of the Camp David agreement helped to unsettle the economic situation still further. The government was also employing more people. In 1973, 23 per cent of the labour force had been employed by the government; by 1980, the figure had risen to 30 per cent. This situation would have been far worse had it not been for American aid. Between 1948 and 1974, the United States granted Israel $1.5 billion in economic and military assistance. Between 1974 and 1981, this figure rose to $18 billion.

By the end of 1980, the inflation rate was approaching 180 per cent, compared to 77 per cent two years previously. There had been a two-thirds increase in the level of unemployment. Industrial investment had fallen 15 per cent, while the small increase in the gross national product had been the lowest for six years. The foreign debt alone was 17 billion dollars. There was a growing public belief that the promises of 1977 had not been fulfilled and that the gulf between rich and poor had widened. By the beginning of 1981, Begin's government appeared to be in total disarray. The general perception was that of a directionless administration led by an ailing premier and a hoard of divided, bickering ministers. Ideological schism within the Likud began to erode the foundations of the broad coalition that Begin had painstakingly constructed. The Democratic Movement for Change had lost its way and disintegrated after the high hopes of 1977. Dayan had formed his own party, Telem, and joined with the Rafi – State List of Hurvitz and Shoval – to fight for the implementation of the autonomy plan. The Sephardim had formed their own ethnic party, Tami, under Aharon Abuhatseira. Those on the far right who had not remained with Sharon within the Likud established Techiya, Brit Ne'emanei Eretz Israel – the Covenant of the Faithful for Eretz Israel. The very name Techiya – 'renaissance' in Hebrew – projected an echo of Avraham Stern and Lehi. Stern had espoused the cause of the militant intellectual who did not belong to the left; the sword and the book came bound together from heaven (Midrash Vayikra Rabba 35:8). This approach was integrated into the founding philosophy of Techiya. The new party encompassed a broad spectrum of intellectuals and professionals, the radical right and the Ein Vered Group representatives of kibbutzim and moshavim. It was also a mixture of the secular and the religious. Rabbi Zvi Yehuda Kook gave Techiya his blessing and urged his followers in Gush Emunim to support the new party.

The party originally wished to project itself as a centrist organization, and there was internal debate about whether former members of Lehi such as Israel Eldad and Geula Cohen should be allowed to join. The persona of Professor Yuval Ne'eman, the party leader, contrasted with that of Rabbi Meir Kahane, whose sensationalism epitomized the hitherto public perception of the far-right fringe. Ne'eman could quietly advocate the annexation of Judea, Samaria, Gaza and the Golan Heights with convincing logic and grave seriousness. As a defence expert and physicist, his central concern was that of security. Ideologically, he was close to the political philosophy of the left-socialist Achdut Ha'avoda – only 40 per cent of which has supported the Camp David Accords – and worked with Yitzhak Tabenkin's sons to establish Techiya. Ne'eman believed that Begin had accepted the Camp David approach to rehabilitate himself in the eyes of history so that he should not be remembered as a 'terrorist'. He regarded the major parties as having acquiesced and thereby undermined the very cause of Zionism. He was shocked at the way in which they readily agreed to evacuate Yamit in Sinai in order to secure peace with Egypt. 'For me, this was the equivalent of the French parliament in support of Petain during the Nazi occupation of France.'[13] The sudden proliferation of parties and groups which had once congregated under the Likud umbrella appeared to herald the end of the Begin era. The great Revisionist dream seemed to have foundered on the rock of Camp David, and the return of Labour under Shimon Peres looked assured.

Yet, in electoral terms, all this was actually of secondary importance. Begin understood that the economic situation of ordinary people was a greater priority for them than questions of ideology. The struggle to make ends meet shaped their daily lives. Begin appointed Yoram Aridor as Finance Minister. In stark contrast to his predecessor, La'am's Yigal Hurvitz, Aridor initiated tax reductions, compensated the low-paid for the effects of raging inflation, and restored subsidies on essential goods. The Israeli public, once released from Hurvitz's economic puritanism, bought consumer goods as if there was no tomorrow. Opinion polls soon began to register an increase in the Likud's standing for the first time in nearly three years. Those who had flocked to Begin's banner in 1977 as a reaction to Labour returned once more to the Likud. Begin seemed to shake off depression, illness and lethagy to recover his fighting spirit and mount a personalized, aggressive election campaign. The Likud ensured that the public did not forget the corruption and bureaucracy under Labour. A campaign was launched to tarnish the image of the Labour leader under the slogan 'Never trust Shimon Peres'. Begin, in contrast, was once again marketed as a straightforward honest man who was strong in mind and body and had no intentions of retiring.

The Sephardim were courted. They were reminded how 'Project Renewal' had linked 100 neighbourhoods and development towns and how Begin had removed the bureaucrats who had hitherto controlled their lives. 'They trusted Begin. They saw that the Leftists were not patriots. Their declarations of equality were not real. They spoke with two voices.'[14] Begin had appointed several Sephardi ministers; in addition, several development town mayors, such as Meir Shitreet and Ovaadia Eli, stood as Likud candidates in the coming election.

Notwithstanding the reinstatement of Rabin and the appointment of a hawkish team of shadow ministers, Likud painted Labour as unreliable as far as the security of the state was concerned. Labour's Jordanian option was perceived as a security risk, paving the way for a PLO state. Begin pointedly arranged to meet Sadat after a considerable interval to remind the Israeli public about his peace treaty with Egypt. In addition, as if to underline public fear and the need for security, he ordered the successful bombing of Saddam Hussein's Osirak nuclear plant. Even the condemnation of this act by the international community seemed to strengthen Begin's position. Thus, by election day, support for the Likud proved to be even greater than in 1977. The Likud achieved 37.1 per cent of the vote and won 48 Knesset seats, while Labour could only manage 36.6 per cent and 47

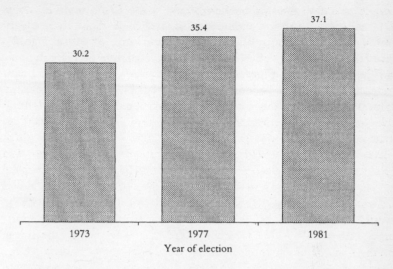

Figure 7.2   Percentage vote for the Likud

seats.[15] Labour, however, could count on the solitary Ratz seat of Shulamit Aloni. The Alignment could thereby muster a greater percentage of the vote and the same number of seats. The Likud, however, could depend on all the other small parties, whether nationalist or religious, to form a coalition of the right. The Labour Alignment could only look to Shinui, a remnant of the Democratic Movement for Change, and the Communists.

Begin's vociferous nationalism during the campaign had been partially directed at the far-right Techiya, which he felt could eat into the Likud vote. In particular, Begin attacked Geula Cohen and his former supporters from Herut. Although Techiya gained 11 per cent of the army vote, Begin's strategy proved successful: the new party gained only three seats and these were based essentially on 23 per cent of the vote in the Territories. Only a tenth of that fraction voted for Techiya in Israel itself. Begin, then, had maintained the strength of the right-wing vote for the Likud in Israel but had suffered a large drop in popularity in the Territories following Camp David. Yet even this had been compensated for by the electorate's steady drift towards the right, the break-up of the Democratic Movement of Change, and the decline in the vote of the National Religious Party. Thus, from a position where his party was on the point of extinction a few months previously and likely to be replaced by a 'land for peace' Labour administration, Begin emerged to head an even more right-wing coalition in a second term of office. Significantly, he formed his government from a coalition of the religious and Sephardi parties. The far-right Techiya was pointedly left out in the cold. The drift rightwards and the acceptability of the pragmatic right under Begin's Likud were very clearly indicated by its rising share of the vote (see Figure 7.2).

CHAPTER EIGHT

LEBANON:
THE ESCAPE OF THE GOLEM

A Shocking Experience

Born of the ambition of one wilful, reckless man, Israel's 1982 invasion
of Lebanon was anchored in delusion, propelled by deceit, and bound
to end in calamity. It was a war for whose meagre gains Israel has paid
an enormous price that has yet to be altogether reckoned.[1]

So wrote Ze'ev Schiff and Ehud Ya'ari in their seminal analysis of
Israel's invasion of Lebanon. The débâcle, the misnamed Operation
Peace for Galilee, was more than a bad war for the Likud: it so
polarized political division within Israel that it made credible other
solutions to the Israel–Palestine conflict. Up until then, Begin's
domination of the political agenda had been complete. Revisionist
philosophy was carried forward on a triumphalist wave, and the
awkward demands of all opponents – the Palestinians, the Labour
Party, the Reagan administration – were simply swept aside. The
cocktail of heady nationalism and total disdain for all those who
questioned the grand design was still readily received by a large part
of the population.

The Labour Party, still shell-shocked after its defeat in 1977,
wrapped itself in an unnatural cocoon of super-patriotism to cope
with Begin's periodic broadsides. Despite the general public's belief
that the Begin administration had mismanaged the economy and was
exhibiting a total lack of direction in government, such cynicism did
not extend to the Likud's approach to the Palestinians and the Middle
East question in general. Begin was seen as tough and effective. The
need for absolute security and the fear of Palestinian terrorism essentially silenced minority views. Although terrorist attacks in 1980 and
1981 had been limited to radical factions – both within and outside
of the PLO – the historical sensitivity to the 'other' in Jewish history

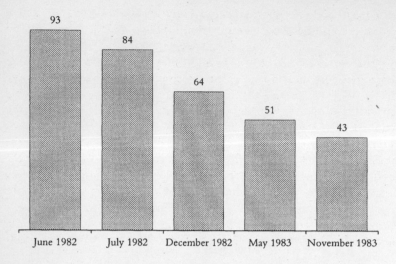

Figure 8.1 Support for the war in Lebanon (%)

was magnified and trumpeted by the Likud. The suggestion that the
PLO could be viewed as a potential negotiating partner was regarded
as treasonous and was the prerogative only of the minuscule far left –
although Peace Now supported the idea in a vague formulation.
Before 1982, opposition to the mind-set that saw the Palestinians as
implacable, eternal enemies was primarily the domain of the Israeli
intelligentsia, the broad peace movement and the small far-left parties
and organizations such as Sheli and Ratz.[2] Few were willing to challenge prevailing political correctness and risk public opprobrium.

The determination to confront Palestinian terrorism and to eliminate the PLO as a military and political power evolved out of a fear
of the PLO's build-up of conventional forces on the Lebanese border.
It also coincided with the Likud's electoral need to mount a cosmetic
exercise to mask the deteriorating economic situation. The events of
the spring of 1981 bore witness to Begin's vigour and to his renewed
determination to settle unfinished business. He had intervened in the
Syrian siege at Zahle in Lebanon to protect Christian Phalangist forces
openly, and only bad weather persuaded him to postpone the bombing of the newly installed SAM-6 missiles in the Bekaa Valley. PLO
positions in Southern Lebanon had come under renewed attack, and
their headquarters in civilian areas in West Beirut had been bombed,
resulting in many deaths. The electoral campaign had allowed Begin

to lambast and ridicule the Labour Party. He was also able to keep at bay the demands of the Reagan White House and to court populist disregard for US and international wishes.

The sense of full-blown triumphalism engendered by Begin in both domestic and foreign spheres appealed to many Israelis – large sections of the population felt confidence in him and his 'strong' approach to every problem. This initiated a mood which, in the context of a state of war, provided the basis of almost unqualified support for the Begin government's policies for the duration of the invasion of Lebanon.[3] Significantly, support remained high during the course of the war, despite its manifold disasters; opinion polls only began to reflect disillusionment well into 1983. In hindsight, public evaluation of the war was a gradual process, and it took a decisively negative turn only when the cost of Aridor's economic hand-outs and the financial drain of the military presence in Lebanon was finally brought home to the ordinary Israeli citizen.

The Rise of Arik Sharon

He is the man most feared in the country for harbouring dictatorial ambitions, and his own colleagues in the Likud government have accused him of unscrupulousness and the capability of establishing concentration camps for political opponents if he ever comes to power.[4]

The Israeli left truly detested Ariel Sharon, but the nationalist right also felt uneasy about him. It was not so much that he emerged from a Labour movement background, but that he exhibited an unrivalled ruthlessness and opportunism both in politics and in the army. He was unpredictable and his reputation was double-edged.

Sharon was regarded as a courageous and brilliant military leader; nonetheless, the aura of self-righteousness and repeated instances of insubordination loomed large. As far back as the Sinai campaign in 1956, his battalion commanders, Raful Eitan, Motta Gur and Yitzhak Hofi, all called for their commanding officer's resignation. They accused Sharon of needlessly sending young men to their deaths in his attack on the Mitla Pass when only a reconnaissance mission had been authorized. Sharon's disregard for the consequences of his actions had been demonstrated earlier when the use of an excess of explosives in an attack on Kibya in Jordan in 1953 had left scores of villagers dead. In 1967, he was investigated and cleared of using excessive force in his pacification programme in Gaza. Few professional soldiers found themselves able to work with him. Indeed, his reputation as a loose cannon blocked his path to the highest military office. He was twice passed over by Dayan. His inability to accept other opinions and to follow orders led to a call for his dismissal in 1973. Moreover, his political philosophy seemed periodically to undergo dramatic change.

On leaving the IDF in 1973, he joined the Liberals and was elected to the Knesset on the Likud ticket. One year later, he resigned his seat so that his reserve commission might be reinstated. Within a few months, the Labour Prime Minister, Yitzhak Rabin, appointed him as his special security advisor. This lasted less than a year and he returned to the Likud once more. He did not remain there for any length of time either. In April 1976, he formed the Shlomzion party and started to advocate negotiations with all the Arab states including the PLO. The party's manifesto for the 1977 elections was shaped by a well-known leftist writer, Amos Kenan; and Sharon was keen to have Yossi Sarid, a leading Labour dove, as his number two on the electoral list. He was open to the idea of a Palestinian state and was interested in meeting Arafat clandestinely in Europe. When this move to the left proved to be electorally unattractive due to the emergence of the Democratic Movement for Change, Sharon turned once more to the right. When he further realized that Shlomzion would bring him very few seats, he made a frantic yet private effort to be included on the Likud list. His return was blocked by his former colleagues in the Liberal Party as well as by La'am.

The elections of 1977 which elevated Menachem Begin to the premiership brought only two seats for Shlomzion. Sharon immediately dissolved the party and merged with Herut. Begin needed Sharon's two seats to strengthen his paper-thin majority in the Knesset. Sharon already coveted the post of Defence Minister at this time, but Begin felt indebted to Ezer Weizmann for securing the electoral victory and running the Likud campaign. Begin proposed instead to establish a Prime Minister's Office for Internal Security and to place Sharon in charge. This horrified the Liberals and the Democratic Movement for Change, with whom Begin was negotiating. Even in Herut, there was considerable opposition as Sharon was still considered an outsider, and besides the whole idea of an Office for Internal Security had something of a 'Soviet' feel to it, especially for those who had experienced Communism in the USSR and Eastern Europe.[5] Begin then offered him the Ministry of Agriculture in June 1977, which he accepted. He spent most of his time restricting the expansion of Arab villages and enacting his programme of the Judaization of the Galilee in Northern Israel. Begin's most important offer to Sharon was to head the Inter-ministerial Committee on Settlement, which placed him in a powerful position to establish many new settlements in the Territories.

Sharon's eye, however, was cast on the prize of the Defence Ministry. He moved closer to attaining this goal when Ezer Weizmann resigned as Defence Minister in 1980. Begin's first choice as Weizmann's replacement was Yitzhak Shamir. Sharon reacted vehemently, commenting that 'this was the price you pay to a prostitute'.[6] In order not to have to choose between Shamir and Sharon, and thereby cause internal problems within Herut, Begin followed Ben-Gurion's example and took on the responsibility for this Cabinet position himself. Begin held the Defence portfolio for fourteen months. Significantly, his first function in that role was to commemorate those who fell when Ben-Gurion ordered the IDF to fire at the *Altalena*, the Irgun arms ship, in June 1948. 'I, the Minister of Defence', intoned Begin, 'come in the name of the IDF to beg forgiveness.'

Sharon's thirst for power and his demand for high office were crudely explicit. His ability to fall out with his colleagues persisted and he castigated Begin during his time as Minister of Defence. Why, then, did Begin appoint him as Minister of Defence in his second administration following the 1981 elections, given that off-the-cuff remarks made by Begin indicate that he was fully aware of the fears that existed concerning Sharon's aspirations? (In his autobiography, Sharon commented that Begin actually wanted to offer him the Defence Ministry in 1977, but had met severe resistance to the idea within Herut.[7]) Begin admired Sharon the military man, but perhaps it was the image of Sharon as the eternal victim that he could most readily identify with on a personal level. Moreover, following the departure of Weizmann, Sharon was now regarded as 'the key security and defence expert in the Likud'.[8] Begin appreciated his support for the Camp David Accords and believed that only Sharon would be able to evict the settlers from Sinai without a bloodbath. Sharon, he felt, was the only man who could stand against the far right. Yet he could also rely on Sharon to slow down the other parts of the Camp David Accords, especially those sections dealing with the autonomy plan for the Palestinians. Begin probably believed that he could extract the best from Sharon and in the process exert control over his actions. Working with Raful, the Chief of Staff of the IDF, Begin believed that Sharon could be restrained from committing excesses and that his energies could be channelled productively.

Begin also needed Sharon to maintain a majority in the Knesset. Without him, Begin could only count upon 60 members of the 120-

seat Knesset to support his policies. Begin had even refrained from naming Sharon as his candidate for the Defence post as a response to Peres' sudden reinstatement of Rabin as shadow Minister of Defence to appeal to the electorate's current appreciation of hawkishness. Nevertheless, unnamed senior defence officers leaked to the press the fact that they thought Sharon's appointment would be 'catastrophic'.[9] Moreover, both Dayan and Yadin warned Begin not to appoint Sharon.

Begin was in a state of euphoria in 1981. He had vanquished his opponents one by one, and all the political constraints to which he had voluntarily submitted over the decades were now virtually non-existent. He no longer needed the psychological restraining support of Dayan, Weizmann and Yadin to ensure a wider popularity. A high-ranking diplomat and former Israeli ambassador to Britain graphically captured the dangerous psychological dimension Begin inhabited – a state of mind that he began to project to his colleagues overtly during his second administration.

> Mr Begin brought with him a style of governance hitherto unknown in Israel. His Cabinet swayed from elation to depression, from stagnation to hyperactivism, from chaotic disarray to monolithic uniformity, always reflecting the shifting moods of its Prime Minister, alternating between ecstasy and apathy. Endowed with a singular political craftiness, an unusual stamina and the patience of a hunter in ambush, Begin's ability to deal with political adversaries – and competitors within his own camp – is unmatched. Weizmann, Dayan, Tamir, Hurwitz had to leave his government when they had reached the end of the rope so lavishly provided to them by Mr Begin. He did not drop them, he squeezed them out one by one.[10]

In addition, the decades of self-discipline were beginning to take their toll as Begin approached the statutory age of three score years and ten. The years of struggle – and the emotional burden that came with that struggle – began to weigh down on him, both physically and psychologically. In 1981 Begin's Jabotinskyian pragmatism, which was dominant in his first administration, competed with a resurgence of his youthful Betar radicalism. Begin had been politically adept at projecting the image of an experienced elder statesman – a co-founder of the state and a disciple of Jabotinsky – when building up a coalition of anti-Labour parties. This led many Israelis to believe that his radical days were now over, a symptom of his youth and the politics of the Irgun. Yet his second administration was far more right-wing than his previous 'peace' government. Yitzhak Shamir, the leader of Lehi, who had little previous experience or interest in foreign affairs, became Foreign Minister. The articulate Moshe Arens was posted to

Washington. Raful Eitan had been installed as Chief of Staff of the IDF in 1979 and was not reticent in conveying his ultra-nationalist views to the public and to his officers. And Ariel Sharon, the Commander of Unit 101, was finally appointed to the Defence Ministry some weeks after the 1981 elections despite widespread advice to the contrary and Begin's own misgivings. Begin, the Diaspora Jew from a provincial Polish town, deeply admired the new strong Jew, gun in hand, ready to defend his country. Notwithstanding everything he knew about Sharon, in Begin's eyes the new Defence Minister epitomized the fighting Israeli, a stark contrast with the frightened persecuted Jew of the past two thousand years who meekly went to the slaughter during the Holocaust. Begin regarded Sharon as 'the most fearsome fighting Jew since the Maccabees'.[11] Polish honour and Jabotinskyian *hadar* apart, it is a measure of the sense of awe he felt for the Israeli soldier that Begin rarely criticized Sharon during either the course of the war in Lebanon or its aftermath, despite all the evidence that he had been misled. Perhaps he saw himself playing out the role of Jabotinsky to Sharon's youthful radical Begin. During his second administration, then, Begin 'created' Sharon as the golem which would do his bidding and protect the Jewish people against its enemies, as had often been described in Jewish folklore.[12] Yet as other legends indicate, the golem could break free from its master and act in an uncontrollable manner.

The Preparations for War

The government will take all necessary measures to prevent the outbreak of a new war. Everyone will remember that the Labour–Mapam Alignment claimed four years ago that if the Likud were to form a government 'war would immediately break out'. Reality and the actions of the government have proved this to be deceptive propaganda. The government has prevented war and achieved the first peace agreement between Israel and the largest of its neighbours.[13]

Although in its election manifesto the Likud tried to project itself as the party of peace, a few days after it had been returned to power Israel resumed air strikes on Southern Lebanon after a six-week interval, even though no Katyusha rocket had fallen on any northern settlement for two months. Pressure on Begin from the right had increased, both from those within Herut and those outside the party, to postpone the evacuation of Sinai. From the other side, the

Americans too had been pressing Begin to return to the autonomy talks. Attacks on PLO positions in Southern Lebanon therefore provided an appropriate distraction. Moreover, Begin never reconciled himself to the presence of the Syrian missiles that had been installed in Lebanon in April and May 1981. Indeed, some military opinion considered the missile umbrella to be the factor which would promote a PLO war of attrition. 'Sometimes one has to wait', Begin later commented to the press.[14] The Palestinians retaliated by shelling the Israeli coastal resort of Nahariya, which caused few casualties. Begin and the Israeli Cabinet responded by endorsing Raful Eitan's plan to bomb the Fatah and the Democratic Front headquarters in built-up West Beirut. This escalation resulted in the deaths of at least 100 innocent civilians and 500 wounded.

The PLO, in turn, replied through continual attacks using Katyusha rockets on Israel's northern border; but, unlike the attack on Nahariya, the Palestinians this time did not pull their military punches. Although the effect could not be compared to the havoc wreaked in Beirut, it nevertheless produced a widespread sense of anxiety, which led to an unprecedented mass exodus from the north. An American-brokered ceasefire eventually forced both sides to desist from their bombardments. The Likud government categorically denied that there was any direct agreement with the PLO, but only with the 'lawful government of Lebanon'. However, there was certainly an indirect understanding on the cessation of military attacks which had been hammered out through third parties. The ceasefire remained in place from 24 July 1981 until the invasion of Lebanon on 6 June the following year.

Begin perceived the build-up of conventional Palestinian forces in Southern Lebanon to be a great danger. For the lesson of this short conflict was that the PLO could now inflict considerable damage on civilian life in Northern Israel. This was comparable to Syria's pre-1967 command of the Golan Heights when they could shell settlements at will. The temporary departure of large numbers of inhabitants from Northern Israel and the proven inability to prevent Palestinian military action, which became evident following the deterrent bombing of Beirut, was psychologically and militarily unsettling for Begin – a chastening experience. He was surprised that military force had not persuaded the Palestinians to desist. Moreover, if frequent attacks continued, they would create severe economic disruption in an area where sections of Israel's less well-off population lived. A gradual population shift towards safer areas therefore became a real possibility. In one sense, this would represent a reversal of Zionist settlement and thus a victory for Palestinian desires to displace the Jews. The presence of the PLO and the Syrian missiles in Lebanon therefore became a major preoccupation for Begin. As with the Osirak nuclear plant in Baghdad, unless the problem was dealt with swiftly the cancer would grow and threaten the entire organism.

Arafat pressured the radical factions to maintain the ceasefire because he did not wish to provoke the Israelis into an all-out attack. The PLO acceptance of the ceasefire had led to dissension even within Fatah itself. A faction sympathetic to Abu Nidal forced a military confrontation, with accompanying arrests and executions – an event 'unprecedented in PLO internal disputes'.[15] Arafat even attempted to distance himself from Palestinian unrest on the West Bank to prevent an Israeli attack. In contrast, Begin, Sharon and Eitan were searching for any excuse to neutralize their military opponents through a breach of the ceasefire. They believed that Arafat was buying time to build up his conventional forces. The Israeli interpretation of the conditions for the ceasefire placed responsibility for any act of Palestinian violence on Arafat's shoulders. It presumed that Arafat had complete control, not only over all factions within the PLO such as the rejectionist Popular Front of George Habash, but also over those outside such as Abu Nidal's Fatah Revolutionary Council and Ahmed Jibril's Popular Front – General Command.

Moreover, in Begin's eyes, the ceasefire was not geographically limited to the Lebanese border. He argued that if Palestinian terrorism struck internationally, then this too would be regarded as a breach of the ceasefire. Begin thus took a stand-off in a local battle as applying to the entire war anywhere in the Middle East or any incident internationally.[16] Eitan commented that there was no difference if a terrorist threw a grenade in Gaza or fired a shell at a Northern settlement – all such acts broke the ceasefire.[17] Sharon similarly did not wish to draw distinctions between different Palestinian factions, since all blame had to be attached to the PLO. He dismissed attempts at more rational evaluation as masking the real issue. In a speech to a Young Herut conference in April 1982, he accused those who tried to take a more objective standpoint of erecting 'a protective wall around the PLO inside and outside Israel'.

On 9 May, the Israeli Air Force bombed Palestinian targets on the Lebanese coast in response to the locating of anti-vehicle mines near the Golan Heights. The PLO replied by shelling the Galilee panhandle. Raful Eitan ordered a military build-up on the Northern border. An

IDF spokesman released figures that showed that there had been 130 attacks in Israel, the Territories and abroad, killing 236 people and injuring 17. Another source later claimed that during the period of the ceasefire, 'the PLO pursued its acts of terror resulting in 26 deaths and 264 injured'.[18] In neither case were these statistics broken down. What is more, no figures were given for the Northern border and no details were given about the Palestinian groups who had been responsible for the violence. While such vagueness seemed to preclude analysis, it also served to encourage public anxiety. Sharon claimed that there had been a total of 1392 victims of Palestinian terrorism since 1967. A retired police officer painstakingly dissected this figure and showed that a quarter had been soldiers engaged in action with the PLO and another quarter had been Arabs killed in the Territories.[19]

Begin undoubtedly did not want further intervention from the US envoy Philip Habib and wanted to finish the PLO militarily. Indeed, Eitan commented in an interview that 'the terrorists can only be weakened by military action and not political action'.[20] Three weeks before the actual invasion, Begin told the Foreign Affairs and Defence Committee of the Knesset that he could not allow Jewish blood[21] to be spilled with impunity. He informed Yitzhak Rabin that he understood the ceasefire agreement as meaning an end to violent attacks on Jews everywhere. Given the propensity of groups outside the PLO such as Abu Nidal to carry out terrorist acts in the international arena on targets such as synagogues and airports, the policy was effectively self-fulfilling. By extending the ceasefire beyond the PLO and Lebanon, Begin ensured that it would be easily violated and thereby provoke a swift Israeli response.

At the beginning of April 1982, two attacks occurred in Paris during the same week: the Mossad operative Yaakov Bar-Simantov[22] was gunned down and there was an attack on the Israeli arms-purchasing-mission building. The unknown 'Lebanese Armed Revolutionary Brigades' claimed responsibility. Yet the Israeli Foreign Ministry called the acts 'PLO-perpetrated terrorism', and numerous Cabinet ministers regarded them as a violation of the ceasefire. This provided the rationale to order the Israeli Air Force to bomb the Lebanese coast and finally induce PLO retaliatory shelling. In turn, this stimulated Begin and Sharon to push ahead with preparations to invade Lebanon to eliminate the PLO as a military force. At a meeting on 10 May 1982, shortly after the PLO shelled the Northern border, the Cabinet voted seven to six to proceed with military action. Begin told his colleagues that up until then they had showed *havlagah* – self-restraint.[23]

By this, he was referring to their failure to approve previous demands to attack Lebanon. One such demand for an invasion had been based on an infiltration of armed Palestinians across the Jordanian border, while another had been the killing of an Israeli soldier in Gaza.

The impending war was delayed only by American appeals not to invade and the reticence of some ministers. A direct appeal from Arafat to Begin[24] did nothing to stop the headlong rush to war. The *coup de grâce* came in dramatic fashion on 3 June 1982 when the Israeli Ambassador to Britain, Shlomo Argov, was gunned down outside the Dorchester Hotel in the centre of London. The assailants belonged to the Abu Nidal group and their weapons, it has been alleged, probably reached them through the diplomatic pouch of the Iraqi Embassy in London.[25] Despite the logic that said it would not have been in Arafat's interests to initiate such an assassination, all too many accepted Begin's assertion that the PLO was responsible.[26]

At the Israeli Cabinet meeting the following day, both Begin and Eitan belittled intelligence reports that the likely culprit was the Abu Nidal group. Begin cut short his own advisor on terrorism, arguing that all Palestinian terrorists were members of the PLO, while Eitan ridiculed the intelligence staff for splitting hairs and demanded to strike at the PLO.[27] Yet Abu Nidal had broken with Arafat and the PLO in 1974 over a fundamental principle: namely, that the Palestinian national movement would adopt a phased piecemeal approach to secure a Palestinian state and embark on a political path. This decision produced, in turn, the first formal contact and dialogue between Palestinians and left-wing Israelis such as Uri Avneri and Liova Eliav. Abu Nidal made common cause with other rejectionist Palestinian groups, some of whom remained in the PLO, and with radical Arab states such as Iraq, Syria and Libya. Abu Nidal's organization of trained killers turned bitterly on those who supported the new approach. A death sentence was passed on Arafat, while Said Hammami and Issam Sartawi, senior PLO diplomats who had openly met Israelis or spoken at Jewish meetings, were assassinated.

The lack of understanding of the difference between Palestinian groups and the total ignorance of Palestinian politics on the part of an overwhelming majority of Israelis and Jews played into the hands of those who did not wish to distinguish between the PLO and the Abu Nidal group. Thus, the president of the Board of Deputies of British Jews demanded the immediate closure of the PLO office in London following the shooting of Ambassador Argov. (Ironically, the British police subsequently confirmed that the assassination squad's next target was to have been the head of that very office, Nabil Ramlawi. This confirmation followed the arrest of two members of the assassination squad. These assailants, students at a London further-education college, had been long-term operatives whom Iraqi intelligence had instructed to carry out general surveillance. Their notebooks contained the names and addresses of Israeli, Jewish and Arab targets and they had detailed knowledge of the layout of the PLO London office, of Jordanian Embassy security arrangements, and information relating to the Saudi-owned Arabic-language newspaper *Sharq-al-Awsat*.[28]) The Israeli Ambassador to the United Nations, for his part, during the Security Council debate, attributed several international atrocities carried out by Abu Nidal's gunmen to the PLO. In a letter to *The Times*, the president of the Board of Deputies similarly attributed Abu Nidal's attack on the synagogue in Vienna to the PLO.[29] Even the publication after the war of selected documents captured from the PLO in Lebanon did nothing to dispel the deliberate confusion of the two organizations.[30] Given the Israeli government's image of the PLO as solely a terrorist organization that wished to push the Jews into the sea, and Arafat's half-hearted and inept attempts to distance himself from that projection, it was easy to load moral blame onto the PLO.

Moreover, even those who did discern a difference between the organizations argued that the PLO, through its apparent intransigence and ambivalent attitude towards Israel, actually encouraged the far more radical groups to carry out atrocities. The *Jerusalem Post*, which traditionally supported the Labour Party, commented in an editorial:

> Whether the outrage in London was in fact sanctioned by the PLO's leadership or perpetrated by a fringe group not entirely subject to PLO discipline, it called for a response in kind. This had to be done, if only to prove to the terrorists that continued violence against Israel's diplomatic representatives abroad would not be countenanced.[31]

No Cabinet minister voiced any reservations regarding this response. No one dared to challenge Begin's angry mood with niceties concerning the ideological differences between the different Palestinian organizations. For Begin, all were guilty. Thus, instead of an initiative to locate the Abu Nidal group in Damascus or Baghdad, the plan to invade Lebanon was activated. Consequently, less than 24 hours after the attempted assassination, Israeli planes hit West Beirut; the PLO in response began to fire Katyushas at the settlements in the Galilee. The 'Oranim' – 'Pines' in Hebrew – scenario to invade Lebanon had been formulated by Raful and 'Yanush' Ben-Gal as a contingency plan long before. Sharon began working on Operation Big Pines as soon as he was appointed Defence Minister at the beginning of August 1981. Its essential features were the elimination of the PLO as a military force, particularly in Southern Lebanon; the neutralization of the Syrian missile threat, using force if necessary; and the forging of an alliance with the Christian Phalangists, who would finish off a weakened PLO and govern Lebanon as a strong ally of the Jewish state. The political implication was that the Palestinians would emerge more compliant and wiser, and be willing to accept the Likud interpretation of Camp David autonomy. An unwritten subtext was the clearing of Palestinian refugees from Southern Lebanon and their transfer away from Israel's border. Begin issued an order during the war forbidding the repair of refugee camps, and thus an unspoken aim was the voluntary yet enforced flight of 100,000 Palestinians.[32]

Begin, Raful and Sharon each projected a different emphasis on different aspects of the original plan as the situation unfolded. Begin's desire to put the plan into action seems to have been stimulated by another phase of hyperactivity. Following his unexpected push to annex the Golan Heights, Begin called a Cabinet meeting at his home on the evening of 20 December 1981. Sharon expounded his plan, Operation Big Pines, to a sceptical and somewhat stunned Cabinet. They clearly did not share Begin's enthusiasm for an advance on the Beirut–Damascus highway. The Liberals and the National Religious Party's Yosef Burg voiced opposition and asked pertinent questions – much to Begin's dismay. The meeting ended quickly with no endorsement of the plan. It transpired at its conclusion that even Begin was unsure of the soundness of the plan. He turned to Sharon with the comment: 'You see, they don't want this plan.'[33] Ministers believed this to be the end of the great design. They understood that any future military action would be limited to incursions into Lebanon to deal purely with security threats to the Northern border.

Sharon, however, was not a man to be thwarted or to bow to the opinion of the Israeli Cabinet, especially on a question which had military ramifications. Begin, for his part, was still concerned about the security of the Northern settlements. In order to clear Southern Lebanon of hostile forces, he would need American approval. An anti-communist, neo-conservative administration had been installed in Washington which he perceived was sympathetic to Israel's aims to defeat terrorism and weaken pro-Soviet authoritarian regimes. Egypt had been eliminated from the political and military equation and was mesmerized by the prize of the return of Sinai dangling before it. Iraq found itself entangled in a much more difficult conflict with Iran than it had anticipated. And the Lebanese election was scheduled for the summer of 1982.

Sharon set out to achieve by subterfuge what he had been unable to secure by Cabinet approval. While Begin was expounding the need for limited action, Sharon was interested in establishing a new political order in Lebanon. In numerous talks with Bashir Gemayel in Beirut and Alexander Haig in Washington during the first half of 1982, Sharon made his intentions clear. It was the beginning of an active and aggressive collaboration between Israel and the Christian Phalangists. Warnings from the head of IDF military intelligence, Yehoshua Saguy, went unheeded. At an early stage, he cautioned Sharon not to place too much faith in the reliability of the Phalangists. He believed that Operation Big Pines would be certain to bring war with Syria and create division in Israel. Moreover, he pointed out that the PLO would simply filter back into South Lebanon and regroup. And the question arose as to how the Phalangists would treat the Palestinians if they ruled Lebanon. Would they be expelled? In his first speech as Minister of Defence, Sharon proclaimed that 'Jordan is Palestine'. Did Sharon hope that the movement of Palestinians from Lebanon to Jordan would destabilize the country and lead to the overthrow of the Hashemites? During the war itself, Sharon exclaimed that if he were Prime Minister, he would tell King Hussein to leave within 48 hours. Yet US dissension from the idea of the Israeli Army marching on Beirut and installing the Phalangists forced Sharon to appease the Americans with a watered-down version of Operation Big Pines whereby the IDF would only clear Southern Lebanon near the Israeli border of PLO forces. This was aptly named Operation Little Pines.

Sharon was by now restricting the flow of information to the Israeli media. US television audiences and the Pentagon seemed more aware of Sharon's plan than did his domestic public. Sharon ensured that he was the only information conduit to Begin. He installed his own candidate as Begin's military advisor and stopped the Defence Ministry's intelligence section reporting directly to the Prime Minister. Mordechai Zippori, who had reservations similar to those of Saguy, was eased out as deputy Minister of Defence. Communication with the Prime Minister was both restricted and selective. A common quip during the opening phase of the war was that 'Begin is Arik's first prisoner of war'. Yet the fact that the Prime Minister often did not know what was happening had its roots in an earlier manoeuvre. Although Begin was indeed in no mood to hear criticism of the general plan, his psychological isolation was reinforced by Sharon's moves. Clearly, he believed as he did in his youth that an iron will and strength of purpose would carry the day when all around were floundering.

Thus, at the crucial Cabinet meeting on 10 May 1982, Begin reacted strongly to reservations expressed by both Zippori and the deputy head of military intelligence. Ministers approved a limited incursion lasting – according to Sharon – no more than 24 hours. Significantly, Sharon used the war maps of Operation Big Pines, which indicated a thrust towards the Beirut–Damascus highway, to illustrate the campaign. No minister questioned this anomaly. In his Irgun days, Begin had trusted his military people and did not interfere directly in such matters. Once again, he effectively passed over control. Sharon utilized this trust by subsequently positioning himself between the ministers and the military, thereby denying the Cabinet access to expert military analysis. In this fashion, both the political executive and the military arm could be fed selectively different information, and the Israeli Cabinet was effectively stripped of its ability to conduct the war.

Operation Peace for Galilee

The Israeli invasion of Lebanon, Operation Peace for Galilee, can essentially be divided into three general phases. The first phase of 6–13 June involved a headlong rush to the gates of Beirut and an inevitable confrontation with Syrian forces. Both Begin and Sharon publicly proclaimed that the aim of the war was to clear Palestinian fighters and terrorists from a 40-kilometre swathe of territory north of Israel's border with Lebanon.

The second phase lasted from 14 June to 22 August. It began with a link-up with the Phalangists on the outskirts of Beirut. There followed a growing Israeli realization that their Christian ally was unwilling to act against the weakened and retreating PLO forces in the western part of the capital. Perhaps even more important was the fact that the Syrians did not collapse and retreat to Damascus. Instead, they reinforced their troops in the Bekaa Valley and also remained in position in Beirut. West Beirut was subjected to a continual artillery bombardment from 1 July. This was followed by heavy bombing at the end of the month and at the beginning of August. The shelling and bombing of PLO positions in built-up areas eventually resulted in civilian casualties, especially after the massive bombing on 12

August. The evacuation of the PLO finally took place in the third week of August.

The third phase lasted from 23 August to 28 September. It began with Bashir Gemayel's election to the presidency of Lebanon and Begin's sudden realization that the new Lebanese president would not openly ally himself with Israel. This was coupled with US repudiation of the war through the announcement of the Reagan Plan.

The Syrian-instigated murder of Bashir upset all plans and possibilities. Both the Phalangists and the Israelis were temporarily numbed by the loss of such a key figure. The assassination was an act which transformed the war into a Greek tragedy. The killing of Bashir embittered his followers; nonetheless the Israelis still permitted them to enter the Palestinian camps of Sabra and Shatilla. Their anger was given full expression in the massacre of old men, women and children in their search for 'terrorists'. The moral outrage both inside Israel and internationally forced Begin to institute a commission of inquiry to examine the issue of Israeli complicity.

The First Phase: 6–13 June

The chronology of events was as follows:

6–7 June   The Israelis conduct a broad sweep against PLO and other Palestinian units in Southern Lebanon. The Israelis land on the Lebanese coast, north of Sidon near the Awali river. There is light Syrian resistance at Jezzin. Israeli forces move centrally through the Shouf mountains towards the Beirut–Damascus highway.

8 June   Syrian aircraft are shot down over Beirut and Southern Lebanon. Although the Syrians are defeated at Jezzin, Israeli forces encounter strong Syrian resistance as they approach the Beirut–Damascus highway.

9 June   The Israeli Air Force attacks Syrian missiles in the Bekaa Valley. The Syrians unexpectedly halt the Israeli advance at Ein Zehalta in front of the Beirut–Damascus highway.

10 June   65 Syrian planes are shot down. The Israeli advance on the Beirut–Damascus highway continues to within 24 kilometres of the Syrian capital.

11 June   An Israeli–Syrian ceasefire takes effect which does not include the PLO.

12 June   The ceasefire is extended to include the PLO.

13 June   The Israelis link up with the Christian Phalangists at Ba'abda, 8 kilometres from the centre of Beirut. The ceasefire with the PLO breaks down and there is further fighting with the Syrians.

The first phase of the operation was agreed at a Cabinet meeting on the evening of 5 June. It met to consider the response to the breakdown of the ceasefire and how to put a stop to the PLO shelling of Northern Israel. Sharon and Eitan requested Cabinet approval to clear a 40-kilometre band of territory to ensure that settlements in Northern Israel were out of artillery range. Significantly, the heads of military intelligence and the Mossad were not invited to speak. Only Zippori, the former deputy Minister of Defence, raised the likely possibility of a clash with the Syrians and escalation of the war. Apart from Sharon, Zippori was the only minister in the Cabinet with military experience. Notwithstanding the overriding need to silence the Palestinian guns after their assault on Northern Israel, he nevertheless challenged the vagueness of the plans. Such probing elicited the explanation that an area from Metulla, Israel's most northerly town, and a line drawn between Lake Karoun and a point south of Sidon would be the IDF operation's target zone. Begin ruled out an attack on the Syrians, while Sharon dismissed any march on Beirut. Twenty-four hours was stipulated as the time required to complete the operation. The entire Cabinet voted unanimously in favour of the plan, with only two Liberal Ministers abstaining.

Cabinet approval was, however, only one piece in a much bigger puzzle. In advance of the Cabinet meeting, Bashir Gemayel, the Phalangist leader, was informed about the possibility of a full Israeli invasion and was asked to permit Israeli units to land at the Christian stronghold of Junieh, north of Beirut and far beyond the 40-kilometre boundary. The day after the Cabinet meeting, the Israeli commander with responsibility for the Lebanese coast was told to land his troops north of Sidon rather than south of the town as the Cabinet had been informed. This automatically exceeded the 40-kilometre limit. Later that day, at another meeting of the Cabinet, Begin asked for approval for an Israeli advance centrally through the Shouf mountains and towards the Beirut–Damascus highway. Whether the Cabinet was aware of the fact or not, such a move also placed Israeli forces beyond the 40-kilometre boundary. Moreover, in replying to two messages from President Reagan, who requested restraint, Begin had once again explicitly reiterated the 40-kilometre limit of the operation in a letter. Washington therefore informed Damascus – in good faith – that Israel did not intend to attack unless in self-defence, but would remain within the 40-kilometre area. Philip Habib, the American special envoy, flew to Damascus to confirm the Israeli stance with President Assad.

On 8 June, the third day of the war, Begin addressed the Knesset using the same 40 kilometre argument and promising that there would be no Israeli move to engage the Syrians. Indeed, he called upon the Syrians to exercise restraint. 'All fighting will end', he said.[34] Yet the first skirmishes with the Syrians had already taken place the day before. On the day when Begin uttered his promises to the Knesset, Israeli forces encountered heavy Syrian resistance at Ein Zehalta in front of the Beirut–Damascus highway and were simultaneously engaging the Syrians at Jezzin. Begin later told the Knesset that the boundary had been 'an intention' rather than a firm Cabinet decision. This hairsplitting approach had permitted Sharon and Eitan to interpret the operation in much broader terms. For example, Eitan's order of the day on 6 June was to force 'the terrorists' war prepara-tions' away from Israel's Northern border. Sharon later justified the presence of Israeli forces beyond the 40-kilometre boundary on the grounds that they were destroying the 'terrorist infrastructure and their stockpiles'.[35]

By late on 8 June, Sharon decided to expand the war – without Cabinet approval. He divided the central force and sent part of it eastwards into the Bekaa Valley. This meant an open confrontation with Syrian forces, which clearly would not retreat without a struggle. The commander of the Israeli units on the coast was ordered to proceed directly to Beirut. Operation Little Pines was being trans-formed into Operation Big Pines without the knowledge of the Israeli government.

At the Cabinet meeting on 9 June, Sharon brushed aside all complaints that the agreed limits of the operation had been exceeded. Instead, he utilized the difficulties that the central force had found itself in at Ein Zehalta to enlist Cabinet support for backup from the Israeli Air Force. Sharon argued that to protect these forces, the Syrian missiles in the Bekaa Valley would have to be destroyed. The Cabinet gradually came round to supporting Sharon's view: how, they reasoned, could they justify putting their troops in danger? Yet Sharon carefully omitted to mention the presence of a simultaneous ground operation against Syrian forces in the Bekaa Valley. The aerial attack

forced the Syrians to respond in such a way that not only were the
missiles destroyed but also large numbers of Syrian aircraft were shot
down with the loss of many experienced pilots.

By 10 June, Sharon was informing the Cabinet that the Beirut–
Damascus highway would be in Israeli hands shortly and that this
would preclude any future Syrian influence on the Lebanese body
politic in Beirut. By 13 June, the Israelis stood at the gates of Beirut,
having defeated both the Syrians and the PLO. The Israeli forces
linked up with the Phalangists at Ba'abda, 8 kilometres from the
centre of Beirut. In all, 130 Israelis had paid with their lives for this
victory. Begin himself discovered that Israeli troops were in East Beirut
from a live radio interview in the Lebanese capital. It certainly seemed
that Sharon's mixture of deception and *faits accomplis* had paid off. A
Jerusalem Post editorial commented that 'there is no question that what
started last Sunday as "Operation Peace for Galilee" will go down in
the annals of modern wars as one of the most brilliantly executed
military campaigns'.[36] The Israeli public overwhelmingly supported
the war. Lone dovish voices such as that of Yossi Sarid, who called
for an immediate ceasefire, and the protests of the Committee Against
the War in Lebanon were drowned out in the euphoria of apparent
victory.

CHAPTER NINE

DEFEAT FROM THE
JAWS OF VICTORY

The Second Phase: 14 June–22 August

The victory over the Palestinians was short-lived. There was no finality
in reaching the gates of Beirut. As the operation became bogged
down, the euphoria began to dissipate and was replaced by a sense of
deep uncertainty. The second phase of the war contrasted dramatically
with the first, but more important, the government's credibility and
Begin's ability to conduct the war was questioned. This is how events
unfolded:

14–25 June	There are intermittent Israeli clashes with both the Syrians and the Palestinians. The IDF consolidates control of the mountains which encircle Beirut. Israeli forces now control most of the Beirut–Damascus highway. There is a new ceasefire.
1 July	The siege of Beirut commences when Israeli artillery bombards the PLO positions in West Beirut.
3 July	Israeli forces seize the Green Line dividing East and West Beirut. Water and electricity supplies to West Beirut are cut.
7 July	Water and electricity are restored following President Reagan's protests.
11 July	There is a new ceasefire and a cessation of artillery duels between Israeli forces and the PLO.
14 July	The PLO requests US diplomatic recognition in return for the evacuation of its forces from Beirut.
21 July	PLO forces once more fire Katyusha rockets into

Northern Israel. The Syrians install three more missile batteries in the Bekaa Valley.

22 July   There is increased PLO infiltration of Syrian positions. The first Israeli air strikes on West Beirut since 27 June take place. The first Israeli attacks on Syrian positions since 28 June take place. Air attacks coincide with diplomatic negotiations.

23 July   Israeli forces destroy the SA-8 missiles in the Bekaa Valley. Water is restored to West Beirut.

30–31 July   New ceasefire.

1 August   A 14-hour Israeli air and naval bombardment of PLO positions in Beirut takes place. The Israelis capture Beirut Airport.

2 August   Israeli forces mass on the Green Line dividing East and West Beirut.

4 August   Three Israeli armoured columns advance 500 yards across the Green Line into West Beirut. President Reagan accuses Israel of endangering negotiations. Israel refuses to return to the Green Line.

5–6 August   Negotiations for the withdrawal of PLO forces from Beirut are completed without US recognition.

7–8 August   A lull in the fighting as an announcement of a breakthrough in negotiations is expected.

9 August   There are renewed Israeli attacks on PLO positions in Beirut and on Syrian positions outside the capital.

10 August   The Israeli government accepts the Habib Plan for evacuating the PLO from Beirut.

11 August   The Israeli bombardment of West Beirut continues.

12 August   Hundreds are killed in a massive bombardment of West Beirut. Reagan telephones Begin to protest. Sharon's authority to initiate moves is withdrawn by the Cabinet.

13 August   The military forces begin to disengage.

14 August   The Syrians announce their withdrawal.

19 August   Israel agrees to the details of the withdrawal of PLO forces from West Beirut.

22 August   The first PLO forces begin to depart from West Beirut.

A Modi'in Ezrachi poll conducted in Israel at the end of June indicated that 93.3 per cent of 1236 respondents thought that the war was justified. Some 90.7 per cent of all Labour voters questioned in the sample concurred. A mere 4.6 per cent of the total believed that the war was wrong. When they were asked 'What is the main feeling Arik Sharon evokes?', 28.7 per cent said 'confidence'; another 15 per cent mentioned 'trust', 12.9 per cent 'affection', and 15.8 per cent 'pride'. They clearly believed that if the scourge of terrorism could be lifted from them by defeating the PLO, it therefore followed that Sharon, warts and all, should be supported. At that point, then, the degree to which Sharon would go to liquidate the PLO was matched by the Israeli public's determination. Even those who had realized that they and their elected representatives had been deceived were willing to ignore this inconvenience if Sharon could finish the job. Yet the Israeli public were psychologically prepared only for a short war with minimal cost to human life. Instead, the opposite happened: it dragged on and on. Sharon was forced into ever more extreme actions, which ultimately many Jews felt increasingly unable to justify.

The tiny minority who were unwilling to tolerate the situation thus increased dramatically with the growing realization of what was taking place. The sense that they were not being told the truth also began to affect the sensitivities of more and more people. Sharon wanted a clear-cut victory against the PLO. He sent numerous messages to Arafat through intermediaries in which he stipulated that he wanted a visible show of surrender from the Palestinians. Arafat did not capitulate. He knew that the longer he could hold out, the greater would be the sympathy for the Palestinian cause in the West. Sharon's heavy-handed tactics had created the best publicity for the Palestinians in living memory. Nearly 15,000 members of the PLO, together with half a million civilians, were holed up in West Beirut.

Sharon's dilemma became increasingly acute as he realized that his Phalangist allies would never move against the PLO. He was also trapped by having no Cabinet mandate to enter Beirut. Moreover, the probable heavy loss of life on the Israeli side incurred by such a step would not be tolerated by the Israeli public. As an interim measure, he ordered his artillery to fire on PLO positions. This pounding of Palestinian and Syrian positions was almost certainly the prelude to entering the city under some pretext. The renewed bombardment of West Beirut forced Begin to return from New York to order his Defence Minister to stop. The Cabinet, in turn, became more frustrated at its inability to control events. Moreover, the sight of a capi-

tal city being continuously shelled began to erode any political advantage that Israel had gained internationally in its crusade to rid the
Middle East of terrorism.

On 1 July, a seven-week siege of West Beirut commenced. By
mid-July, Sharon publicly resolved to take West Beirut within a stipulated period of 48 hours. To have left the PLO forces intact or under
the control of a weak Lebanese government would have posed too
many awkward questions about the *raison d'être* of the entire operation. Moreover, Sharon's triumphalist demand for outright victory
would not have been satisfied. He was willing to gamble as he had in
the past; and, as in the past, there was immediate opposition from
most of his commanders. One of these, Colonel Eli Geva, concluded
that the IDF was not prepared for such an operation either militarily
or morally. He believed that the conquest of West Beirut in order
formally to defeat an already weakened PLO would cause the deaths
of untold numbers of Israeli soldiers and Arab civilians. He had begun
to ask himself questions which many Israelis – soldiers and civilians
alike – were asking themselves. He concluded that the honourable
way to resolve his inner trauma was to renounce the command of his
brigade. He asked to stay on as a tank commander, but Sharon denied
this to him. Instead, attempts to make him stay were initiated by
Eitan, Sharon and even Begin himself. Geva stood his ground and
was eventually dismissed from IDF service, even though he had asked
to remain as part of his brigade's medical team. His bold initiative in
opposing the decision to take West Beirut in fact questioned the very
purpose of the Israeli presence there and the methods which had
been and were being used to extend the war without any political
accountability. The Geva affair arose from an act of conscience which
proved to be a turning point in the attitudes of the Israeli public to
the war. Begin, Sharon and Eitan had been anxious to convince Geva
of the error of his ways because they well understood that this act
would be perceived as the breakdown of the consensus that they had
striven so hard to portray.

The Change in Public Opinion

On 6 July, Sharon told a delegation of the British Joint Israel Appeal
that Israel would not lay down its arms until the last terrorist had left
Lebanon. He commented that 'we never said that we were going to
leave the terrorists to act beyond the [40-kilometre] line.... We did
not go to war to change the political structure in Lebanon.'[1] In an

address to the IDF's Staff and Command College, he told his audience that Operation Peace for Galilee was a pre-emptive strike: it had forestalled a war with the PLO and Syria, which would have taken place within one to three years. In an address to the Knesset Likud faction, Sharon conceded that there had been heavy casualties, but claimed that the government had been well aware of this likelihood when it decided to launch the invasion. Both Begin in the Knesset, and Sharon to two leading British Joint Israel Appeal activists, justified the move beyond the 40-kilometre line as being due to Syrian provocations. A week previously, Sharon had told *Yediot Aharonot's* Yeshayahu Ben-Porat that he had been planning the entire operation ever since he had taken office.

These publicly aired and contradictory explanations sowed the seeds of public disillusion. Even so, Israelis somehow still hoped that Sharon would be able to complete the task of ridding the country of the PLO. Yet this was not the view in the IDF itself. Many serving soldiers began to feel that there was no purpose to the operation and were unwilling to be used as mere cannon fodder. A growing number of ministers now closely monitored Sharon's political manoeuvres and had become adept not only at detecting what had been omitted, but also at asking the right questions. At the end of Cabinet meetings, the ministerial watchdogs would even meet to exchange notes.

Ministers had to discern what was politically possible, given the wave of populism that had swept the country. For example, while Israeli ministers were very well aware that an entry into Beirut could bring about US and EC sanctions, Sharon's statement that 'the Israeli sword is now resting on the throats of the terrorists' was nevertheless well received by the Israeli public. By mid-July, at the beginning of the third week of the siege, a Dahaf survey in *Monitin* magazine showed that 80 per cent supported the operation while only 20 per cent believed that it had got out of hand. Electoral support for the Likud had mushroomed. According to the survey, an immediate election would have secured 61 seats, an overall majority for the Likud alone, and only 39 for Labour.

Begin's behaviour, however, veered towards the erratic as the war continued. As the pressure mounted on him from both inside and outside Israel, his explanations were increasingly seen to be transparent by a growing number of people. On 4 August, Begin explained the war's evolution to US donors from the United Jewish Appeal. He told them that no civilians had been killed on 4 June when the Israeli Air Force had raided the centre of Beirut after the attempted

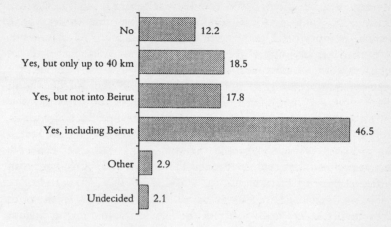

Figure 9.1 If you had known before 6 June all that you know now, would you have supported the government's decision to launch the operation? (%)

assassination of Shlomo Argov. He reaffirmed 'the absolute truth that we didn't intend to reach Beirut'. He reasoned that after the PLO broke the ceasefire on 11 June, 'we had no option but to go on'. He subsequently offered a similar explanation for the IDF's advance into West Beirut at the beginning of August. Begin told his Diaspora audience that there had been PLO terror attacks on Israeli targets for the last seven years, citing the killing of children at Misgav Am and Ma'alot. 'The IDF hits hard against anyone who raises his hand against a Jewish child', he stated. Although an ill-informed American Jewish audience may have appreciated it, the inconsistencies and inaccuracies of Begin's account gave Israeli journalists a field day. They showed how the Prime Minister's version simply did not fit the known facts. Even Begin's understanding of the military danger was mistaken. For example, he stated that the Palestinians had enough war materiel to arm fifteen brigades, whereas the IDF had formally stated that it was only sufficient for five brigades – some 20,000 men.

Another Dahaf poll in *Monitin* in August registered continuing support for the war – 75 per cent in favour, as in the previous month. This was confirmed by a Modi'in Ezrachi poll of nearly two thousand people in the middle of August. Yet this poll also included more specific questions regarding the nature of that support. The pollsters asked the pertinent question: 'If you had known before 6 June all that you know now, would you have supported the government's decision to launch the operation?' (see Figure 9.1). The poll showed that, despite continued general support for the war, there was a distinct current of opposition to its extension. Clearly, almost half the Israeli public – 46.5 per cent – broadly supported all the stages of the war, but significantly 36.3 per cent expressed reservations about the deviation from the stated aims of the operation. Some 17.8 per cent did not wish the IDF to enter Beirut. There was also an increase in the number of those who now totally opposed the war – up to 12.2 per cent. This meant that 48.5 per cent questioned the conduct of the war at a time when it appeared that Sharon was working towards a conquest of the Lebanese capital. This poll was taken during the sixth week of the siege of Beirut and at the time of the heaviest bombing and shelling. There was thus clearly no consensus in support of any attempt to enter West Beirut, and there was wider questioning of the war's purpose. The Modi'in Ezrachi poll also asked whether Israel should conduct peace negotiations with the PLO. Although 60.7 per cent registered a categorical 'No!', 17.9 per cent said 'Yes', and another 19.8 per cent said 'Yes under certain conditions'. Labour voters were divided equally. The pounding of Beirut and the lack of control by the Likud government over the direction of the war had clearly given rise to what had hitherto been unthinkable: the loss of public support.

The Responsibility of the Media

Although opinion polls indicated that the population had been carried away by a display of national fervour and wishful thinking about their Palestinian adversaries, it was also clear that many were not receiving objective information that would allow them to form an opinion contrary to that of the government's stated aims. There was not even an awareness that there existed a partial information vacuum. A Modi'in Ezrachi poll at the end of June showed that 64.4 per cent regarded information from the media as 'largely credible'.

The Likud government had never been warm towards the media. Since 1949, the editors of the Israeli press had held periodic meetings with state leaders; but with the advent of the Likud to power, this ongoing contact changed dramatically. Begin had not met the Editors' Committee for three years and Sharon ensured that it was not convened for the duration of the war. Sharon did not give any direct briefings throughout the course of the war. The Likud exhibited an extremely negative and disparaging attitude towards the media. On one occasion the Israeli censor changed a report for *Ha'aretz* to suggest that the Syrians had attacked the IDF on the Beirut–Damascus highway. The reality was the exact opposite of the reported events – the IDF had attacked the Syrians. Some interpreted this intervention as a move to tailor the facts to fit Sharon's version of events for Cabinet consumption. Journalists were perceived as left-wing agitators whose motives could not be trusted. Indeed, on television in July, Sharon referred to his media critics as 'poisoners of wells'. Sharon, then, was keen to ensure that no overt opposition to his presentation of the war should be conveyed through the media. What is more, he also felt that objective reporting should not contradict the government's version of events. Such an approach could easily be camouflaged under the blanket of national security – a sacred precept for the vast majority of the population. Yet journalists are a breed of professionals who do not readily accept such restraints. The *Jerusalem Post*'s military correspondent explained to his readers at the end of June:

> Have we military correspondents been able to report the real story from the front – the human dimension? No, and for good reason. Censorship has been most strict and the Army spokesman less credible than ever before. Never before have journalists been more self-restrained, more careful in describing this war, lest they be accused of political and personal bias.[2]

Journalists, in turn, became the target of bitter rebukes from serving soldiers, who accused them of only repeating mindless official explanations. Paradoxically, many Israeli soldiers turned to Lebanese radio for a different and perhaps more accurate version of events.

On only the third day of the war, the head of Israel Television ruled that no politically motivated commentator could appear on the news or on the current-affairs programme *Mabat*, which was compulsive viewing for the Israeli public. At a press conference on 27 June, Sharon referred to the 'journalistic poison' which was demoralizing the troops. He was more interested in the presentation of positive images of the war such as the glowing comments of Jane Fonda or Sammy Davis Jr, who had been drafted in to promote the Israeli case for an American audience. As opposition and general questioning of the war became more vocal, so did the attempt to suppress any unpalatable reporting. Inside Israel Television there was a split between the media professionals and the Likud appointees. The Likud member of Knesset, Meir Cohen-Avidov, proposed that the government should take over television under the terms of the 1965 Broadcasting Act in

order to stop 'the lies and calumnies'. The deputy Minister for Education and Culture, Miriam Taasa-Glezer, attacked the lack of balance
in the war's coverage on the grounds that it would create 'genuine
doubts in the public's mind about the very justness of the war'. The
deputy Minister of Defence even raised the possibility that the government might ban all rallies and demonstrations in wartime. Sharon
countermanded Raful Eitan's agreement to appear in a discussion on
television between pro-war and anti-war wounded soldiers at an army
rest home. A critical interview conducted by the *Ma'ariv* journalist
Aharon Abramovich was dropped because of his comments about
exceeding the 40-kilometre boundary.

Some Herut members of the Knesset regarded the press as almost
a fifth column. At the end of August, Dov Shilansky told the Knesset
that the media showed 'a lack of critical sense and national responsibility. It encouraged and served as a spur to the enemy.' There was
concerted pressure on Galei Zahal, the Army radio station, to toe
the official line. The station, formally under the control of the
Ministry of Defence, terminated the reserve duty of two programme
editors after they were perceived by the Ministry to have uttered
statements contrary to the official line. Dan Shilon raised the question of 'how we will ever get out of this *plonter*'[3] – referring to the
siege of Beirut. On another occasion, he challenged the historical
basis for Begin's statement at a Likud rally that 'no war had ever
been as just as this one'. Ariel Cohen, the editor of a classical music
programme on Galei Zahal, was informed that he would not be
allowed to serve on the station again. He had signed – as a civilian
– an anti-war petition before he was called up. The Ministry tele-
phoned almost daily with complaints and there was pressure to oust
the station head.

The veteran novelist Yitzhak Ben-Ner was suspended after two
meetings with Eitan. Another employee monitored the station's output
for leftist sentiments – such as quoting the Voice of Damascus – and
communicated his views to Eitan. This led to an argument between
the Labour-led Knesset Education and Culture Committee and the
Foreign Affairs and Defence Committee, which supported Sharon.
Eventually, it was shown that, under the terms of the 1968 Broadcasting Act, Galei Zahal was considered to be independent of the direct
authority of the Ministry of Defence. Even so, the effect of such
pressure, both actual and psychological, took its toll. The media began
to absorb the contemporary newspeak and to disseminate it to its
readers. That expert practitioner of language, Abba Eban, commented:

There is a new vocabulary with special verbs 'to pound' 'to crush' 'to liquidate' 'to eradicate all to the last man'; 'to cleanse' 'to fumigate' 'to solve by other means' 'not to put up with' 'to mean business' 'to wipe out'. It is hard to say what the effects of this lexicon will be as it resounds in an endless and squalid rhythm from one day to the next. Not one word of humility, compassion or restraint has come from the Israeli government in many weeks, nothing but the rhetoric of self-assertion, the hubris that the Greeks saw as the gravest danger to a man's fate.[4]

The Likud had always, paradoxically, been sensitive to foreign media opinion. This was an embodiment of the contradiction between ignoring the outside world and expressing indignation at its criticism. The Likud could point to genuine inaccuracies which often stemmed from Palestinian sources. For example, the figures for those killed and wounded were promulgated through the Lebanese Red Crescent by its chairman, who was also Arafat's brother.

Israeli dissemination of information was uncoordinated, a situation exacerbated by the fact that the Cabinet were often still unaware of Sharon's latest tactic. A young member of the Knesset, Ehud Olmert,[5] was proposed as coordinator of information with the rank of deputy minister. This was later vetoed by Shamir, who felt that the Ministry of Foreign Affairs was being deprived of part of its political birth-right. Yet Olmert, ironically, tried to show that the march on Beirut was a consequence of events rather than a specific aim of Arik Sharon. If Israeli forces intended to reach Beirut, he asked, why were between five and seven thousand terrorists allowed to retreat from the South? Why wasn't the main arterial road north to Damour blocked to prevent the flight? Why wasn't there a simultaneous attack on PLO positions in the South and Beirut? Despite Olmert's eloquence, smooth public relations could not explain away confusion; the attempt simply testified to the degree of deception practised at the highest level and the desire to mould Israeli perceptions of the war through limited access to information.

Still Small Voices

Opposition to the operation began on the first day of the invasion of Lebanon. The leading Labour dove, Yossi Sarid, called for an imme-diate ceasefire. Mapam and Sheli cautioned against what they termed 'a dangerous adventure'. While Peace Now was initially reticent and indecisive about its tactics, the Committee Against the War in Lebanon was established and decided to demonstrate. Its first major rally on 26

June attracted 20,000 people. At a press conference the next day, Sharon commented that such protests affected the morale of the soldiers at the front. He took particular offence at the charge that the Cabinet and the Knesset were being kept in ignorance.

Many of Israel's intellectuals and academics were strongly opposed to the war. The opinions of Amos Oz, A.B. Yehoshua and others were dismissed because of their political allegiance to the left and a populist disdain for the intelligentsia. From the right, the humorist Ephraim Kishon railed against 'the Jewish self-hatred of the progressives'. He complained about the intellectuals who criticize 'in prose and rhyme'. From the left, Yeshayahu Leibowitz, a leading Israeli religious thinker and philosopher, described government policy in Lebanon as 'Judeo-Nazi' at a press conference on 20 June of intellectuals opposed to the war. Such an inflammatory description moved two coalition members of the Knesset to call upon the Attorney General to put Leibowitz on trial. By the end of June, when it was becoming clear that Israel was being sucked into a more complicated and more drawn-out scenario than had been anticipated, Peace Now became more active and called for a ceasefire. This, in turn, stimulated a response from the government and their sympathizers. Organizations such as 'Citizens for Zahal' called upon citizens to support the fighting soldiers on the front line and condemned 'a vocal minority' for causing demoralization. Further advertisements appeared in the Israeli press sponsored by 'the Voice of the Silent Majority'. In what appeared to be an orchestrated campaign, 'slanderers at home ' were condemned for instigating 'waves of defeatism'.

When Uri Avneri, the editor of Ha'olam Ha'zeh, crossed the Green Line in Beirut and met Arafat, it created an apoplectic reaction from the Likud and the right. They particularly resented the fact that Avneri had broadcast his impressions on Israel Television and informed the viewers that Arafat had accepted the eight-point Fahd plan to evacuate Beirut. Ehud Olmert termed Avneri 'a traitorous collaborator', while other Likud Knesset members called for legal action to be taken against him. Right-wing commentators evoked the imagery of treachery in headlines and articles. The daily Yediot Aharonot published several pieces with inflammatory titles such as Herzl Rosenblum's 'A Stab in the Back', Natan Brun's 'Poisoning the Wells', and Eliahu Amikam's 'Peace for the PLO Operation: The Deeds of Lord Haw-Haw and his Cohorts'.

The increasingly influential lobby Peace Now spearheaded opposition in the absence of a coherent line from the Labour Party.

Their sophisticated tactics and mainstream character made them a difficult target to discredit and marginalize. Peace Now so antagonized the Israeli right by their stand that all manner of verbal weapons were deployed to berate them. Aharon Papo, a member of the board of directors of the Broadcasting Association accused them of a lack of Jewishness since they exhibited the 'Jesus syndrome' through their 'sanctimonious self-righteousness'. This was balanced by the assertion of a hidden agenda inasmuch as 'Peace Now had a lust for Putsch Now'. The deputy Minister of Agriculture, Mikhail Dekel, asked the Defence Ministry to investigate a number of officers who had formulated a Peace Now petition while on active service which called for the dismissal of Sharon. He termed it 'the first act of mutiny in the IDF'. On 3 July, 100,000 people turned out to participate in a Peace Now protest. At the Cabinet meeting the following day, Begin condemned the demonstration. He dismissed the huge protest as being anti-democratic since only the government had been elected to govern. Moreover, he did not regard Peace Now as an autonomous organization, but as an extension of his political enemies – in this instance Mapam. Perhaps Begin was unable to acknowledge the possibility of an autonomous grassroots movement on the left and the fact that demonstrations and rallies were no longer the prerogative of the right. It also served him politically to tar the Alignment with the brush of dissension and, by extension, a lack of patriotism. Sharon argued that the Labour Party had broken with the tradition of Ben-Gurion, Golda Meir and Yigal Allon by following the leftists.

Begin had always shown a weakness for 'the fighting Jew'. The Peace Now movement, however, was itself founded by reservists. Begin attempted to redefine them, labelling them 'pacifists' or using the more damning Biblical epithet 'rotten fruit'. Yet soldiers at the front began to write to Begin with their complaints. To avoid the dilemma involved in recognizing that some military people were bitterly opposed to the war, he stated that he would not reply to collective letters but only to individual appeals. By July, there was a growing body of reservists who openly opposed the war. Ninety-two reservists wrote to Sharon to demand his resignation. This move spawned a public meeting organized by 'Soldiers Against Silence'. Other reservists went further and formed Yesh Gvul – 'There's a Limit'. The members of this group pledged not to serve in Lebanon, which effectively meant that they preferred to go to prison rather than participate in Sharon's war. Such a move on an organized scale was unprecedented in Israel, since the IDF was a hallowed institution at the heart of the nation. The right called those involved 'pacifists' and 'traitors', and even Peace Now distanced themselves from them. In addition, there were Likud members of the Knesset who suggested that Peace Now supporters in active units should be excused all reserve duty. The Herut member of the Knesset, Mikhail Kleiner even accused Peace Now of obtaining funds from Saudi Arabia. Support for the government also came from bereaved parents who had to believe that their sons had died for a valid cause. In an advertisement in the *Jerusalem Post*, they stated that,

> our loved ones did not fall in vain. We bereaved families whose dear ones fell in the 'Peace for Galilee' campaign wish to raise our voices in protest against the terrible exploitation of the deaths of our dear sons by certain political elements. Stop the incitement – leave us in our hour of grief.[6]

Eitan utilized this approach when relieving Eli Geva of his command, claiming that he 'would not have the courage to look in the eyes of the parents of soldiers who would be killed in West Beirut'.

In an address to officers on 12 July, Sharon defended the right of soldiers to express their views. He differentiated, however, between those opinions he considered independent and objective and the views of political agitators who wished to undermine the spirit of the nation. He attacked organized groups of discharged officers as a threat to democracy. Sharon conjured up images of subversive leftist revolutionary cliques working in military units. Begin himself declared that the discussions and activities of people in the IDF opposed to the war reminded him of Bolshevik efforts to undermine the Russian war effort in the summer of 1917. As with Peace Now, independent protest had to be explained away in conspiratorial terms. Yet Begin clearly had to take note of such discontent in the IDF. Significantly, when he received the peace activist Avrum Burg and two other serving soldiers, the meeting received only a mention in the press.[7]

The Response of the Likud

The Likud's reply to the increasing protest was to mount a huge rally of its own supporters. This was intended as a response to the pointed criticism and to reclaim the popular ground from organizations such as Peace Now. Begin believed that he could use his rhetorical ability to bring back waverers into the Likud fold and thereby stop the political rot. It also fulfilled an inner need in Begin for total support from the masses.

An estimated 200,000 attended a demonstration of support for the government on 17 July in Tel Aviv. Begin told his audience that 90 per cent of the terrorists would be liquidated by the end of the war; there would be a peace treaty with Lebanon and 'a free confederation between Israel and Jordan, between Western Eretz Israel and Eastern Eretz Israel'. Once again opposition protests were said to be politically motivated. A contrast was drawn between Likud's loyal support during past wars and the Alignment's present ambivalence, and the latter promoted as a reason for the current lack of consensus. Begin suggested that those who 'resisted this holy war' had overstepped the limits of democratic behaviour by turning 'freedom of expression into freedom of defamation'. He attempted to capitalize fully on the anti-Labour animus of his loyal supporters by resorting to the underdog language that had been his hallmark in the Irgun underground:

> If you, the ones responsible for the Yom Kippur War, will defame us, will libel us, will supply our enemies with material, are we not allowed to answer in kind? We shall come back, we shall go to the people when election day comes and we shall exact the full price for your misdeeds during these days of war.[8]

The Likud felt that both Labour and 'the vocal extreme left' were exploiting the international media for their own purposes. The frustration of the Likud intensified as the difficulties increased. The National Religious Party's Yosef Burg attacked Peace Now for 'encouraging the terrorists' — even though his son, Avrum, was a leading member. Such arguments were used by Begin shortly afterwards in a Knesset debate. He accused 12 Alignment leaders of attending a Peace Now rally. This was quite untrue. The irony was that the leadership of the Labour Party was doing its best to keep its distance from Peace Now.

Since the beginning of the war, the Labour Party had been internally split between its hawks and its doves. In January 1982, there had been a debate in the party's Political Committee about the conditions that would trigger a war with the PLO. Motta Gur had argued strongly that a full-scale war would end in tears. With the outbreak of war, Yossi Beilin had called for a withdrawal from Lebanon in *Ha'aretz*. Yet the party leadership desperately tried to maintain a façade of public unity and looked for any sign of public disapproval of government action. It was not willing to be wrong-footed by the Likud declarations of disloyalty.

The Labour position on military action, as articulated by its two prominent former soldiers, Rabin and Gur, was that it was far better to maintain the ceasefire with the PLO than to find any excuse to rationalize its collapse. This was not an argument which impressed Begin or Sharon. And Raful Eitan, the head of the IDF, had argued in favour of a military solution to the problem of the PLO in Lebanon long before the actual intervention.[9] On the second day of the war, Peres and Rabin had their third meeting with Begin during the course of a Cabinet meeting. As in previous meetings, the Alignment leaders felt uneasy about the vagueness of aims and lack of defined purpose. There was also a clear sense in the Labour camp that the norms of political and consensual support for the aims of a war were being placed in abeyance. As Eitan later admitted:

> We were the initiators in this war. We initiated it. We determined the plan in advance. We determined the timing.... This is the first war in which the war aims were determined from beginning to end in the General Staff master plan, subject, of course, to Cabinet approval.[10]

The Labour leadership were particularly concerned about the possibility of increased involvement with the Syrians. Given the degree of public support for the war and the stated public aims regarding its scope, the Alignment supported the government in the Knesset when the Communist-dominated Democratic Front for Peace and Equality proposed a motion of no confidence. The scale of the defeat of that motion, 93 to 4, was indicative of the political consensus, albeit a somewhat shaky one, that existed at the start of the war. Even Shulamit Aloni, Yossi Sarid and Mapam – whose followers formed the nucleus of the peace movement – abstained. As the government's stated aims were continually being breached, and with no sign of a conclusion to the war, the doves within the Labour Party started to become more vocal and to make common cause with those from other parties who opposed the invasion. Initially Peres ambiguously backed the government when the siege of Beirut commenced in early July. Begin told Alignment leaders at a meeting on 6 July that he believed that a negotiated settlement would force the PLO to leave Beirut. Yet the following day, almost in disregard of the leadership's approach, the leading Labour doves, Yossi Sarid, Motta Gur and Uzi Baram, met to consider their tactics. They argued that they should take a clear stand against Likud rather than be viewed as a pale imitation of it. Such an attitude obviously infuriated the party's hawks, but it also annoyed the leadership. Rabin, in particular, reasoned that the time was not opportune for such a stand in view of strong public support for the war. Party loyalists such as Chaim Herzog openly condemned the Labour doves as 'a vocal minority' and criticized any attempt to differentiate between the aims of the government and those of the Army. He contended that war was inevitable and fully backed the government's approach, including its confrontation with the Syrians. In the early days of the siege of the Lebanese capital, he entertained the possibility of the IDF entering West Beirut – an option to which Peres was opposed. The hawkish Herzog echoed Begin in proclaiming that Arafat and the PLO were 'the most virulent enemy that the Jewish People had known since Hitler'.[11] Indeed, Herzog as a native English speaker with good military credentials was a valuable asset in explaining the government's position when he visited the United States during the course of the war. The Labour leadership tried very hard to rein in its young doves. Chaim Bar-Lev, the party secretary-general, ruled that a full discussion of the situation could only take place once the fighting had ceased and the soldiers had returned.[12]

The Labour doves had meanwhile formed a loose grouping called Ometz – 'Courage' – with members of Mapam and Ratz. The Labour leadership, however, faced in both directions. A statement by the party's bureau on 29 July called upon Begin to order a cessation of the bombing of West Beirut because it was severely damaging 'Israel's image as a democratic state based on humanitarian values'. Nevertheless, the statement also requested Labour Party members not to participate in anti-war demonstrations. Yet the Labour doves were paradoxically more conservative than other opponents of the war, notably those on the far left. Significantly, Yossi Sarid turned down the opportunity to meet Arafat, whereas Uri Avneri had been happy to do so. By early August when the bombing had intensified and the IDF's entry into Beirut seemed imminent, the party's political bureau seemed to adopt a more dovish tone. There was a call for a mutual ceasefire on all fronts, no crossing the Green Line into West Beirut, and the eviction of the PLO through diplomatic means. Bar-Lev took a more centrist position this time and condemned both doves and hawks. Rabin was criticized for advocating a tightening of the siege through aerial bombardment and the cutting off of water supplies. Yet even Rabin was disturbed by the course of the war: he told a visiting group of US Conservative rabbis that Lebanon might become Israel's Vietnam. Serious consideration was given to the possibility of a Labour Party demonstration.

Labour's division and its leadership's ambivalence were characterized time and again as anti-patriotic by Begin. At one point, Begin considered appointing a commission of inquiry to consider the conduct of the Opposition during the war. He repeatedly termed them 'Labour's team of slanderers' and tried to show how Peace Now was in reality merely a front for the party. David Magen, a right-wing Likud member of the Knesset, termed the Labour leader, Shimon Peres, 'a hotbed of incitement and sedition, full of hatred and spite'. Techiya's Geula Cohen accused the Alignment of taking on the role of 'national informer' and of adding 'its own drop of poison to the bonfire that has been lit around us by our enemies'.

The Likud's attempt to keep the lid on criticism by mounting virulent counter-criticism and thus maintaining Labour's silence was by default successful throughout the war. When the Likud deputy minister Dov Shilansky circulated a letter to all members of the Knesset requesting that they should not openly criticize any aspect of the war, 'to increase national unity during these days of glory', the majority of Labour members effectively acquiesced. Begin used this tactic to deflect many legitimate questions. When Peres asked Begin in the Knesset at the end of July why he had not foreseen difficulties in the operation, the Prime Minister replied that Gahal had refrained from raising such questions during the Yom Kippur War. Begin repeatedly contrasted the Likud's loyalty, and thus their patriotism, during past wars when a Labour administration had been in power, with Labour's present lack of solidarity with a Likud government. He referred to the stigma of the Yom Kippur War several times during the summer of 1982. This, too, was a criticism of Labour, who had presided over the lack of preparedness and the unsatisfactory outcome.

Likud members publicly defended Arik Sharon against the charges that he was exceeding his authority. They pointed out that during both the Six Day War and the Yom Kippur War, military decisions were taken without notifying either the government or the Knesset Foreign Affairs and Defence Committee. Moshe Dayan, they argued, had taken the decision to attack the Golan Heights in 1967 without any consultation with his colleagues in government or the then Chief of Staff, Yitzhak Rabin.[13] In this war of words, the frustration mounted and the criticism continued.

CHAPTER TEN

BEGIN'S
HOLOCAUST TRAUMA

Begin's Burden

Begin's use of patriotism as a propaganda weapon against Labour was relatively ineffective against the outspoken doves, who were quite clear in their objectives. After the PLO had left Beirut and when it appeared that Operation Big Pines had been militarily successful despite all the deceptions, Begin questioned Yossi Sarid as to whether in fact he really wasn't sorry that the terrorists had been beaten. Sarid replied 'We belong to different worlds in Zionism.' For the doves and those aligned with Peace Now, that comment spoke for a different value system and a different way of reading history.

Begin inevitably compared the present to the past. On more than one occasion he stated that the war in Lebanon was a means of overcoming the trauma of the Yom Kippur War, upon which he conferred Vietnam-like characteristics. Like many of his generation, Begin understood contemporary events primarily through the filter of his own terrible experiences during the Holocaust. Many enemies and opponents featured as reincarnated Nazis. He had originally cast the British occupation of Palestine in a Nazi mould. The Irgun Zva'i Leumi, he said, had brought about the expulsion of 'the Nazi-British enemy'.[1] When he emerged from the underground, he had referred to the British as 'both the teacher and pupil of Hitler' in his speech on Irgun radio.[2] The Reparations controversy showed how Begin could simultaneously exhibit the survivor syndrome and manipulate a charged situation for political ends. The revelations and machinations of the Kastner trial allowed Herut to accuse Mapai indirectly of collaborating with the Nazis.[3] If in the 1950s and 1960s Begin had passionately directed his bile against the Federal Republic of Germany, it became second nature for him to see Palestinian nationalists as latter-day Nazis, following the rise of the PLO after 1967. In 1970, Begin pulled Gahal out of the government coalition in response to Golda Meir's acceptance of the Rogers initiative and told the Knesset that such 'a repartition of the Western Land of Israel' would lead to the return of the PLO to Judea and Samaria. This, he argued, would provoke 'the cruellest and bloodiest war in the history of mankind'. He then called upon US Jews 'to take to the streets' – in contrast to their passive conduct in the 1940s – and bring down the American plan.

The PLO's campaign of terror and violence after 1967 undoubtedly assisted Begin in his determination to retain the Territories and severely weakened any moderate riposte. The PLO's advocacy of international terrorism reached new heights particularly between 1971 and 1974 in the aftermath of King Hussein's military confrontation with the organization during 'Black September' 1970. The campaign certainly succeeded in that it turned the world's attention to the Palestinian issue, but it also strengthened the concept of Fortress Israel and gave Begin a growing audience for his denunciations. Unlike Jabotinsky, Begin saw the Arabs as 'Europeans'. Jabotinsky, who died before the Holocaust, believed that Arab hostility was a natural reaction to the Zionist experiment. It was self-evident that there would be conflict. He certainly did not see the Arabs as anti-Semites. Begin's outlook was totally different, since he was first and foremost a product of the terrible times through which he had lived.

Following an attack on women and children in Kiryat Shemona by the Popular Front for the Liberation of Palestine, Begin told the Knesset:

> For years, our mourning mind's eye has seen the massacre of infants on alien soil which is soaked in our blood. Today on Israel's soil, our mourning mind's eye saw our children thrown out of top-storey windows so that their bones were crushed, their heads smashed, as the German Nazis did in Europe. Two legged beasts, Arab Nazis perpetrated this abomination.[4]

The theme was repeated a few months later when three members of the Democratic Front for the Liberation of Palestine took over a school in Ma'alot and killed 21 children:

> We are confronting a continuous attack on the Jewish People by renewed Nazism.... The terrorists have vowed 'to disembowel every Jewish man, woman and child'.... This blind hatred of the Jewish People has been expressed diabolically throughout the generations by harming Jewish children.[5]

No doubt these atrocities deeply affected Begin; such comments were clearly not simply a knee-jerk reaction to garner political capital. But the unspoken message was that the Labour government was not doing enough to protect its citizens. Not only was Labour incompetent in matters of security; in Begin's eyes, it was a display of considerable weakness to propose trading territory for peace. When he was told by other members of the Knesset that the analogy with the Nazis was unjustified and distorting, he rebuked his questioners by reminding them that during the life of Irgun underground not one single English woman or child had been hurt.

Begin spoke for the Holocaust generation of the destroyed East European Diaspora; consequently he found himself at odds with a succeeding generation who did not experience what he had experienced and did not perceive the present in terms of the past. Moreover, Begin did not recognize the existence of a new awareness about the Palestinians, especially amongst the post-war young. The propagators of the campaign after 1967 to bring the Palestinian issue to public attention – including the ascendant new left – were labelled 'dark reactionaries' by Begin.

Reacting to PLO participation at the UN Security Council in January 1976, Begin again resorted to analogies with the past:

> My generation remembers propaganda that was more successful than that of Farouk Kadoumi. The Germans merely demanded to be reunited with the three million Germans living in the Sudetenland of Czechoslovakia. The propaganda succeeded tremendously, being accepted by the British Cabinet and many sections of the French nation.... The choice today is between submitting to wicked false propaganda which creates the possibility of destroying a nation or not. The experience of our generation proves that we must not.[6]

The demand by the PLO for a state in Judea and Samaria and the knowledge that among them there were perpetrators of violence against unarmed civilians persuaded Begin to build the Likud's iron wall even higher. The PLO, Begin maintained, was fighting to destroy a nation, not to liberate one. A Palestinian homeland would simply become a Soviet base 'along the lines of "Independent" Angola'. Not only was the Popular Front's George Habash a Soviet agent, he claimed, but so were the nationalist Yasser Arafat and the PFLP–GC's Ahmed Jibril, who broke with the Marxist Habash in the late 1960s. Shortly after he became Prime Minister, Begin called the PLO 'an organization of murderers and the Jewish People's most implacable enemy since the Nazis'. 'Their objective', he said, 'is destruction, therefore their method is Nazism. They should be expelled from every civilized forum. They are the representatives or instigators of the blood orgies from Rome to Athens, from Munich to Lod.'[7] This attitude was not softened by the responsibility of government. At a news conference to explain the Israeli bombing of the Iraqi nuclear reactor in 1981, Begin informed the world's press that 'there will not be another Holocaust in history'.[8]

The epithets 'Nazi' and 'fascist' were tossed around with abandon by all sides in the political struggle in Israel. It was a technique of ideological warfare that predated the state. After 1945, the horrors of the Holocaust did not create a moral moratorium on the use of such terminology, whether it be against Israel's hostile neighbours or domestic political foes. It became instead an instrument in a political armoury – to expound the reality about an enemy, to reveal to the people the unfettered truth. In fact, the use of such language exacerbated tensions by releasing emotions best held in check. The opponents of the present had been turned into the ghosts of the past.

Begin's reductionist approach served to concentrate all the historical fears of the Jews, and his deep-seated beliefs were often widely shared by large sections of the Israeli populace. To the accusation that all this amounted to paranoia, Begin's response was that paranoia was sometimes justified. Others dubbed him 'the High Priest of Fear' because of his expertise in uncovering and playing on the innermost anxieties of the population.[9] After 1967, Begin politicized the Holocaust like no other Israeli politician had. The feeling prior to the Six Day War that the Arabs would exterminate – l'hushmid – Israel was widespread and deeply felt. This coincided with an increased prominence of the Holocaust in the Israeli psyche. There was also an element of fantasy in Begin's exposition of past and future Holocausts. The execution of his father by the Nazis took place at the head of his community while he was heroically singing the Hatikva, the Israeli national anthem, Begin claimed – an account dismissed by his sister.[10]

Some surmised that Begin's ability to locate the psychological weakness of a group – whether it was dread of an Arab-instigated repetition of the Holocaust, the hatred of Labour by disaffected former members, or Sephardi humiliation by insensitive Ashkenazim – was the key to his political strength. The trauma of the Holocaust and the potential for its recurrence had always been a feature of Begin's approach, but it seems to have become more pronounced and less focused in his old age. During the invasion of Lebanon, Begin's obsessively repeated references to the past were seen by many – especially opponents of the war – as the key to his political strategy.

Holocaust imagery indeed loomed large in Begin's mind. In 1939, he was unable to enact the Talmudic empowerment *im ba l'horgach hashkem l'horgo* (Sanhedrin 72a) – 'If someone comes to kill you, rise up so as to kill him'. For the tragic truth was that the Jews, including every Revisionist, were powerless. Instead, Begin fled before the advance of the German army in the certain knowledge that any resistance, though heroic, was also futile, and that nothing more could be done for the cause of Zion in Poland. Symbolically, the building that housed the *Betar* newspaper had been bombed and destroyed. The sense of frustration, of nagging doubt, of leaving others behind, which afflicted many who escaped the Nazi occupation of Poland, must have affected Begin. By 1982, however, the course of political events presented him with an opportunity to act as he would have wished to have done in 1939.

At the beginning of the war in Lebanon, on 14 June, Begin responded to criticism from the Knesset Foreign Affairs and Defence Committee about civilian casualties caused by the attacks on West Beirut:

> If in World War II, Adolf Hitler had taken shelter in some apartment along with a score of innocent civilians, nobody would have had any compunction about shelling the apartment even if it had endangered the lives of the innocent as well.[11]

Begin naturally reacted strongly to claims that Israel was imitating the Nazis in its actions against the Arabs. For such comments tended to be picked up by Western leader writers and run together with misleading statistics – it made good copy to turn the Jews into Nazis and Begin into Hitler in order to condemn the war. This often had the effect of turning unpalatable reports into inaccurate ones, with the result that such distortions persuaded many confused Diaspora Jews to attack the press as a way of escaping their bewilderment and to align themselves with the government of Israel. Even President Mitterrand, a one-time Vichy official, saw fit to call the siege of Beirut 'an Oradour-type incident', thereby recalling the Nazi massacre of the inhabitants of a French village in 1944. There was particular resentment when young Germans condemned the policies of the Israeli government. All this confirmed Begin in his total distrust of the outsider given the path of killing and destruction that coloured Jewish history.

Perhaps the most bizarre manifestation of Begin's own use of analogies to the Nazi period was his telegram to President Reagan:

> Now may I tell you, dear Mr President, how I feel these days when I turn to the creator of my soul in deep gratitude. I feel as a Prime Minister empowered to instruct a valiant army facing 'Berlin' where amongst inno-cent civilians, Hitler and his henchmen hide in a bunker deep beneath the surface. My generation, dear Ron, swore on the altar of God that whoever proclaims his intent to destroy the Jewish state or the Jewish people, or both, seals his fate, so that what happened from Berlin – with or without inverted commas – will never happen again.[12]

These comments, made at the height of the bombardment of Beirut, outraged many Israelis. They felt that the Holocaust had been co-opted to provide the *raison d'être* for the war. Many believed that such sentiments characterized Begin's reversing of traditional Jewish norms in a war he had lost control of. Despite Jewish sensitivity to the trauma of the Holocaust, many came to believe that he had lost touch with reality and was merely chasing the ghosts of the past.

The writer Amos Oz, who had termed Operation Peace for Galilee 'a typical Jabotinskyian fantasy', accused Begin of the urge to resurrect Hitler from the dead each day so as to kill him once more:

> This urge to revive Hitler, only to kill him again and again, is the result of pain that poets can permit themselves to use, but not statesmen ... even at great emotional cost personally, you must remind yourself and the public that elected you its leader that Hitler is dead and burned to ashes.[13]

Chaika Grossmann, a Mapam member of the Knesset who had actually fought in the Warsaw Ghetto, conveyed a similar message to Begin: 'Return to reality! We are not in the Warsaw Ghetto, we are in the State of Israel.'[14] One lecturer in Holocaust Studies wrote:

> Are we really to view the miserable refugee camps as Munich and Nuremberg? Are we to understand that the flattened hovels outside of Sidon represent the 'Palestinian Dresden'? Are we to see the thousands of old people, women and children bereft of all and exposed to the elements as the paragons of the master race?[15]

Begin's outbursts provoked survivors of the Warsaw Ghetto and Buchenwald to go on hunger strike outside Yad Vashem, Israel's memorial to the Holocaust, in protest. One of them observed:

> The Germans in Buchenwald forcibly starved us, but in Jerusalem today, I freely starve myself. My hunger is no less terrible. When I hear people

talk about the 'filthy Arabs', I remember the talk about 'filthy Jews'. I see Beirut and I remember Warsaw.[16]

Raful Eitan banned army visits to Yad Vashem after some of the guides openly opposed the war. Herut's Dov Shilansky, a Holocaust survivor from Lithuania, asked the director of Yad Vashem to dismiss Israel Gutman, a leading Holocaust scholar and a survivor of Auschwitz, because he had condemned the bombardment of Beirut and Begin's rhetorical use of the Holocaust.

Yet behind the rhetoric was Begin's determination that the vacillation of the West in the 1930s should not be repeated by the Israel of the 1980s in the Middle East. He believed strongly, therefore, in the pre-emptive strike against potential foes. Indeed, he believed that France's pro-Palestinian policy arose out of their 'jealousy of Israel' because they did not have the courage to strike down the Algerian FLN before it became too strong. Begin viewed US pressure on Israel as similar to that of the imperial powers on small European nations in the 1930s to kneel before Hitler. At the beginning of the Lebanon war, he told the Presidents' Conference of Major Jewish Organizations in the USA that Israel would not act as Czechoslovakia had acted in 1938 when it had succumbed to Western pressure. In an interview three months later, alluding to the United States, he commented that 'Israel is not Chile and I am not Allende'.[17] The central reason for the prolongation of the war and its transformation from Operation Little Pines into Operation Big Pines was the fact of Israel's dependence on the Phalangists, who in the event remained neutral and refused to honour their promise to fight with the Israelis. Sharon clearly overrated their military capacity and misread their political allegiance. Begin, however, viewed them through the eyes of a Holocaust survivor. The Christian Phalangists were – like the Jews – a small people constantly being attacked and persecuted by a hostile Muslim world bent on genocide. As early as May 1981, he told the Knesset that the Syrians had treated the Christian population of Lebanon as the Nazis has dealt with the nations of Europe. He compared Beirut to Rotterdam and the siege of Zahle to the destruction of Coventry.

Yet there had also been much internecine bloodletting between the leading Christian families – such as Bashir Gemayel's authorization of the murders of Tony Frangieh and his family. Begin did not begin to comprehend the byzantine intrigues of the Lebanese warlords. His reference point was growing up in Catholic Poland where he had witnessed Christian anti-Semitism first hand. The idea of Jews saving Christians from their fate appealed to him as one of history's ironies. Begin explained his rationale in an address to the National Defence College on 8 August by taking issue with the consensual view that war was an option only when all other channels had failed. He characterized the operation in Lebanon as a war with no alternative: Israel was forced to take the initiative to stop a greater calamity befalling the country in the future. In particular, he invoked the Six Day War of 1967 as a conflict where Israel had no choice but to fight, and this, he suggested, was the precedent for the invasion of Lebanon:

> The Egyptian army concentrations in the Sinai approaches did not prove that Nasser was really about to attack us. We must be honest with ourselves. We decided to attack him ... [to] take the initiative and attack the enemy, drive him back, and thus assure the security of Israel and the future of the nation.[18]

This statement effectively reversed all official Israeli explanations about the cause of the Six Day War – most Israelis had hitherto believed that the state had been in mortal danger and that there had been no option but to attack Nasser's forces. Furthermore, Begin described in graphic detail how the Syrian tanks had almost swept into Israel at the beginning of the Yom Kippur War, in order to convey how fragile the existence of the Jewish state really was. In this way, Begin was able to justify the human cost of the war in Lebanon as being far less than if a full-blown war had been forced upon Israel. 'There is no moral imperative that a nation must fight only when its back is to the sea or to the abyss', he insisted. 'Such a war may avert tragedy, if not a Holocaust, for any nation; but it causes it terrible loss of life.'[19] Yet many Israelis by that stage had come to regard the war as an option which Begin had taken rather than a last resort without choice – a war of no alternative.

The Third Phase: 23 August–28 September

The events that shaped the final phase of Operation Peace for Galilee were as follows:

23 August	Bashir Gemayel is elected president of Lebanon.
1 September	President Reagan announces his plan for a settlement of the Israel–Palestine question.

5 September	Israel rejects the Reagan Plan.
14 September	Bashir Gemayel is assassinated when the building in which he is speaking is blown up.
15 September	The IDF moves into key positions in West Beirut.
16–18 September	The Phalangists are permitted to enter the Sabra and Shatilla camps to search for terrorists but instead massacre Palestinian civilians.
20–23 September	Begin refuses to initiate an inquiry into the massacre and rebuts internal and international criticism.
24 September	An estimated 400,000 Israelis demonstrate in Tel Aviv at a Peace Now rally.
28 September	Begin authorizes the establishment of the Kahan Commission to investigate the massacre.

With the exit of the PLO from Beirut and Bashir Gemayel elected as President of Lebanon, Begin felt that a major part of Operation Big Pines had succeeded. He felt vindicated in the political path he had followed. One way of concluding the process would be to bring the vanquished Palestinians to the negotiating table and achieve their acquiescence in the Likud's understanding of the autonomy plan envisaged in the Camp David Accords. On 21 August, when the PLO was still in West Beirut, Sharon called upon 'the Arabs of Eretz Israel' to commence negotiations with Israel. It was trumpeted as a historic opportunity and the start of a new era.

The Foreign Minister, Yitzhak Shamir, justified the invasion of Lebanon in terms of this ideal outcome on the very first day of the war. He told an international banking conference that 'the elimination of PLO terrorism would be an important contribution to the well-being of the Arab inhabitants of Judea, Samaria and the Gaza District and to their chances of joining the peace process'. He had nevertheless told younger colleagues privately that he was distinctly unhappy about the decision to initiate the invasion.

The rearrangement of the Middle East map to suit Israeli interests was perceived by Begin also to be in America's interest. Yet Begin's euphoria was not shared by the White House. The growing rift between the Begin and Reagan administrations had induced a decisively negative feeling towards Israel, especially following Alexander Haig's resignation. Both George Schultz and Caspar Weinberger were perceived to be critical of Israel's policies and they would not drop the crucial question of Palestinian nationalism. In a speech to the American people on 1 September, the president unveiled the Reagan Plan. He pointedly mentioned that 'the military losses of the PLO have not diminished the yearning of the Palestinian people for a just solution of their claims'. Although he stipulated that there would be no Palestinian state and that the PLO would not be the negotiating partner, Reagan insisted on a clear link between the West Bank and Jordan. He proposed an immediate freeze on the settlement drive and rejected the notion that Israeli sovereignty over the occupied territory was compatible with Palestinian autonomy.

This was a great blow to Begin. When victory appeared to be in sight, the Americans, in Begin's opinion, were willing to throw away all the gains. The Cabinet opposed the Reagan Plan through their own interpretation of the Camp David Accords – even though the Americans had argued from the same premise. Begin pointed out that Camp David made no mention of anything more than a three-month settlement freeze or of any links with Jordan. He reiterated the arguments he had put forward during the disagreements with President Carter over interpretation. Thus, although he had won the war, the political way forward was far from a settled matter. Begin had believed that a virulently anti-communist, neo-conservative US administration, harbouring its own obsession with terrorism, would behave differently from its Democratic predecessor. On the Israel–Palestine question at least, seemingly little had changed.

Even the Phalangists did not appreciate Begin's vision of the future. Bashir Gemayel would not sign a peace treaty with Israel and preferred a 'peace by stages' approach. He would not take the step of effectively weakening his links with the Arab world or indeed renounce Lebanese Muslims and Druzes. In one sense, the situation threw into sharp relief the lack of understanding about Lebanon that permeated Israeli thinking. Sharon, for his part, believed that there were clearcut solutions to everything if only the will to implement them was there: 'In Lebanon, everything is a compromise ... all the time compromises. The question is, can we, the Jews live here with a compromise, and I think the answer is "no".'[20]

Religious Arguments for the War

The National Religious Party's Rabbi Druckman had voted with the far right against the government during a vote of confidence two months before the war. During the course of the operation, however, the party became Sharon's staunchest ally. The remnant of La'am merged with Herut, while Telem and Techiya joined the government. The government which fought the war was therefore even further to the right. Techiya called for the annexation of Southern Lebanon, while religious elements produced maps indicating it to be 'the territory of the tribe of Asher'. Indeed, the party's chairman, Yuval Ne'eman, viewed the war as merely a continuation of Israel's war of independence. He called the invasion 'the last act of the war for this country, the whole of Eretz Israel'[21] and advocated joint use with the Lebanese of the waters of the Litani river. This proposal, of course, flew in the face of government policy as articulated in its first statement on 6 June that 'Israel continues to aspire to the signing of a peace treaty with independent Lebanon, its territorial integrity preserved.' Techiya's demands revived Zionist claims to Southern Lebanon as far as the River Litani from the time when borders were in the process of being defined by the imperial powers at the end of World War I. There were precedents for this line of thought. Ben-Gurion was also an enthusiastic advocate of a Christian state in Lebanon in the 1950s; yet he was strongly opposed on this by the more pragmatic Moshe Sharett.[23]

Such arguments were supported by many religious Jews who considered large tracts of Lebanon to be the domain of the tribe of Asher. Beirut was even Hebraized to Be'erot – the Hebrew for 'wells'. Members of the IDF's rabbinate issued a leaflet which quoted the inheritance of Asher in the Book of Joshua. Chapter 19, Verses 24–31 delineate both territorial boundaries and cities. Although some places are unknown today, the references include Tyre, part of the Jezreel Valley, and the land around Sidon.[22]

Forty American rabbis who had been brought to the hills surrounding Beirut to view the besieged capital declared that Operation Peace for Galilee was, Judaically, a just war and a *milchemet mitzva* – an obligatory war. A leading American Torah scholar, Rabbi J. David Bleich, suggested that a verse from the Song of Songs supported the acquisition of Southern Lebanon: 'Come with me from Lebanon, my bride, with me from Lebanon you shall come' (Song of Songs 4:8). Bleich interpreted this as another step towards complete redemption. He suggested, remarkably, that any evaluation of the ethical basis for an episode on the road to redemption was an irrelevance. Referring to Operation Peace for Galilee, he wrote: 'There are events in the lives of men that, irrespective of their morality or immorality, are nevertheless harnessed by God and utilized by Him as instruments of divine providence.'[24]

The Ashkenazi Chief Rabbi of Israel, Shlomo Goren, went further and, following Maimonides, cited three categories of obligatory war. The first was Joshua's battle to clear Eretz Israel when the Israelites crossed over into Canaan. The second was the battle against the Amalekites,[25] who became symbolic of the enemies of the Jews down the centuries. The final category of an obligatory war was to fight in order to save any Jewish community under threat. Goren interpreted the settlements in Northern Israel and in the Galilee panhandle as in this category. He generalized the idea of *pikuach nefesh* – the saving of a Jewish life – to that of saving an entire people.

The air attacks on and the bombardment of Beirut – even before the war – had been criticized by both the Labour Party and representatives of Israel's intelligentsia. Begin accused the opposition of double standards and reminded them of the Israeli shelling of Egyptian cities during the war of attrition just after the Six Day War when a Labour government had been in power. Religious moderates such as Avrum Burg, the son of the NRP leader, asked Begin if he would have shelled Beirut and effectively targeted innocent civilians as well as terrorists if those civilians happened to be Jews. Burg argued that all human beings, regardless of their race or religion, were created in God's image. Therefore if the IDF would have avoided the bombing and shelling of Beirut to spare Jewish lives, then the criterion would also apply to sparing non-Jews.

Goren significantly referred to Chapter 20 of the Second Book of Samuel to justify his position. This concerns the revolt of Sheva Ben Bichri of the tribe of Benjamin against King David. Ben Bichri led the northern tribes, Israel, against Judea, which remained loyal to David. The King's commander, Yoav Ben Zeruiah, was a mighty, ruthless soldier who finally laid siege to Sheva Ben Bichri in Abel of Beit Maacah with his followers, the Barim. As Yoav prepared to batter the city, 'a wise woman' appealed to Yoav that there were some within who were 'peaceful and faithful'. She asked: 'Why do you wish to destroy a city and a mother in Israel? Why do you want to devour the inheritance of the Lord?' Yoav, in all reasonableness, replied that he only wished to capture the rebel Sheva Ben Bichri: 'Deliver him only and I will depart from the city.' The woman obliged and located Ben Bichri, cut off his head and tossed it to Yoav who – satisfied that he had completed his task – blew the *shofar* (the ram's horn) and departed for Jerusalem with his army.

Goren clearly saw a typological example here in that the peaceful people of Beirut – perhaps the *Barim* – should deliver Arafat and his henchmen to Sharon. If this did not transpire, then the IDF should take the city by force, saving the innocent, the women and children if possible. The saving of life was justified through the Mishnaic saying that 'he who saves one life, it is as if he has saved the entire world' (Sanhedrin). Yet Goren did not fully explain the analogy, which, if taken to its logical conclusion, would have been politically counter-productive. The characters in the story of Sheva Ben Bichri clearly related to the current war. According to Goren, the position of the Prime Minister, labelled by his supporters *Begin, melech Israel* ('Begin, King of Israel'), was based on that of King David, who was for-bidden to build the Temple because he was a man of war. Ariel Sharon was depicted as a modern-day Yoav Ben Zeruiah. Yoav, the uncontrollable tool of his master, King David, while showing great loyalty to him, was also power hungry and adept at settling personal scores. For example, Yoav murdered Avner, who had made a covenant with King David, accusing him of being a spy. He also killed the King's son, Avshalom, who had rebelled against his father despite David's wish that his son should be spared. In the story of Sheva Ben Bichri, Yoav/Sharon disposes of a seemingly lukewarm ally, Amasa. Yoav tugs Amasa's beard as a sign of friendship and kills him with his sword held in the other hand, leaving the dead man 'wallowing in his blood in the midst of the highway'. Amasa had been promised the post of commander-in-chief by David and had thereby become a rival to Yoav. David's response to this series of brutal unauthorized acts was simply to rebuke him, but not to dismiss him. David feared the power of Yoav and his followers: 'these men the sons of Zeruiah are too hard for me'.

Like Sharon in Israel's conflicts, Yoav was active in each of David's wars. In Edom, he created terror by remaining for six months in order to exterminate all the male population. Moreover, rabbinical literature did not regard Yoav as having been endowed with powers of analysis or understanding. In the Talmud (Baba Batra 21a, b), he explains to King David that he committed genocide against the male Edomites because it is written, 'You shall blot out the male (*zachar*) Amalekites' (Deuteronomy 25:19). Whereupon, David points out Yoav's stupid error: he should have read the word as *zecher* – 'remembrance'.

One of the midrashes has Yoav besieging Kinsali, the capital of the Amalekites, (B.H. 146–148). When the siege does not prevail, he

enters the city incognito, proclaiming 'I am an Amalekite'. He then
proceeds to kill not only the soldiers and mercenaries but also all the
inhabitants, including the young woman who has given him food
and shelter. When the Israelites see the blood flowing from the city
gates they know that Yoav had been successful in liquidating the
legendary enemy of the Jews.

Significantly, Yoav came to an untimely end when he supported
Adoniyahu's claim to the throne over David's chosen heir, Solomon.
As he prepared to die, David instructed Solomon to pursue Yoav in
revenge for his slaying of Avner and Amasa and for all the destruction
and loss of life that he had caused in the king's name. Yoav fled to
the Tent of Lord, in which sanctuary he should have been given the
right of asylum. Instead, Solomon ignored this and ordered Benaniah
Ben Yehoiada to kill him. Yoav, the model for Sharon, is described in
a standard reference work as 'a loyal and willing tool in the hands of
his master, David; a sturdy, unscrupulous military chieftain, such as
surround Asiatic despots and leaders of freebooters'.[26]

CHAPTER ELEVEN

THE MASSACRE AT SABRA AND SHATILLA AND ITS CONSEQUENCES

The Massacre in the Camps

On 12 September Bashir and Sharon agreed – in violation of the evacuation agreement – that the Lebanese Army would root out the remaining two thousand Palestinian terrorists which Sharon believed to be present in West Beirut. The implementation of this vague plan might have led to the demolition of the Palestinian camps and the transfer of a large part of their populations to Syria and Jordan – thus confirming that Jordan was indeed Palestine. Two days later, however, Bashir was assassinated by a bomb which had been planted by a member of the Syrian National Party. A few hours after the killing, Sharon ordered the IDF to move into West Beirut to take over key strategic points, and discussed with Eitan the possibility of the Phalangists entering the Palestinian refugee camps to locate terrorists. This move to authorize entry into the Muslim half of the city was taken by Begin without Cabinet consultation or approval. Moreover, many Israelis had cautioned Sharon about the Phalangists' state of mind after the killing of their leader. Sharon balanced such warnings against his desire to complete the job – to flush out all remaining armed Palestinians and to locate and confiscate their weapons caches. The official reason for the Israeli move into West Beirut was to maintain order and to avoid bloodshed. Sharon clearly wished to utilize this opportunity to its full advantage. The Phalangists, for their part, agreed that they would not harm civilians in the camps. Yet the Christian soldiers understood that this responsibility, bestowed upon them by Sharon, offered an unparalleled opportunity to avenge their leader's assassination and to provoke a mass flight of all Palestinians from Beirut by turning the camps into killing fields.

While the Phalangists were actually in the camps, Sharon reported to an angry Cabinet, who had asked why they had not been informed about the entry into West Beirut. In placating them, Sharon said nothing about the Phalangists' move into Sabra and Shatilla. When Eitan finally did inform the Cabinet that they were actually in the camps, their main fear was that the Phalangists would be trapped and systematically eliminated by an estimated force of 2000 Palestinian fighters. This was also the view of the moderates in the Cabinet. David Levy's concern was with the statement that the IDF had entered Beirut to prevent bloodshed, when in fact a Palestinian–Phalangist conflict already in progress would show this to be transparently untrue. The Cabinet was worried that the IDF would have to enter the camps to help the Phalangists, such was their low opinion of the military capabilities of their Christian ally.

The lack of perception exhibited by even the moderates within the Cabinet became abundantly clear within hours of the meeting. Throughout the duration of 16 and 17 September, there were hints and signs that something terrible had happened. Yet all messages by concerned individuals to those in authority were either put to one side on the eve of the Jewish New Year, *erev Rosh Hashanah*, or simply ignored. Early on Saturday morning, 18 September, the full horrific details began to seep out. Israeli intelligence estimated that between 700 and 800 people had been slaughtered. Other estimates put the number of deaths even higher. The sense of outrage in Israel – particularly from those who had questioned the war – was immeasurable. The upper echelons of the IDF were deeply bitter at Sharon's leadership and at the Phalangist killers with whom they were supposed to be cooperating. Many senior commanders felt that Sharon had brought great dishonour to the reputation and ethical code of the Israeli fighting forces.

The world held the Israelis morally responsible for the massacre, the details of which filled the television screens of millions. The killings bore witness to how far this war had taken the Israelis. The failure to predict the consequences was symptomatic of the lack of humanity and insensitivity which the Begin government had projected throughout. Ze'ev Schiff, the doyen of Israeli military correspondents, wrote in *Ha'aretz*:

> In the refugee camps of Beirut, a war crime has been committed. The Phalangists executed hundreds of old men, women and children and even more. Once pogroms used to take place against the Jews in just the same way. It is not correct, as official spokesmen are claiming, that we learned of this crime only on Saturday at noon, through reports of foreign corre-

spondents in Beirut. Already on Friday morning, I heard about the slaughter in the camps and informed a senior figure – and he, I know, took immediate action. In other words, the slaughter had already begun on Thursday night and there is no doubt that what I had heard on Friday night was known to others before me.[1]

Begin was in synagogue during the Jewish New Year and only heard the news about the massacre later from the BBC World Service. At a Cabinet meeting, Sharon and Eitan explained to shocked ministers that there had indeed been coordination between the IDF and the Phalangists. Begin's initial reaction to all this was that it was simply another atrocity committed by the warring tribes of Lebanon. Begin's instinctive response was to turn his back on his international critics. He appealed to the Cabinet to close ranks in an act of solidarity against a hostile world. 'Goyim [non-Jews] are killing goyim', he reputedly commented, 'and the whole world is trying to hang Jews for the crime.' In addition to invoking such historical Jewish suspicion, he obfuscated the difference between Israeli moral responsibility for the crime and the actual crime itself which was committed by the Phalangists. In this, he was helped by Palestinian propaganda and Western reporting that ambiguously attributed the actual massacre to the Israelis. The government's communiqué distanced Israel from any connection and labelled 'a Lebanese unit' the culprits.

In the days that followed, the more Begin attempted to play down the incident, the greater was the clamour for a judicial inquiry. In the Knesset on 22 September, he praised the success of the war with the claim that no more Katyushas were falling on the Galilee. The more he attacked critics and refused to acknowledge that something terrible had happened, the more vociferous was the next wave of criticism. The Israeli playwright Yehoshua Sobol wrote that,

> Begin's characteristic response was a moral autism, accompanied by hypocrisy and self-righteousness. After turning the Holocaust into an oversized symbol, after using it like a dishcloth with which to wipe one's dirty hands clean, he has revived the notion of a 'blood libel' in the quagmire in which he and his government are floundering and into which he has dragged the people as a whole.[2]

When the storm of indignation finally broke, Sharon went to ground and was incommunicado for several days. Subsequently, he utilized the hitherto untarnished reputation of the IDF and its high standing amongst the Israeli public as a shield to ward off criticism. In Beirut, Sharon's commanders were in a virtual state of rebellion against his authority, so deep was their animosity. For the first time, they began to analyse the motivation behind and conduct of the war.

While Likud functionaries tried to divert discussion away from the need for a judicial inquiry, the impetus to mount a cover-up succeeded only in persuading the country's elite to join the call for such an inquiry. The Liberal Energy Minister, Yitzhak Berman, tendered his resignation from the Cabinet, as did Amram Mitzna, the head of the IDF College. Significantly, Mitzna, a kibbutznik, was put under pressure by his kibbutz organization not to resign, in order to prevent the army being placed under the control of right-wing officers. But it was President Navon's call for an inquiry which placed the greatest pressure on Begin:

> We owe it to ourselves and to our image in the world ... and to the cultured world of which we see ourselves a part, to find out quickly and exactly what has happened.[3]

This permitted leaders of Jewish communities in the Diaspora who had hitherto acquiesced in the official version of the war to appeal to Begin to support Navon's plea. This move, however, simply confirmed the Likud in their perception of a weak-kneed Diaspora. Thus, the Speaker of the Knesset accused the American Jewish leadership of not possessing 'the spiritual and cultural backbone to stand up to the barrage of criticism'.[4]

Labour members of the Knesset called upon Begin and Sharon 'to draw the immediate personal conclusions because of their responsibility' in the matter. Peace Now had approached Yossi Beilin, the party's spokesman, with the idea of a joint demonstration. Beilin enthusiastically relayed the idea to Peres, yet it was strongly opposed by many on the party's right, such as the veteran Israel Galili. Uzi Baram and other doves persuaded a meeting of the party bureau to give Peres the mandate to meet Peace Now.[5] When a record 400,000 demonstrated at a Peace Now rally in Tel Aviv – possibly the largest demonstration in Israel's history – it provided a channel for the anger and resentment that had welled up. The uncharacteristic decision of the Labour Party to take part in a public protest, after months of vacillation and attempts to be all things to all people, was an index of the sharp political polarization that had taken place in the country. The Likud, however, was not prepared to be challenged on its own territory. It began to prepare a counter-rally of similar size. However, unlike in the case of the pro-government rally at the height of the war, few ministers from the other parties in the coalition now wished to be seen supporting Begin, and the idea was dropped.

In the Diaspora, the long-derided opponents of the war became the dominant voice, displacing the hitherto compliant communal and philanthropic leadership. American Jewish leaders such as Julius Berman of the Presidents' Conference and the Anti-defamation League's Kenneth Bialkin had preached the doctrine of solidarity with Israel and now had to work hard to cope with the barrage of criticism. They had supported Sharon's approach that the war was inevitable and that 'the basic consensus of American Jewry is solidly in support'[6] – a dubious statement at the time, given the lack of hard statistical evidence. The Likud government expected Diaspora Jews to give their unconditional support to its war effort. They were expected to repeat the latest government statement whether it made sense or not. Thus, the task of the Diaspora leadership was to wage a *hasbarah* campaign in the belief that any event could be explained positively by means of good public relations. Likud functionaries interpreted the growing international clamour against the war as a matter of poor public relations rather than a question of misguided policies.

The Likud directed its political influence at the philanthropists and the donors, whom they wrongly believed were opinion-formers. Many had been bussed to selective areas of Lebanon and given the official explanation. Abba Eban condemned this exercise as 'the vulgarity of the fundraisers'. The Jewish press was also wooed, and it slavishly followed the official line during the early stages of the war.[7] Begin told a leading US Reform rabbi that 'to be a good Jew means to give full support to the government of Israel and to back the Prime Minister unequivocally on all issues whether you agree with him or not.'[8] Given the intellectual and dissident tradition of the Jews, many disagreed with that formulation. Yet a number of attempts were made to marginalize or to distort the motivation of the growing band of critics. For example, when two Jewish Labour MPs in Britain criticized the war, the Board of Deputies of British Jews issued a statement which cast aspersions on their 'Jewishness':

Neither of the Jewish Members of Parliament who have seen fit to make statements criticising Israel is a practising member of the Jewish faith or represents Jewish opinion in this country which remains convinced that only the total evacuation of Lebanon by the PLO will lead to peace in that sad country.[9]

As the war became bogged down both militarily and in terms of its rationale, Jewish leadership moved from a position of advocacy to one of studied neutrality. Thus, no comment was made when Sir Isaiah Berlin and Jacob Rothschild later called for an inquiry into the Sabra and Shatilla massacre. At a special meeting of the Board of Deputies of British Jews in London to discuss the massacre, the leadership remained silent and simply acted as a neutral chair mediating between speakers for and against the war. Although the Board also added its voice for an inquiry, its president, along with other Diaspora leaders, had attacked the statement of Nahum Goldman, Philip Klutznick and Pierre Mendes-France made earlier during the war calling for the siege of Beirut to be lifted and for negotiations with the PLO. Many Diaspora Jews now openly called upon both Begin and Sharon to resign. Arthur Hertzberg, a rare example of an American Jewish communal leader who actively opposed the war, prophetically took the argument further:

> Menachem Begin may not resign next week, but he has lost the power to govern effectively. A Prime Minister of Israel can survive blunders at home, deep strains with the US and disagreements within World Jewry, but he cannot remain in office if he has squandered Israel's fundamental asset – its respect for itself and the respect of the world.[10]

Despite such protestations, Begin did not immediately budge from his stand of self-justification. It was not a moral argument that finally persuaded him to appoint Judge Kahan to head an official inquiry but a political one. Although the National Religious Party ministers took heed of the moral arguments, they did not initially support the demand for an inquiry. It was only when private pressure from leading scholars and teachers, such as Rabbi Joseph Soloveitchik in the United States, emphasized the importance of such an inquiry to the National Religious Party ministers that the first rumblings of a coalition crisis were heard – and noted by Begin. Yet, a day after he had initiated the inquiry, in a letter to US Senator Cranston, he painted a picture of an anti-Semitic world once more turning against the Jews. It seemed more important for Begin to correct misreporting and to deflect the argument:

> Levelling false accusations is a repeated feature of our own experience. It is almost inexplicable but true, the astonishing fact – Jews condemned as the poisoners of wells, the killers of Christian children for the Pesach ritual, the spreaders of the Black Plague … and now this.[11]

The question of responsibility for the massacre quickly moved beyond the political to the realm of morality. A demonstration of religious Jews outside the main synagogue in Jerusalem, Hechal Shlomo, proved to be the forerunner of Netivot Shalom (Paths to Peace), the religious peace movement. Typical of the advocates of settlement in the Territories was the response of Rabbi Chaim Druckman, a leader of Gush Emunim and an NRP member of the Knesset. He accused those who called for an inquiry, of being *yefei nefesh* – do-gooders.

Significantly, the course of the war and the massacre in the camps became almost a struggle for the correct interpretation of Jewishness. Assimilated Jewish intellectuals in the Diaspora and devout Israeli secularists looked to religious sources to support their understanding of Jewish values. A leading scholar, Dr Jonathan Sacks, later to become the British Chief Rabbi, recalled the reaction to his support for President Navon's demand for an inquiry:

> Among my congregation in Golders Green at the time was an old and distinguished rabbi, *zichrono livracha* [may his memory be for a blessing], the leading spokesman of the yeshiva world who then held the senior position on the London Bet Din [Rabbinical Court of Law]. My custom had been to extend the pulpit to him at various times during the year. One of his favourite themes was the denunciation of the State of Israel for its secularity, choosing the streets of Tel Aviv as the part that represented the whole. On this occasion, however, as I finished my *derasha* [sermon] he mounted the pulpit, and declared to the congregation that my call for an inquiry into Sabra and Shatilla was tantamount to *chillul ha'Shem* [the desecration of God's name]. There was little doubt in my mind that the sympathies of the congregation were with him.
>
> Here, then, was as neat an irony as one could wish. Those who had hitherto been avowedly secular Jews, for whom the State of Israel constituted a significant part of their self-definition, were to be found appropriating religious terminology and values in order to criticize and dissociate themselves from the actions of the State, while those whose identity was religious and had hitherto been vociferous critics of Israel, leapt to its defence.[12]

The Aftermath

The Kahan report[13] into the massacre in the Sabra and Shatilla camps delivered its full complement of justice. Raful Eitan was severely criticized for his 'acts and omissions', Begin for his lack of involvement, and Shamir for ignoring reports of the massacre from Zippori.

The Commission reserved its clearest and most damning judgement for Sharon. They found that the Minister of Defence bore personal responsibility for the matter and that he should draw 'the appropriate personal conclusions regarding the failings revealed in the manner in which he discharged the duties of his office'. It pointedly suggested that Begin could exercise his authority to remove a minister from office. The problem, however, was that Sharon did not want to resign and neither did Begin wish to dismiss him. Despite the fact that the entire Cabinet was now arraigned against him, Begin dithered and could not bring himself to dismiss Sharon. Begin's sense of personal responsibility for appointing Sharon in the first place and then failing to control him was self-evident. (He had begun to realize what was really happening in early August when the prolonged bombardment of Beirut commenced. He had already decided to curtail Sharon's authority when Reagan's dramatic telephone call to him on 12 August, protesting at the saturation bombing of Beirut, sealed the matter.) After days of debate, a compromise was finally struck whereby Sharon was shunted sideways to be Minister without portfolio.

Yet significantly, notwithstanding the massacre and the 400,000-strong demonstration, Begin's support did not plummet. A Modi'in Ezrachi poll at the beginning of October 1982 showed that the Likud would still attain 60 seats in an election. Another poll conducted just after the massacre showed that in answer to the question 'Who is best suited to be Prime Minister?', Begin's standing fell only 7 percentage points, from 49.8 per cent to 42.9 per cent. Clearly, most people were not ready to undertake a political reckoning of what had happened. A Dahaf poll in July 1982 recorded that 83 per cent of respondents thought that it was right to start the war. This view was held for some considerable time, and opposition to the decision to go into Lebanon only gradually increased.

The central concern of most people was undoubtedly that of security – a theme Begin had repeatedly emphasized in order to build and maintain support for the war. The minimal objective of the war was to neutralize the Palestinian military threat on the Northern border. In the short term, this was successful, as was the evacuation of the PLO from Beirut, but it provided neither a long-term solution nor absolute security. Israel's international image was severely dented – no longer 'a light unto the nations'. In part, this was due to the successful public-relations campaign waged by the Palestinians and their allies in Europe and the United States. The inadequacy and

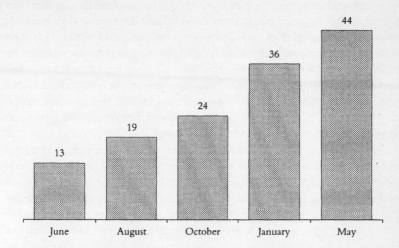

Figure 11.1 'Was it right to start the war?' – negative answers to the Dahaf surveys, June 1982 to May 1983 (%)

confusion of the Likud government and its inability to respond compounded the problem.

Several military analysts and historians who subsequently examined the Lebanon war considered the question of whether or not the IDF's response was proportionate to the threat and whether it was sufficiently discriminating in terms of minimizing damage to property and loss of human life. In looking at specific stages of the war, one commentator stated that,

> Israel substantially met its standard of 'battle ethics'.... Serious efforts were made to minimize civilian casualties and damage in the drive to Beirut. These efforts were rendered very difficult by the PLO's tactic of fighting from civilian areas. In the siege of the PLO in West Beirut, the problem of fighting with proportionate and discriminate means became even more difficult.[14]

Significantly, although he concluded that Israel did act proportionately and discriminately during the siege of Beirut, he also argued that this was not the case after 6 August when Habib had succeeded in negotiating a withdrawal of the PLO from Beirut. He observed that,

> In most evaluations of war there is a mixed record of compliance with and deviation from the law of war.... Judgements about war conduct tend to be influenced by judgements about the legal permissibility of the war.[15]

Some military commentators – as opposed to media pundits and political opponents – suggested that the IDF did appear to have upheld the doctrine of *tohar ha'neshek* – the purity of arms. This was achieved in a catastrophic military situation and despite the leadership of Sharon and Eitan, who placed minimal value upon such ideas. Yet there were plenty of examples that testified to the contrary. All this was counterbalanced and underplayed by selective media coverage of the war with its accompanying emotive and harrowing imagery, and Israeli opposition to Sharon's military aims.

In the Likud and in some sections of the Israeli right, the blame for the Lebanon war was laid at the door of Sharon, who was perceived to have misled both Begin and the nation. The admission of failure, albeit implicit, did not stimulate any real analysis of fundamental Likud positions. It was an aberration and not original sin.

The Lebanon war most immediately affected those who favoured a rational resolution of the Palestinian question. Israeli academics and the intelligentsia in general had been stunned by the wave of unthinking nationalism which had swept the country. There was a shocked awareness at the political direction in which Begin and the government had taken the Jewish state and of the needless deaths and wanton destruction that had been caused. To the outside world which was familiar with a Labour-dominated Israel, the state seemed to have renounced its self-imposed restrictions on the use of power and to have relegated past values. At its inception during June and July 1982, the Lebanon war seemingly turned the Jews of Israel from being a people of non-conformists and dissidents into one which remained obedient to the prevailing political wisdom of the day. As the war progressed, this abandonment of such historical characteristics proved to be a transient phenomenon as the protests increased in size and number. Yet this sense of responsibility for the moral and intellectual values of Jewish tradition permeated the psyche of thousands of Israeli Jews and became a central preoccupation as the war aims were realized.

The editor Jacobo Timmerman was in exile in Israel at that time, following his flight from Argentina and a narrow escape from the brutality of its ruling junta. In a book written during the Lebanon war, he related the present to his previous experience:

During Juan Peron's second and third presidential terms, I saw Argentina seized by a collective madness, sometimes violent, sometimes peaceful; living in a mystical state, translating hallucinations into daily routine. There have been other countries in the past few years where I was able to confirm such transports which allow a government to manipulate collective fears and impose an escape from reality through hallucination or messianism. This happened in Chile and Uruguay after 1972, and in Argentina after the military dictatorship took over in 1976.

I have relived this experience in Israel.[16]

What happened in the summer of 1982 was for many Israelis, in one sense, a challenge to their very identity as Jews. Was Israel now no different from Latin American countries such as Argentina? Was Israel merely a state of the Jews like any other state rather than a Jewish state with a special vision of how humanity should conduct its affairs?

It was certainly true that the Begin government had finally been forced to hear the rising tide of protest, but the fundamental questions persisted: How were we dragged into this war? Why did we allow it to happen? The sense of isolation, and indeed betrayal, was deep. The war in Lebanon was thus a watershed for a great many people. Something fundamental had changed. The lesson that many Israeli Jews learned was that it was very important not to retreat intellectually into the wilderness, but instead to participate in the struggle for the soul of Israel. The political activities that arose from this realization formed the basis of opposition to the policies of the Likud for the next decade, and proved to be an important influence on the Labour Party in moving them to negotiate with the PLO in 1993.

Although Sharon succeeded in removing one military threat, he nevertheless awakened other sleeping dragons in the Arab world. He forfeited the possibility of succeeding Begin as the leader of Herut and was now marked as a figure who could not be trusted with high office. For the PLO, it was on the surface a glorious débâcle which promoted the Palestinian cause as never before. It propelled some West Bank Palestinians to re-examine their approach towards attaining a homeland. Some were persuaded to embark on the road of political compromise, while others believed that the armed struggle should be intensified. For Begin, it was the end of a dream. The dignity and ideals of his youth had been undermined. He could no longer hold back reality. The death of his wife and lifelong partner at the end of 1982 was a tremendous blow. The devastating import of the Kahan report and the gradual realization of what had actually happened during the war led him into a self-imposed isolation from the world. A member of a delegation of striking medical personnel who witnessed Begin's behaviour at this time suggested that it bore all the hallmarks of depressive psychosis.

In August 1983, the new Chancellor of West Germany, Helmut Kohl, decided to take up the invitation which Yitzhak Rabin had extended in 1976. Although Begin never cancelled the invitation, Kohl's predecessor, Helmut Schmidt, had delayed taking it up – probably much to Begin's satisfaction. Schmidt's comments that Germany bore some responsibility for the Palestinian problem – thereby implying that the Holocaust was responsible for the establishment of the State of Israel – had infuriated Begin. Begin, for his part, accused Schmidt of taking part in Nazi ceremonies to celebrate the failure of the July Plot in 1944 to kill Hitler and the hanging of the conspirators. Schmidt thus never met Begin. The Israeli Prime Minister clearly could not put off Kohl, however. Begin had almost certainly decided to resign by this time; he was thus confronted with the prospect that his last act as Prime Minister of Israel would be to salute the German flag and respectfully listen to *Deutschland Über Alles*. This was something he simply could not face.

During the Lebanon war, Begin had received a letter from Yaakov Guterman of Kibbutz Ha'ogen, who had lost his son during the battle for Beaufort Castle at the beginning of the war. Guterman was the descendent of a rabbinical family and the only son of a Jewish fighter in the Warsaw Ghetto. He ended his harrowing letter thus:

> And the voice of our sons' blood cries out from the earth.
> Remember: the history of our ancient people will judge you with whips and scorpions and your deeds will be a warning and a verdict for generations to come.
> And if you have a spark of conscience and humanity within you, may my great pain – the suffering of a father in Israel whose entire world has been destroyed – pursue you forever, during your sleeping hours and when you are awake – may it be a mark of Cain upon you for all time.[17]

The pain of the murder of 3 million Polish Jews had turned full circle. In September 1983, Menachem Begin resigned and retreated to his home, a recluse and seemingly a broken man – perhaps reclaiming once more the psychological security of the Irgun underground. The emotional and often fanatical dedication which coloured his way of life, with all its deep depressions and high elations, had finally overcome him.

CHAPTER TWELVE

SHAMIR:
THE MAN FROM LEHI

The New Leader

Security – his whole life. Always at the hub of responsibility and authority. Always far from the limelight. Yet whoever needs to know has always known that this man is made of the stuff that makes national leaders. They believe – and rightly so – that his word is always kept. Israel's friends respect him, Israel's enemies fear him. The people of Israel are what he cares about. The life of each citizen and the future of every child are important to him. His pleasant smile hides an iron will. Pressures won't bend him. He has a heart to feel with, a mind to judge with and a hand to act with. (Likud election advertisement, 1984)[1]

On 1 September 1983, at Tel Aviv's Ohel Shem auditorium, Herut's Central Committee elected Yitzhak Shamir to lead the party following the sudden resignation and dramatic withdrawal of Menachem Begin. Begin's failure to leave in place an obvious successor was a commentary on the absolutism of his position. Shamir, on the other hand, was perceived as a safe pair of hands to maintain the establishment's interests and to soothe the political anguish of an 'orphaned' party. He had built his support originally on opposition to Ezer Weizmann's campaign to become Begin's successor, and, later, on his increasingly liberal policies towards the Palestinians. At the age of 68, he was seen – and indeed probably saw himself – as a caretaker and compromise candidate. Yet Shamir stayed in office until 1992, with a hiatus of two years as deputy Prime Minister in the rotational National Unity government of 1984–88. With the exception of Ben-Gurion, no other Israeli Prime Minister has served longer.

The fact of Shamir's long tenure certainly serves as a commentary on the political divisions and weaknesses which characterized his domestic opponents and Arab enemies alike. But it was also an indication of Herut's desire to shut out both Arik Sharon and David

Levy from the party leadership. Sharon, a latecomer to the movement, was especially feared following the débâcle of the Lebanon war, and many senior Herut politicians clearly regarded him as an electoral liability. Shamir himself considered Sharon to possess 'a degree of inborn extremism and recklessness'.[2] David Levy, although a standard-bearer for the Sephardi underclass, was considered a political light-weight and was perceived by the public as both unsophisticated and lacking in *gravitas*. For the party old guard, he had no association with the establishment of the state and was not connected with the Fighting Family aristocracy, the guardians of the Irgun legend. Instead he represented the aspirations of the other Israel, those Sephardim who had joined Herut in the 1960s and 1970s to oppose the Align-ment's paternalism and apparent indifference to their plight. David Levy appeared distant from the philosophy of the revered *Rosh Betar*, Jabotinsky. He also seemed to be distinctly un-ideological, displaying little obvious concern about the fate of Judea and Samaria. Moshe Arens, Sharon's successor as Minister of Defence, who would have posed a serious challenge to Shamir, could not be considered because he was not a member of the Knesset.

The Liberals voted to back Shamir and he also had the support of all the Herut Cabinet ministers. Although Sharon attracted the younger and right-wing elements in the party, he did not offer himself as a candidate. Instead, he met Shamir at an early stage in the campaign to conclude an alliance to stop Levy, probably in the belief that given Shamir's age his own day would soon come. Shamir was also chosen for his greyness of character and his lack of charisma – a dull but necessary antidote to the drama and passions of the Begin years. Some Likud members saw him as a sort of Israeli Attlee in terms of temperament and reliability, and thus well suited to follow a distinctly Churchillian period. When Begin's resig-nation was announced, supporters gathered around his home to implore him to reconsider. One placard read: 'Without you, we have no king, no saviour, no messiah.' Shamir was no such father figure. He was quiet, economical with his lacklustre rhetoric, and virtually invisible on the political stage. He did not project Begin's sense of pomp and circumstance, was uninterested in ritual and religion, possessed no intellectual pretensions, and was relatively detached from the Revisionist mythology. If Begin reached both the heights of elation and the depths of depression, Shamir proceeded on an unmelodramatic even keel all the way through. Unlike Begin, he did not care about his public image or what people thought about him. The award of the Nobel Peace Prize would never have excited him. Even in the days of the Lehi underground, there was always a certain disdain for the cult of the personality which the Revisionists bestowed upon their leaders. Although publicly Shamir deferred to the adulation of Begin, privately he could not stomach the theatrics:

> I wasn't a particular admirer of Begin's famous speeches; I felt them often to be filled with pathos and overstatement – though who could remain unimpressed by their power, sarcasm and careful architecture? I was impatient with his deference to titles, his being awed by generals or professors, and I disliked his acceptance of flattery and fawning and wished always in vain, that he were not so hungry for popularity.[3]

In one sense, Shamir exhibited a greater affinity with Ben-Gurion in that he had understood political reality far better than had the emotional Begin. Although he played the political game, such thoughts remained in the private domain. He had seemingly become disillusioned with the Lebanon war, later claiming in his memoirs that there had been 'a lack of national consensus' and that he had 'no hand or say in the conduct of the war'. Yet at the time he had made no discernible move to oppose it as had other Cabinet ministers. What is more, he had earned condemnation from the Kahan Commission, which commented that it was difficult to find a justification 'for his disdain for information' following his inaction on receiving early reports of the massacre in Sabra and Shatilla camps. Indeed, he argued in Cabinet that they should 'not be too hasty in acting' on the findings of the Kahan Commission. During that period, Shamir maintained a relative silence – a fellow traveller with the spirit of the times – and became adept at offering plausible explanations in dealing with controversy and upheaval.

Shamir was chosen because he was seen as having emerged from the same ideological milieu as Begin. He was similarly perceived as stubborn and firm. Yet unlike Begin, he did not espouse Jabotinsky's liberalism – which he had renounced long ago. He was known instead for his caution and his secrecy, a political shadow boxer whose skills were developed in Lehi and in the Mossad. Ironically, he was proclaimed party leader beneath the portrait of Jabotinsky, whom he had disowned nearly half a century before. Yochanan Bader, a long-time Herut stalwart, remarked sarcastically: 'Shamir is a real man of principle and most suitable to lead an underground movement.'[4]

Who was Yitzhak Shamir?

As Yitzhak Yezernitsky, Shamir had known and met Begin in Poland during his student days and had similarly espoused the Revisionist cause. He too was impressed by the zeal of revolutionary Russia and the dedication of purpose exhibited by other contemporary national movements such as the Irish struggle for independence. Shamir's exemplars were Lenin and Trotsky, Michael Collins, and the protagonists in the centuries-long Polish fight for an independent state. Above all, he looked to Jabotinsky, who had broken with the Zionist establishment and was then beginning to challenge their dominance. The riots in Hebron in 1929 persuaded him to join Betar. The trial of Abba Achimeir and his far-right circle for Arlosoroff's murder a few years later induced a life-long disdain for Mapai and the Labour movement. In Shamir's eyes, the blame that was heaped upon the Revisionists for the killing helped to safeguard Labour Zionist influence for decades to come.

After his arrival in Palestine in 1935, Shamir studied history at the Hebrew University and worked as a building labourer in Kerem Avraham. He then moved to Tel Aviv to work for the Braude accounting firm.[5] Shamir logically adhered to the radical position of the young Betarniks who demanded military action against the British. He was particularly inspired by Yonatan Ratosh's pamphlet *Aiming for Government: The Front of the Liberation Movement in the Future*, which advocated that a revolutionary minority could – and should – catalyse the masses into action. Unlike Jabotinsky, Ratosh wanted to declare a Jewish state immediately, before a Jewish majority had been attained. It was the advocacy of the formation of a national liberation movement to oust the British and the prospect of the armed struggle that appealed. The official Revisionists, who ultimately believed in diplomacy, were totally unimpressed by this thesis and, apart from Begin, voted against it at the Revisionist General Conference in Prague at the beginning of 1938. Yet Ratosh's views were overwhelmingly popular amongst the Betarniks and the radical wing of the Revisionist movement. The pamphlet proved to be the bridge which connected Shamir with Avraham Stern, who regarded Ratosh as a teacher and mentor.

Like many other members of Betar, the influence of the intellectual far right in the Yishuv – figures such as Ratosh, Abba Achimeir and Uri Zvi Greenberg – gradually proved more attractive than the considered moderation of Jabotinsky. Shamir joined the Irgun in 1937 to oppose Ben-Gurion and the policy of *havlagah* ('self-restraint') and was inevitably drawn towards Avraham Stern. The lack of progress with the British, the Arab revolt, and the darkening Nazi shadow over Europe's Jews forced some members of Betar and the Irgun to break with formal Revisionism. Shamir's disappointment with Jabotinsky, who 'sounded not unlike Ben-Gurion',[6] continued throughout his days in Lehi until he formally joined Herut 30 years later and was then duty bound to embrace the Revisionist legacy once more.

In Lehi, Shamir viewed the war as a conflict between the forces of evil – between Gog and Magog – and saw little distinction between the British oppressor and the German persecutor. Few in the Yishuv at that time believed that such persecution was the precursor of extermination. It was therefore but a short step for Shamir to understand the *raison d'être* behind Stern's approaches to the Nazis in the hope of raising an army to evict the British and thereby declare a Jewish state.[7] It was a policy forged in the depths of adversity and in ignorance of the unimaginable murder of millions, including Shamir's own family. Yet significantly, in his memoirs, Shamir does not – even in hindsight – criticize this approach. He offers the remarkable comment that at that time 'it was reasonable to feel that there was little for Jews to choose between the Germans and the British'.[8] This was not a view shared by the vast majority of the Yishuv's Jews, who clearly perceived a greater distinction, but it did indicate where Lehi's priorities lay and show the likely direction of Shamir's politics – the establishment of a Jewish state by whatever means it took to oust the British. Indeed, it is significant to note that Lehi embarked on the path of armed struggle as a direct result of the White Paper published in 1939. For the Irgun, the moment was the impending defeat of Nazi Germany. The threshold for the Haganah was the British Labour government's about-turn in 1945.

Jabotinsky's ambivalence over the question of the military revolt and his reinstatement of David Raziel persuaded Shamir to side with Stern in the split in the Irgun in 1940. Shamir did not join Stern straight away, but waited several months before leaving the Irgun. His hesitancy may have been motivated by a desire to see how the Irgun's policy of cooperating with the British developed. He probably deliberated on the wisdom of leaving the Irgun and believed that tactically it was better to work from within. He later commented that, 'if the split had been put off for another three years, it would have been avoided, for by then, Begin had arrived and taken over the Irgun command and agreed with Yair's conclusion.'9 Shamir almost certainly remained in contact with Stern while he was still a member of the Irgun. Possibly he attempted to persuade Stern to work with the Irgun. When he did leave, he immediately joined Stern's high command in a senior position at a time when contact with the German legation in Beirut was being appraised. Yet in 1944, Shamir opposed any reunification with Begin's Irgun and refused to accept Jabotinsky as the supreme mentor.

To become a member of the Stern Group, Shamir had to adhere to Stern's national *Weltanschauung* which was embedded in his 'Eighteen Principles of National Renewal'.10 Under the heading, 'the Principles of Rebirth', the borders of the Land were defined by a quotation from Genesis (15:18): 'To your seed, I have given this Land from the River of Egypt to the great River, the River Euphrates.' The third clause in the document stated that 'the Land of Israel was conquered by the Jews by the sword. It was here they became a nation and only here can they be reborn. Not only has Israel the right to ownership over the land but this ownership is absolute and has never been or can ever be rescinded.' In the light of the approaches to Germany and Italy, Stern proclaimed that 'treaties will be signed with any power interested in supporting the struggle of the Organisation and willing to give direct assistance.' The document's hopes for the future provided for the ingathering of exiles, the cultivation of the desert wasteland, and the revival of the Hebrew language. It also proposed the rebuilding of the Third Temple and the transfer of the Arab inhabitants of the Land through an exchange of populations.11

Following Stern's death, the organization fell apart. In September 1942, Shamir escaped from Mazra prison and together with Natan Yellin-Mor and Israel Eldad reorganized Lehi. A year spent analysing Stern's failure produced a different and more sophisticated approach. Lehi began to move beyond individual assassinations and bank robberies as its main vehicles of struggle. Guerilla warfare and attacks on military installations assumed a higher priority. More emphasis was placed on propaganda and public relations. As the revelations of the Final Solution began to be understood by Lehi, the group began to compare itself to the French resistance, the Maquis. In this scenario, the British played the role of the Gestapo, whilst the Jewish Agency leadership became the collaborators, Petain, Laval and the Vichy government.

Stern was mythologized into a figure of Promethean stature, yet his mystical inspirational approach was replaced by a hard-core pragmatism. As the mysterious 'Michael', Shamir was the chief of operations for Lehi and his work involved the planning and carrying out of numerous assassinations. Shamir took his *nom de guerre* from the Irish revolutionary, Michael Collins. In the view of an authoritative biographer, Collins was 'the founder of modern guerilla warfare, the first freedom fighter, or urban terrorist ... a role that sometimes took priority over sensitivity.'[12] Clearly, Shamir must have been acquainted with Collins's theories and activities. Collins had taken part in the Easter Uprising and the occupation of the General Post Office in Dublin. In the arbitrary selection of those to be placed in front of a British firing squad, Collins was overlooked and instead imprisoned. After his release, he worked assiduously to establish an intelligence network, bomb-making factories, highly trained hit squads and an underground press. Collins attempted to perfect a system to facilitate arms smuggling and to refine the mechanics of mass breakouts from prison. All these techniques became the stock-in-trade of Lehi under Shamir's direction in the 1940s. A colleague on the editorial board of *He'Hazit*, the group's publication, referred to Shamir as 'the man who pulled all the strings of the Lehi'.[13]

The use of individual terror in the context of military struggle was fervently embraced by Lehi. Such activity defined the group's identity and existence. The instrument of assassination was also used occasionally by Lehi – and, indeed, by the Irgun and the Haganah – against Jews who worked for the British or acted as informers. Between September 1942 and July 1946, when Shamir was finally arrested and exiled to Eritrea, there were 14 Lehi assassination attempts. Most were carried out against Jews who were working for the British. Others were against members of Lehi or the Irgun who were suspected of passing information to the British. There was even a plot to kill Stern's successor, Yitzhak Zelnik, who subsequently gave himself up to the British, possibly because he felt safer with them than with his erstwhile colleagues.[14]

Lehi under Shamir also attempted to strike at the British leadership of that time. There were seven assassination attempts on the life of the British High Commissioner, Sir Harold McMichael, and several more were planned – for example, against Ernest Bevin, the British Foreign Secretary, as well as members of British Intelligence. Shamir – using the code name 'Baratz', the Hebrew for 'breaking through' – sent two young members of Lehi, Hakim and Bet Tsouri, to Cairo to kill the British Minister Resident in the Middle East, Lord Moyne. The assassination was later justified by Shamir and others on the grounds of his alleged anti-Semitism and anti-Zionism. Moyne's famous comment on meeting Adolf Eichmann's messenger, Joel Brand, 'What would I do with a million Jews?', in the 'trucks for Jews' controversy, was, it turned out, a flight of fancy. In his auto-biography, Joel Brand in fact attributes the remark to a conversation with an Englishman over a drink at the British–Egyptian Club. Nevertheless, this didn't stop Shamir from repeating the remark over 50 years later in his memoirs.[15]

Moyne's reputation amongst the Jews was that he was generally hostile to the Zionist cause. In a debate in the House of Lords in June 1942, Moyne had made a speech which was, indeed, highly antagonistic. He stated that neither the Mandate nor the Balfour Declaration had intended Palestine 'to be converted into a Jewish State against the will of the Arab population'. He opposed 'the racial domination by the newcomers over the original inhabitants', and turned the 'Nazi' epithet back on the Zionists – 'If a comparison is to be made with the Nazis, it is surely those who wish to force an imported regime upon the Arab population who are guilty of aggression and domination.' What is more, Moyne's interest in anthropology seemingly led him to make racist observations, such as when he remarked that the Arabs were the real Semites and referred to the 'Armenoid features' of Sephardi Jews and the 'Slav blood' of the Ashkenazim.[16] Yet privately, Moyne had advocated the establishment of a partitioned Jewish state attached to a Greater Syrian Federation. Several historians have argued that, ironically, if Moyne had lived, the State of Israel may well have come into existence in 1945.[17]

The Labour Zionist leadership were aghast at the assassination, not simply because it marked a different set of mores, but because of the political implications, since Moyne was a minister of state and a close friend of Churchill. There was vehement and bitter condemnation by the Labour movement and no effort was made to seek an overturning of the death sentences on the captured assassins. Hakim and Bet Tsouri were abandoned to their fate.[18]

Stern had instilled in Lehi the remembrance that the Land of Canaan had been conquered by the Israelite sword. Ben-Gurion was outraged not simply at the act itself, but at Lehi's dismissal of the necessity for diplomacy, however distasteful this might be, and at their rejection of *havlagah* – political and military self-restraint. Ironically, over 30 years later as Knesset Speaker, Shamir eulogized Ben-Gurion on the fifth anniversary of his death as 'the stiff-necked fighter who put not his faith in foreign princes and drew on the well-springs of his people to do battle'.

The British Foreign Office described Shamir at the time as 'among the most fanatical of terrorist leaders'. Whereas the British regarded the killing of Lord Moyne as cold-blooded murder,[19] Lehi viewed such actions as a totally justified use of individual terror or *hisul* – the Hebrew for 'elimination'. They considered such assassinations to be moral acts which demanded great courage. Although Lehi was the smallest of the three Jewish military organizations, it nonetheless carried out 71 per cent of all political assassinations between 1940 and 1948.[20] Moreover, 48 per cent of Lehi's killings were of fellow Jews, most of whom worked for British Intelligence or passed information to hostile opponents.

The Jewish Agency and the Haganah considered Lehi to be poorly trained and lacking in military professionalism; nevertheless, the courage and conviction of the organization earned it respect:

> There was intense horror in the Jewish community against their acts, combined with respect for their motives and often for their motives as human beings. Our own efforts to uncover and control them, like those of the British, foundered on the most contemptible word in the Hebrew language, *mosser*, the word for informer.[21]

Significantly, while Lehi passionately endorsed the idea of individual terror, the Irgun adamantly rejected claims that it was a terrorist organization. Indeed, in due course, the assassination of Lord Moyne set the character of Lehi, showing it to have an identity distinct from that of the Irgun. At root, the difference lay in the fact that Begin reinterpreted Jabotinsky rather than rejecting him. Although by advocating a Jewish state outside the British Empire and embarking on the Revolt, Begin effectively distanced the Irgun from the official Revisionists, the New Zionist Organization, he nonetheless argued that the political process still had to take precedence over the armed struggle – and was indeed served by it. Begin, then, still regarded himself as a disciple of Jabotinsky even if a growing number of Revisionists did not accept this. Begin's insistence on recognizing the political inheritance of Jabotinsky duly proved to be a fundamental difference between Lehi and the Irgun, one which prevented full cooperation and subsequent unification. Shamir comments in his autobiography that Begin

> hadn't approved of, or understood, Lehi's modus operandi: he opposed all assassination. Going to war when there was no alternative was all right, but

the singling out of one person, even of an informer, for execution was morally wrong in his eyes. He wanted courtrooms, trials, validation; cautious legal procedures that were impossible in the underground. Even there he cared, much more than I ever did, about what people said or thought.[22]

For the members of Lehi, there were countless Biblical examples of 'noble' assassinations which were carried out for the good of the cause. A Judge of Israel, Ehud Ben-Gera, assassinated Eglon, King of Moab, who had subjected the Jews to his rule for 18 years. Indeed, Natan Yellin-Mor took his *nom de guerre*, 'Gera', from this example. In addition, there was Yael, who murdered Sisera the leader of the King of Hazor's army. There were also contemporary models such as Hirsch Lekert, the Bundist bootmaker who attempted to kill the authoritarian governor of Vilna in 1902; or Shalom Schwartzbard, the assassin of Semion Petlyura, who was held responsible for pogroms in the Ukraine during the Russian civil war. Yet it was the Sicarii, two thousand years before, who were the supreme example for Shamir and Lehi. They specialized in killing Jews who had cooperated with the Romans by utilizing their sicae or daggers and then melting away into the crowd. During the first Jewish Revolt, 66–70, the Sicarii or daggermen killed many notables who had advocated an accommodation with the Roman Empire. Yet the Sicarii were also noted for their courage. They were responsible for taking the upper city in Jerusalem and were the legendary defenders of Masada who killed themselves and their families rather than surrender to the Romans.

Avraham Stern used the name 'Yair' as his *nom de guerre* in the underground, after the leader of the Masada zealots, Elazar Ben-Yair. Uri Zvi Greenberg wrote poems glorifying the example of the Sicarii. Thus Lehi could justify the killing of both foreign rulers and Jews who pursued a more moderate course, on the basis of a selective reading of Jewish tradition and history. Yet those who vehemently opposed Lehi's strategy could quote Josephus, the historian of the first Jewish Revolt, who castigated the Sicarii for their violence and blamed them for the destruction of Jerusalem and the Second Temple. The course of ancient Jewish history therefore played an important role in the thinking of Lehi as well as in the discussions of the Irgun and the Haganah. All were determined to learn from the past and not to repeat the mistakes made by their ancestors. Yet each group perceived and interpreted that history differently.

In the context of perpetrating violent acts for the sacred good of the cause, Lehi could thereby justify killing one of their own if the need arose. Thus Yehuda Arie Levi was executed by Lehi in early

1948 when he wished to leave to join the Haganah. Yitzhak Shamir was himself directly involved in the killing of his fellow escapee from Mazra prison, Eliahu Giladi. After Stern's death, both men played a crucial role in reorganizing Lehi at the end of 1942. Yet clearly they were unable to work together. As one commentator has observed: 'Yezernitsky-Shamir, a greyish, serious and thorough person liked to double check and be very sure before acting; he consulted a lot, was thoughtful and non-charismatic. Almost the exact opposite of Giladi who was stormy, self-assured, charismatic and fast.'[23] Although the murder of Giladi is still shrouded in mystery, it appears that he tended towards a more erratic, anarchist position than Shamir, Yellin-Mor and Eldad. In one sense, Giladi was closer to Stern's philosophy and had been involved in the propagation of the 'Eighteen Principles of National Renewal'. Giladi had planned terror on a much wider scale and reputedly wished to assassinate many members of the Zionist establishment, including the heads of the Haganah and the Jewish Agency. Giladi was said to follow the ideas of the Russian nihilist Dmitry Pisarev, who espoused the doctrine of 'rational egotism'. Yet Shamir and others have claimed that Giladi was killed for his 'irrationality', and in this context they feared for their own lives. Giladi, for example, proposed that female Lehi operatives work as prostitutes for the British. Given the conspiratorial nature of Lehi, the struggle for its direction and soul resulted in Shamir's operational decision to kill Giladi after consulting other members in the organization.[24] In his autobiography, Shamir comments 'that the decision was made and carried out', without clarifying the central question of who actually pulled the trigger. Even today, Giladi's family do not know the whereabouts of his body.

Shamir's belief in the importance of political assassination was indicated when a founder member of Lehi, Avraham Vilenchik, was killed in February 1943, a few days after his release from prison. He was believed to have bought his release by passing information about Lehi to British Intelligence. Shortly after the killing of Giladi, Lehi settled a long-standing score by assassinating the former head of the Haifa branch of the Irgun intelligence network, Israel Pritsker, who had supported the Irgun's pro-British policy under Raziel and acted with zeal against Lehi members. Two of his agents, Michael Waksman and Joseph Davidesku, were also killed on separate occasions.

Similarly, Shamir showed no opposition in 1948 to the plans of a Lehi splinter group, the Fatherland Front, to assassinate Count Folke Bernadotte – even though the State of Israel had come into existence.

In a communication to the UN Secretary General, Trygve Lie, Moshe Shertok (Sharett) described Bernadotte's assailants as 'desperadoes and outlaws who are execrated by the entire people of Israel'.[25] This assassination, which was also condemned by Menachem Begin, led to the suppression of Lehi and its subsequent evolution into a political force, the Fighters' Party. Natan Yellin-Mor was placed on trial and sentenced to eight years' imprisonment. The young Shimon Peres gave evidence against Yellin-Mor, based on correspondence between the Haganah and Lehi.[26] Natan Yellin-Mor was elected the candidate of the Fighters' Party in the first election to the Knesset. The party gained one seat and Yellin-Mor thereby earned an early release from a long prison sentence.

Shamir's involvement with the Fighters' Party exposed him to the political contradictions within Lehi which the common struggle against the British had obscured and made seemingly less important. Lehi's fundamental approach of embracing Britain's opponents began with the contacting of the Polish military just before World War II. After Poland's fall, Stern approached Fascist Italy and Nazi Germany in turn, but to no avail. With the beginning of the Cold War, Soviet Russia became the logical 'ally'. This, however, created the seeds of schism in Lehi. Eldad, following the anti-communism of Jabotinsky and Stern, saw this as merely another tactic which would bring about British withdrawal from Palestine. Yellin-Mor, however, appreciated the ideological imperative and moved to a left-wing, genuinely socialist, position especially where the cause of anti-imperialism was concerned. Yellin-Mor came to see the struggle in an international context and advocated alliances with other anti-imperialist movements which were striving to overthrow the colonialist order. This, of course, meant alliances with the Palestinian Arabs and with progressive movements within the Arab world itself. In 1947, though, appeals to the Palestinians fell on deaf ears and Lehi was persuaded to participate in the general military war against the Arabs. However, the involvement of Lehi in the attack on Deir Yassin, which left over two hundred dead, led to a private confrontation between Yellin-Mor and Eldad.

Shamir's return from Africa in the early summer of 1948 led him to align himself with Yellin-Mor rather than Eldad. In embracing the centre-left and 'socialism' rather than the right, Shamir probably reckoned that the possibilities of building a strong yet national organization were greater with Yellin-Mor than with the highly volatile Eldad. Whilst he was not overtly keen on the pro-Soviet orientation of Lehi, he would quote approvingly of the well-organized Communist underground in Greece. His idea of an economic model for the new state was 'a body which will have extensions in every sphere of life and which with its thousands of eyes and ears will prevent any attempt at sabotage and defection ... such an example is the Communist Party in the USSR and in the Peoples' Democracies'.[27]

Unlike his radical mentors such as Abba Achimer and Uri Zvi Greenberg, Shamir did not join Herut in 1948. His involvement in Lehi had distanced him considerably from Revisionism in all its varieties. At the first – and last – conference of the Fighters' Party in March 1949, Shamir's pragmatism and his disdain for intellectuals led to an implicit criticism of both Yellin-Mor and Eldad:

> 'Intelligent' individuals play an important and necessary role in any political movement, but they have a tendency to show detachment and disregard for realistic factors when implementing their ideas. Without their ideas we are nothing, but without an understanding of reality, their ideas will forever remain strictly in the realm of theory.[28]

Clearly such criticism could also have been applied to Avraham Stern.

The Fighters' Party subsequently collapsed in the absence of a clear ideological message. Yet, although Shamir embraced the left-wing stance of Yellin-Mor and his supporters, he did not follow him into the left (from which position Yellin-Mor came to advocate reconciliation with the Palestinians and negotiations with the PLO). Shamir did not forget the territorial stand of the Fighter's Party, which, despite its progressive nature, supported a large Jewish state from the Nile to the Euphrates. In one sense, he was closer to Eldad's maximalist view on the Palestinians and the exodus of 1948. Many years later as Speaker of the Knesset, in an address to the Tel Aviv Rotary Club, he commented on the expulsion of the Arabs of Lod and Ramle:

> What is important is not whether they were driven out or left of their own accord, but what would have happened if they had stayed. By now, these 60,000 Arabs would have multiplied to hundreds of thousands and then what would have been our situation today?[29]

Shamir was said to be interested in foreign affairs but he found his way barred, like all other former members of Lehi. Significantly, Shamir does not mention this short phase of his life in his memoirs, but devotes more comment to failed business ventures and his general frustration with life outside Lehi. In the mid-1950s, Ben-Gurion lifted his ban on the entry of members of Lehi into positions of authority. Isser Harel, the head of the Mossad, immediately inducted Shamir and other Lehi operatives into Israel's intelligence network. Shamir was, for instance, believed to have been the mastermind behind a letter-bomb campaign in the early 1960s against German scientists who were working for Nasser's Egypt. This allegedly brought Shamir into conflict with the Mapai establishment and especially with the deputy Minister of Defence, Shimon Peres. They did not consider the German scientists' endeavours to be as dire a threat as did Harel and Shamir.

After a decade in the Mossad, Shamir developed a deep interest in the fledgling Jewish emigration movement in the USSR following the Six Day War. Indeed, he joined the National Council for Soviet Jewry. The first refuseniks were passionate nationalists whose idealism about Zionism matched their detestation of the moral bankruptcy of the Soviet system. Some had been former democrats who had moved from the general dissident movement to a position advocating emigration to Israel as they reclaimed their Jewish identity from Soviet assimilationism. Others such as Leah Slovina seemed to have imbibed Zionism with their mothers' milk. Slovina had inherited Jabotinsky's philosophy from her parents, as Riga had once been a stronghold of Revisionist influence.[30] Indeed, some of Jabotinsky's works were circulated in Riga in samizdat in the early 1960s and, through contacts in other cities, his writings reached a large number of Jewish activists in the USSR. In addition, there were also a disproportionate number of Betarniks who had survived the war by fleeing to the safety of Central Asia or who had been imprisoned in the Gulag, but who had been unable afterwards to emigrate to Israel. They and other older Zionists acted as teachers and guides to a new generation who were groping for an identity in the Soviet vacuum. Official Israeli policy had hitherto been concentrated on quietly promoting the national, cultural and religious rights of Soviet Jews rather than openly calling for their emigration. Although the emigration of Soviet Jews recommenced in the autumn of 1968, the situation had changed dramatically as a result of Israel's victory in the Six Day War with the emergence of a Jewish national movement in the USSR. Yet the cautious policy of the Eshkol government was still to distance itself publicly from openly embracing the emigration movement for fear of KGB reprisals. It preferred quiet diplomacy as a means of helping Soviet Jews. Such an approach antagonised Jewish activists in the Soviet Union – especially those who leaned towards Jabotinsky and classical Revisionism – and their growing band of supporters in the Diaspora.

The USSR severed its diplomatic ties with Israel after the Six Day War, and thus the prime reason for such timidity was removed. Israel had little to lose by publicly leading the campaign for Soviet Jewry, which Golda Meir eventually did in her formal speech to the Knesset in 1969. Yet it was the Revisionist bare-knuckled approach which appealed to many of the younger frustrated refuseniks in the USSR. Thus, when Slovina and several Riga activists finally reached Israel in early 1969, they immediately quarrelled with the less than radical, methodical approach of the government office responsible for dealing with Soviet Jewish emigration, which insisted on tight control over what was essentially becoming a mass popular movement. Begin was quick to pick up on any dissatisfaction with the ruling Labour Party and thus easily attracted many early 'heroes' of the Jewish movement in the USSR. This dissatisfaction was fuelled by the many Soviet Jews who became outraged and perplexed by Israeli bureaucracy and who felt quite powerless to help family and friends left behind.

Shamir was drawn wholeheartedly into this campaign through the idealism, conviction and energy of these early refuseniks in Israel. It appealed to his sense of patriotism as well as to his sense of conspiracy to maintain contact with activists in the USSR. This was also a pragmatic cause to serve, for, as in Lehi and the Mossad, it called for organizational skills and was free from the intellectual turbulence of a Yellin-Mor or an Eldad. Shamir's path throughout had been a pragmatic one, coupled with a fundamentalist ideology. Indeed, he had joined Stern to fight a war of national liberation. The journey from seemingly left-wing statements in 1949 – albeit with a nationalist veneer – to helping Soviet Jews twenty years later was one which led Shamir to appraise Herut as the only political vehicle in which he could, realistically, travel. Shamir's immediate future after his work with the Mossad lay in the managing of a rubber factory in Kfar Saba. Having followed Stern out of the Irgun and away from Jabotinskyian thought in 1940, Shamir made a calculated decision to return by applying for membership of Herut in 1970, whereupon he was appointed to head the party's immigration department. For Shamir, Herut remained the only party which had not abandoned the idea of an Israel 'from the Nile to the Euphrates'. Unlike Yellin-Mor and other members of Lehi, Shamir had not accepted the principle of partition. The conquest of Judea and Samaria in 1967 and the presence of Begin in government suggested to him that this was the way forward. Although Begin regarded him as a considerable catch inasmuch as it helped him unite all the elements of the nationalist camp under his leadership, Shamir was clearly never a true disciple of undiluted Revisionism. He belonged ideologically and emotionally on the far right; but his sense of pragmatism told him that power lay with the centre-right – with Begin and the Irgun old guard.

CHAPTER THIRTEEN

ABOVE AND BELOW GROUND

The Jewish Underground

Shamir's emotional and ideological loyalty to his Lehi past remained unwavering as he climbed the political ladder. Although the activities of the Stern Group became generally more acceptable to public opinion in Israel as time receded from the actual events and after the political demise of Ben-Gurion, Shamir nevertheless remained consistent in his attitude to 'individual terror'. Shortly after the massacre of Israeli schoolchildren at Ma'alot in 1974 by members of Naif Hawatmeh's Democratic Front for the Liberation of Palestine, Shamir condemned its leader's statement that he was opposed to 'individual terror'. He observed – clearly with the Giladi case in mind – that Hawatmeh required countless victims in order to make its point. Shamir followed Lehi's philosophy that selective terror was 'a more humane method of killing'. After he became Knesset Speaker in 1977, Shamir was questioned about the killing of Sergeant T.G. Martin on a tennis court some 30 years earlier. In his reply, he reaffirmed his position:

> There are those who say that to kill is terrorism, but to attack an army camp is guerrilla warfare and to bomb civilians is the professional way. But I think it is the same from the moral point of view. Is it better to drop an atomic bomb on a city than to kill a handful of persons?[1]

Unlike Natan Yellin-Mor, who became an activist in the Israeli peace camp, Shamir remained faithful to the idea of an unpartitioned Land of Israel. In April 1974, a few months after his election to the Knesset, he appealed to Golda Meir to annex the Golan Heights – some seven years before Begin actually carried it through. Although the Sternist conception of a Land from the Nile to the Euphrates undoubtedly clashed with his sense of political pragmatism, Shamir opposed Begin on the Camp David Accords and did not accept the return of Sinai to the Egyptians. In early 1976, before Sadat's visit to Israel, he condemned in the Knesset Egyptian violation of the Interim Agreement:

> President Sadat has not changed his tune since he worked for the Nazis and spearheaded the surprise attack on Yom Kippur. He is adopting new tactics, although he appears in the guise of a lover of peace, he is consistent in his adherence to the dominant Arab demands – that Israel shall not benefit by one inch of land and that the right of the Palestinian Arabs must be recognized.[2]

Despite his reference to stripping off 'Sadat's Nazi face' – language strongly reminiscent of Begin's rhetoric – Shamir was nevertheless quite happy a year later as Speaker to introduce Sadat to the Knesset when the Egyptian president visited Israel, and to talk of the necessity of beating swords into ploughshares.

Shamir was given the office of Knesset Speaker in 1977 as a poor substitute for not receiving a post in the Cabinet. Yet he was able to use this office to build a base of support. If the coalition partners had succeeded in keeping him out of the first Cabinet, they nonetheless indirectly allowed him to attain the post of Foreign Minister when Dayan resigned. Both the Democratic Movement's Yigal Yadin and the National Religious Party's Yosef Burg turned down the opportunity. In order to head off Liberal claims to the post, Begin offered it to Shamir – four months after Dayan had stepped down. Many Labour figures thought it the 'height of absurdity' to offer such an important position to someone who had opposed Camp David. From the other side of the fence, Techiya's Moshe Shamir spoke for many of Yitzhak Shamir's comrades from the Lehi when he asked Shamir to decline Begin's offer. 'What', he asked, 'does a serious, responsible man, like him, have in common with the adventurers and chatterboxes who today constitute the Israel government?'[3] Shamir paid no attention to the critics and cynics, and conducted Begin's foreign policy in a low-key and undistinguished fashion for three years.

Within months of succeeding Begin as Prime Minister in 1983, Shamir was faced, ironically, with a situation where his background as an advocate of individual terror could no longer remain submerged. The practice of his stewardship of Lehi seemed to rise up and challenge the pragmatism of his policies as Prime Minister. At the end of April 1984 and shortly before the national elections, several dozen West Bank settlers were arrested as members of the Machteret

Yehudit – the Jewish Underground. The group, which was centred on the settlement of Kiryat Arba, adjoining Hebron, was held responsible for a series of retaliatory attacks on Palestinians. Following the killing in 1980 of six yeshiva students who were returning to Beit Hadassah in Hebron, the group waited for the traditional 30 days of mourning and reflection to pass and then mounted an attack on the five leaders of the Palestinian National Guidance Committee. By wiring the cars of their intended victims with explosives, they succeeded in maiming the mayors of Nablus and Ramallah.

The second initiative of the Underground was an assault on the Hebron Islamic College in retaliation for the murder of a yeshiva student. Three Arab students were killed and another 33 wounded. The final attack, in 1984, was in response to the Bus 300 incident where Palestinian terrorists hijacked a bus and drove it to the outskirts of Tel Aviv, where they murdered a large number of the passengers and bystanders.[4] The Jewish Underground wired the fuel tanks of five buses belonging to the Kalandiya-Atarot Bus Company with explosives and primed them to go off late on Friday afternoon – to coincide with both the Muslim festival of Isra wal me'eraj and the approach of the Jewish Sabbath, when few Jews would have been walking the streets. The timers used were the kind utilized by observant *shomer Shabbat* Jews in order to keep the sanctity of the Sabbath by avoiding the use of electricity. However, through intensive intelligence monitoring of the group, the Jewish Underground was literally caught in the act at five villages in and around Jerusalem, thus saving not only the lives of many Arab passengers, but also those of 50 German tourists who had been scheduled to travel to Jericho on that Friday.

The psychological preparation for such an act did not take place overnight. In 1978, Raful Eitan, then the IDF chief, had permitted the inhabitants of settlements to share in the defence of their own areas instead of serving normal military service in other units. This, however, had encouraged a vigilante mentality where the dividing line between respect for the law and law-breaking became very blurred. Notwithstanding the encouragement to engage in self-defence, why had hitherto peaceful people taken the law into their own hands? Successive governments – even if sympathetic to the settlers – were by 1980 perceived by the inhabitants of the Territories to be unable to stem Palestinian violence. Some settlers concluded that the law had therefore to be implemented on the ground by those most capable of doing so. Official government attempts at dialogue with the Palestinians were frowned upon since they weakened the political position of the settlers. What is more, such overtures were seen actually to foment violence. Ezer Weizmann's establishment of the National Guidance Committee from among the municipal West Bank leaders thus provided not only a Palestinian body with which government could converse, but also a nationalist focus at which the settlers could direct blame. Settlers in places such as Kiryat Arba, situated in the militant heartland of Palestinian nationalism, were radicalized over time and became more isolated from the norms of Israeli society as the violence grew. Rabbi Moshe Levinger, a founder of Kiryat Arba and one of the first West Bank settlers, opposed the idea of a surgical strike at the Palestinian mayors, advocating instead a wider, more violent act. Levinger was overruled. Yet three years later, the premeditated random attack on students at the Islamic College proved to be acceptable to the group and to their rabbis. Thus, within four years, the Jewish Underground moved from individual terror, the maiming of the mayors (of which Lehi would have approved), to indiscriminate mass violence – the planned destruction of the buses and their passengers. The path from the maiming of Palestinian instigators to the murder of Palestinian innocents was taken relatively easily by members of the group. Even though there was dissent in the Underground itself as the killings became indiscriminate, all the acts were discussed within the context of *halakhah* – religious Jewish law – and eventually received rabbinical authorization.

Those arraigned for the planned attack were all known figures within Gush Emunim – people of hitherto good character who could not be marginalized as American misfits or peripheral extremists. Benzion Heineman and Yitzhak Gamiram had come with Levinger to Hebron in 1968. Yehuda Etzion was the son of one of the founders of Gush Emunim and a former member of its secretariat. Moshe Zar was a leading land dealer on the West Bank. Yeshua Ben Shoshan, a respected IDF captain, came from an old Jerusalem family stretching back eight generations. Hagai Segal was one of the editors of the Gush magazine *Nekuda*. One of the principal defendants, Menachem Livni, was head of the Committee for the Renewal of Jewish Settlement in Hebron. Some of the others had familial connections with earlier underground organizations. Although Gilad Peli was a graduate of Zvi Yehuda Kook's yeshiva, Merkaz Ha'Rav, he was also the son of a Lehi veteran. Finally, the arrests of the sons-in-law of Rabbis Levinger and Waldman revealed the Underground as emanating from the heart of Gush Emunim.

The existence of the Underground therefore sent shock waves

through Israeli society. There had been no Jewish terrorism since the early 1950s, when Lehi veterans, organized as Machteret Malchut Yisrael – the Kingdom of Israel Underground – were caught by police carrying explosives. Gush Emunim was strongly admired by Israelis for its dedication to settling the Land. They were seen as surrogate pioneers by many who preferred to live settled, secure lives in Israel proper. With the decline of secular Zionism and the loss of socialist ethics, Gush Emunim filled the vacuum, rekindling both ideals and nostalgia – a return to Zionist values. The genuine fervour of the religious settlers served another purpose, however. It provided an acceptable screen for the rise of the far right in Israeli political life.

The Resurrection of the Far Right

The conquest of the Territories in 1967 had been the kiss of life to a hitherto moribund far right. Between 1948 and 1967, few had been willing to follow figures such as the Lehi veteran Israel Eldad into the wilderness of confrontational ultra-nationalism. The acquisition of Judea and Samaria had turned the ideological clock back to 1937 and spawned new groups such as the Land of Israel Movement, which was dedicated to reclaiming all the land which it maintained had been promised to them by the British. It brought together maximalists from the left and the right, and provided a forum where present similarities proved more important than past differences, where the followers of Avraham Stern and Vladimir Jabotinsky could sit with the disciples of Yitzhak Tabenkin – and indeed David Ben-Gurion. The acquisition emphasized the ideological weakness of the new Labour Alignment, the Ma'arach, which included the dovish Mapam and the maximalist Achdut Ha'avoda. Such an ideological schism proved to be a paralysing factor in Labour governments during the 1970s, which Gush Emunim and the far right exploited to the full. Leading Labour figures would seemingly espouse opposing policies. Thus Yigal Allon could visit Rabbi Levinger's group at the Park Hotel in April 1968, while a few years later Liova Eliav would engage in dialogue with leading PLO figures.

The central purpose of ousting the Labour elite was the prime unifying force that bound together the Likud, the far right, the religious maximalists and the Labour splinters. It was held together through the personality and sense of purpose of Menachem Begin. Once faced with reality and responsibility in government, the alliance began to fall apart with the Camp David Accords and Begin's apparent willingness to return territory such as Sinai. The formation of Techiya – mainly from the Likud's right wing in 1979 – and, subsequently, of Tsomet by Raful Eitan in 1983 from Labour movement adherents was symptomatic of the growing influence of the far right and the move away from the official Revisionist umbrella. Even so, the Lebanon war with its sharp division into opposing camps once more rallied the far right to Begin's standard, and Techiya entered the government coalition in July 1982. In the agreement with Techiya, Begin refused to renounce the Camp David Accords, but suggested that his government was doing little to enforce them at that time.[5] Techiya's Yuval Ne'eman was appointed deputy chairman of the all-important settlements committee on the understanding that Simcha Ehrlich would soon resign. Ne'eman thus quickly succeeded to the position and directed settlement policy for two years. Although the far right exerted a fair degree of influence on Likud government policy, so long as Begin was in command there was still a semblance of unity.

The ties of the past were considerably loosened when Begin was replaced by the lacklustre Shamir. Lehi veterans such as Geula Cohen who found themselves in the ultra-nationalist Techiya asked why Shamir had not followed them. The religious parties did not feel close to Begin's successor either, and bemoaned the fact that Shamir had little overt interest in Judaism. A National Religious Party election advertisement in 1984 exclaimed: 'Begin's *B'ezrat ha'shem* [with the help of God] has disappeared from the Likud lexicon'. Yet Begin's traditionalism seemed to obscure the fact that many Likudniks were secularists. Indeed, a Smith survey for the American Jewish Committee a few years later showed that 43 per cent of Likud voters favoured equal status for Conservative and Reform rabbis.[6]

By 1984, there existed in Israel a general sense of political fatigue that no solution of the conflict with the Palestinians was in sight. While there was profound disillusionment with Labour, it was generally conceded that the 68-year-old Shamir had no answer either. The tendency to seek political solace outside Labour and Likud was indicated in the proliferation of parties which achieved up to four seats each in the 1984 election. In 1981, there had been only 7 such parties. Three years later, the number had risen to 13. In addition, Shamir was perceived as only a stopgap leader in a divided Herut. Yoram Aridor, the former Likud Finance Minister, characterized Shamir as lacking 'Jabotinskyian noblesse', while David Levy criticized him for his 'autocratic style'. In April 1984, Shamir was challenged by Sharon for the leadership of Herut. Despite a prediction that he would receive only 10 to 15 per cent support, Sharon actually secured 42.7 per cent of the vote of the Herut Central Committee. As it happened, on the very evening of the vote, the Bus 300 incident took place, with its attendant loss of Jewish life at the hands of Palestinian terrorists. It is quite likely that Sharon, posing as the hard-line candidate, would have secured an even greater percentage of the vote if the hijacking had taken place only a few hours earlier.

The discovery and arrest of the Jewish Underground and the election of Rabbi Kahane to the Knesset finally dissolved the gloss with which Begin had coated his wide-ranging anti-Labour coalition, and revealed the extent of the influence of ultra-nationalism and religious fundamentalism in Israel. Some understood the Jewish Underground to be the result of a synthesis of the thought of Rabbi Zvi Yehuda Kook, the mentor of Gush Emunim, and the legacy of Avraham Stern.

Although many saw the settlers as a continuation of the Zionist past, there was in fact a fundamental difference between the religious Zionism of the pre-1967 National Religious Party and the post-1967 Gush Emunim. The founders of the Religious Zionist Movement, Mizrachi, at the end of the nineteenth century, did not associate their work with either messianism or redemption. Moreover, they originally suggested that 'not all forms of "active messianism" should lead necessarily to the endorsement of an extremist or radical political style'.[7] The hitherto normatively passive and relatively apolitical aspect of messianism – that the Messiah would arrive in his own good time – was abandoned for a dynamic, youthful 'hands-on' approach. The Messiah's actual arrival became more important than the manner of his coming. The Lubavitcher Rebbe, a Hasidic leader who held court in Brooklyn, had invigorated an international movement to return Jews to their Jewish roots. The Lubavitch movement's educational activities were renowned throughout the Jewish world, but this overshadowed the Rebbe's less publicized stance in support of retaining the Territories. Indeed, he fiercely opposed Israel's withdrawal in 1985 from Lebanon – the 'North Bank', which had been part of Biblical Israel. The Rebbe severely castigated the National Unity government for its decision to leave Lebanon and pressured Shamir specifically. Lubavitch had popularized the messianic idea through its culture. Its popular slogan 'We want *Meshiach* [Messiah] now' had implicit political connotations in the context of post-1967 Israel. It characterized a sense of immediacy – the magnetic pull of many religious people to settle in the Territories and build Eretz Israel. The spiritual experience that was defined in the establishment of the state and in the victory of the Six Day War in 1967 convinced the heirs of Mizrachi that the normative viewpoint, of passively waiting for the Messiah, had had its day. A new situation had arisen and it had to be acknowledged.

After the hiding of God's face and the agony of exile for nearly two thousand years, the Zionist enterprise was seen by some as a divine signal of a redemptive process already in motion. To perceive reality was a measure of holiness. The unknowing instruments of the plan were the atheistic socialist Zionist pioneers who drained swamps and made the desert bloom. In fact, many adherents of Gush Emunim believed that 'Herzlian Zionism is not real Zionism'. For Rabbi Levinger, the state was merely a vehicle to facilitate the Age of Redemption and the coming of the two Messiahs, Meshiach Ben-Yosef (Messiah, son of Joseph) who would lead the way for Meshiach Ben-David (Messiah, son of David). 'The essence of Zionism', according to Levinger, was 'the vision of the Jewish People during the period of the First and Second Temples. This spiritual message must be the essence of the Third Temple. The task of the Jewish state in our day is to enable the people to broadcast the true vision of justice and righteousness and the rest of the principles expressed by the Prophets and Scholars of Israel'.[8] According to this school of thought, true Zionism – redemptive Zionism – only began when the followers of Rabbi Eliyahu of Vilna emigrated to the Promised Land at the beginning of the nineteenth century. By extrapolating backwards in time, it became possible to reclaim figures such as Rabbis Kalisher and Alkalai and Rabbi Avraham Yitzhak Kook. Thus a pre-Herzlian Zionist history, grounded in the idea that the era of redemption had already begun, could be constructed.[9]

Such was the respect and admiration of many religious people for the new pioneers of Judea and Samaria that it was difficult to propose a different course of action. For many, the religious Zionist had come of age, and was no longer a figure merely tolerated by the secular socialists, no longer a focus of condemnation by the anti-Zionist ultra-orthodox. The warnings of religious intellectuals were disregarded and the protests of the religious peace movement were ignored. The ascendant nationalism of the religious Zionists integrated secular motifs, such as the example of Shimon Bar-Kochba who led the second revolt against the Romans. Others pointed out that the Bar-Kochba revolt had ended in total disaster with the expulsion of virtually the entire Jewish population. Opponents of contemporary messianism suggested that, following calamitous and dramatic events in Jewish history, a false Messiah had always arisen to provide solace and psychological escape. They pointed out, for example, that, according to Talmudic legend, Bar-Kochba had actually been killed at the behest of the sages, who did not believe that the leader of the revolt against the Romans was the true Messiah. They further invoked the figure of the false Messiah, Sabbatai Sevi, who, after the massacre of Jews in Poland in 1648–9, had deluded thousands with his hopes and dreams. Nathan of Gaza, a leader of the Sabbatean movement, wrote that the soul of Bar-Kochba had been reincarnated in Sabbatai Sevi.[10]

Yet the group which formed the Jewish Underground did not simply emerge out of the messianism of Gush Emunim and the teachings of Zvi Yehuda Kook. There was also a direct connection with Lehi, Avraham Stern, and the nationalist teachings of the 1930s. In addition to retaliatory attacks on Palestinians, one section of the Underground conspired to blow up the Dome of the Rock in Jerusalem, one of Islam's holiest sites, which was constructed on or near the site of the Second Temple. Moshe Dayan had left the Temple Mount in Arab hands after the Six Day War, and Jews were not permitted to pray there despite the fact that the Second Temple had been situated near the spot. The Dome of the Rock therefore became a focus of resentment for many religious Jews, and even more so after the Camp David Accords. As early as 1978, two members of the Underground, Yehuda Etzion and Yeshua Ben-Shoshan, discussed what could be done to remedy a situation wherein the process of redemption was seen to have been impeded if not retarded by the Camp David Accords. Etzion believed that Jewish history since the time of the destruction of the Temple by the Romans had been conditioned by paralysis and compromise. The removal of the 'abomination' from the Temple Mount would ensure the free yet directed flow of history once more. The elimination of the Dome of the Rock before the withdrawal from Sinai, they argued, would create such a cataclysmic upheaval that it would trigger a spiritual renewal in the House of Israel. The momentum driving the era of redemption would thus be restored.

Etzion and his fellow conspirators surveyed the Temple Mount for two years and acquired precision bombs and other material from the Golan Heights. Despite such meticulous advance planning, no rabbi – including Levinger – would give unqualified approval to the plan.

A visit to Zvi Yehuda Kook by Ben-Shoshan was similarly inconclusive. Although Etzion and Ben-Shoshan were prepared to go ahead,
the plan foundered on the rock of rabbinical equivocation and was
shelved.[11]

During the Camp David trauma, Yehuda Etzion discovered the
writings of Uri Zvi Greenberg and the works of a little-known
religious writer, Shabtai Ben-Dov, who in his youth had been a
member of Lehi. The ailing Ben-Dov persuaded Etzion to participate
actively in the redemptive process. Like Avraham Stern, he believed
that the Third Temple should be speedily constructed. This would lead
to the establishment of a world government, based on Torah values
and governed by a Sanhedrin (the major political, judicial and religious
assembly of the Jews during the Roman period). The Jewish Underground provided, in one sense, the linkage between the messianic
redemptionist philosophy of Zvi Yehuda Kook and the mystical nationalist tradition of Greenberg and Stern. The political lineage of
Greenberg, Stern, Ben-Dov and finally Etzion was an evolution galva-
nized by a spiritual evaluation of the return of Judea and Samaria in
1967. Ben-Dov effectively redirected Greenberg's mystical nationalism
into a fundamentalist channel. The descendant of a long line of *tsadikim*
(wise scholars), Greenberg wrote poetry, the mystical religiosity of
which evoked the glory of the past and the redemption of the future.
He was a maximalist whose words were intended to recapture the past
in order to vanquish the enemies of the present.

> Here are my brothers the money changers, the pedlars
> whose life goes on forever
> The Temple Guards are gone, but these remain
> And here is the rubble of the ruined Hebrew Temple
> and on the rubble, made of solid marble
> a temple of crescents for Arabia's prayers
> Here are my cousins, here the braying of donkeys
> and here the excrement of sheep and men
> This is the City of David[12]

Greenberg's poetry embraced the themes of redemption and
messianism. It impressed and stimulated the radical wing of the
Revisionist movement. He passionately attacked the leaders of the
Labour movement in his poetry – especially after the Hebron massacre
in 1929 and the Arab uprising of 1936. Many Labour leaders blamed
Greenberg and the members of the Brit Ha'Biryonim (League of
Hooligans) for inciting the assassins of Arlosoroff to commit their act
of murder. Yet Greenberg's poetry touched and inspired Stern, Begin,

Eldad and Shamir – they began to translate his words into political realities. Greenberg certainly influenced Stern's messianic tendencies. Indeed, Stern wrote a series of articles on messianic movements in Israel in the underground journal *B'Machteret*. Stern also understood the significance of Meshiach Ben-Yosef and Meshiach Ben-David in the context of the struggle against the British. Indeed, one authoritative writer has commented that 'Stern had reserved for himself the position of messiah son of Joseph (Meshiach Ben Yosef) ... such that his personal failure would not mean the failure of his movement.'[13] In one sense, Lehi was a true reflection of Greenberg's lyrical nationalism.[14]

A Cause Célèbre

The trial of the Underground provided the far right with a *cause célèbre* which served to illustrate graphically the lesson that what was unacceptable yesterday may be readily permissible today. Thus, the shock that greeted the arrests soon gave way in the Shamir era to an 'understanding' of such acts by many sectors of Israeli opinion. The defendants seemed like any other well-meaning law-abiding citizens. The 15-month trial, punctuated, as it was, with the cries of running children, appeared more like a family picnic. It was sufficient that the defendants gave their word to their wardens that they would not escape. As Yehuda Etzion commented to reporters during the trial: 'Do I look like a terrorist?' None of them did. But as several commentators pointed out, they were not being judged on their appearance and *mensch*-like bonhomie.

The Lehi legacy of extra-legalism characterized the Underground and its supporters on the far right. It also posed a dilemma for the pragmatic Shamir – still a Lehi loyalist, but now the purveyor of the anti-terrorist tradition of the Irgun and, as Prime Minister, the inheritor of the moral and legal norms of the Haganah and Ben-Gurion's Israel. Such contradictions raised questions from both the Likud's left-wing critics and supporters of the Underground. The writer Amos Elon saw the country's rulers as strongly characterized by their underground sojourn in the Irgun and Lehi, and given to recalling this inheritance in countless ceremonies, postage stamps and school textbooks. 'Their past is in their bones', he observed, 'What does it do to their judgement, their sensibilities?'[15]

When an enterprising journalist managed to interview imprisoned members of the Underground just a few weeks after their arrest, they placed the blame for their acts on the government for not taking action to secure the safety of the inhabitants of the Territories. This, they argued had forced their hand: 'We acted as they once did in the Haganah, the Irgun and Lehi, like Ben-Gurion, Begin and Shamir.'[16] Depicting themselves as 'prisoners of Zion', the defendants did not accept that they were terrorists and refuted the charge that they were an underground acting against the state. They claimed instead to be working 'on behalf of the people', despite 'the helplessness of the government and its weakness due to pressure at home and abroad'.

The Likud and the far right adopted different techniques to avoid condemning the Underground. Gush Emunim and the settler movement in general initially refused to condemn the defendants, but differences eventually came to the surface when several more moderate rabbis from the Gush Etzion bloc expressed their dissent. In settlements such as Ofra and Kiryat Arba, there developed an 'understanding' for the Underground. Rabbi Moshe Levinger was a leading protagonist of this viewpoint:

> When the attack on the West Bank mayors was carried out, I expected the government to issue a statement, explaining that the assailants' motives were understandable. When the government was silent, I convened a press conference. I said that in my view, the Jewish people considered those mayors to have generated an atmosphere conducive to the murder of Jews and that we could therefore understand those who committed the acts.[17]

This was a theme taken up by the far right in general, both within the Likud and outside it. Although terrorism could not actually be approved, the attack on the mayors constituting the Palestinian National Guidance Committee was held to be within the realm of legitimate action. A distinction was made between controlled individual terror, as in the case of the attack on the mayors, and indiscriminate terror, such as the proposed destruction of the Arab buses. This, of course, was a distinction that Shamir had advocated in Lehi 40 years earlier.

Yuval Ne'eman, the Science and Development Minister and head of the far-right Techiya, argued that the maiming of the mayors curbed the actions of the major instigators of Palestinian terrorism without killing anyone else. He consequently condemned President Herzog for calling the defendants 'traitors' in his Independence Day speech. Indeed, he went further: with regard to the possibility of individual terror going wrong, he insisted that, 'by no means may one classify counter-terrorist activity, even if it constitutes the killing of innocent people, as "treason"'.[18]

Several supporters of the Underground differentiated between Jewish and Arab terrorism, thereby creating a distinction between 'good' terrorism and bad terrorism. Israel Eldad, the Lehi ideologist, wrote that the group could not be accused of being a 'hostile underground' since they were not like the PLO, an enemy of the state: 'The Jewish group that is suspected of attempting to sabotage the Arab buses committed both a crime and an act of foolishness, but it cannot be called 'hostile' ... they were more offences against commonsense, political logic and sheer responsibility.'[19] In the context of Arab terrorism, Ne'eman pointed out that Lehi's killing of Lord Moyne could also be described as a criminal act. 'There are acts which are acceptable ... after all neither Begin nor Shamir killed women and children. Whoever denounces all acts of terror determines that the Irgun and Lehi acted wrongly.'[20]

Religious interpretations and selective justifications of the attacks were also invoked. One American religious academic, the coordinator of the Committee for the Sanctity of Human Life, Rabbi Avraham Weiss, argued that since law and order were not deeply rooted in Judea and Samaria compared to the position in Israel itself, the attack on the mayors had to be judged in the context of the security problem for the Jewish settlers. He asked whether the application of the principle of *rodef* (assailant) was justified in the case of the actions against the mayors. If it was so justified, then the Underground constituted a legitimate self-defence group; it therefore followed that while their actions were illegal inasmuch as they were not sanctioned by the state, nevertheless 'they may be morally justifiable'. Their patriotism was utilized to invoke a rationale for their actions: 'Their intention was to strengthen rather than weaken the State. They are idealists and great lovers of Zion whose lives are inextricably bound up with the people, land, government and Torah of Israel.'[21]

The defendants were supported by Israel's two Chief Rabbis, who requested that they be released to celebrate the Jewish New Year and other holidays with their families. This plea was turned down. The Sephardi Chief Rabbi, Eliahu Mordechai, had actually been a member of Brit Ha'Canaim, a small religious underground group that had operated against the state in the 1950s and whose members had previously been associated with Lehi. He had also sponsored a conference the year before with the Ateret Cohanim yeshiva on the building of the Third Temple. He believed that the Third Temple would descend from heaven and devour the Dome of the Rock in a wall of flames: 'The Lord said: I set Zion afire and I shall build her by fire.'[22]

In a visit to the settlement at Shilo in December 1983, Eliahu claimed that the person held responsible for the recent killing of an Arab girl was not a murderer; he supported this claim by invoking the traditional response that 'if someone comes to kill you, rise up so as to kill him' (Sanhedrin 72).

Rabbi Dov Lior, the head of the Kiryat Arba yeshiva, for his part, saw divine retribution in the apprehending of three members of the Israeli mission in Beirut by the Syrians. This, he argued, was an expression of God's anger towards the government for permitting the arrest of the Underground. Another leading radical settler, Rabbi Yisrael Ariel, argued that the arrest of the detainees was inconsistent with *halakhah*, religious Jewish law, and quoted a dayan (religious judge) to the effect that 'if the detainees were to come before a court over which I presided, they would be acquitted and receive a commendation'.[23] On another occasion, Ariel commented that the commandment 'Thou shalt not kill' was never meant for universal application.[24]

At the conclusion of the trial, a number of prominent members of the far right, such as Rehavam Ze'evi, who advocated transferring the Palestinians out of the Territories, and the Likud MK Yigal Cohen-Orgad, appeared as character witnesses for the defendants. The trial judges sentenced three of the accused to life imprisonment, and the other twelve to sentences of between four months and seven years. The prosecution regarded such sentences as remarkably lenient – indeed, supporters of the group in the courtroom started shouting 'We've won, we've won' when the sentences were announced. Most of the defendants expressed regret; and Ya'akov Bazak, the most lenient of the three judges, took into account 'humanitarian and extraordinary personal reasons'. Bazak's three sons, observers noted, lived in Gush Emunim settlements, while a fourth studied Third Temple rites at the Ateret Cohanim yeshiva.

Some 20 members of the Knesset campaigned on the defendants' behalf – while condemning their acts – and these included representatives of the right-wing and religious parties, Techiya, Ometz, the National Religious Party, Shas, Agudat Yisrael and Morasha, as well as members of the Likud itself. Yosef Shapira, the Morasha Minister without portfolio was subsequently dubbed the 'Minister for the Underground'. In November 1984, Shimon Peres – as Prime Minister – was presented with a letter signed by 25 members of the Knesset which complained about the conditions in which the prisoners were held. The signatories claimed the support of another 25 Knesset members who did not wish to be identified.

The vociferous campaign by the collective far right and the inertia projected by the government unnerved many Israelis, who felt that the moral basis for their world had been turned upside down. The playwright Yehoshua Sobol commented that Israeli society was effectively driven by two artificial Freudian concepts – the pleasure principle and the reality principle:

> When the pleasure principle overrides the reality principle, one quickly arrives at the language of the kindergarten.... The Likud rose to power after the Yom Kippur War, in a frustrated, frightened, jittery society that lacked the chief gratification to which it had become accustomed in the course of a generation – that of victory. It was a society in which the rational person in touch with reality demanded a pitiless stock-taking, whereas the instinctual person craved instant gratification – and to hell with reality. Instinctual man has won the day.[25]

The Likud government had been warned by Avraham Achituv, the head of the General Security Services (GSS) that the Gush Emunim settlements were becoming 'a psychological hothouse' for terror. He was particularly worried by the zealotry of growing numbers of American *ba'alei teshuva* – those who had newly returned to the faith. Such warnings were ignored and indeed the Minister of Justice, Moshe Nissim, was quoted as saying in 1983 that there was no possibility of a terrorist underground being established.

The 1984 Election

The rise of the far right and the very openness of its politics presented the pragmatic Shamir with a real problem in that he had to adopt a line both centrist and able to accommodate the radicals. A poll by the magazine *Monitin* on the eve of the election showed that 32 per cent of the electorate favoured a regime of strong leadership that was not dependent on political parties – an attitude which clearly favoured the far right. Shamir's difficulty was compounded by the fact that the affair involving the Underground broke in the weeks leading up to the 1984 election. The great anti-Labour coalition which Begin had constructed was already beginning to unravel in 1981. By 1984, the magic of the Likud promises of 1977 had dissipated to a significant degree. In addition, there were now 100,000 new voters. Likud was in considerable danger of losing votes to Techiya, Morasha and Kahane's Kach on the far right. This was perceived by Likud strategists to be a greater threat than a swing to Labour.

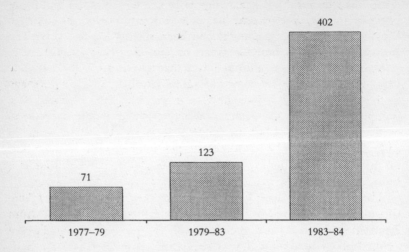

Figure 13.1   Inflation under the Likud, 1977–1984 (%)

Yet despite the legacy of 600 dead in the Lebanon war and its huge cost – a $20 billion external debt since 1977, a 400 per cent annual rate of inflation, and the erosion of workers' incomes – there was nevertheless, according to the opinion polls, a gradual recovery by the Likud during the first half of 1984. The deterioration of the economic situation under Aridor's free-for-all economic policies had as yet scarcely affected the Israeli public.

Labour was still perceived as stale and corrupt. The character assassination of Shimon Peres by the right had been extremely successful. Polls showed that both Rabin and Navon would have secured more votes for Labour. After the death of Ben-Gurion, Peres seemed to have moved out of his mentor's shadow to develop his own political personality. He became a politician in his own right, with his own ideas. Yet he was perceived as a wheeler-dealer – a man who had won the Labour leadership as a hawk only to turn 180 degrees to espouse the cause of the peace movement. For the right, Peres' endorsement of and participation in the Peace Now demonstration after the killings in the Sabra and Shatilla camps was a watershed. The Likud also tried to paint Peres in the colours of Abba Eban – a European intellectual and not too much of an Israeli. Peres also made a tactical error when he allowed the election to take place in July rather than during May – his original proposal. It was estimated that between 100,000 and 150,000 Israelis were abroad during the summer. Most of them were higher-income earners and Labour voters. In electoral terms, this meant between six and nine Knesset seats.

Shamir's problem, as indicated, was that he had to adopt a middle way to shore up the Likud vote while controlling the haemorrhage to the small factions of both the secular and religious far right. There was pressure within the Likud not only from his political rivals, in particular David Levy, but inevitably from the party's right wing. In addition, there were moves to increase the number of Herut members on the Likud list at the expense of the Liberals. The hawkish fragment from La'am under Ehud Olmert returned to merge with Herut.

The case of the Jewish Underground could not be ignored during the election period. If the far right were to be deflected from capitalizing on the issue, then Shamir had to create an image of public solidarity with fellow Jews, while frowning – albeit half-heartedly – on law-breakers. Shamir's office immediately reacted to the arrests of the Underground by commenting that if the explosives had been detonated under the buses, 'the catastrophe which would have befallen the State of Israel would have been indescribable'. The first approach was therefore to indicate that the interests of the state were paramount rather than other concerns – to adopt an authoritative national stand and thereby to isolate the Underground as both unrepresentative and irrelevant.

Shamir also wished to differentiate between support for the settlers and for the Underground. A few days after the arrests, he commented that 'there are those who are exploiting this affair to assail the character of the settlement enterprise in Judea, Samaria, Gaza and the Golan. An injustice is thereby being done to those who are doing great things for their country and their people'.[26] Ignoring the connections to Levinger, Druckman, Waldman and Rav Kook, Shamir characterized the Underground as nothing more than 'a small group of suspects'. Moreover, he found comparison with Lehi to be 'grotesque' and insisted that only the government was responsible for security in the Territories. Shamir clearly saw this as a damage-limitation exercise on excusable behaviour. Both Sharon and Raful Eitan significantly refused to comment on the discovery of the Underground.

Initially, the Council of Settlements in Judea, Samaria and Gaza vehemently denied the existence of an Underground; such protestations quickly evaporated, however. Shamir met Gush Emunim leaders and urged them to conduct an educational campaign which would effectively purge deviants. Shamir, who strongly admired the organization and compared them to the founding fathers of Israel,[27] tried to convince the Gush leaders to be more realistic and to pull back from the edge. Yet many religious settlers believed that the law of the state was of secondary importance and indeed had to be circumvented if the process of redemption was to continue unimpeded. This adherence to a higher authority was also used by the far right to enlist support from religious groups and to prove their own greater commitment to the cause in comparison with the Likud. Eliakim Ha'Etzni, one of the lawyers for the defendants and later a Techiya member of the Knesset, wrote that,

> a State of Israel that relinquishes sovereignty over Judea and Samaria will do so in name alone. By that very act, they will have become estranged from the Jewish People and abandoned its role as their emissary. The Jews in Judea, Samaria and Gaza will not be bound by such an act of alienation and disavowal.[28]

Two Herut Knesset members, Meir Cohen-Avidov and Dov Shilansky, were extremely active from the beginning in support of the Underground. At a demonstration at the Russian Compound in Jerusalem, Cohen-Avidov blamed the government's failure to take a stronger line against Palestinian terrorists as the reason for the rise of the Underground. On another occasion, Cohen-Avidov called the Jewish Underground 'the pride of Israel' and criticized a weak-kneed government that bowed to 'pressure from Peace Now'.

A month before the election, the Likud held a rally at the site of the 127th settlement since 1977, Shilat, and Shamir urged all God-fearing Jews to obey the religious injunction to settle 'all of Eretz Israel' up to the Jordan. Shamir continued to suggest that the Underground was 'the fault of individuals' and not of the settler movement. To emphasize this point, the Finance Ministry allocated 500 million shekels for the settlements three weeks before the election.

The results of the election indicated that Shamir's strategy had worked reasonably well. Although the Likud lost seven seats and 120,000 votes, it was returned with a respectable 41 seats. In a Likud without Begin, this was quite an achievement. But the price paid for appeasing the far right was, ironically, to further its advance and, in effect, to redistribute the nationalist vote. The combined vote of the Likud, Techiya and Kach in 1981 was 768,769. In 1984, it remained static at 769,500. Techiya increased its representation to five, and

Morasha was returned with two seats. But the major upset was that Meir Kahane had succeeded in attracting sufficient votes to secure a seat in the Knesset. He had picked up the vote of the poorest elements of Israeli society, including many in the army. His number two, Yehuda Richter, had been imprisoned for Kach activities. Baruch Goldstein, the perpetrator of the Hebron massacre in 1994, was number three on Kahane's list. Shamir underplayed the event by referring to it in mild terms as 'a negative phenomenon'. Even Sharon dissociated himself from Kahane, adding only that the radicalism on the left was far worse. Yet many commentators felt that Kahane's election was a sign of the times: it reflected both the sense of stagnation and the demoralization of the people. A Dahaf opinion poll which was published ten days after the election showed that many young people favoured the expulsion of the Arabs. Some 43.5 per cent suggested that they should be permitted to remain, but without civil and political rights – including the right to vote.[29]

The electorate had split evenly. The combined votes of the Likud, Techiya, the NRP, Morasha and Ometz totalled 875,001. Labour, Yahad, Shinui and Ratz amassed between them 874,821. Despite Peres' inducements behind the scenes to prise Shas and Agudat Yisrael away from Shamir, they still seemed to be more comfortable with their more natural ally, the Likud. The Labour Alignment, with 44 seats, could only depend on Ratz, Shinui and Ezer Weizmann's newly formed Yahad. Shamir and Peres concluded that a National Unity government was the only way of avoiding dependency on the far right and the minor religious parties. The premiership would therefore be shared equally between Peres and Shamir in rotation. Yet this precipitated the end of the Ma'arach, the Labour Alignment, when Mapam walked out rather than serve in a government with the Likud. The leading Labour dove, Yossi Sarid, broke with Labour and joined Shulamit Aloni in Ratz. They were not alone. The formation of a National Unity government – even under Peres – was enough to crystallize the first tentative steps towards a broad alliance on the part of the peace camp.

CHAPTER FOURTEEN

OUTLAWING THE PALESTINIANS

Shamir's Domestic Problems

As Foreign Minister and deputy Prime Minister, Shamir was reduced to playing a secondary role in the rotation scenario. He paled into political insignificance before the debonair brilliance of Shimon Peres. The Labour leader was fêted by European politicians and praised by many who had been bitterly hostile to the Likud governments. Peres started to win back the alienated intelligentsia and attracted European literati such as Simone Signoret and Alberto Moravia, as well as the philosopher Claude Lévi-Strauss to his standard. It seemed like a return to the pre-1967 days. Indeed, many political observers believed that Shamir would not succeed Peres in October 1986. The cunning Peres, it was argued, would break the gentlemen's agreement at an opportune time for Labour and go to the country. A second possibility was that Shamir would be toppled in the internecine warring within Herut. In March 1986, at the first party conference since 1979, Shamir controlled only half the delegates. Another 35 per cent looked to David Levy, while Arik Sharon led the remaining 15 per cent. In fact, David Levy had broken ranks with Shamir and supported Peres' intention to withdraw from Lebanon – and had not seen his support in Herut dwindle.

The vacuum left by Begin manifested itself in an unseemly power struggle, which was exacerbated by the shakiness of the internal workings of the Likud party procedure. Indeed, the party convention was marred by constant disruption and factional brawling. Some opposition commentators remarked that such behaviour mirrored the party's origins in the 1930s. One left-wing editor cited Ignazio Silone's *La Scuolla dei Dittatori* (The School for Dictators):

The superiority of the fascist leader over his competitors lies mostly in that he aspires to rule – only to rule and nothing else. With capitalists or with proletarians, with priests or with the devil – those considerations are all secondary – the main thing is to rule.[1]

The writer questioned whether the schismatic Herut could be trusted, or indeed should be allowed, to take over from the Labour Alignment in October 1986. Without Begin, the party bore only a cadaverous resemblance to its former self. Shamir was naturally desperate not to upset the political apple cart, so as to gain power in his own right as well as contend with a successful Labour leadership. This permitted Peres to press ahead with Labour policies while the Likud bore it all in silence. Likud opposition to negotiating with Egypt over the fate of Taba dissipated because they feared that Peres would use the issue to break up the coalition. Thus Shamir endured the first phase of the National Unity government as deputy Prime Minister under Peres with gritted teeth. The prize of the premiership awaited him at the end of a 25-month period if there were no upsets.

Peres, for his part, was riding high on a wave of popular support. He had dramatically reduced inflation and pulled the army out of Lebanon. Understandably, he now felt ambivalent about his agreement with the Likud. The Consumer Price Index had been reduced from 445 per cent to 22.8 per cent in the two-year period from 1984 to 1986. Inflation levelled out at 3 per cent as 1986 began. Peres benefited from his fair share of political luck as well: there was a drop in oil prices and Israel received $4 billion in aid during 1985–6 from the United States. Several opinion polls consequently showed support for Peres at 50 to 60 per cent with Shamir struggling at 20 per cent and below. Peres tried – perhaps half-heartedly – to find ways out of the agreement. This involved instigating coalition crises over the conduct of Sharon and Modai – their clear lack of loyalty to the National Unity government – and vain attempts to entice the less nationalistic religious parties such as Shas and Agudat Yisrael into a narrow coalition with Labour. As hard as he tried, Peres was unable to buck the right-wing trend and to uncouple any of the religious parties from their nationalist allies. The interest of the small religious parties was to preserve the status quo as this maximized their political influence. A secular Labour government would also be far less sympathetic to religious views. Moreover, despite his success as Prime Minister, Peres was still regarded with suspicion by the Israeli public and had to struggle to overcome his Nixonesque image. He therefore felt an inner need to prove himself and turned down opportunities to resign during the course of the National Unity government. Both the Likud and his rivals in the Rabin camp in Labour therefore covertly ensured that the mud stuck at every turn.

Within Herut and in the nationalist camp in general, Shamir had to devise a way forward which would please the radical faithful while appearing a pragmatic and responsible policy in public. The Shamir–Arens alliance, bolstered by the young 'princes' of the Likud – the succeeding generation of Olmert, Milo, Meridor and Netanyahu – wanted to retain Israeli sovereignty over the Territories while resisting the catcalls and criticism of the increasingly influential far right, the opposition of Labour and the peace camp – and, of course, outside interference from the United States and Europe. Shamir, like Begin before him, adopted a pragmatic approach to the question of securing the integrity of Eretz Israel, based on the practical yet ill-defined framework of the Camp David Accords.

By the beginning of 1984, 112 settlements had been established, which were inhabited by 28,000 Jews. Nearly half of them lived in the relatively few larger settlements such as Ariel and Ma'ale Adumim. Yet the World Zionist Organization's master plan for the settlement of Judea and Samaria called for a Jewish population in the Territories of 530,000 by the year 2010.[2] Unlike the experience of his predecessor, Menachem Begin, the pressures on Shamir became more diverse and more numerous. In the years of the National Unity government such pressures were still manageable. The main threat to Shamir in the mid-1980s was the growth of the far right both within and outside the Likud; and this was coupled with the fact that the party itself had moved even further to the right after the war in Lebanon.

The benevolent, laid-back Reagan–Shultz attitude to the Israel–Palestine conflict was convenient for Shamir, since any potential difficulties could be circumvented in the name of the close friendship between the Israeli and American peoples. Both the Reagan and Shultz plans were placed in comradely abeyance. Unlike Jimmy Carter, Reagan remembered that New York's Jews had deserted the president's standard in droves in the Democratic primary in 1980; and even though American Jews were not traditionally supporters of the Republican Party, he was not willing to cause any further irritation with new American initiatives for peace. Moreover, the Palestinians were in a continuing state of confusion, with the PLO unable to present a coherent policy. Indeed, following its evacuation of Beirut, the PLO had fragmented into three groups: a much weakened PLO under Arafat; a Syrian-dominated Palestine National Alliance comprising the Fatah rebels under Abu Musa; and an Iraqi-controlled Democratic Alliance consisting of the rejectionist Popular Front of George Habash and the Democratic Front of Naif Hawatmeh.

To the far right, Shamir's public stance was perceived as one of potential appeasement. He was therefore at pains to soothe the sensibilities of the settlers, especially where security was concerned, and to adopt a paternalistic attitude. In Shamir's eyes, the Jewish Underground were essentially wayward children:

> I love you with all my heart and I have expressed it, but I also know your mistakes. The history of the people of Israel is full of examples. The best people with the best intentions have sometimes harmed, out of miscalculation, their own ambitions.[3]

Shamir was therefore always positive in his attitude towards Laor,[4] the support group for the Jewish Underground and their families, which dissociated itself from the latter's activities but focused instead on a 'humanitarian understanding' of the defendants' plight.

Two months before the verdicts on the Underground were announced, Yitzhak Rabin, Minister of Defence in the National Unity government, authorized the exchange of 1150 Arab prisoners for 3 Israeli soldiers held by Ahmed Jibril's Popular Front for the Liberation of Palestine – General Command. The lack of wisdom displayed by this decision, involving as it did an extraordinary lack of symmetry, was registered by the Israeli population, thereby providing the Likud with a golden opportunity to show support for the defendants in the Underground trial. Shamir argued that, if it was right to free convicted Palestinian terrorists, then why shouldn't the same rationale apply to the Jewish Underground? Why should Jewish terrorists pay the penalty for their crimes when Palestinian terrorists patently did not? 'There's no connection, heaven forbid, between boys who erred, but are basically good boys who have done much for the nation, and, on the other hand, terrorists, enemies, murderers. We will do everything we can to get them a pardon.'[5]

Shamir's qualified support was only for those 'who have admitted and will admit their mistakes and express remorse for their deeds'. An opinion poll showed that 73 per cent of respondents endorsed the principle of clemency for the defendants; at the same time, 81 per cent favoured the death penalty for Arab terrorists.[6] This overwhelming support for Shamir's position was an indication of the sheer dread of Palestinian terrorism in Israeli society. It was a crucial psychological factor which Peres could not gloss over. Despite the reticence of many senior figures in Labour to interfere in the judicial process, Peres asked the Attorney General if there was any legal basis on which to free members of the Underground even when the trial was still in progress. Peres promised Shamir that he would consider the possibility of pardons once the trial had finished. Significantly, he was virtually silent when the defendants were sentenced. The Labour Police Minister, Chaim Bar-Lev, later submitted a plan to release 400 prisoners which would include the Jewish Underground, but it was rejected by President Herzog. Peres clearly felt it to be electorally too risky to give an unequivocal message condemning the Underground to the Israeli public. Less than two months after the verdicts, the first amnesty was given to a member of the Underground.

The PLO and the Use of Security

The deep need for security for the Jewish people was a policy which all Israeli political parties understood and espoused as a cardinal principle. With its Revisionist heritage and its reputation as the standard-bearer of mainstream nationalism, the Likud embraced the security issue with zealous conviction. It looked for any deviation, for any weakness that the Labour Alignment might exhibit. The Likud was able to articulate the deep-seated historical fears of the populace – and electorally it was seen to be the party which was strong on security. Yet this psychological condition of post-Holocaust Jewry could be utilized for purposes other than that of strengthening security.

Most people who wished to retain the Territories advocated this course of action on grounds of security. Judea and Samaria formed a protective belt around the state and provided strategic depth. Even those who wished to trade land for peace suggested retaining some military presence in the Territories as an early-warning system against unexpected invasion from the East. The disciples of Jabotinsky, however, had ideological reasons for wanting to retain the Territories that had been promised to them by the British some 60 years before. Two partitions had been partially reversed in 1967, and no member of Herut could contemplate the surrender of Western Eretz Israel to foreign sovereignty once more. Although few in Israel in 1985 held to the old Revisionist dream of a Jewish state on both sides of the Jordan, the security issue nevertheless helped to cloak the ideological issue and gained the Likud wide support within the country.

The leadership of the Likud sought to shore up its ideologically inspired policy of settling and retaining Judea and Samaria by emphasizing the scourge of terrorism at home and abroad and thereby delegitimizing the PLO as a future partner in negotiations. It sought to stifle any possibility that some sections of the PLO could conceivably turn away from terrorism and take the political road. Through the device of association, they could tar those Palestinians who expounded a two-state solution of the Israel–Palestine conflict with the brush of rejectionist terrorism. Their formal platform maintained that the only Palestinians who could be considered suitable partners in a peace process were those who effectively accepted the Camp David Accords and the proposed open-ended five-year autonomy period. This latter principle would permit the Likud still to claim Israeli sovereignty at the end of the interim period.

Despite all this, Shamir kept some private back doors open to the Palestinians. Herut's Moshe Amirav and the leftist Liova Eliav regularly reported back on their discussions with pro-PLO Palestinians in the Territories and senior PLO figures abroad. On one occasion, Shamir sent his advisor, Yossi Achimeir, in the dead of night to meet Charlie Biton, a Knesset member and a leader of the Sephardi underclass, following a meeting between Biton and Arafat. Shamir was said to be in receipt of a letter from Arafat and to keep open intermediary channels through Ceausescu's Romania.

Shamir forcefully opposed Peres' campaign to initiate an international conference sponsored by the permanent members of the UN Security Council, the Arab States and Israel. Shamir believed that the term 'international conference' was in reality code for forcing Israel to relinquish the Territories, based on the unacceptable Brezhnev Plan. It would avoid the necessity of face-to-face negotiations with Jordan and Syria and effectively neutralize the Likud's interpretation of the Camp David Accords. Superpower pressure, together with Soviet influence and old opponents such as the United Nations, would press for a solution based on 'land for peace'. Worst of all, the Likud feared that Peres would allow the PLO to slip into negotiations through the back door. Some had noticed that he downplayed the option of attacking the PLO even during the most difficult of terrorist crises.[7]

At the beginning of February 1985, Hussein and Arafat signed an agreement which implied a 'land for peace' approach and a Jordan–Palestine federation. This *rapprochement* came about after many years of mutual hatred, following the bloody civil war in September 1970 when the PLO had been decimated by Hussein's army. Peres' first half of the rotation was seen by Hussein as a window of opportunity. The Hashemite monarch believed that he could 'do business' with Shimon Peres.

Hussein was also interested in developing negotiating positions with the Likud because he was deeply worried that Shamir would be toppled or would resign and be replaced by Sharon. This, he believed, could lead to a policy of 'transfer' which would transport undesirable Palestinians to Jordan and effect the destabilization of his regime.

Peres' secret negotiations with King Hussein were carried out with the knowledge of Shamir at the home of Lord Mishcon, a leading British Jew and a former home affairs spokesman for the British Labour Party. The London agreement in 1987 advocated an international conference to which the five permanent members of the UN Security Council and the protagonists in the conflict were to be invited. The resolution of the Arab–Israeli conflict was to be based on Resolutions 242 and 338, and negotiations would be conducted through bilateral committees with the Palestinians forming part of the Jordanian delegation. Peres informed Shamir of the contents of the agreement, but the Likud leader gave no commitment to it. Such was the suspicion between the two that Peres did not give a copy of the agreement to Shamir for fear of leaks to the press. Although the terms of the agreement allowed for no imposition of a settlement on either Jordan or Israel, Shamir understood too well that this opened the door to withdrawal and the possible renunciation of Israeli sovereignty. Shamir therefore sent Arens to Washington, where he privately met Shultz in a bid to scupper the agreement. The Americans' reaction to Shamir's opposition was both docile and lethargic. Shultz accepted Arens's point that if the United States took up this initiative, it would be 'a crass interference in Israel's internal affairs'.[8]

Shamir's approach to any prospective deal with Jordan was to go on the offensive and to proclaim that a witch-hunt was in progress against Jews who had bought land in the Territories. One settler magazine commented that, 'any government which turns over sovereignty to the enemy will be considered illegal and should not be obeyed.'[9]

If the Likud held the upper hand in the Israeli public-opinion stakes with its proclamation of total war against the PLO, it was aided and abetted by the PLO itself. In 1985, a total of 538 people were killed and injured at the hands of Palestinian terrorists. This compared with only 18 deaths during the previous year. There was also a sharp rise in the number of international incidents: 73 in 1985 compared to 35 in 1984. Over 60 per cent of these were committed by Palestinian groups which had rejected any dialogue or deal with Israel; just over 20 per cent were carried out by formal members of the PLO – and many of these were instigated by those who espoused a hard-line approach in the organization.[10] Many rejectionists had targeted Jordan because it had been quietly negotiating with Israel. This initiative moved Arafat in 1984 to reposition himself for fear that Hussein might eventually control the West Bank, thereby excluding any independent Palestinian voice. Ironically, when Hussein first recognized the PLO in the 1960s, the PLO agreed that it had claims only on Israel and not on the West Bank, which was Jordan's domain.

Both Israeli and Palestinian leaders were subject to the internal constraints operating within their own camps. Shamir and the far right refused to allow Peres to proceed with the idea of an international conference, while the politically hesitant Arafat was persuaded of the error of his ways in dealing with King Hussein by rejectionists both inside and outside the PLO. Even if Arafat had been prepared to consider embarking upon the political road, the Palestine National Council – even without the rejectionist PFLP and DFLP – were not. They were indifferent to Hussein's entreaties and even vetoed the possibility of contacts with dovish Israelis by reverting to the traditional line of the 1960s of only agreeing to dialogue with anti-Zionist Israelis. By the end of the year, then, the Hussein–Arafat agreement was null and void; Jordan formerly abandoned it in February 1986. Arafat's capitulation had been accompanied by new acts of PLO terrorism, in particular the involvement of Fatah's Force 17 in the killing of Israelis in Larnaca and the Palestine Liberation Front's hijacking of the Italian cruise liner, the *Achille Lauro*. The activity of the PLF under the guidance of Abul Abbas, a PLO executive member, not only outraged the West and strengthened the Likud; it also indicated the considerable chaos caused by the lack of direction within the PLO itself. The concerted attempts of the PLO leadership to mount a cover-up and to sidetrack the issue with misleading statements only added fuel to the fire and provided an easy target for Likud publicists.

In addition, Syrian Intelligence utilized the services of several rejectionist Palestinian groups who accused Arafat of collaborating with the 'murderer' Hussein. Moderate Palestinians were also viewed as targets. Thus British Intelligence uncovered a plot to assassinate PLO officials in London, which led to the arrest and deportation of an eight-member hit-squad belonging to Ahmed Jibril's PFLP–GC. Some of the group carried Syrian diplomatic passports, and four members actually stayed at the Syrian Embassy during their sojourn in London.

The Abu Nidal group, possibly under Syrian authorization, sub-sequently carried out attacks on El Al counters at airports in Rome and Vienna. These acts resulted in wholesale carnage, including the deaths of many passengers, thereby extending the scope of Palestinian terrorism on an unprecedented international scale. The Abu Nidal group carried out a third of all Palestinian actions in 1985, a year in which 331 Westerners fell victim to Palestinian terrorism, compared with only 5 in 1984. These highly publicized acts of indiscriminate terror were coterminous with a series of Shi'ite hijackings of aircraft and Hezbollah kidnappings of Westerners in Beirut. The world looked on aghast as terrorism became a growth industry. The United States seemed unable to do anything about the escalation and the Europeans and Arab states were only too pleased to release convicted terrorists or deport those caught in the act just to avoid being drawn into a byzantine embroilment. The prospect of a terrorist international, backed by the twin evils of rampant communism and Islamic funda-mentalism threatening to devour the civilized world, was an image that enabled the Likud to enlist powerful forces in the United States in an attempt to delegitimize those Palestinians who had chosen the political path to a resolution of the conflict.

Netanyahu's Campaign against Terrorism

Prime Minister Shamir, like Begin before him, employs demagoguery to warn the public only of the dangers of withdrawal; he glosses over the dangers of annexation. When the national dialogue does not include a full-scale analysis of the advantages and disadvantages of the available options, but focuses instead on the disadvantages and dangers of one option only, the level of discussion becomes dangerously simplistic and emotional. Instead of stimulating a debate on the real issues, Begin and Shamir consciously exploited antagonistic sentiments. A further mani-festation of this trend has been the focusing of attention on Palestinian terrorism, as if this were the main challenge to Israel.[11]

So complained Yehoshafat Harkabi, the military writer and analyst, in 1986. Like many others, Harkabi had watched the Likud's projection of the rising tide of terrorism and the emotional response it evoked from an overwhelming majority of Israelis and Diaspora Jews.

By the early 1980s, an alliance was slowly emerging between Likud pragmatists and the neo-conservative forces of the new right in the United States – many of whom were Jewish intellectuals who had renounced their liberal pedigree. The Israeli Embassy in the United States under Moshe Arens and Benjamin Netanyahu found it relatively straightforward to make common cause with the Reagan White House and with figures such as Daniel Moynihan and Jeane Kirkpatrick in a crusade against international terrorism. Both Arens and Netanyahu had received their education, and subsequently spent considerable time, in the United States. Arens had been the *natziv* of Betar in the United States when Israel declared its independence in 1948. At that time, he followed the Irgun's line of condemning the partition of Palestine, 'a midget state, a monstrosity composed of three oddly shaped pieces of land isolated from each other, forced to carry the economic burden of the rest of Eretz Israel which will be controlled by Arab feudal landlords and their British masters'. He bitterly condemned Ben-Gurion, Weizmann and the Jewish Agency for 'condemning the Jewish people to a small ghetto in Eretz Israel'.[12] In Israel, he had pursued an academic career and developed Israel Aircraft Industries. Arens seemed to place more emphasis on security than on ideology. Unlike Shamir, Arens was not attached to the formulae of past ideologies. For example, by October 1994, he strongly supported the peace treaty with Jordan and regarded Jabotinsky's claims to both banks of the Jordan to be irrelevant.[13] He had voted against the Camp David framework on security grounds, but supported the Accords once they became a reality.

Both Arens and Netanyahu implicitly rejected the anti-intellectual culture and antiquated thinking of the Likud and projected themselves as the modernizers of their movement. They envisaged a model of the Likud shaped in the image of Jabotinsky's philosophy and Begin's pragmatism. Netanyahu's father, an academic and long-time Revisionist, lauded Jabotinsky's powers of analysis and insight in a public lecture in 1981. On the question of the Palestinians, he commented that

> according to Jabotinsky, their [Arab] resistance will not cease so long as they maintain even a 'glimmer of hope' of eliminating our presence here. And who will deny that they have such a glimmer – and indeed much more than a 'glimmer' only? Thus, there is no possibility of peace with the Arabs – that is, a true peace – at this time, for they have not yet been convinced that it is impossible to destroy us or drive us into the sea.[14]

The strong Revisionist legacy was passed from father to son. Netanyahu's brother, Yonatan, who had been involved in several anti-terrorist operations, had met his death in the dramatic rescue of passengers in the Entebbe operation in 1976. The manner of his death clearly propelled Netanyahu away from his architecture studies into the world of Revisionist politics. Netanyahu was responsible for the establishment of the Jonathan Institute in his brother's memory, the purpose of which was to communicate to a complacent world the danger of international terrorism. The Institute's first conference was held in Jerusalem in July 1979. A second conference was held five years later in Washington with the heavy involvement of the Israeli Embassy. Its participants included the US Secretary of State and the Israeli Minister of Defence, as well as leading neo-conservative intellectuals and writers. Its high-profile, businesslike approach was a far cry from the 'blood and fire' melodramas of the Begin era.

Netanyahu himself laid the blame for the perceived crisis – the international community's apparent impotence in the face of the terrorist threat – at the door of pusillanimous governments, 'not for their lack of knowledge but for their lack of courage and moral clarity'. Yet, although his speech at the Washington conference was in the tradition of a Jabotinskyian call to arms, Netanyahu implicitly recognized that the killings did not arise from a void. Yet the line which he and American Jewish representatives took was to oppose strongly the often superficial school of thought that believed terror would only fade away once its root causes were confronted. One American Jewish writer commented that 'understanding' terrorism was 'a form of moral confusion'. 'Mass murder is mass murder and no grievance can justify it, nor will pusillanimous "understanding" or "explanation" avert, ameliorate or eliminate it.'[15] Despite Jewish emotion over the slaughter of innocents and Netanyahu's comments from the podium of the United Nations that 'nothing, no political cause, justifies the murder of children', Palestinian terrorism disputed this. They argued that it was not killing for killing's sake, but a means of promoting their political platform. The political motivation and advantage gained in the wider world were factors central to the act and justified it. The morality of any atrocity was a secondary matter and perhaps irrelevant in the world of *realpolitik*.

The PLO explanation for its early acts of terrorism had been that they drew attention to the Palestinian question. With the slow evolution towards a political rather than an armed struggle after 1974, many Palestinians in the pragmatic mainstream began to realise that, although they had indeed brought their cause to the world's attention, acts of terrorism against Israel had become increasingly counter-productive. A growing number of Palestinians over the years began to ask the question whether international terrorism actually advanced their cause. They came to realize that terrorism would neither under-mine the confidence of the Israeli public nor defeat their military machine. Israeli society would not collapse from within, and the 'Zionist entity' would not wither away under terrorist salvos.

In due course, the gradual renunciation of international terror by Fatah and the PLO mainstream led to murderous schisms within the organization itself. In 1974, Abu Nidal broke away. In 1983, after the Lebanon war, it was the turn of Abu Musa and the Fatah dissidents. The Marxist groups under Habash and Hawatmeh moved uneasily in and out of the PLO, while the intelligence services of Syria and Iraq controlled smaller Palestinian factions which could be activated at a moment's notice to serve their own state interests.

Notwithstanding these impediments, the PLO's slow movement towards a political approach was an ideological threat to the Likud. If this was allowed to develop, then the tactic of subsuming the ideo-logical necessity of retaining Judea and Samaria within the common need for security through territorial protection would become trans-parent. If the Israeli public felt that a self-governing Palestinian entity was not a security threat, then why keep the Territories? Although Palestinian terrorism was deeply abhorred by the Israeli right, it para-doxically strengthened their position amongst the Israeli electorate. The existence of a siege mentality benefited the Likud: it allowed them to suggest that any dialogue with Palestinians was offensive and unpatriotic.

Netanyahu understood that there was a political dimension to the fight against Palestinian terrorism and that it was a political imperative to block off any discussion of the Palestinian case:

Slowly, imperceptibly, the initial horror recedes and in its place comes a readiness to accept the terrorists' point of view.... Before we know it, the hijackers and killers have spokesmen and commentators of their own and the terrorists have been transformed into merely another type of political activist that has to be 'considered' and even given equal time.[16]

Clearly, it was morally wrong to foment death and destruction in order to promote a policy, but was it also wrong to state such opinions in open discussion without resolution to violence? An argument could be made that such opinions represented an incitement to violence;

however, the Likud feared Palestinians not only for what they did, but also for what they said about the political situation.

During the second Reagan administration, Bibi Netanyahu proved himself to be a brilliant operator in the American media – the master of the sound-bite. Netanyahu realized that there was a crucial need to counter the increasingly sophisticated propaganda of the Palestinians and to change totally the hitherto crude approach of the Revisionist old guard. He even publicly chastised past Likud governments for their ineffective work in the media. He argued that they did not heed the teachings of Jabotinsky regarding 'the need for an unrelenting effort of persuasion and pressure to protect Jewish interests'.[17] Netanyahu believed that the lack of a credible effort to explain Israel's position had led to 'one political defeat after another'.

Israel's public-relations effort had been relatively low-key up until 1967. At that time few doubted the case for Israel, which had appeared to arise phoenix-like from the ashes of the Holocaust. Israel was simply Leon Uris's *Exodus* writ large and there was really no need for an overt public-relations exercise. Indeed, symptomatically, the post of Prime Minister's press secretary was only instituted in 1975. But the combination of a new post-war generation un-acquainted with the Jewish question, the social consciousness of the 1960s, and growing Palestinian nationalism challenged the certainty of that approach. Labour governments under Golda Meir and Yitzhak Rabin attempted to meet that need by appointing Shimon Peres and then Aharon Yariv to the newly established office of Minister of Information. Both were short-lived appointments, since the Foreign Ministry objected to such a poaching of its territory. With the advent of National Unity governments, control of such a position could give credence to a specific policy – a policy which might be disputed or interpreted differently by the other major party in the government. Neither Labour nor the Likud could afford the risk of estab-lishing a Ministry of Information, since it could all too easily become an agent of propaganda.

In addition, after 1977, the belligerence of the Likud approach and Begin's verbal bellicosity made a calm explanation of Israel's official point of view more difficult. The distortions in the inter-national media during the Lebanon war dismayed and indeed shocked the Israeli right. Yet the world could not be ignored or dismissed as a bunch of anti-Semites. The competitive age of electronic media required instant reaction. The snapshot news clip had replaced con-sidered analysis. Such abbreviated reportage often led to inaccuracy and distortion. The packaging of current events into neat consumable bundles also brought about the evolution of the spin-doctor. In one sense, Netanyahu was the long-awaited answer to Israeli problems in this area, since he was both presenter and spin-doctor. Netanyahu believed that language and ideas in the media circus shaped foreign policy – and particularly in America. His smooth appearance, good looks, faultless command of English, and articulate rebuttal of barbed questions made him a courted commentator on the networks. Netanyahu's efforts were thus much appreciated by the Likud and also by American Jews who resented media coverage of the Middle East. Yet the price of the immediate sound-bite was a reduction in detailed debate and a subtle submerging of Revisionist ideological aims.

CHAPTER FIFTEEN

BETWEEN INFORMATION
AND PROPAGANDA

The Hasbarah Industry

Benjamin Netanyahu developed *hasbarah* to a new level during his time in the United States. *Hasbarah* is a Hebrew word that means 'explanation'; but it is not a neutral term, since one person's explanation of an event can differ substantially from that of another. Thus *hasbarah* is far from being an objective exercise in conveying information. On the contrary, according to Ehud Olmert, another of the young 'princes' of Likud, 'the aim of *hasbarah*' should not be to convince people of the veracity of a political position; rather, the intention 'should be more modest, namely, to make the world reconsider its position – to raise doubts, to alter the approach taken towards our adversaries'.[1] Professionals like Netanyahu and Olmert clearly could not hope to promote controversial issues such as settling the Territories in the absence of a consensus in Israel or in the Diaspora. Nevertheless, controversial Likud policies that were less obvious, and therefore less readily discernible, were able to be projected in a favourable way. In this sense, the ever-present propaganda aspect of *hasbarah* became not only a weapon to counteract hostile Arab interpretations in the public arena, but also a means to provide often simplistic accounts of complex events to Diaspora Jewry, who would then digest, repeat and propagate them. This inevitably often led Netanyahu into severe disagreements with Shimon Peres, both when he was Prime Minister and, far more often, when he was Foreign Minister in the National Unity government under Shamir.

Netanyahu was a contracted political appointee, rather than a career diplomat, whom Arens had recommended as his successor in 1982. Despite his standing as a senior representative abroad, Netanyahu had no reservations about criticizing the Labour Party even if it headed his government. Thus, under Peres as Prime Minister, Netanyahu told American audiences that Israel would be committing political suicide if it gave up the West Bank. He also condemned Rabin's exchange of 1200 Palestinian prisoners for three Israeli soldiers. Following a visit to the United States, Ora Namir, a leading Labour member of the Knesset, complained that,

> the national consensus is not reflected by our official spokesmen especially our Ambassador to the United Nations, Binyamin Netanyahu, who in his almost daily appearances on the television networks speaks as if Labour does not share power with the Likud.... I watched his daily television appearances where he shocked not only me but many prominent people by his arrogant manner of handing marks to various countries in his role as an expert on terrorism.[2]

Labour, then, felt acutely aggrieved that Peres' stewardship of the National Unity government was being perceived by millions of Americans through the prism of the Likud. Indeed, Peres was criticized within the Labour Party for allowing Netanyahu to interfere in American communal politics, such as pushing right-wing candidates into key positions or promoting mainly Likud speakers at leadership functions. Netanyahu was thus a political asset to the Likud in his position in the United States. Shamir made sure that this situation continued. On his last day as Foreign Minister before the rotation, Shamir ensured that Peres inherited Netanyahu and eight other Likud political appointees by extending their contracts for two years.

Arik Sharon as Minister of Defence in the second Begin government promoted the idea that the Palestinians already had a homeland – the Hashemite Kingdom of Jordan. Yet the foundation for this view had been laid a decade earlier by Golda Meir, who, while disputing the existence of the Palestinian people, suggested on occasion that 'they had a state in Jordan anyway'. What is more, Shamir himself had already floated the idea when he was Foreign Minister in Begin's second government.[3] Yet, unlike Sharon, Shamir believed in the idea that 'Jordan is Palestine' as purely a propaganda tool. While Begin had refused to meet King Hussein privately because he was unwilling to compromise the historic claim to the East Bank, Shamir had no such problems. In the context of pragmatic *realpolitik*, it was important to remain in contact with the Hashemite monarch. A propaganda exercise to delegitimize the Palestinians was something else though. Thus, with the blessing of Shamir, Netanyahu developed the idea to the extent that a network of 'Jordan is Palestine' committees were established, linking most major Jewish communities. He had already referred to Jordan as 'eastern Palestine' in an article in the *Wall Street Journal*.[4] He argued that the demand for another state in Eretz Israel had nothing to do with Palestinian self-determination; it simply provided the basis for an irredentist drive to destroy the State of Israel. Netanyahu referred to the West Bank as a time bomb which would start to tick if Israel withdrew from the area.

When challenged about the right of self-determination for the Palestinians, Jewish leadership would thus expound this line and invoke the Camp David autonomy plan for the Arabs of the West Bank, and finish by pointing out that 60 per cent of the population of Jordan was Palestinian. Why then, it was argued, should there be another Palestinian state? The Palestinians were concentrated in the eastern part of Mandatory Palestine while the Jews were settled in the western half. From a *hasbarah* point of view, though, the argument had the advantage of making Palestinian demands seem greedy in that they now wished to have two Palestinian states, while the Zionists, for their part, were generous in giving up the East Bank, Eastern Eretz Israel. It also suggested that if the Palestinians wanted to adopt a full Palestinian identity, they should go and join their brethren in Jordan. This, in practical terms, was a hidden encouragement to emigrate and thereby solve the pressing demographic problem. At worst, the argument accepted the far-right position in that it implied wholesale population transfer.

The PLO did not accept the idea because they did not wish to substitute the West Bank for Jordan as their homeland. Jordan did not accept it for obvious reasons, even though Hussein did use the cultural closeness of the two banks to integrate the Palestinians into his kingdom. Yet comments by leading Jordanians could be used to prove the soundness of the 'Jordan is Palestine' equation. Thus, in 1970, Prince Hassan told the Jordanian National Assembly that 'Palestine is Jordan and Jordan is Palestine. There is one people and one land with one history and one destiny.' Militarily, however, it did not make any sense for Israel to advocate this approach. For example, a Palestinian state in Amman under Arafat, allied to Saddam Hussein's Iraq during the Gulf War, would have posed a serious threat to Israel. Moreover, it did not make sense in historical terms.

Although the Zionist movement had laid claim to the East Bank at the Versailles Peace Conference and at Zionist Congresses in the 1920s, British imperial *realpolitik* had to rationalize making promises to the Arabs (the McMahon Correspondence), the French (the Sykes–

Picot Agreement) and the Jews (the Balfour Declaration) over a similar area of the Ottoman Empire at intermittent intervals during World War I. The delineation of Palestine at that time was extremely vague. The *Encyclopaedia Britannica* of 1910–11 comments that, although the River Jordan naturally divides the area, 'it is practically impossible to say where [Palestine] ends and the Arabian desert begins'. The British first used the term 'Mandate for Palestine' in 1920, some two years before the League of Nations formally granted mandatory status. The British included Trans-Jordan in their understanding of 'Palestine' for eight months from July 1920 until March 1921. Two recent commentators have observed that 'it is preposterous to base today's major decisions of war and peace on the transient interests of the British Empire after World War I. That Jordan was briefly part of the Palestine Mandate does not establish a vital link; it merely recalls a historical curiosity.'5 Yet the 'Jordan is Palestine' explanation gained wide currency amongst Jews and non-Jewish Zionist sympathizers, even spawning an entire conference in Jerusalem. It helped to marginalize the autonomy plan and effectively delegitimized the very idea of Palestinians as negotiating partners. A diversionary measure in support of Likud policy thus came to be presented as *hasbarah*.

Although Netanyahu avoided overtly controversial, non-consensual issues, there still existed the belief that good, efficient, modern management of *hasbarah* would create the right mind-set in the corridors of power. A silver tongue uttering magic words at the right time at the right place could accomplish a great deal. Winning the propaganda war was vital to any struggle. Given both the power and vacuity of the electronic age, this seemed to be a rational approach. Instant sound-bites through CNN and other networks would reach an international population at the same time as the White House. This in turn demanded an immediate reaction from the US administration. Lack of reaction could be interpreted as vacillation. However, that said, Likud leaders often acted as if they did not understand that foreign political leaders pursued a different agenda and were motivated by different interests from those of the Israeli government. Media hype and public campaigns, no matter how sophisticated, could not replace the stuff of political analysis. For many, public relations was not the same as public reality despite the shallowness of political life in the 1980s.

Yet, for sophisticated operators such as Netanyahu and Olmert, the 'one more push' heritage of the founders of the Revisionist movement licensed the disconnection of public relations from actual events. Thus, even the most difficult of situations could be explained if the right form of words and the correct imagery were deployed. For example, it did not seem to matter that much of the media criticism of Israel's conduct during the Lebanon war in 1982 arose from misconceived policies – policies which Shamir in his memoirs criticized – and was not simply manipulation of adverse news. Although there was indeed much ill-informed commentary and distortion, Likud spokespersons made no distinction between unpalatable reporting and biased reporting. Thus, disregarding Sharon's duplicity and Begin's errors, Olmert commented in a *hasbarah* conference in 1984 that, 'despite the differences concerning the correctness of the [Lebanon] war's objectives and its achievements, it is now universally accepted that, as a result of this campaign, Israel faced *hasbarah* problems to an unprecedented degree'.[6]

The growth of the *hasbarah* industry served to mobilize large numbers of Diaspora Jews and the mass deployment of prepared – though often ill-thought-out – arguments in the propaganda war. This activity conveyed a genuine sense of solidarity with the embattled Jewish state, a sense of sharing in Jewish destiny; yet this transmission of a siege mentality also tended to shut out any independent thinking on how to go beyond the current static situation. The measure of loyalty to the State of Israel was reduced to who could shout loudest and longest in a megaphone war. The idea of seeking peace was reduced to a cliché rather than being actively pursued as an option. A by-product of this process was to cast the notion of dialogue with the Palestinians into an anti-patriotic mould – an activity left to the marginalized left and clandestine meetings. If there was no discussion with the enemy – the other – then it was possible to deny their existence and their humanity, thereby giving credence to the proposition that there was no one to talk to.

Netanyahu accused those who did not believe in the *hasbarah* crusade of being unrealistic – leftists who chose to focus on the 'sin' of Israel's conquest of the Territories in 1967. This view appealed to the new Jewish politics in the Diaspora after the Six Day War, which were predicated on an assertive survivalism. If effective *hasbarah* was to be deployed to combat Palestinian propaganda, then similar methods could be sanctioned against internal opposition. 'In the Leftist revision of history', Netanyahu wrote, 'the incorporation of the territories into Israel during the Six Day War was the beginning of all evil, Israel became smug and self-satisfied, insensitive and inhuman, repressing the Palestinian Arabs and tarnishing the Israeli soul in the process.'

Such selective polarizing of a complex process permitted Netanyahu's Diaspora audience to avoid the fact that Israel had in fact changed and that there were real problems which had to be confronted. Such 'dreamers' who did not accept the Likud's iron-wall philosophy were condemned and often ostracized. Those who were prepared to question the veracity of the propaganda war were also compared to the religious settlers on the West Bank: 'A mirror image of this messianism is found on the religious right where it is believed that the act of settling the land is in and of itself sufficient to earn divine providence and an end to the country's woes.'[7] This juxtaposition – of leftist dissidence and right-wing religious zealotry – served to convey an impression of strength and realism to anyone who followed Netanyahu's line. Yet, unlike with Begin and Shamir, it openly indicated a limit to the courting of settlers.

Sinking the PLO

The pragmatic Shamir–Arens camp pursued a peace policy which admitted little deviation from the Camp David Accords on the issue of Palestinian autonomy, believing that they would permit the continuation of Israeli sovereignty over the Territories. Moreover, it was assumed that the situation would become more permanent with each new settlement. The strategy of seeking peace on these terms, it was argued, would minimize the degree of interference from the international community, and indeed from the Israeli Labour Party and their allies in the peace movement. It was therefore in the Likud's interests to reject or drag out any political initiatives which hinted at the possibility of withdrawal and the renunciation of Israeli sovereignty over the Territories. The prospect of a PLO that was moving away from the armed struggle to embrace the political path and eventual negotiations was a dangerous ideological development for the Likud despite the benefits it stood to derive from the cessation of terrorism. Such a development thus had to be obscured or reinterpreted for lesser motives. The very idea of a dialogue between Zionist Israelis and Palestinian nationalists without preconditions suggested the beginning of PLO recognition of Israel. If reality broke through the propaganda to show that some PLO members did not conform to the imagery of bloodthirsty terrorists, then the Likud's containment of calls for negotiation with the PLO would become increasingly difficult. The PLO had to be demonized and kept outside the norms of political discourse. This had always been a Likud policy, in fact;

however, in the mid-1980s, Netanyahu's talents were necessary to inject credibility into an eroding strategy.

Netanyahu termed the PLO 'the quintessential terrorist organization of modern times'.[8] In this definition, he was greatly assisted by the PLO itself and by its chairman. Yasser Arafat's great ability to survive in the treacherous world of Palestinian politics has largely been due to his adeptness at changing position. Arafat has always placed great emphasis on the unity of the Palestinian people. Yet from the very beginning of its renaissance, Palestinian nationalism has been beset by factionalism and fragmentation, generated by both ideological and personal differences. The organizational framework of the PLO and the Palestine National Council came to serve a coordinating function for an ever-increasing number of groups. This promoted the PLO as the nerve centre of an otherwise diffuse Palestinian nationalism and its voice in any eventual negotiations. The lack of homogeneity in Palestinian politics allowed Arafat the maximum degree of independence. He was thus able to play off one sponsor against another in the conflict-ridden Arab world. The price he had to pay was that PLO strategy often lacked coherence and resolution, and the organization tended to speak with many voices. Arafat's manoeuvrability also fluctuated with the influence of rejectionist groups within the PLO and the whims of the radical Arab states such as Syria and Iraq who sponsored and manipulated them.

The years of the National Unity government began with a weakened Arafat reaching a *rapprochement* with Hussein, and effectively embracing the idea of land for peace and accepting UN Resolution 242. Within months, however, he was being pulled in the opposite direction. He was forced to bow to pressure from the rejectionists and hardliners within Fatah to pursue international terrorism once more when he clearly believed that it had become counterproductive. Thus, 1985 may have started with the Hussein–Arafat agreement, but it soon gave way to the granting of lukewarm approval to the operations of Force 17 and the botched attempt to take the *Achille Lauro*. This about-turn allowed Netanyahu to berate Western Governments who 'parrot endless incantations about Mr Arafat's "moderation" and "reasonableness"'.[9] Indeed, by 1987, Arafat had formerly renounced the accord with Hussein and welcomed Habash and Hawatmeh as well as the Communist Party back into the PLO. At the PNC meeting in April 1987, Fatah began to cooperate with the fundamentalist Islamic Jihad and there were even rumours of a secret meeting between Arafat and Abu Nidal in an attempt to broaden the membership of the PLO. The reunification of the PLO provided a clearer focus for Palestinian aspirations than did King Hussein. Yet there were still many rejectionists who remained outside the framework of the PLO, such as Jibril and Abu Musa, who warmed to Syrian and Libyan influence. They condemned UN Resolution 242, Camp David and the Reagan Plan, and denounced Arafat's abstention from international terrorism.

Although Arafat survived and the PLO duly recovered from its self-destructive urge, the movement's lack of direction and political immobility at this time became easy propaganda for the *hasbarah* industry. Clearly, there was an obvious contradiction between endorsing PLO discussions with members of the Israeli peace movement and welcoming Abul Abbas back into the PLO executive, given his complicity in the murder of an elderly Jewish passenger on the *Achille Lauro*. The twin-track approach may well have prevented further schism within the PLO and kept open Arafat's political options, but it also projected the image of an organization that was two-faced and untrustworthy.

As Netanyahu consistently pointed out, 'It must be remembered that what counts with the PLO, as with all dictatorial regimes, is not what it tells the outside world, but what it says to its own people'.[10] This statement regarding the duplicitous nature of the PLO contains a ring of truth which only apologists would dispute. The claims of the Likud that Israeli–PLO discussions amounted to terrorism by other means, which would result in the destruction of the State of Israel, sounded all too credible. Even within the Israeli peace camp there existed doubt about which policies the PLO leadership really espoused. Were they being used by convinced rejectionists in a phased plan to achieve a Greater Palestine? Which was the true face of the PLO? Moreover, such uncertainty undermined both their own efforts amongst Israelis and those of their Palestinian counterparts in the Territories.

The US Congress stipulated that the prime condition for the initiation of an American–PLO dialogue would be the renunciation of terrorism. Few Israelis or Diaspora Jews had any notion of the labyrinthine nature of Palestinian politics. Many were unaware of the multitude of factions, and the differences between those who embraced terrorism and those who distanced themselves from it. The depths of Israeli emotion generated by the massacres and the murders of ordinary people overshadowed the possibility that sections of Fatah were attempting to find a language of rational discussion with Israelis and Jews. All killings were deemed to be the work of the PLO regardless of who had carried them out. No distinction was made between Abu Nidal outside the PLO, the Popular and Democratic Fronts inside, and those who had clearly renounced cross-border and international terrorism. All were lumped together and perceived as one great Satan.

Moreover, in Jewish history the enemy had often been bent on expulsion and extermination – not on compromise, but on extinction. In this psychological realm, the Likud mounted an operation of obfuscation and distortion. Such tactics were not new. One Israeli journalist wrote shortly after the Lebanon war that,

> it is not cynical to conclude that the Israeli government is making use of the bloody deeds of Abu Nidal and his murderers as ammunition in its total war against the PLO, which before and after the war in Lebanon is viewed as the number one enemy – not because it constitutes a military threat or because of the potential damage of its terrorism, but by reason of its political pay-off. In Israel, these tactics are successful because the public is hardly aware of the differences between the various organizations and the deadly rivalries between them: terrorist attacks are carried out by organisations of murderers – and that means the PLO.[11]

Little was done by the official face of Israel to bring such details to public attention. For example, while there was extensive coverage of the large number of atrocities that Abu Nidal had committed, little official information about him was given out. In neither Shamir's autobiography nor Netanyahu's books does the name of Abu Nidal appear once. In real terms, the terrorist mercenary Abu Nidal, the Likud reasoned, was politically unimportant and should therefore be ignored. Likud politicians saw the PLO as the real threat. Coverage of Abu Nidal was left to foreign journalists or Israeli authors. The fact that Abu Nidal was sponsored by Baghdad and Damascus was thus never promoted by the *hasbarah* industry. The fact of this sponsorship was not in doubt; take, for example, the revealing information reported in *The Economist* in October 1982, as part of an interview with Saddam Hussein, which was explicit about Iraq's protection of Abu Nidal. Such reports were allowed to pass without comment.

> Grinning broadly, he [Saddam Hussein] said that Abu Nidal, like any other Arab, was welcome at all times in Baghdad: sometimes he stayed only a day, on other occasions it could be for a week or even a month. It was not the President's business to interfere in his politics. In any event, Abu Nidal was not a terrorist, he was an Arab *munadil*, a struggler.[12]

Thus, the central concern of Likud strategists was not to issue moral condemnation of Abu Nidal but to ensure that his terrorist outrages could be linked to the political aspirations of the PLO. Most Diaspora public-relations organizations – which of course received much of their information from Israel – duly republished the inaccurate material that attributed terrorist incidents to the PLO rather than to Abu Nidal. The efforts to confuse the two organizations were helped by the fact that Abu Nidal had given his own organization a deliberately misleading name: the Fatah Revolutionary Council. For these reasons, then, the PLO often found itself accused by Israelis of actions in which it had played no part. For example, when Pan Am Flight 103 exploded over the small Scottish town of Lockerbie, killing all its 259 passengers and crew, Netanyahu, Arens and Shamir all allocated the blame for this atrocity to the PLO.[13] Such comments were made before any examination of the wreckage had been carried out and after Israeli academic experts had discounted any PLO involvement. Since the PLO had by this time embarked whole-heartedly on the political path and was in the process of dialogue with the Americans, it was highly unlikely that they would risk a confrontation with the United States. If it was the case that Palestinians were involved, they were more likely to belong to one of the rejectionist groups or those in the service of the intelligence services of Libya, Syria or Iraq. Time has indeed shown this to be the case, as Libya is believed by Britain and the United States to have instigated the incident. Others have questioned this official explanation and have implicated Syria and Iran. None has laid the blame at the door of the PLO. It goes without saying that, if the allegation of PLO involvement had been made to stick, the US–PLO dialogue would have ended immediately.

In the summer of 1986, the Likud leadership decided to clamp down on the growing number of contacts between Zionist Israelis and members of the PLO that were taking place in a series of well-publicized conferences and seminars in Europe. Labour support for an amendment to the Law for the Prevention of Terrorism was enlisted in exchange for the Likud's support for an anti-racism bill. (The Israeli left felt very strongly about Kahane's influence in the classroom. Several surveys of high-school students and young people revealed a growing antagonism to and considerable ignorance about their Arab neighbours. Opinion polls disclosed that Meir Kahane would certainly increase his representation in the Knesset at the next election – with one poll citing as many as ten seats.) The amendment to the Law for the Prevention of Terrorism proclaimed that 'a citizen or resident of Israel who knowingly has contact in Israel or abroad, without authorization, with any person who fulfils a function in the executive, council or any body belonging to an organization which the government has declared to be a terrorist organization' was liable to a maximum prison sentence of three years or a fine. The outlawing of the actions of those Israelis who sought dialogue with PLO members was intended to halt any drift towards open negotiation with the Palestinians and the possibility of withdrawal from the Territories. Such legislation allowed both the Likud and the far right to enact a witch-hunt against Israelis who breached or circumvented the law. Some suffered individual harassment, while others, such as the peace campaigner Abie Nathan, were imprisoned for short periods. The amendment to the law banned 'contact' with the PLO, regardless of the purpose of the contact. Even a member of the Likud, bent on remonstrating with the PLO and explaining the Revisionist attachment to Judea and Samaria, was forbidden from engaging in any kind of dialogue.[14] This ban was extended to radio and television to deny to the ordinary Israeli the possibility of hearing what Palestinians thought and believed. Thus, Ehud Ya'ari's interview with Arafat was never broadcast on Israel Television.

This denial of the right to explore even the slimmest of opportunities was perceived by some Israelis as an attack on civil liberties. Israeli government officials even protested to the Bucharest authorities when left-wing Israelis planned to discuss the conflict with PLO Palestinians in Romania. Likud members of the Knesset called for the Israeli delegation's arrest on their return. The very idea that there could be someone to talk to within the PLO was regarded as subversive.

Confusion in the Diaspora

This division of opinion was also reflected in the Diaspora where intellectuals and writers took a stand against the often mindless repetition of official Israeli viewpoints on the part of Jewish leaderships. Even so, Likud leaders took little notice of appeals from international figures such as Sir Isaiah Berlin, Isaac Stern and Saul Bellow, who with others called upon Shamir to accept the Shultz Plan. Shamir termed them 'a discordant minority', openly preferring the views of the often ill-informed herds of young fundraisers, who were more irritated by what they considered to be media misrepresentation than motivated by a considered understanding of the intricacies of internal Israeli politics.[15]

Jewish leaders often complained that Israeli governments of National Unity were very troubling for the Diaspora since they actually had to make a decision as to which policy – either that of Labour or the Likud – they chose to follow. In the rotation government of 1984–88, they tended to support the party which held the premiership. When Peres appealed for American Jewish support for an international conference in May 1987, it fell on deaf ears since Shamir was the Prime Minister at that time. AIPAC, too, vocally refused to take a stand and even the liberal American Jewish Committee and the American Jewish Congress were lukewarm in their support.

The Likud denied Diaspora Jews the right to voice dissenting opinions in public. A majority of Jewish leaders accepted and followed this line. Some followed out of habit, others out of opportunism, and still others out of sheer ignorance of the political situation. Some conservative Jewish leaders argued that Jews did indeed have the right to dissent, but not in areas involving national security where Israelis exerted greater rights than Diaspora Jews. Abe Foxman, a stalwart of the Anti-Defamation League, commented: 'If I dissent, it won't affect my children. That's why I believe that public criticism by American Jews of Israeli security policies is arrogant and irresponsible'.[16] Shamir confirmed this line in a letter to the chairman of the Presidents' Conference of Major Jewish Organizations in 1987. He defined matters such as the existence of the state and security as those which only Israeli citizens could decide upon. But as American Jewish critics pointed out, the issue was in fact all about interpretation. Could Israeli security policies really be separated from the policies of the Israeli government? Yehoshafat Harkabi spoke for many Israelis when he insisted that,

> Israel must distinguish between the fate of Herut's policy and the fate of the State of Israel. There is no cause to assume that the two are inextricably linked. Rejecting the Jabotinsky–Begin ethos has become imperative for Israel's survival.[17]

Others pointed out that Meir Kahane and the Lubavitcher Rebbe had been intervening in Israel's affairs for years without any comment from mainstream organizations. The Likud had actually inherited this policy of quiet compliance from its Labour predecessor. During the Vietnam War, for example, Israeli representatives had attempted to quell vociferous Jewish dissent since they felt that it would ultimately affect the Israeli national interest.

Likud activists went further in blurring the distinction between the state and the government. Criticism of government policies was often transformed into accusations of 'criticism of Israel', 'anti-Zionism' and 'Jewish self-hatred'. Unity was confused with uniformity. Yet demographic surveys among American Jews indicated liberal attitudes towards the issue of returning the Territories providing that Israel's security remained intact. In 1988, an American Jewish Committee survey of 'American Jewish Attitudes towards Israel and Israelis' showed that opinion was split three ways. One third unreservedly supported Israeli government policies and blamed media bias for any problems; another third raised 'severe moral objections' to government policies; while the remaining third preferred to keep their misgivings to themselves, although they did express resentment at the media portrayal of Israel. For most of the 1980s, the Likud managed to keep the lid on mainstream Jewish criticism by invocations of solidarity and the state-of-siege syndrome. The pursuance of *hasbarah*, the campaign to combat terrorism and correct media bias, deflected any attempt to examine the ideological agenda of successive Likud governments. Yet in spite of all this, dialogue groups flourished in Israel and proliferated in the Diaspora during the second half of the decade. For example, in London, a group of British Jews and PLO Palestinians began to meet clandestinely on a monthly basis shortly after the Lebanon war.

The *Jerusalem Post*, the English-language daily, was effectively Israel's window to the wider world. It was also a thorn in Shamir's side, since it projected a critical point of view to the Diaspora as well as to the White House. The paper's liberal credentials and independent stand were often attacked by the Israeli right. It was therefore in the Likud's political interests to undermine this focus of opposition which inhabited such a sensitive position, since it presented a negative image of the Shamir government to the English-speaking world. The *Post*, in the eyes of the Likud, underrepresented the government's approach and failed to play a real part in the *hasbarah* campaign.

During the rotation government, David Radler, the chairman of the Canadian-based Hollinger Corporation, was visiting Jerusalem and asked to see Shamir. The request was turned down and Radler was passed on to an aide, Aryeh Mekel. Radler was a passionate Reaganite while his colleague, Conrad Black, was a great admirer of Margaret Thatcher's policies. Hollinger already owned the British *Daily Tele-*

graph. Radler asked Mekel if there was anything that he could do to help the Likud government. Mekel and another aide, Yossi Ben-Aharon, detailed Shamir's irritation with the *Jerusalem Post.* Two years later, the owner of the newspaper, Koor Industries, which had been established by the Histadrut, decided to sell the *Post* to ward off severe economic difficulties. Britain's Robert Maxwell, together with the North American Bronfman family, were foremost in attempting to purchase the *Post.* On hearing this, Mekel contacted Netanyahu in New York and asked him to visit Radler in Canada. The Hollinger Corporation subsequently bid $16.9 million for 51 per cent of the paper's shares in order to establish control, followed by another $4.6 million later for the rest of the shares,[18] an offer that was duly accepted. This large amount seemed to most observers to be far in excess of the real worth of the *Jerusalem Post.* It did, however, give a measure the ideological commitment on the part of the Hollinger Corporation to help neo-conservative forces worldwide, and especially the Israeli right. Hollinger installed Yehuda Levy, a military man with no background in newspapers, as publisher. This, in turn, led to management intervention and the undermining of editorial independence. The editors of the *Post* soon stepped down and were followed by many of their most experienced reporters. In due course, the *Post* took a sharp turn to the right under its new editorials' editor, David Bar-Illan, who had been appointed to guide the paper in a new direction. Bar-Illan was a former speechwriter for Netanyahu and an organizer of his conferences on terrorism for the Jonathan Institute.

Likud activists were themselves not reticent in pressuring Diaspora Jews to intervene in Israel's internal political scene by endorsing Likud policies through donations to party funds. Fundraising campaigns for the party by figures such as Ehud Olmert reached their apogee during election years. While the Palestinian Diaspora and Gulf petrodollars had effectively fuelled the PLO machine for many years, Jewish donors living overseas were reluctant to publicize the relatively small amounts by comparison which they gave to Israeli political parties. In part, this was due to the fear of being accused of split loyalties. Yet there was also a feeling that such overt political support ran counter to the stand of neutral – indeed explicitly apolitical – philanthropic munificence that was paraded in public. The myth of non-interference would thereby be dispelled.

In 1988, the Israeli State Comptroller made a ruling that information relating to such political donations should be made public. In her annual report for 1988, she stated that 49 donors had each given 50,000 Israeli shekels ($30,000) or more to the election coffers of the party of their choice. Twenty donors had given to the Likud, with the rest supporting the Alignment, with the exception of one Viennese supporter of the Civil Rights Movement. The North American philanthropist Charles Bronfman made a huge donation of $1,250,000 directly to the Peres election campaign in 1988, and the Likud raised between $5 and $6 million in the Diaspora. The Likud's donors included André Marcus, a Swiss businessman; Martin Gross, a New York commodity dealer; Max Landa, a London financier; and Shlomo Zabledovitch, an arms manufacturer in Finland. It was further reported that 'most of the money is not given directly but laundered through institutions like the Golda Meir Foundation on the Labour side and the Tel Hai Fund on the Likud side. These donations have the advantage of being tax deductible whereas direct contributions to the parties do not.'[19]

After the 1992 election, the State Comptroller published an even more detailed report of direct donations to party funds. It listed 49 donors who had given at least $10,000 each to the Likud campaign, making a total of nearly $700,000. Over half the donors lived in the United States. One section dealt with Diaspora donors who gave to more than one party: some had indeed hedged their bets by giving to both Labour and the Likud.[20]

The willingness of Diaspora philanthropists to support the party financially further illustrated the Likud's coming of age and the shedding of its anti-establishment image. This may have been welcomed by Diaspora donors, but it was a development with which some sections of Israel's underclass found difficulty in identifying. They thus turned away from Likud in the 1988 elections to the growing plethora of groups on the far right and to ethnic parties such as Shas.

CHAPTER SIXTEEN

THE YEAR OF RECKONING

Another Victory for the Likud

1989 is remembered as the year that Communism began to enter into its death throes. It was also the year that the seemingly eternal Israel–Palestine conflict turned the psychological and political corner. In 1989, fundamental developments occurred which eventually led to the signing of a peace accord between Rabin and Arafat in September 1993. Unprecedented changes spawned a common language between yesterday's enemies. This, in turn, exerted new pressures on – and within – the pragmatic Likud leadership, which they were forced to confront immediately.

1988 had ended on a relatively good note for Shamir, when the Likud was returned as the party with the most seats in the national elections. The Labour Alignment had fared badly and was forced to play a secondary rather than an equal role in the new National Unity government. This time there would be no rotation of Prime Ministers. The high hopes of a real movement towards reconciliation with the Palestinians that had been generated during Peres' time as Prime Minister dissipated under his successor, Yitzhak Shamir. Moreover, the continuation and indeed escalation of Palestinian terrorism moved the Israeli public to maintain an extremely vigilant attitude.

The advent of the Palestinian Intifada in December 1987 caught the Israeli defence establishment unawares and disconcerted an already worried population. In addition, innumerable acts of revolutionary fervour from a range of PLO sources drowned out any moderate noises. The 'Iron Fist' policy of Shamir and Rabin to suppress the Intifada was applauded by a majority of the Israeli public. Yet this solution had a disquieting effect on those who looked for deeper reasons for this outburst of Palestinian militancy. Despite the Palestinian use of the media to gain maximum political capital from the daily events, the very idea of the Israel Defence Force acting as a police squad appalled a growing minority of Jews in Israel and in the Diaspora. Rabin's approach, however, had the advantage of keeping at bay the far right, which advocated total suppression of the Intifada. In opposition to this controlled approach, there were those in the Likud who advocated a stronger line. Bibi Netanyahu, for example, took exception to the comment made by the head of the IDF, Dan Shomron, that there was no military solution to the Intifada.

In contrast, Labour in 1988 looked unchanged and jaded. Peres, for all his brilliance, had not overcome his image problem. He was still not trusted by the population and his proposal for an international conference and direct negotiations had cut very little electoral ice. The Likud, on the other hand, had taken the political offensive. Early in 1988, Shultz's proposal for negotiations with the Palestinians and an international conference came under direct attack from Netanyahu because the US Secretary of State had met members of the Palestine National Council. The Shultz Plan was effectively scuppered when Shamir told Schultz shortly before the election that UN Resolution 242 was not applicable to negotiations with the Palestinians and Jordanians since the resolution had been 'exhausted' by the withdrawal from Sinai.

Shultz had suggested some revisions to the autonomy plan, such as decreasing the interim period from five to three years and an international conference which would involve face-to-face negotiations with Syria, Lebanon and a joint Jordanian–Palestinian delegation. Despite Shultz's softly-softly approach, Shamir commented that there was no plan as such, only 'ideas'. The stonewalling tactic on the part of the Shamir government was certainly appreciated by the population since it provided a psychological barrier, a breathing space, from the traumas of the Intifada and outside intervention. Even so, there existed a deep public disillusionment with the two major parties. Shamir's political immobility was at the same time a discouragement to anything new and innovative. If Begin-style pyrotechnics were no longer wanted, Shamir at 72 was uninspiring and seemingly unable to move forward. The Likud had in fact lost its radical veneer and was now increasingly seen as just another part of Israel's establishment. Significantly, in Herut's list of candidates for safe seats for the Knesset, not one of the first 40 actually lived in Judea or Samaria. The elections in 1988 indicated a turning away from the two major parties. Taken together, support declined from 85 seats in 1984 to 77 four years later.

The decline in the vote of the Labour Alignment, producing the loss of five seats, was far more dramatic than the relatively static vote for the Likud and its allies on the far right. Despite the fact that the violence of the Intifada favoured the Likud in electoral terms, there was considerable anguish on the left that Peres had still not been able to achieve an election breakthrough after four attempts. Many felt a sense of personal sadness that he had failed, and he was regarded as the symbol of defeat, despite his still powerful standing in the Labour Party. As Foreign Minister for the second half of the rotation government, he had been thwarted at every turn by Shamir. Even the doves in the Labour Party were critical inasmuch as Peres did not take their advice and resign after the London Agreement had been vetoed by Shamir.[1] They were surprised that Peres essentially abandoned his own peace initiative and entered the National Unity government on the Likud's terms. One journalist wrote that, 'only the wings of the planes in which Peres flies have not been clipped'.[2] Moreover, Labour had lost control of the Foreign Ministry to the Likud.

Peres had the misfortune to be espousing liberal policies when Israel seemingly turned to the right in reaction to the Intifada. A Modi'in Ezrachi poll in June 1988 suggested that 41 per cent supported the idea of transferring the Palestinians out of the Territories. What is more, 45 per cent believed that Israel was too democratic, while 55 per cent were against equal rights for Israeli Arabs. King Hussein's decision to renounce political responsibility for the West Bank in the summer of 1988 effectively annulled his grand-father's annexation of the territory nearly 40 years before. It finally sealed the fate of the Jordanian option and it thereby opened up the distinct possibility that Israel would, in due course, deal directly with the PLO. Meanwhile, reflecting on the opprobrium heaped on Arafat and the PLO by Israeli public opinion, Peres was unable to give a clear lead to a worried and confused public. In the popular mind, this fortified the Likud – despite their perceived faults. Shamir was a safer bet: he, at least, was the devil they knew.

The election had come too early for the Palestinians to have spelt out the changes that had been made to their position, or for these to have been perceived by their Israeli adversaries. In the meantime, for the left and the peace camp there was a sense of total impotence arising from the failure to alter Israeli perceptions. Amos Oz raged against 'the tragic fossilization of most political thought in Israel', and blamed Golda Meir for laying the psychological foundations of the notion of the Palestinians' non-existence – and thereby preparing the way for the ideological victory of the Right.[3]

The major unexpected development in the 1988 elections was the rise in the vote of the religious parties, which increased their representation in the Knesset by 50 per cent. With an all-time high of 18 seats, they benefited from a swing away from the nationalist camp. This was in part an expression of Sephardi ethnicity, but it was also a symptom of disillusionment with secular culture – identified with both the state and its major parties. It marked the recognition that the Likud had moved away from Begin's traditionalism. With the decline of idealism, many looked for a new spiritual home. Unlike Zionist ideology, an interpretative religion such as Judaism could explain all phenomena. In addition, the religious parties were no longer dominated by the heirs of Mizrachi, the religious Zionist movement. Instead, the ultra-orthodox *haredi* parties were in the ascendancy. Although they lived and took part in the affairs of the state, their ideological beliefs ranged from anti-Zionism to non-Zionism. Unlike Gush Emunim, they did not believe that the establishment of the state and victory in the Six Day War heralded the era of redemption. Some strongly believed that the State of Israel was merely a transient phenomenon, a Zionist carbuncle on the face of Judaism, and would be superseded by the real thing when the Messiah arrived.

The early leaders of the state certainly had to contend with the ultra-orthodox in their time, but the numbers were far smaller then and their influence was virtually negligible. The *haredim* coexisted with the state rather than integrating into it. In the 1950s, Moshe Sharett was invited as the Prime Minister to attend the convention of Agudat Yisrael. When Sharett mounted the podium, the doyen of the party and a much revered religious figure, the Gerer Rebbe refused to stand and instead covered his face with a handkerchief – a Biblical gesture – so as not to look directly at the Prime Minister, the symbol of the Zionist state and secularism. Since that time, Prime Ministers of Israel have rarely been invited to such meetings and conventions. Parties such as Agudat Yisrael and Degel Ha'Torah are more concerned with the world of Jewish learning and acquiring funds to maintain their ever-expanding institutions and seminaries. It is this need for continuous financing and the authority of their rabbis' rulings that have guided the decisions of their representatives in the Knesset rather than any strong feelings about land or peace.

The Lubavitcher Rebbe, Menachem Schneerson, resident in Brooklyn, advised those of his followers who held Israeli passports to fly to Israel from all over the world and to vote for Agudat Yisrael in the 1988 election. His formidable opponent, Rabbi Eliezer Menachem Schach, a leading figure of the Lithuanian school of Torah study, had broken with Agudat Yisrael. He formed his own party, Degel Ha'Torah – the Flag of the Torah – and urged his followers to vote for it. Schneerson was by then in his late 80s, while Schach was in his mid-90s. Thus, many *haredim* hitherto in retreat from the world stepped back and into the polling booths at the behest of their rabbis. The spiritual leader of Shas, (Sephardi Torah Guardians), Rabbi Ovadia Yosef, had wider ambitions. He had founded the party in 1984 not simply to generate and receive funds for yeshivot, but as a vehicle to ameliorate the social conditions of the Sephardim. In contrast to his constituency – many of whom were formerly Likud voters – the rabbi was a political dove who had made a number of moderate statements over the years. His televisual blessings over the airwaves to potential Shas voters and inspired campaigning succeeded in increasing the party's standing to six seats in 1988.

The religious parties were thus, in the main, both religiously and politically hawkish in 1988. A new dovish religious party, Meimad – the creation of religious intellectuals and Western immigrants – was formed for the election, to promote tolerance and peace. It failed abysmally at the polls. During the negotiations to form a new administration, the controversial issue of 'Who is a Jew?' was soon raised by the Likud's potential religious partners in government. They defined the sense of belonging to the Jewish people in *halakhic* terms through matrilineal descent. The rabbis wished to incorporate this *halakhic* principle into the Law of Return – which allowed anyone who considered him- or herself Jewish to emigrate to Israel. The accompanying uproar in the Diaspora produced widespread protest and a plethora of anguished visiting delegations – particularly from the Reform movement whose conversions were not recognized by the Orthodox. This and the threat of losing American Jewish donations to the state and to his party, made an impression on the secular Shamir. His choices were strictly limited: he could either form an administration with the far-right parties and accept the demands of the rabbis, or he could continue with another National Unity government. The pragmatic Likud leadership of Shamir and Arens decided that Labour as a partner would be preferable and would present fewer problems.

Palestinian Changes

The Intifada and Rabin's attempt to contain it changed perceptions of the Palestinians in Western minds. Once more, they were seen as the underdog in the Israel–Palestine conflict. The Shamir government increasingly came in for international condemnation and was the catalyst for the growth of an ever vociferous Israeli peace movement. The international media no longer emphasized the image of the PLO as a terrorist organization, but instead depicted Israel as a foreign occupier suppressing a civil uprising. Thus, the Intifada had once more focused the world's attention on the Palestinian problem and at once served to strengthen Arafat's position within the PLO. This happened at a time when the use of terrorism to publicize the Palestinian case was bringing diminishing returns politically.

Ironically, the Intifada arose despite the PLO and not because of it. The first mass opposition by the Palestinians to Israeli rule since the Six Day War, it was carried out by the post-1967 generation, who had been influenced by the occupation in so far as they were much more worldly, assertive and independent than their parents. Some 60 per cent of the inhabitants of the Territories had been born after the Six Day War and a further 20 per cent were still only children when it broke out. These young Palestinian city dwellers looked neither to the old established families nor to Tunis for leadership. The symbolic leadership of the PLO was accepted, but the National Unified Command of the uprising was an indigenous body which made its own decisions. Advice could be given by the PLO, but did not necessarily need to be taken.

The intellectual leadership of the Palestinians around Faisal Husseini urged Arafat to make the most of this turnaround of events in the Territories by espousing a political programme which would allow for an Israeli response. Arafat and his chief advisors, however, found it exceedingly difficult to respond to the new situation. Like Shamir, they looked to the past rather than to the future. For too long, they had been prisoners of their own inconsistencies and were roped in by their own propaganda. As early as January 1988, Husseini had suggested that the PLO declare a State of Independent Palestine which would invest its authority in a ruling body, half of whose representatives would come from the Territories and the other half from the PLO in Tunis. Municipal elections would be held and deportations would end. Following this path, Husseini argued, would result in a peace agreement with Israel. For some time, however, Arafat resisted the temptation and the subsequent risk that changing his hardline position involved.[4] Yet in June, a former member of the Popular Front for the Liberation of Palestine, Bassam abu Sharif, who was close to Arafat, told an Arab summit that the PLO's prime objective should be the achievement of a Palestinian state and not the destruction of the Israeli one. This change of emphasis and the desire to pursue a political path towards a two-state solution did not please hardliners within Fatah such as Abu Iyad or PLO rejectionists such as Habash and Hawatmeh.

King Hussein's decision, a few weeks later, to cut legal and administrative links with the West Bank produced a vacuum which the PLO had to fill. Any new ideas had to be aimed at convincing its own people – including the rejectionists and the dissenters – as well as a section of Israeli public opinion. The White House, for its part, looked for a renunciation of terrorism, recognition of Israel, and the acceptance of Resolution 242 as the preconditions for opening a dialogue with the PLO. The PLO's new programme reverted, ironically, to a formal acceptance of partition, in that it endorsed UN Resolution 181 of 1947, which proposed both a Palestinian and a Jewish state. Both Menachem Begin and the Irgun, and Yitzhak Shamir and Lehi, had at the time virulently opposed the Labour movement's acceptance of the resolution and the partition of Western Eretz Israel. Now, over 40 years later, there came an implicit Palestinian acceptance of that partition. Although Ben-Gurion had agreed to partition, the Palestinians and the Arab world had found common cause – for clearly different reasons – with Begin in opposing it. Now history had finally caught up with the Palestinians, who on the face of it seemed to be giving up their maximalist aspirations, renouncing the dream of a Greater Palestine, and joining the minimalists. This, the Likud realized, could form the basis for negotiations between the minimalists of both sides. It was therefore in the interests of maximalists on both sides to prevent this coalescence.

The Palestine National Council's meeting in Algiers in November 1988 bore witness to the theatricality of the Declaration of Palestinian Independence. The fine print punctured all the pomp and circumstance, however, since it soon became clear that ambiguity and ambivalence coloured all official PLO declarations and pronouncements. On the one hand, there was a qualified acceptance of UN Resolution 242. On the other hand, there were bellicose references to the armed struggle and 'the Zionist entity'. The PLO rejected terrorism but seemed to glory in its own violence of the mid-1980s.

The bottom line was that it could mean all things to all parties, be they American diplomats or Palestinian rejectionists. Arafat clearly did not wish to split the PLO and obviously wanted to ensure his own survival.

Behind the scenes, the Americans urged Arafat to be specific; and he duly gave private assurances to American Jewish peace activists at a meeting in Stockholm. Publicly, however, Arafat seemed unable to accept partition and to renounce terrorism. An agreed promise to expound the new line failed to materialize at the special UN General Assembly session in Geneva in December. Arafat found it very difficult to give up the phraseology of an insecure existence, the habits of a lifetime. The symbiotic relationship between that part of him which advocated peace and coexistence and that which advocated an end to the Zionist enemy through armed struggle had now outlived its expediency. After 20 years of conflict, there was little to show for it in concrete terms. Israel was thriving and the Palestinians had moved in every direction except forward. For the inhabitants of the camps, who lived in squalor and deprivation, there was no amelioration of the Palestinian condition.

At a subsequent press conference in Geneva – and presumably under intense pressure from the Arab world and his own advisors – Arafat took the psychological leap and stated his acceptance of the rights of all parties to exist in peace and security in the region and renounced all forms of terrorism, 'including individual, group and state terrorism'. The deed was finally done and within hours the White House announced the commencement of a US–PLO dialogue. Shamir's observation on Arafat's speech at Geneva was that 'the PLO is inherently incapable of accepting US conditions which contradict its very existence'. The Likud response was that the statements were mere subterfuge, aimed at deceiving the United States and Israel. Palestinian rejectionists also repudiated the Geneva press conference and claimed that Arafat had actually gone against PLO policy as determined in Algiers. Even within Fatah, the new line was interpreted by some as a means to dismember Israel in stages. Some suggested that UN Resolution 181 could be interpreted selectively in that it only recognized the establishment of a Palestinian state and bypassed the recognition of a Jewish state. At the Fatah Congress in August 1989, journalists were barred because the discussions featured the old intransigent language of the past. There was no mention of UN resolution 181 within its implicit recognition of a Jewish state and selective interpretation of the line of the Algiers PNC. Arafat's cautious approach seemed to preclude promoting the new line amongst the Palestinian faithful.

The confusion and unease within the PLO concerning the true meaning of Algiers and Geneva allowed Netanyahu to use selected statements of hardliners and rejectionists as well as those of Arafat himself to suggest that the PLO's alleged recognition of Israel's right to exist was a mechanism for an ongoing deception. He argued that the erroneous perceptions of the Western media had all been produced by rhetorical legerdemain. The magic words which 'were extracted from the PLO [by the Americans] the way one pulls a tooth' did not, he insisted, amount to much.[5] Netanyahu chose to accentuate the negative while eliminating the positive. His easy dissection of Arafat's speeches and his condemnation of 'declaration and retraction' was predicated on the belief that the main aim of the PLO was merely 'to conquer Washington'. He believed that the PLO agenda rested on their belief that only the Americans could bring pressure to bear on Israel. The following years were to prove that Netanyahu's fear of the Americans was essentially justified.

The Bush administration was forthright in its approach to Israel where its predecessor had simply gone through the motions. The PLO, for its part, believed that it could remain unchanging in its relations with the Arab world and could – more often than not – count on the USSR. It consequently believed that it could resist American pressure whereas Israel could not. Yet no one could have foreseen Saddam Hussein's invasion of Kuwait or anticipated the Gulf War and its effect on the Arab world. The realignment of former enemies and the isolation of the PLO by the oil-rich states severely weakened the Palestinians. The swift extinction of the Soviet Union and its Eastern European satellites removed another pillar of support. American pressure therefore came to count for far more in 1991 than the PLO would have believed in 1988.

The PLO was certainly pleased that it had achieved its long-term aim of securing official discussions with the Americans. But it was far from clear what the organization wanted from this new situation. Some wanted an international conference, while others thought that the Americans could bring about a unilateral Israeli withdrawal from the Territories. Some truly accepted the two-state solution, while others saw it as a means to regain the whole of Mandatory Palestine. Others seemed to hold maximalist and minimalist views virtually simultaneously. Netanyahu and other Likud leaders viewed the confusion in the PLO as the inevitable price that the Palestinians had to pay in order to catalyse American action on the Israel–Palestine conflict and ultimately to place pressure on Israel. The Israeli public, however, reacted favourably to Arafat's pronouncements at Geneva; a newspaper poll suggested that 54 per cent were willing to enter into talks with the PLO.[6] The official Likud counterattack therefore set out to exploit the contradictions and confusion at every turn and thereby undermine the US–PLO dialogue in the hope that it would finally fall apart. Another way of achieving this was to show that the PLO had not in fact renounced terrorism.

Interpreting Palestinian Terrorism

The third component of the Israel–United States equation was American Jewry. Even before the Palestinian Declaration of Independence, American Jewish leaders were finding it more and more difficult to support the Shamir government. The growing gap between their public statements and private views became increasingly troublesome. Years of acting out the policies of others had taken their toll. Now a difficult bridge had to be crossed. Diaspora Jews were deeply divided, and American Jews were no exception. Even Israel's friends in Congress began to take issue with the direction of the Israeli government – especially over its 'Iron Fist' policy. When 30 US senators protested in a letter in March 1988, Netanyahu complained that if such a situation continued, any future Israeli government of whatever political stripe would lose the ability to command support in Congress. 'The letter represents a very serious breach of principle that has not been breached before. We have never before incorporated [Israeli] partisan politics in the US in this very dangerous way'.[7] For Netanyahu, what mattered was not the substance of the criticism, but the effect on the political lobby. In the Likud, the complaints of Diaspora Jews about Israeli government policy were considered at best an irrelevance, at worst an irritation. They only mattered when they led to a refusal to act upon Likud directives to expound a specific policy or to pressure the American administration. Thus, when no American Jewish organization – including the right-wing Zionist Organization of America – forcefully condemned the White House for initiating the US–PLO dialogue, the Likud leadership believed that their authority in directing the Diaspora's Israel policy had been severely undermined. There was clearly reticence on the part of American Jewry to criticize Reagan and Shultz or subsequently to get off to a bad start with the new Bush administration.

Some of the more conservative leaders eventually issued a number of meaningless and diversionary statements. The chairman of the Presidents' Conference, which had close ties with Jerusalem, pointed out that there would be no progress if the PLO Charter was not revoked. Others like the ADL's Abe Foxman openly said that he did not believe the PLO, and suggested that the role of the Jewish Community was 'to keep the administration honest and remind it of its commitments', and these included opposing an imposed settlement and an independent Palestinian state.[8] There was thus initially no direct opposition to the dialogue, only advice by some of the more conservative organizations to proceed cautiously and not to pressure Israel into dealing with the PLO. When Arens asked the Presidents' Conference in February 1989 to condemn the US–PLO dialogue, they publicly came up with a mild request to President Bush to reassess the situation. Even Netanyahu's plea to the Conference that the Likud government was being subjected to 'tremendous propaganda and political pressure' was only heeded by its more right-wing constituents. Nevertheless, the Presidents' Conference and the ADL began at this time to monitor Arafat's pronouncements more closely and to compile details of terrorist incidents. If the intention was to prove to the new US administration that the PLO had violated the terms of the dialogue, then it was not difficult for Shamir's government and its US supporters to locate evidence. They also tried to persuade more liberal Jewish organizations that any public perception of weakening Jewish support for Israel would have serious implications for the future of American–Israeli relations.

The campaign to undermine the dialogue was not only carried out by the Likud Foreign Ministry and certain American Jewish organizations. Palestinian rejectionists inside and outside the PLO, as well as the radical Arab States, also wished to see it collapse. Although Rabin reported to the Knesset that Fatah had not conducted cross-border attacks on Israel, the same could not be said of the PFLP, DFLP and PLF – all of whom were represented on the PLO executive. Arafat's interpretation of a renunciation of terrorism was the stopping of such cross-border raids into Israel. (He had formally abandoned international terrorism in the Cairo Declaration of November 1985.) Arafat's lack of control over Palestinian actions inside Israel and the Territories meant that he had no option but to define all incidents within these borders as part of the ongoing armed struggle. His lack of authority over the rejectionists within the PLO was indicated by the fact that the vast majority of cross-border attacks were being carried out by them alone. The Israeli government press office released figures showing that attacks within Israel and the Territories had risen 9.4 per cent in 1989 compared to the previous year. The number of cross-border incidents, however, had fallen from 50 to 33 in 1989. Fatah outside the Territories heeded Arafat and ceased attacks across the borders; however, Fatah within the Territories – where it was less under the control of Tunis – continued with the Intifada. Even if Arafat had wished to call for an end to incidents within Israel and the Territories, it is highly doubtful that this would have been heeded by the youthful Palestinian footsoldiers of the Intifada. The Likud government clearly perceived that the rejectionists were Arafat's Achilles' heel. Whereas Labour was willing to recognize that the mainstream Fatah had ceased its cross-border attacks, this was an irrelevant fact to the Likud. Indeed, to them it was merely inconvenient that Dan Shomron, the head of the IDF, had told the Knesset Foreign Affairs and Defence Committee that there was no evidence that Fatah had participated in cross-border incidents. The Likud's main task, then, was to attach responsibility to Arafat and Fatah for the actions of the rejectionists in the hope of diverting their political trajectory and wrecking the dialogue with the United States. Arafat inadvertently aided this perception by always refusing to condemn those sections of the PLO which had not renounced cross-border terrorism. In this, he clearly violated the original US guidelines, which required the leader's clear denunciation of such actions when they occurred.

In a State Department report in March 1990, the Americans reported that they felt that none of the cross-border attacks were made with the knowledge of Arafat and that he was clearly unable to control his rejectionist factions. They also believed that the Intifada was not controlled by the PLO in Tunis but was under the direction of 'indigenous elements who look to the PLO for political support and coordination, but operate by and large independently on a day to day basis'. Shamir labelled the report 'tendentious', while the ADL in New York, which had been monitoring Palestinian terrorism, called it 'flawed on many counts'. In a report of their own, the ADL held Arafat accountable for the activities of the rejectionists, including their cross-border raids and several incidences of Fatah attacks within Israel itself. Shamir's office reported that, in the year after Arafat's declaration of a Palestinian state, there had been 79 attacks by Fatah operatives against Israeli civilians.[9] The sharply differing interpretations reflected diametrically opposed views regarding current PLO strategy,

Arafat's grandiose proclamations notwithstanding. The Likud and their allies in the American Jewish community adopted a fundamentalist approach: they stood by the letter of the PLO's pronouncements. The White House preferred to accept the spirit of the PLO leadership's actions. Both sides were selective in their deliberations. Clearly, the ADL wanted to find the PLO guilty as charged. On the other hand, mistakes were sometimes made. Both the ADL and the Israeli government press office pointed to two Fatah-sponsored cross-border attacks in the Negev in February and December 1989 and berated the State Department for failing to draw due attention to them. These actions were, in fact, the work of former Fatah members who had gone over to the Islamic Fundamentalists following Arafat's pronouncements in Algiers and Geneva. Yet these incidents emphasized the continuing differences of opinion within Fatah itself.[10]

The US–PLO dialogue itself did not actually get very far in 1989; indeed it quickly ground to a discouraging halt. Yet the very fact of this level of contact represented an ideological and political danger for the Likud if the attempts at *rapprochement* were not quickly suppressed. Despite the lack of progress in the talks throughout 1989 and 1990, the Shamir government, together with domestic Jewish organizations, strenuously lobbied in Congress to weaken the dialogue by dissecting every Palestinian action and word. As rejectionist attacks increased across the Lebanese border, Congressional pressure against the dialogue mounted. When Egypt privately asked Arafat to condemn such attacks, he pleaded 'the frail unity of the PLO'. In September 1989, 68 senators sent a letter to President Bush opposing a visa for Arafat on the grounds that he had retreated from his original obligation to condemn terrorism. Jewish organizations that supported the Shamir government proceeded to endorse the Helms Amendment. This threatened a cessation of the dialogue should any party involved be found to have 'directly participated in the planning or execution of a particular terrorist activity which resulted in the death or kidnapping of an American citizen'. This attempt to create a linkage between the past and the present was defeated because there were still many in Congress and in the Jewish community itself who were willing to allow the PLO an opportunity to show that it had indeed embarked on the political road. Yet the combination of no progress in the dialogue, the ongoing cross-border attacks of the rejectionists, and the selective categorization of information by pro-Israel government organizations forced even those who were originally sympathetic to the idea of eventual negotiations with the PLO to think again.

The Mack-Lieberman legislation obliged the US State Department to report three times a year on PLO compliance. The State Department had few allies willing to challenge the selectivity of the Likud version of compliance. Thus they too were forced to become selective and to hide behind ambiguous phraseology to protect the faltering dialogue. For the State Department, what were once 'conditions' had now become 'expectations'. An emboldened Netanyahu attacked the Bush administration on IDF Radio for 'engaging in a policy based on lies and distortions'.[11]

On 30 May 1990, the Palestine Liberation Front launched an incompetent and badly planned assault from the sea at Nitzanim beach near the Tel Aviv seafront, which was crowded with holidaymakers celebrating a Jewish festival. Fortunately, this instance of cross-border terrorism was stopped before there were any casualties. But it bore all the hallmarks of an attempt to deliver the death blow to the moribund dialogue and to tarnish severely the growing respectability of the PLO in the West. Abul Abbas – of *Achille Lauro* infamy and prominent figure of American demonology – had been brought out of seclusion to launch the PLF on a seaborne expedition. Libya had supplied the naval back-up, while Iraqi intelligence had sponsored the plan. The entire episode had been hastily put together, with ill-informed Palestinian youngsters deployed as cannon-fodder. Rather than launch yet another failed attack along the Lebanese border, the plan was to achieve international publicity through the mass slaughter of civilians at a well-known seaside resort in the heart of the country.

The day after the incident, 33 senators sent a letter to Secretary of State Baker to denounce the attack and to request the expulsion of Abul Abbas from the PLO. Even liberal Jewish organizations such as the World Jewish Congress were aghast at the political consequences of the PLF attack. US diplomats met PLO officials four times in an attempt to persuade them to condemn the attack and to expel Abul Abbas from the PLO executive. The PLO refused, and on 20 June 1990 Bush suspended the dialogue. Eighteen months of dialogue had proved futile. The PLO's standing had in fact worsened. The inner composition of the PLO had led to political paralysis. From the other side, pressure from the Israeli government had made the State Department cautious. By 1990, this static situation had weakened Arafat's position both within the Territories and within the PLO itself. Once more, Arafat moved – this time, away from political compromise to seek the hardline support of Iraq's Saddam Hussein.

CHAPTER SEVENTEEN

THE SHAMIR PLAN

The New Secretary of State

In 1988 and 1989, opinion polls showed that a majority of both the Israeli public and American Jewish community were willing to give the PLO an opportunity to show that they had indeed turned away from terrorism and were following the road of political compromise. It was a development which the new Bush administration followed up enthusiastically, having inherited a legacy of formal contacts with the PLO from the Reagan–Shultz era. Unfortunately for the Likud, this new conjunction of events coincided with changes that proved to be beyond its control.

The new Bush administration was more aware of the Arab world than was its predecessor. Despite the fact of overwhelming Jewish support for the Democratic Party, in line with their shared espousal of liberal values, Ronald Reagan projected a personal inclination to support Israel. Bush, though, was far more of a classic Republican. He felt strongly about America's inherent right to the oil reservoirs of Saudi Arabia and Kuwait – as he was later to show in his prosecution of the Gulf War. The gradual ending of the Cold War and the slow death of Communism persuaded Bush to turn his attention to the volatile Middle East. If America's oil interests in the Gulf were to be safeguarded, then there obviously had to be a measure of stability in the region. His association with the CIA had made him aware that failure to resolve the Israel–Palestine problem and a continuation of the Intifada would encourage the rise of Islamic militancy. Bush remembered that the Carter administration had been humiliated by Ayatollah Khomeini and he therefore continued strongly to support Saddam Hussein in his ill-conceived war against Iran.

Shamir perceived the Bush administration to be projecting a 'less than neutral attitude towards the PLO', and viewed the new Secretary of State, James Baker, as an 'ever-inflexible pragmatist'.[1] This was indicative of the changing relationship between the two countries. The sense of moral commitment forged in the aftermath of the Holocaust and during the establishment of the state had given way to Israel's transformation into a 'strategic asset' during the Reagan years. The formal alliance and mutual understanding had arisen very much at Begin's behest. It followed that, if the moral basis of Israel's relationship with the United States had indeed been diminished, there was no good reason why the Bush administration should not pursue its own interests in the Middle East conflict.

The Likud component of the new National Unity government had to respond to this development in the White House or be overtaken by events. For a political vacuum now existed due to King Hussein's political withdrawal from the West Bank. Some, like Dan Meridor, advocated talks with the West Bank leadership in the hope of finding a solution and at the same time splitting them away from the PLO in Tunis. The Likud pragmatists had to steer a path which would appear eminently reasonable to the Israeli public, to its Labour Party partner in government, and to the international community in general, whilst not antagonizing the anti-Shamir factions within Likud and the far right in general. Peres and Rabin had agreed to join the Likud as part of the National Unity government for a probationary period of nine months. If there was no breakthrough to peace at the end of that time, they stipulated that they would both resign from the government. Shamir was thus under pressure from Labour as well as from America and the participants of the Intifada to find a solution.[2]

The Shamir Plan was not really Shamir's plan. Shamir's instinctive reaction to Arafat's declarations in Algiers and Geneva and the initiation of dialogue was to create a smokescreen of activity but to give little away. This was not the approach of the new Likud Foreign Minister, Moshe Arens. Unlike Shamir, he espoused traditional Revisionist principles and the liberal democratic principles of Jabotinsky. He understood that the present situation could not continue forever and that a practical solution had to be formulated. Moreover, Arens placed security before ideology. Indeed, he believed that Gaza had never been a part of Israel and was less concerned about the British Mandate definition of the borders of the Jewish state.[3] Thus Arens proposed the Shamir Plan to Shamir. It specified that the peace process would be based on the Camp David Accords and UN Resolutions 242 and 338, and that there would be no participation by the

PLO and no Palestinian state. Negotiations on the final status of the Territories would commence after three years of interim arrangements. The most significant part of the Shamir Plan was the staging of elections to select Palestinian negotiators to sit with Israel during the interim settlement.

The very attraction of elections divided Shamir's Israeli opponents. Some believed that it was an advance, whilst others interpreted it as just another smokescreen tactic to draw out the proceedings. In one sense, these reactions reflected the respective approaches of Arens and Shamir. Naturally, the leaders of the Labour Party, Finance Minister Shimon Peres and Defence Minister Yitzhak Rabin, reacted positively. Rabin, in particular, had been consulted in the later stages of the formulation of the plan. There were some in the Likud, like Dan Meridor, who strongly supported Arens and the proposals of the Shamir Plan. Others on the right of the party, such as Sharon, were opposed. The Shamir Plan certainly unnerved the settlers, who were already worried about the prominence of the emerging Palestinian leadership under Faisal Husseini and its acceptance by the Likud government. Some settlers connected with Meir Kahane's Kach even suggested that ties with Israel should be severed and a new State of Judea established in the Territories. Above all, though, the Shamir Plan cast light on the political immobility of the Palestinians. They were now forced to respond to Shamir's initiative.

Before the plan was presented to President Bush, it was important to re-entrench American and Diaspora Jewry in its support for the National Unity government – which, in reality, meant support for Likud's approach to the Israel–Palestine conflict. US Jewry's lack of commitment to participation in the campaign to undermine the US–PLO dialogue sounded warning bells in the Likud. Not only did there appear to be a difference between the US and Israeli governments on a major issue – that of acknowledging that the PLO could be potential negotiating partners. It also seemed that the US Jewish leadership had reached a crossroads in terms of decision-making. With the exception of liberal organizations such as the American Jewish Congress and the American Jewish Committee, there had hitherto been a refusal to commit US Jewry to policies other than that of the Israel government. The refusal to recognize the fact that no consensus for Likud policies existed in either Israel or in the American Jewish community had finally been overcome. American Jewish leaders now had to choose whether or not to follow a line that was independent of, and substantially different from, that of the Israeli government.

Thus it was that, from the beginning of 1989, the leadership began to reflect the more liberal views of the American Jewish community at large, and perhaps even to act on the basis of their own personal convictions.

The Likud's vehicle for drumming up Diaspora support for the National Unity government in preparation for Shamir's visit to the White House was The Prime Minister's Conference of Jewish Solidarity with Israel.[4] The very title of the conference betrayed a sense of political insecurity, since it was absurd to suggest that most Jews did not express solidarity with Israel on a continuous basis. It also illustrated the fact that it was felt necessary to display support for the government as the Diaspora mainstream began to voice dissent. Peres surprisingly agreed to the staging of the conference. Yet it was predicated on the basis of support for the National Unity government – and therefore differences of opinion would only be permitted within the parameters of the Likud–Labour divide. Those who supported the peace movement or the far right were effectively barred from the conference. It was therefore a safe, orchestrated affair. Even so, only a fraction of the delegates invited were able to attend at such short notice while a number of Diaspora grandees actively boycotted it. Moreover, those who did attend tended to be compliant communal leaders and unthinking philanthropists. Youth and the intelligentsia were effectively ignored. Ironically, the international media gave as much coverage to those Jewish critics of Shamir's policies who had not been invited as to those who willingly listened to one ministerial speech after another at the conference. Clearly, the event was less than successful in conveying an image of unity and solidarity to Bush and to American Jewry.

The build-up to Shamir's visit to the White House to present the plan was further coloured by a statement from Bush that Israel should end its occupation of the West Bank. Shamir also dampened expectations by dismissing any comparison between Sadat's peace initiative in 1977 and the PLO's apparent turning over of a new political leaf. Indeed, he went considerably further and threatened to imprison Arafat if he flew to Israel to talk about peace. 'Hitler and Arafat belong to the same family of demagogues', Shamir said, 'enemies of the Jewish people who think nothing of killing millions in order to achieve their objective.'[5] Yet this rhetoric apparently fell on deaf ears; for a Smith Research Centre poll revealed that 58 per cent of Israelis would favour talks with the PLO if it officially recognized Israel and ceased terrorist activities.[6]

Although Bush welcomed Shamir's plan, he asked him to submit concrete proposals for the elections. The resigned tolerance for Likud policies which the Reagan presidency had found an acceptable response now dissipated with the promotion of James Baker to Secretary of State. After Geneva, there was clearly an impetus to solve both the Israeli–Palestinian and the Israeli–Arab conflicts. Unlike their predecessors, the new holders of office did not mince their words. This Republican administration decided that it had little need of the Jewish community either in terms of votes or in donations. After all, since the time of the New Deal, American Jews, irrespective of their increasing affluence, had always shown great loyalty to the liberal principles of the Democratic Party. Indeed, only American Blacks voted proportionately in greater numbers for the Democrats. By 1989, the no-nonsense approach of Baker soon made the Reagan era seem like a golden age in US–Israeli relations.

Acknowledgement of the new tough approach by Bush and Baker unsettled the divided American Jewish leadership. Their division was all too obvious when half of them decided to meet Hosni Mubarak while the other half stayed away – all because the Egyptian president refused to meet Shamir when both leaders were in the United States. The chairman of the Presidents' Conference, Seymour Reich, tried to counteract the new language emanating from the White House: 'The President's use of the word "occupation" was very disturbing. "Occupation" and "occupier" are harsh words that do not take into account the historical context in which Israel came into control of Judea and Samaria.'[7] The enthusiastic espousal of the Shamir Plan by conservative elements of the American Jewish leadership was based in part on the assumption that it would divert attention from the 'land for peace' scenario. Moreover, when Shamir addressed the Presidents' Conference, he was at pains to swing the liberals behind his plan. Thus, for the American Jewish Congress, the idea of Palestinian elections was very appealing. Shamir even provided touches of moderation in referring to Judea and Samaria as the 'administered territories'.

The pleasantries which Bush and Shamir exchanged during their meeting belied the resolve by the White House to 'get tough' with Israel and the Palestinians. The Israeli–American honeymoon, which had begun in 1948, had worn thin following the rise of the Likud to power in 1977. Whereas Begin could impress and deflect Carter and mollycoddle Reagan, Shamir's quiet and determined, yet often unsophisticated, stonewalling seemed to outrage the Americans. Moreover, the special relationship between the two countries had been based in part on memories of the past – and the past was remembered by fewer and fewer people. The Likud understood that once again they would have to struggle using all possible means to retain Israeli sovereignty over Judea and Samaria. As one Shamir aide to the Washington talks exclaimed to the press: 'We know what the game is. Nobody is going to get Shamir pregnant.'[8]

The following month, Baker was invited by AIPAC, the main lobby organization for Israel on Capitol Hill, to address them. His speech called for American support for the 'reasonable middle ground'. His appeal to the Arab world to end violence, reach out to Israel, end its economic boycott of Israel, and repudiate the UN Resolution that 'Zionism is Racism' were all well received by the delegates. He further admonished the Arabs for believing that the United States would 'deliver Israel' to them. He also did not overtly circumvent the Shamir Plan when he said that 'a properly constructed international conference would be useful at an appropriate time, but only if it did not interfere with or in anyway replace or be a substitute for direct Arab–Israeli talks'. His next remarks, however, were heard in total silence. He told the AIPAC delegates that Israel should turn aside from 'the unrealistic vision of a Greater Israel, forswear annexation, stop settlement activity, allow schools to open, and reach out to Palestinians as neighbours who deserve political rights', and that 'land for peace' was the only genuine channel for a real peace process. The term 'Greater Israel' had never before been used by a US representative despite American opposition since 1967 to settlements in the Territories. The term had hitherto been the prerogative of the Israeli peace movement, and its use by Baker clearly indicated the influence of Peace Now ideas on the State Department.

New Pressure from the Right

On a visit to London, Shamir termed the Baker speech 'useless and unhelpful' – 'treif' (not kosher). He and his allies in the American Jewish leadership were disturbed by the 'no-holds barred language' of this political bombshell. Shamir also commented that Baker's words would reinforce 'Israel's extremists and weaken the National Unity government'. Such a comment was not only directed at Peace Now and the dovish wing of the Labour Party, but also at the increasingly restless far right both within the Likud and outside it.

Both Levy and Modai were sceptical about the Shamir Plan when it was discussed on Shamir's return. Together with Sharon, they voted against the Plan at a Cabinet meeting in May 1989. Levy was trying to position himself as a leadership contender and probably opposed it out of sheer frustration at continually being marginalized by Shamir. Modai was trying to redefine the Liberal faction of the Likud, whose identity was rapidly being lost within the new merged party. With Sharon, the standard-bearer of the far right within the Likud, they formed the 'Constraints Ministers'. They were referred to by their opponents within the Likud as 'a coalition of ambition',[9] yet they represented a formidable opposition to the pragmatic Arens group in the Likud. They counted on the support of the newly formed Eretz Israel Front of Knesset members from Techiya, Tsomet, Moledet, the National Religious Party and the right wing of Likud – all of whom refused to make any concessions. In an advertisement in the Israeli press on the day following the Cabinet vote, the Front charged that 'elections would be a submission to terrorism' and would lead to a relinquishing of the right to all of Western Eretz Israel and to the foundation of a Palestinian state. They stipulated that the Intifada would have to cease before elections could be staged. Moreover, since Jerusalem was a united city under Israeli sovereignty, no Arab inhabitant of East Jerusalem would be permitted to vote. Thirty Knesset members signed the statement, including Netanyahu, who, despite being deputy Foreign Minister under Arens, was beginning to cultivate his own leadership chances.[10]

Techiya proposed a vote of no confidence – in which all the right-wing nationalist parties voted against the government. Several members of the Likud refused to vote or absented themselves from the Knesset chamber. Shamir's dilemma was that he gone too far for the right but not far enough for the Americans and the peace camp in Israel. The Baker speech to AIPAC exacerbated the tensions within Likud. It severely weakened the pragmatic Shamir–Arens wing of Likud, whose conciliatory approach had received a political slap in the face.

The PLO in Tunis initially opposed the idea of elections for fear of being sidelined by a new indigenous leadership. Yet this matter was subsumed by Shamir's apparent inability to move in any direction. The Palestinians characterized this situation as Shamir's three 'noes': No to a Palestinian state; No to talks with the PLO; No to an international conference. This expressed the new confident Palestinian approach, since the original three 'noes' were the collective Arab response to Israel after the latter's victory in the Six Day War. That is, the intransigence of the Arabs at Khartoum in August 1967 – no peace, no recognition, no negotiations – had been replaced by the refusal of Shamir twenty years later.

Arafat eventually accepted the idea of elections – but only after the termination of the Israeli occupation. Despite the resulting stalemate – which Shamir may well have calculated – the plan had awakened the right generally and given them and Shamir's political opponents within Likud the opportunity to depict him as deviating from true Revisionist principles – a heretic rather than a true believer. The degree of internal turmoil was indicated by the fact that there was still no agreed agenda the day before the Likud Central Committee was due to meet to discuss the Shamir Plan. Moreover, Shamir's standing was far from secure. In December 1988, Shamir had barely secured a majority from the Likud Central Committee to form a National Unity government instead of a narrow coalition with the far right and religious parties.

However, by July 1989, Arens, Meridor and other leading members of the Likud believed that Shamir had secured a large majority for his plan in the party's Central Committee. To their collective astonishment, Shamir refused to put the plan to a vote, pleading that party harmony was more important. Instead, he had to settle for a hardening of its details at the behest of the Constraints Ministers. He agreed not to negotiate as long as the violence of the Intifada continued. There would be no foreign sovereignty imposed on Judea, Samaria and Gaza. Settlement activity would continue unabated and there would be no negotiation with the PLO and no Palestinian state. Shamir could clearly have overcome his opponents if he had wished to, but he clearly had no real desire to move along the path delineated by the plan which bore his name. The Constraints Ministers helped Shamir to constrain himself.[11] From this point on, Shamir no longer posed as a free agent in the direction of policy. This was politically convenient since he could offer an excuse to those who wished him to make a decision; but it was also the case that he was being pulled in too many directions to be able to navigate a straight course. Despite Baker's rumbustious determination to move the peace process forward, Shamir now stonewalled to the point of saying that a dialogue with the Palestinians was no longer relevant. An exasperated Baker spoke disparagingly about the Israeli tactics at the House Foreign Affairs Committee: 'I can only say "Take this number 202-456-1414" [the White House] and when you're serious about peace, call us.'[12]

In September 1989, President Mubarak put forward his own ten-point plan. He suggested that Israel should accept the results of the poll and that international observers would be present. The IDF would withdraw from the balloting area; there would be a ban on any Israeli presence on election day; and there would be complete freedom to disseminate election propaganda. Israel should commit itself to a 'land for peace' platform and put an end to all settlement activity. Furthermore, the Arab inhabitants of East Jerusalem should be permitted to participate in these elections. Shamir duly objected to obvious points such as 'land for peace' and the cessation of settlement activity just as he had done before.

The Mubarak Plan was discussed by the inner Cabinet and only narrowly rejected. This effectively destroyed the understanding between Shamir and Rabin which had been operating for several years. Despite the fundamental difference in the meaning of 'land for peace' between Shamir and himself, Rabin had become one of the main supporters of the Shamir Plan. He was also very positive towards the Mubarak Plan, especially since it did not mention the PLO. Moreover, he did not object to Mubarak's acting as an intermediary with the PLO. The Palestinians were also more accommodating where the Mubarak Plan was concerned, and Rabin argued in the Labour Party Central Committee that it made no sense to follow Shamir's line that there was nothing to discuss. The Intifada had had a sobering effect on Rabin and he had quietly been engaging in discussions with Palestinians from the Territories. The Mubarak Plan thus marked a turning point for Rabin and the first stage in the disintegration of the National Unity government.

In October 1989, Baker kept up the pressure by putting forward his own five-point plan. He said that an Israeli–Palestinian dialogue should take place in Cairo and that the Mubarak government should consult with the Israelis, Palestinians and Americans. Israel would attend subject to its approval of a list of Palestinians. The United States would attend on the basis of the Shamir Plan. The Palestinians would be free to discuss the elections and to raise any matter. In order to facilitate this process, the Foreign Ministers of Israel, Egypt and the United States would meet in two weeks.

The End of the National Unity Government

Baker's plan encouraged Labour to press Shamir for an answer to the Secretary of State's proposal. In February 1990, Arens tried to save the initiative and proposed a series of amendments to Baker. The US Secretary of State, in turn, required answers to two questions which would permit talks with the Palestinians to resume. One, would Shamir agree to Jerusalemites who also had a residence in the Territories forming part of the Palestinian delegation? Two, could deportees be members of the delegation? Moderates in the Cabinet, such as Arens and Meridor, argued strongly in favour of giving positive answers to these questions. Shamir, however, did not feel any sympathy for this approach. From the other side, the Constraints Ministers called upon Shamir vigorously to oppose the Baker Plan. Shamir therefore took the unsatisfactory middle course and refused to give any reply. Rather than gain time for the Likud, this response persuaded Peres that the National Unity government had reached the end of the road. He thereupon resumed his approach to the small religious parties he had been cultivating. Peres believed that it would be possible to form a narrow Labour-led coalition government with parties such as Shas and Agudat Yisrael. The Constraints Ministers asked Shamir to call a meeting of the Likud Central Committee, their power base. Shamir refused the request, but the Constraints Ministers were not perturbed – they called an informal meeting of the Central Committee instead. The 500 members that turned up heard Sharon, Modai and Levy attack Shamir and Arens for violating the terms of the July agreement of the Central Committee, and for appeasing the Americans and the Labour Party.

A visit by Shamir to the United States resulted in little clarification of the situation, and 1990 began with the National Unity government showing clear signs of rapid decay. Despite the best efforts of a large number of Likud ministers, Shamir would not change his mind over the composition of the Palestinian delegation. At the beginning of the meeting of the Likud Central Committee in mid-February, Sharon dramatically announced his resignation. He later told Israel Television that 'we have a paralysed government, a Cabinet which is incapable of taking decisions.'

Within Labour, Rabin had his doubts about the possibility of forming a Labour-led government and made efforts to save the National Unity government. Rabin had invested a considerable amount into the peace process and hoped to find some way of working with the Likud pragmatists. He was also concerned about the distinct possibility that his old rival, Shimon Peres, might once again become Prime Minister. Peres, on the other hand, attempted to bring down the government by all means possible. In particular, he had no problems with the proposed inclusion of deportees and East Jerusalem Arabs in the Palestinian delegation.

Even with Sharon gone, Shamir deliberated further; he finally decided not to proceed with his plan for elections in the Territories. The hole into which Shamir had fallen was illustrated by an interview he gave to Israel Television:

> Q: Mr Prime Minister, the US Secretary of State, James Baker, has presented the Israeli government with a question and he is waiting for an answer. Will this answer be affirmative?
>
> A: This is not the only question he has posed; there is a series of questions. We are currently engaged in a discussion of these issues and when we conclude our discussions, we will make decisions of which the US Secretary of State will be duly appraised.
>
> Q: Will the decisions be made this week and are they expected to be endorsed by the inner Cabinet?
>
> A: It is hard to say whether it will happen this week or later. After all, these are very important and serious matters that cannot be decided under the pressure of timetables.[13]

Time was running out for Shamir. The PLO had accepted Baker's latest suggestion, which allowed the Palestinian delegation to consult with 'any Arab element', including deportees. They also accepted the principle that East Jerusalem Arabs could be included if they also possessed an apartment on the West Bank. The Likud, moreover, was in serious internal disarray and seemed directionless. Netanyahu wanted to end the entire process because 'it had been infiltrated by the PLO'. He told IDF radio that 'the United States is holding us at gunpoint on one side and the [Labour] Alignment is holding us at gunpoint on the other.'[14]

In Cabinet, Shamir refused to take a vote on a Labour Alignment proposal to reply favourably to Baker's question regarding the composition of the Palestinian delegation. The failure to reply and the refusal to clarify the issues indicated the impotence of the pragmatic wing of Likud; they were unable to move in any direction or to change Shamir's mind. Despite advice urging him to act otherwise, Shamir seemed destined to follow a path of political self-destruction: he found it impossible to extricate himself from an intractable situation. After several weeks of prevarication, Shamir's way out of the dilemma was to dismiss Peres and to opt for the possibility of a narrow coalition with the far right and the religious parties, or indeed for early elections, which he felt would result in a Likud victory. Arens and other Likud ministers believed that this was a grave mistake. They thought that no progress could be made in harness with the far right. Moreover, if the situation subsequently deteriorated, Labour would not be blamed by the electorate since it would be in opposition.

At first, Shamir tried to justify his approach through diversionary tactics. He told the Likud Knesset group that the PLO was only interested in 'a crushed and disintegrated Israel'. He significantly blamed American Jewry for not coming to the aid of the Israeli government. Rather than resign, Shamir pushed the situation to the limit. Even Rabin, despite his best efforts to go on with negotiations, came to the conclusion that Shamir wished to immobilize the peace process. Shamir's precipitate dismissal of Peres triggered an inevitable vote of no confidence in the Knesset. In the debate which Labour had called for, Shamir told the Knesset of the gulf he perceived between the PLO and Israel: 'between us and them, there is an unbridgeable abyss'. Peres' motion was passed by 60 votes to 55; Shamir thus became the first Israeli Prime Minister to have fallen because of a no-confidence motion.

Peres triumphed in the Knesset due to the absence of five of the six Shas MKs from the chamber. Unlike the other ultra-orthodox religious parties, Shas had come into existence with a social mission – to ameliorate the conditions of the Sephardim. Their point of reference in relation to the state was not simply the acquisition of funds; unlike Degel Ha'Torah and Agudat Yisrael, Shas was actively involved in the affairs of the State of Israel. Indeed, their mentor, the former Sephardi Chief Rabbi, Ovadia Yosef, had appealed to Shamir to reply positively to the Baker Plan.

Logic would have dictated the formation of a narrow Labour government coalition including Shas and some of the smaller left-wing and religious parties. The religious mentor of Degel Ha'Torah, Rabbi Schach, however, appeared to fear the secularists in the Labour movement more than he disliked the far right. He thus proceeded to instruct the Shas MKs to support the party that they had just driven from government, the Likud. In an address to the Degel Ha'Torah faithful, Schach pointedly commented that the main issue was not territory, but the survival of the Jewish people. Indeed, he had been suggesting for some time that the population of the state was 'un-Jewish', and, through his paper *Yated Ne'eman*, he continued to claim that there was a profound difference between Torah-true Jews and atheistic Israelis. Unlike other Israeli parties, Degel Ha'Torah's non-Zionism and disregard for the trappings of the state were pronounced. There was no playing of the national anthem or the obligatory presence of the formal head of state, President Herzog, at their national conference.

Peres tried to patch up this deficiency, caused by Shas's sudden defection, by gaining the support of Agudat Yisrael. However, this too fell apart when one Agudat Yisrael MK received an instruction from the Lubavitcher Rebbe that he should not support Peres because of his dovish policies. Thus, Peres' support from Agudat Yisrael soon began to dissipate, and no matter which permutation or combination he tried in order to attain the necessary 61 seats – the blocking majority to stop a Likud-led coalition – the goal always eluded him. After several weeks of trying and claiming premature success, he was finally forced to return his mandate to form a government to President Herzog.

Shamir, for his part, was speedily able to form a narrow right-wing coalition with the far-right Techiya and Tsomet and several religious parties. Against all predictions, then, Shamir had managed to remain in power. Yet he was the leader of a Likud with diminished political clout and was now forced to swim with ultra-nationalist and religious fundamentalist demands in the most right-wing coalition that had so far governed Israel.

CHAPTER EIGHTEEN

FORWARD TO THE EDGE

Shamir's Last Government

The new Shamir government was undoubtedly a radical administration in which the far right exerted unprecedented influence, but there was a sense of fatalism about its prospects of longevity. Composed of a plethora of two-seat and three-seat parties whose views were highly unrepresentative, this volatile political cocktail would clearly be short-lived. Shamir told the Knesset that his new government contained 'all the national forces which have fought for the sake of Eretz Israel, for settlement in all parts of Eretz Israel'. Yet any possibility of progressing with the Shamir Plan and the peace process in general was highly dependent on the whims of a Hassidic rabbi in Brooklyn and his mitnagdic opponent in Bnei Brak.

Although, significantly, Shamir had not restored Arik Sharon to the coveted position of Minister of Defence, many observers regarded this as Sharon's government. He had instead been appointed Minister of Housing, in control of a large budget and responsible for immigrant absorption projects. In defiance of American wishes, this heralded the implementation of new settlements and the expansion of old ones. In April 1990, the Ateret Cohanim yeshiva in the Muslim quarter of the Old City in Jerusalem announced that it had purchased the sub-lease to a hospice which belonged to the Greek Orthodox Patriarchate and renamed it 'Neot David'. The Council of Jewish Settlements in Judea, Samaria and Gaza, together with the far-right parties, published a document that proposed increasing the number of settlements – an issue that had been placed in abeyance during the lifetime of the previous National Unity government.[1] In May 1990, Shamir authorized the dedication of a Torah scroll at the yeshiva of Joseph's Tomb in Nablus.

The decline of the pragmatic wing of Likud was all too visible. Ehud Olmert remarked that the establishment of the new government was 'not the happiest moment in my public life'. Shamir finally had to recognize David Levy's faction and he was duly appointed Foreign Minister – the first in Israel's history who was unable to speak a word of English. Notwithstanding the far right's opposition to any meaningful negotiations over the Territories, Shamir still defined his government's attitude towards the peace process on the basis of the Camp David Accords and his own plan of May 1989. He even managed to convince the dovish spiritual mentor of Shas, Ovadia Yosef, that he would reply positively but indirectly to Baker. Shamir justified his subterranean tactics by suggesting that new ideas from Washington and Cairo would have emasculated his own plan and that he was not sorry to have arrested the political process: 'This way we prevented the degeneration of our own initiative.... One should know how to defuse landmines and avoid dangers and examine any move proposed by others accordingly.'[2]

Peres, for his part, had failed yet again; but, more importantly, he was now seen by his own party to be a liability. Rabin, on the other hand, had been vindicated in all his warnings about the wisdom of trying to form a narrow Labour-led government. All Peres' courting of the different religious parties had come to nothing. Rabin told Israel Television that the collapse of the Labour initiative was 'not only due to a technical hitch, but also because of a conceptual error'. Rabin's support for the idea of another National Unity government even produced an unrealistic suggestion from the Likud that he join Shamir – but without Peres. Significantly, a telephone poll at the end of March 1990 indicated that 37 per cent of respondents thought that Rabin was the best choice for Prime Minister. Peres polled only 18.8 per cent and Shamir 16.8 per cent. It was not simply Peres' failure to form an alternative government that irked Labour Party members, it was the manner of that failure. The attempted seduction of the religious parties and the promises made to encourage defectors from the Likud brought Israeli politics to a new low. There was a real sense of anger that wholly unrepresentative religious minorities could exact such a high price from the two main party establishments.

The view of the Labour Party about the way forward was also changing. Peres had warned the Likud in 1987 that Shamir's veto of the London Agreement with Hussein and the effective marginalization of Jordan as a negotiating partner would become a calling card for

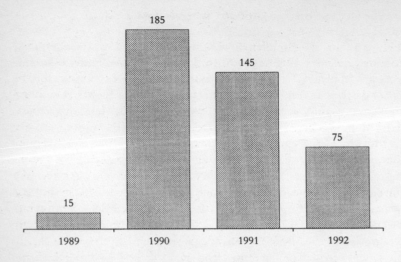

Figure 18.1   Soviet immigration to Israel 1989–92 (thousands)

the PLO. Shamir was rigidly opposed to the international conference that Hussein needed as a necessary umbrella to guarantee his position. The PLO, on the other hand, was now willing to negotiate directly with the Israelis without the aid of an international conference. By 1990, with the apparent elimination of the Jordanian option and the Likud's insistence on a narrow interpretation of the Camp David Accords, many Labour Party members were coming round to the view that any solution should now include the PLO. The Allon Plan, which sought to return 60 per cent of the West Bank – the heavily populated areas – to the Jordanians while retaining mountain ridges close to the border for security purposes, now appeared to be redundant. This fact was later underlined when, during the Gulf War, Labour members witnessed the incapacity of the Jordanians under Iraqi pressure to deliver on any past promises. In an address to the Labour Party Central Committee in March 1990, Peres elucidated the new thinking:

> It is important for us that a Palestinian side be created with which we can negotiate…. If we say 'no', there will be no more Palestinian side and we will be left with a Tunisian address. Who created this situation? Was it not Shamir? Was it not the Likud? By stopping the Jordanian option – and I hope that they did not kill it – they have opened all the doors to the Palestinians, the PLO and Arafat.[3]

Paying for Soviet Jews

By 1989, the slow collapse of Communism in the USSR had increased Soviet immigration to Israel from 2000 the previous year to 15,000 (see Figure 18.1 for Soviet immigration to Israel 1989–92). In 1990, the floodgates truly opened and Shamir's dream of a huge immigration was realized. This tempted Shamir to hint, in January 1990 at a meeting of Herut veterans, of mass settlement in the Territories. This was probably a manoeuvre to outflank his rivals, Sharon and Levy, for Shamir later reinterpreted his comment as meaning that Soviet Jews could settle wherever they wished. Baker, though, understood that the real significance of the emigration was the vast expense involved in settling and integrating these new immigrants into the fabric of Israeli society. This could be used as a lever to extract concessions from the Shamir government. The cost of absorbing a family of three in 1990 was $62,000. Israel asked the Bush administration for $10 billion in loan guarantees over a five-year period. At the end of March 1990, Baker implied that the granting of such guarantees would effectively free funds for new settlements. Whether this was true or not was irrelevant; it was, quite simply, something which the Americans had loudly stated they would not allow to happen. Baker wished to link a cessation of settlements to the granting of loan guarantees for as long as negotiations relating to the peace process continued.

By 1991, the cost of settlement of Soviet Jews had become a major source of tension in US–Israel relations. Baker complained on several occasions that Israel had not supplied the necessary information on its settlements policy. In a report by the US State Department, it was estimated that 4 per cent of the 185,000 Jews who had immigrated in 1990 had settled in the Territories. This compared with the figure of less than 1 per cent which the Israeli government had put forward. The Americans, however, had signalled their determination to confront Shamir by including in their statistics the expansion of new suburbs in and around Jerusalem – a factor which not even the Israeli peace movement had considered in their calculations.

Sharon enlarged settlements near Jerusalem such as Ma'ale Adumim and Givat Ze'ev. By now it was becoming difficult to differentiate between these settlements and the outlying suburbs of Jerusalem. Since 1967, a belt of settlements including French Hill and Gilo had already effectively expanded Jerusalem; the line dividing this Greater Jerusalem and the West Bank was called the Purple Line – to differentiate it from the Green Line of the pre-1967 borders. Sharon now resolved to push beyond the Purple Line and to develop a second belt of settlements to expand Jerusalem further into the Territories. Even if Shamir wished to downplay the settlement programme, the far right would not allow it. Sharon's Ministry of Housing announced in March 1991 that some 13,000 homes would be built on the West Bank to provide 'strategic depth'. Sharon made it easy for the new settlers to buy apartments beyond the Green Line by providing heavy subsidies and loans on very generous terms. In April the first new settlement for two years was established at Revava. This was followed by settlements at Talmon, Kanaf, Mevo Dotan and Avneh Hafetz. Baker told the House of Representatives that he regarded settlements as the greatest obstacle to peace. This cut no ice with Sharon, who argued that settlements were in fact the greatest obstacle to war. He inaugurated Mevo Dotan on the day after Bush had criticized the government's policy.

Baker, however, was able to block other routes to the loan guarantees Shamir had been counting on. For instance, Germany withheld loan guarantees of $1 billion following American pressure. In September 1991, despite the granting of Congressional approval, Bush asked them to delay the provision of the loan guarantees by 120 days in the belief that the peace process which was then crystallizing in the Madrid Conference would be harmed. American Jewish organizations who accepted the Likud approach campaigned for the loan guarantees on 'humanitarian grounds'. Since the United States had provided $3.5 billion in loan guarantees to Saddam Hussein, they argued, why not help Jews who had left the 'evil empire'. Bush did not give way and instead castigated the instigators of pressure: 'I heard today that a thousand lobbyists on the Hill are working the other side of the questions. We've only got one lonely little guy here ... I don't care if I only get one vote.' Bush's reference to 'some powerful political forces' was unprecedented – no president of the United States had ever used such language about the pro-Israel lobby.

It was suitably ironic that Bush presented himself as the all-American David against the Jewish Goliath. Nevertheless, the approach succeeded in making Jewish organizations wary of proceeding. It awakened traditional anti-Jewish images from the past – primarily that of a vast international Jewish conspiracy bent on subversion. Even those organizations who wished to help the Soviet Jewish immigrants were unhappy about the Israeli government's settlement policy, and they backed off immediately at Bush's words. Moreover, they did not warm to the implication behind Shamir's comment that 'the momentum of increasing immigration goes hand in hand with the momentum of settlement'.

From the Gulf to Madrid

The invasion of Kuwait and the subsequent Gulf War temporarily alleviated American pressure on the Shamir government. The structure of the grand alliance that set out to reclaim the oil reserves in Kuwait and to safeguard Saudi interests ironically lined up Israel with lifelong enemies such as Syria. Despite Arens's opposition, Shamir agreed to the United States' request not actively to attack Iraqi targets, but drew the line at any Iraqi advance into Jordan. This restraint was based, in part, on a military appraisal of the Iraqi threat as well as the possible political consequences. As far back as September 1988, when Saddam Hussein had committed terrible atrocities against Kurdish villagers, the head of the IDF, Dan Shomron, reported that Iraqi ground-to-ground missiles were inaccurate and would cause little damage. What is more, Shomron calculated that Saddam would not use chemical weapons against Israel as he had done against the Kurds and Iran because he feared Israel's capability to retaliate on a massive scale.[4]

The political demand by the United States that Israel should remain above the struggle to retake Kuwait led to a thawing of the icy relationship between Bush and Shamir. The peace process and other contentious issues were meanwhile placed on hold. Even so, while he expected no real favours from the Bush administration, Shamir believed that there was political capital to be gained in the isolation and marginalization of the PLO. Arafat had found himself badly positioned when Saddam Hussein marched into Kuwait. Only a few months earlier, he had unwisely sought out the Iraqi leader as the new protector of the Palestinians in the aftermath of the virtual collapse of his initiative at Algiers and Geneva. It had been yet another episode in the ongoing saga of keeping the PLO together and ensuring his own survival. This time, he found himself on the opposite side of the fence to the Gulf States which funded the PLO. Once again, ill-chosen words rebounded on him, and his sudden well-publicized warmth for Saddam won him few admirers. His attempts to mediate in the dispute were interpreted as merely acting out the role of a surrogate for the Iraqi regime. The 'neutral' partisanship of the PLO and its failure wholeheartedly to condemn Saddam came as a tremendous blow to many members of the Israeli peace movement and undermined its efforts within Israel. It also weakened the indigenous Palestinian leadership, who gave confused and ambiguous answers on their stand in the crisis.

Initially, angry articles by leading peace campaigners such as Yossi Sarid indicated a bitter sense of betrayal. He remarked that 'compared to the crimes of Saddam Hussein, the Israeli government's actions [towards the Palestinians] are as white as the driven snow'[5] Yaron London even attacked local Palestinian leaders such as Faisal Husseini and Sari Nusseibeh:

> [T]his week you proved to me that for many years I was very foolish, pretending to support your aspirations, which are not mine at all. When you next ask for my support for your 'legitimate rights', you will find that your cries of encouragement for Saddam have plugged my ears.[6]

In an address to the IDF National Defence College on 9 August, Shamir capitalized on this profound disillusionment and remarked that the PLO was now showing its true face after years of dependence on Saudi and Kuwaiti funds: 'It is high time that the heads of the countries of the world open their eyes and disengage themselves from this hypocritical and murderous organization and expel their representatives from their territories.' Moreover, opinion polls indicated the polarization of both Israeli and Palestinian views. They showed that a majority of Palestinians supported the invasion of Kuwait, while Israelis were adopting more hardline opinions further to the right. There was undoubtedly resentment at the Palestinians' perceived stand. Any emerging trust between Jews and Arabs was at once dissipated. Once more a siege mentality prevailed in Israel. Shamir comforted his people, on television, with a policy of restraint. 'It is', he claimed 'similar to the war waged against us by the terrorists, by people like Arafat and therefore hard to fight.'[7] The Israeli media once more reverted to the pre-1988 terrorist image of the PLO.

The far right used the invasion to attack the advocates of territorial compromise. They also targeted King Hussein, who did not wish to antagonize his Iraqi neighbour. Geula Cohen, a Techiya MK and former member of Lehi, revived the Revisionist claim to the East Bank when she suggested that if Israel was forced to invade Jordan in order to repulse Saddam, then the country should not be given back to the King. Rehavam Ze'evi, the leader of Moledet, which advocated the transfer of Palestinians out of the Territories, told the Knesset that the Palestinians should be taken from their homes to face any invading Iraqi forces – that is, used literally as a Palestinian human shield. When the scud missiles began to hit Tel Aviv, three Cabinet Ministers – the Likud's Sharon, Tsomet's Raful Eitan and Techiya's Ne'eman – all called for immediate retaliation. Significantly, Netanyahu told Israeli television that 'there must be a reaction. I will not say what this reaction will be or how it will take place ... it is important that the world knows that the times when Jews were beaten without retaliating have passed. This will not happen again.'[8] This semi-official reaction was designed to stop Saddam escalating the war. It also implicitly aligned Netanyahu with the Likud's right wing.

Shamir throughout believed that it would be easier to find pliable Palestinian partners after the Gulf crisis and that the grateful Americans would not press him to negotiate with the PLO. At the beginning of February 1991, Moledet joined the coalition, thereby strengthening the far right in the Cabinet. The party's leader, Rehavam Ze'evi, told Israel Television that 'the [real] war will begin the day after the [Gulf] war, when the great struggle over the future of Eretz Israel starts. This is why we want to be in.'[9]

The new constellation of political forces in the Middle East following the Gulf War persuaded Bush and Baker to move quickly. In March, the US House of Representatives approved a package of $650 million in aid to help meet the cost of the Gulf War to Israel, but this was accompanied by Bush's statement that there was now a rare window of opportunity for Israel and the Arab states to achieve a lasting peace. Baker was in Israel virtually every month in 1991 to meet both Shamir and the Palestinians in an attempt to devise a formula which would bring both parties to the negotiating table. Israel and the Arab States had faced a common enemy in Iraq and that sense of common purpose had to be exploited. Yet Shamir's basic dilemma, of trying to appease both the Americans and the far right at the same time, remained. As one journalist commented:

> Shamir continues in his transparent efforts which to him seem sophisticated – to play for time, while speaking in two voices; a moderate tone in English in face-to-face meetings with Baker and through his moderate Ministers in Washington and New York; and an extremist tone in Hebrew with the right wing hawks. He does this in a bid ... to defy President Lincoln's timeless saying that you cannot fool all of the people all of the time.[10]

Shamir was perceived to be engaging in an 'Assad' type of politics[11] where issues would be handled pragmatically on the surface and yet little would be given away unless it proved absolutely unavoidable. In the autumn of 1991, Shamir finally agreed to Baker's format for a

Middle East peace conference within the framework of UN Resolutions 242 and 338. Shamir argued that, following the Gulf War, the Arab world was forced to meet Israel on its own terms. Syria had agreed to face-to-face negotiations with Israel without any prior conditions involving the surrender of territory. The PLO agreed to its absence from any negotiations and allowed a delegation from the Territories to represent the Palestinians in its stead. The ally of the PLO and the radical Arab states, the USSR, was in terminal decline. The Intifada was fast running out of steam without any visible success and the prospect of a huge immigration of Jews from the Soviet Union was psychologically threatening for the Palestinians. Shamir stated that the basis for the conference was still the Camp David autonomy plan.

The Americans accepted Shamir's demand that the Palestinians would be represented in a joint delegation with the Jordanians and that this would not include any covert PLO affiliates. The conference would begin with a ceremonial opening; this would initiate bilateral meetings with Syrian, Lebanese and Jordanian–Palestinian delegations and multilateral meetings where regional issues such as water resources, environment and arms control would be discussed. Baker had secured promises of attendance from all the parties, and thereby sidestepped the PLO's demand for a UN-sponsored international conference. Shamir, for his part, argued that the Madrid Conference was based on the Likud's long-held position regarding direct talks, and in so doing averted Peres' demand for an international conference. Shamir told the Knesset that Israel would not sit with Palestinians who were appointed by or who represented the PLO.

The reality was somewhat different. It was an open secret that Faisal Husseini and Hanan Ashrawi were closely connected with the PLO leadership and were even rumoured to have attended the Palestine National Council in Algiers in September 1991 – almost certainly with the help of the Spanish government. Even Shamir accepted the reality that the PLO might indeed pull the strings behind the scenes. He told Israel Radio: 'To my regret, we cannot banish this organization from the face of the earth, so it will be somewhere.'[12]

The far right felt that the Madrid Conference was nothing less than a capitulation to American pressure. During the Cabinet discussion to approve the Israeli government's attendance, Sharon compared the situation to that of Czechoslovakia on the eve of World War II, and Shamir to Benes. He predicted that the peace talks would lead to war and advocated the enlistment of world Jewry to resist American pressure. He finally called upon Shamir, Arens and Levy to resign.

Techiya's Yuval Ne'eman saw no difference between this conference and Peres' much vaunted idea of an international conference. He argued that it was self-delusion to believe that the PLO would not be represented. Moledet's Ze'evi threatened Shamir with the withdrawal of support of the smaller parties such that the government would lose its majority in the Knesset. All three voted against going to Madrid. Sixteen ministers accepted Shamir's assurances, despite the fact that the PLO would be represented, albeit covertly.

Techiya's Geula Cohen called the Madrid Conference 'a sacrificial altar' and urged 'the Eretz Israel faithful' to wage war.[13] Netanyahu did not believe that the conference would lead anywhere 'except to bring about Israel's return to the 1967 borders and the neutralizing of its deterrent capability'.[14] He wanted Israel to wage a vociferous information campaign against the Bush administration's tactics. Although Shamir packed his delegation with hardliners, even asking the Council for Settlements in Judea, Samaria and Gaza to send a representative, the general gloom descending on the right – and particularly on the far right – was unmistakable. Despite a right-wing rally 'Peace for Peace', on the eve of his departure, Shamir was not in a positive state of mind. Nevertheless, a Dahaf Institute telephone poll showed that an overwhelming 91 per cent supported participation in the conference, although only 37 per cent believed it would produce concrete results.[15] Significantly, 80 per cent of Palestinians hoped for a useful outcome,[16] and 3000 Gazans demonstrated their hopes by marching with olive branches in support of peace.

It was not only the Likud which had severe reservations about the Madrid Conference. Fifteen Labour Alignment MKs, together with another 46 from other parties, signed an advertisement sponsored by 'The Campaigning Group for the Golan Heights'. The 61 – significantly the blocking majority figure in the Knesset – declared that retention of the Golan was necessary for Israel's security, and stressed that in negotiations the government should insist on Israeli sovereignty over the Heights. Labour had colonized the Heights after 1967 with kibbutzim and moshavim: it never occurred to the socialist pioneers that one day they might have to contemplate giving up their homes.

At Madrid, Shamir depicted the gathering as the end-product of a sustained American effort based on his plan of May 1989. In a speech that reviewed 4000 years of Jewish civilization, Shamir warned his audience that 'the issue is not territory, but our existence. It will be regrettable if the talks focus primarily and exclusively on territory. It is the quickest way to an impasse.' It was a speech that was designed primarily to impress a domestic audience. The Arab world naturally expressed a diametric view. The Jordanian Foreign Minister emphasized this fact when he pointed out to Shamir that he could have either peace or territory, but not both. The Israeli far right were also quite clear about their direction. They responded to the Madrid Conference by announcing that more settlements would be built and a larger budget drawn up for the purpose. They proved the point by immediately establishing the settlement of Kela in the Northern Golan Heights in the presence of three ministers.

Why did Shamir decide to go to Madrid at the end of 1991? He obviously believed that conditions were much more favourable to Israel following the Gulf War. Shamir felt that he could stonewall and prevaricate as he had done before and, like Begin, render those areas of the peace process that did not accord with the Likud's position totally meaningless in a morass of diplomatic hairsplitting. For Shamir, the Madrid Conference was little more than a glitzy, media-dominated occasion. The bilateral discussions which would follow could be drawn out at will. Indeed, the process of agreeing the final status of the Palestinian authority, and the period between the interim and final definition of that body, would allow time for more settlements to be created.

In those discussions where there were no impediments to progress, genuine negotiations took place. Thus, 80 per cent of the agreement signed with Jordan in October 1994, including on water, was concluded at this time.[17] Shamir wished to gain time and to make the minimum number of concessions in what he perceived to be a hostile environment. He would therefore sign an agreement only after detailed and lengthy negotiations, and even then its implementation could easily be postponed for a variety of reasons. Shortly after the 1992 election, Shamir told the daily *Ma'ariv* that he intended to drag out the autonomy talks for ten years.

The far right did not perceive events like that. They saw the Madrid Conference as the first step down the slippery slope to a Palestinian state. The apocryphal comment by Shamir that 'for the sake of Eretz Israel, it is permitted to lie' did not ring true for them in this instance. They perceived Shamir as a tough bargainer who, like Begin before him, would eventually concede after extracting the maximum possible concessions. They believed that the Americans and international opinion would gradually erode the Israeli position. They pointed to American duplicity at Madrid, namely the discovery by Shamir that the two components of the Jordanian–Palestinian delega-

tion had been allotted equal time. In reality, this meant American –
and international – recognition of the fact that the Palestinians should
speak for themselves and not be submerged within the Jordanian
delegation as the Israelis intended. Even Shamir himself was surprised
to learn that the Americans had also issued extra invitations to six
advisors to the Palestinian delegation: these included their real leaders,
the East Jerusalemites Faisal Husseini and Hanan Ashrawi, who were
also the prime contacts with the PLO in Tunis.

The Inevitable Elections

Within a few weeks of the Madrid Conference, the Israeli government coalition began to break up. Tsomet left because the Likud
Central Committee had opposed direct elections for Prime Minister.
Moledet and Techiya decided to withdraw in January 1992 because
the Israeli delegation for the third round of bilateral talks in Washington had submitted a document which implied Palestinian self-
government. They argued that this opened the way to territorial
concessions and the abandonment of the settlers.

Shamir could now only count on 59 members of the Knesset to
support his government. Although this proved sufficient to see through
five votes of no confidence, he nevertheless agreed to bring the
elections forward from November to 23 June. According to the
opinion polls, the Likud ratings had plunged dramatically. The party
stared electoral defeat in the face. Moshe Arens commented after the
election that 'the Likud was perceived as a factor that was standing
still. There were statements by Shamir that helped to create this
image.'[18] To be sure, Shamir and the Likud after 15 years in power
were seen as tired and jaded, but the essential point was that the mood
of many Israelis had changed. A growing number now saw Yitzhak
Shamir as Israel's Chernenko – a rigid apparatchik for whom innova-
tion was an alien concept. By the spring of 1992, he was regarded as
almost a lame-duck premier.

Israel, however, was changing. It was no longer a land of socialist
pioneers, but of a people who wanted to enjoy the benefits of a
normal life. Israel, like most Western countries, worshipped the god
of consumerism. The economy was no longer considered a secondary
matter and it had become harder and harder to justify to the ordinary
citizen the billions of dollars that were being poured into Judea and
Samaria. The age of ideology had passed: the electorate was looking
for someone who would solve their practical problems. Few people

warmed to the sentiments of the Likud election platform that 'the State of Israel has a title and a claim to sovereignty in Judea, Samaria and Gaza. Israel will raise this claim at the end of the interim arrangements and will act to implement it.' Opinion polls suggested that over 70 per cent of Israelis wanted a freeze in the settlement programme.

The Likud insisted that the change in the electoral system, the addition of direct elections for the premiership, should not take place until 1996. They knew that in a straight fight with Rabin, or even Peres, Shamir would attract very few votes in 1992. His very projection as the Likud candidate and potential Prime Minister was played down by campaign managers. Rumours of a coup by the princes to dethrone Shamir and replace him with one of their own, possibly Benny Begin or Bibi Netanyahu, were rife. Arens privately questioned Shamir's commitment to his own plan and to the autonomy talks. Others, like Meir Shitrit, the Jewish Agency treasurer, openly came out for a settlement freeze.

Shamir's poor relationship with David Levy plummeted even further. A few months before, Levy had refused to attend the Madrid Conference when Shamir suddenly decided to head the Israeli delegation himself. The dovish Levy could not be trusted to mount a hard-line defence at such an unprecedented international gathering; Shamir had to ensure that he had strict control over Israeli deliberations. What is more, Levy found himself marginalized when he discovered that he had been ranked eighteenth in the candidate stakes by the Likud Central Committee. An alliance between the Shamir–Arens faction and Sharon's camp had effectively eliminated Levy's previous strong standing when he had secured 31 per cent to Shamir's 46 per cent in the leadership contest. The threat of resignation and desertion to Labour soon forced Shamir to promise Levy that he would retain the Foreign Ministry. This, in turn, did not please Arens, who had beaten Levy only to see the result overturned. Arens privately tendered his resignation to Shamir.

Such byzantine manoeuvrings failed to impress the public. The State Comptroller's report subsequently revealed incompetence and inefficiency on a massive scale in Sharon's Ministry of Housing. It was estimated that $2 billion had been wasted over the previous two years. Moreover, the State Comptroller hinted at corruption. It appeared that the drive to construct settlements quickly and on a large scale had presented the ideal opportunity for graft. For example, Sharon had increased the number of 'housing companies' competent

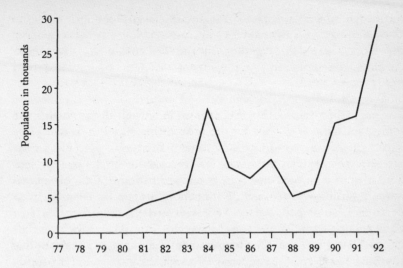

Figure 18.2   Annual settlement in the Territories 1977–92

to carry out major building projects from 70 to 500; it later transpired that a number of these were extremely minor construction
companies owned by members of the Likud Central Committee. In
another case, Mikhail Dekel, the deputy Minister of Agriculture
between 1981 and 1984, was later found guilty at a trial in 1993 of
requesting payment to the Likud in return for recommending con-
tractors for building projects in the Territories. The Likud had seemingly forgotten that the party came to power on a wave of discontent
at the corruption within the Labour Alignment. The Israeli public
had given its verdict when it elected Menachem Begin Prime Minister
in 1977. There was now a widespread belief that the Likud, too, was
affected by a similar malaise – that it had been in office for too long
and it was time for a change.

Sharon had worked at breakneck speed to increase the settlement
drive – perhaps in the almost certain knowledge that the government's term of office would be relatively short. Since he had become
Housing Minister, the number of units planned for the Territories
had increased fourfold. In March 1991, he announced that 2150 units
begun the previous year would be swiftly completed. Another 4670
would be added by the end of 1991 and a further 6200 in 1992. An
analysis of the annual population growth in the Territories showed
that under Shamir that there had been a marked increase compared

to the Begin era. Since Sharon's appointment as Housing Minister in the Likud coalition with the far right and religious parties from 1990, the annual population growth in the Territories had more than doubled. The projected figure for 1992 was ten times that of 1982 (see Figure 18.2).[19]

Shamir's assurances to audiences of settlers during the election campaign that he would not accept an American diktat to halt the settlement drive may have won him some votes; yet it undoubtedly also hardened the stand of the Bush administration, especially on the question of the loan guarantees. Baker told Jewish leaders in May 1992 that Israel would not receive the $10 billion in loan guarantees because Shamir had reneged on his private promise in February 1991 to restrict settlements. No doubt Baker used the loans issue, in fact, to influence Shamir's electoral downfall. Shamir, in turn, told the Likud faithful that the US administration had promised the Arabs that it would not permit the granting of the loans guarantees. His subsequent comment to one settlement that 'even 120,000 [settlers] is not enough' was clearly not going to win over the Americans.

Shamir hoped that a Likud victory would finally turn the tide against the Americans, since Bush would shortly be preoccupied with his own election at the end of 1992 and thus susceptible to pressure. However, the practical effect of no loans guarantees for the foreseeable future was that Shamir's ability to massage the debilitated economy was limited. In addition, many questioned the wisdom of antagonizing the remaining superpower – historically Israel's supreme ally. Shamir had continually rejected the advice of his ambassador in the United States, Zalman Shoval, to strike a compromise deal with Baker. For the US Secretary of State, Shamir's refusal in January 1992 to accept US terms effectively destroyed the last vestiges of American confidence in the workings of the Likud government. This duly catalysed a feel-bad factor in the Israeli electorate, which had still supported Shamir in the euphoria of the Madrid Conference. Ironically, Shamir only accepted Shoval's advice on the issue of the loan guarantees in April 1992. By then, it was far too late to make any impact on the electorate.[20]

Unemployment in Israel had reached a high of 11 per cent in the general population; 35 per cent of new immigrants were unable to find work. A report prepared by the Ministry of Finance predicted a 16.2 per cent rate of unemployment by 1996 if Israel did not secure the loan guarantees. If an anticipated one million immigrants arrived from the former Soviet Union during the next five years, then Israel would require a massive $26.5 billion to absorb them all. Moreover, Shamir's lack of flexibility did not impress the 240,000 new voters from the former USSR. Conditioned under the Soviet system, they did not respond well to bureaucracies that did not hear their appeals. Labour's promise to freeze the settlement drive, divert money back into Israel, and secure the loan guarantees from Bush were clear attractions to new immigrants, to the Sephardim, and to those below the poverty line. Moreover, the 'Soviet' votes counted for eight or nine Knesset seats.

The immigrants from the former USSR were also committed secularists; they thus found the power wielded by the small religious parties unacceptable. An example of this undue influence was the Lubavitcher Rebbe's reported pressure on Shamir not to negotiate away any part of the Land of Israel, quoting God's admonition to the Children of Israel 'to cast out the peoples of the Land, to smite them, to destroy them, to make no covenant with them, nor show any mercy unto them' (Deuteronomy 7:2).[21] The Rebbe's bitter opponent, Rabbi Schach, had for his part ordained the merger of two parties, Agudat Yisrael and Degel Ha'Torah, to form the Yahadut Ha'Torah list – the United Judaism list. Schach and Schneerson agreed an electoral truce since they now supported the same party. No new accusations of 'false messianism' against Schneerson and the Lubavitch movement appeared in Schach's *Yated Ne'eman*. Rabbi Schach had broken with Shas and hoped to lead a large number of its voters away from Ovadia Yosef to the new party. Schach's unfortunate remark that the Sephardim were not ready to lead the country and that they should study for many more years did not go down well with Shas voters.

The right was even more fragmented than ever – a plethora of parties that could not hope to achieve the new 1.5 per cent threshold for a Knesset seat. In addition to the small nationalist parties and religious parties which had been part of the coalition in the Shamir government of 1990–92, new factions of fragments and new fragments of factions appeared, each trying to secure a Knesset seat. The far right looked to the past to justify its claim to be involved in the formation of the next government. Sharon told the press that without the military campaign for 'Peace for Galilee' in 1982, 'there would be no diplomatic process with the Arab states today'. Only when the Palestinians had been defeated and evicted, he reasoned, did they turn away from the military option. Thousands more had died, he argued, in Labour-initiated wars.

In contrast, the three parties of the peace camp – Mapam, Ratz and Shinui – united to form Meretz. Labour, too, reformed itself. A one-person, one-vote system of over 100,000 party members elected numerous doves to high positions on Labour's candidate list. Moreover, it produced a more youthful, dynamic and attractive package to the electorate. In 1988, only a handful of Labour's candidates for the Knesset were in their thirties and forties; in 1992, the number was 24.

The most important change was the ousting of Shimon Peres as party leader. Many Labour members felt that he should not be allowed to lead the party to a fifth election fiasco. The débâcle of trying to form a Labour-led administration following the collapse of the National Unity government had drastically undermined Peres' position. There was a sense that kowtowing to the religious parties had been damaging as well as totally futile. Rabin articulated the frustration of the secular Israeli public with the peripheral yet electorally important religious parties when he stated that he opposed 'extreme dependence' on such groups. This distanced Rabin from Peres' policy of courting parties such as Agudat Yisrael and Degel Ha'Torah. Yet Rabin was careful not to alienate the religious public. He instigated a change of wording in a controversial resolution which had already been passed by the Labour Convention: 'a separation of state and religion' was rephrased as 'a separation of religion from politics'. In addition, he gained the support of much of the religious intelligentsia and those who had supported the moderate religious party, Meimad, in 1988. The National Religious Party, however, had shown where its political allegiance lay when it openly declared in an election advertisement that 'every vote for the NRP will also be a vote for a government led by the Likud as well as a vote that will determine the Jewish State'.[22]

Rabin, moreover, possessed the tough, security-minded image that would attract undecided voters and move seats from Likud to Labour. He was seen as a man who would transcend ideology and seek practical solutions to long-standing problems. In 1988, Rabin defended his policy of containing the Intifada by explaining that 'no one dies from a beating'. This naturally infuriated many Israelis and Jews with more liberal leanings. Since then, though, he had clearly changed his position. He had moved towards a more dovish position as a result of rationalizing that the Intifada was more than a little local disturbance. Rabin had also become disillusioned with the lack of progress with the Shamir Plan, which he had helped to craft. All these changes appealed to the peace movement and especially to Meretz, which, while closer to Peres politically, understood that only Rabin could win the election.

The new system of one-person, one-vote in the Labour primaries was an unknown factor. Yet Rabin secured the necessary 40 per cent to become party leader after an absence of 15 years. The vote for Peres suffered because of the high poll for Yisrael Kessar, the Histadrut secretary-general, who attracted 18.77 per cent. A considerable personal following within Labour enabled the luckless Peres to register a creditable 34.5 per cent. But it was not enough and thus, after 15 years as party leader, Peres finally stepped down to make way for his predecessor and his successor, Yitzhak Rabin. This development, too, was unwelcome to the Likud, which had been counting on the re-election of Peres. Rabin was a much more difficult target to attack – and indeed to slander.

The election campaign of 1992 inherited many of the hallmarks of the 1980s. However, this time it was coloured more than ever by slick PR techniques, brash publicity and authoritative spin-doctors. Both Labour and the Likud orchestrated barracking at their rival's rallies and instigated no-holds-barred personal attacks, often against the wishes of their leaders. Rabin was characterized as a sometime alcoholic who cracked under strain. Shamir was rumoured to be suffering from Parkinson's Disease and said to be unfit for office. The Likud did, however, refrain from using a book by Rabin's former son-in-law as part of their electoral arsenal.

In essence, Rabin played all the traditional Likud cards without the ideology. He distinguished between 'security' settlements and 'political' ones. He could afford to produce general responses, where Shamir had to justify his government's record on specific issues. The Labour slogan, 'Israel is waiting for Rabin', adapted from a Six Day War popular tune, underlined the campaign's presidential approach. The normally reticent Rabin gradually adopted a warmer, populist persona – much to the chagrin of Shimon Peres, who complained in private about the ascendancy of the personality cult.

The election results were dramatic. The Likud vote dropped from 40 seats to 32. There was a movement away from the Likud towards Labour and to Tsomet. Labour and Meretz increased their vote, while the far right declined dramatically. Techiya lost all their seats and their vote was divided mainly amongst Moledet, Tsomet and Rabbi Levinger's list. The moderate Shas retained its vote, whilst that of Yahadut Ha'Torah dropped by nearly half. Labour, Meretz and the Arab parties thus achieved the blocking threshold of 61 seats. The heyday of the Likud had come to an end.

Years of Hope and Despair, 1992-1999

Two days before his defeat, Shamir recalled his days in Lehi:

> We went to war, although we were few. We knew then that there was no choice but to pay the price and it never crossed our minds that perhaps it was not worth it or that living is the most important thing. We were broken and exhausted, but remained steadfast in our faith that nothing could crush us. No matter how many casualties, we would never be defeated, even if we remained alone.[23]

Netanyahu, Shamir's successor as leader of the Likud, attempted to modernise such radicalism. His projection as a thinking neo-conservative and a practitioner of modern managerialism meant a recasting and a softening of the Likud image which would make the party more acceptable to the centrist voter. This also meant a distancing from the past and an adaptation of ideology to the problems of the present. But Netanyahu's attempt to establish himself in office suffered a setback when the Oslo Accords in 1993 suddenly emerged as Rabin hesitantly shook Arafat's hand on the White House lawn. Netanyahu's strategy after a short period of indecision was to outflank his opponents on the Right by espousing a radical populist approach if for no other reason than to safeguard his precarious position as leader of the Likud. His sound bites reverted to the traditional imagery of Peres as Chamberlain and Oslo as Munich. Netanyahu thus played an important role in the incitement of the far Right against the agreement when others from his party such as Benny Begin and Dan Meridor refused to mount this bandwagon. Fulltime activists and settlers operated a network, which was targeted on breaking Rabin mentally. Several months before the murder of Rabin, Sharon commented to the Mayor of Kiryat Arba, a stronghold of radical settlers that 'Rabin hates you. It's simply hate that knows no boundaries and has no measure.'[24] In a private poll carried out for him a few weeks before his assassination, Rabin was informed that an estimated 800 Israelis were willing to commit murder to halt the peace process and some 6000 were prepared to take up arms.[25] Part of the outrage at the assassination by Yigal Amir who was neither a habitual loner nor a deranged fanatic was therefore directed at Netanyahu. Some accused him of a dereliction of his moral and political duty in permitting an atmosphere of potential violence to develop.

Yet within months Netanyahu had beaten Peres in the 1996 election due to the insecurity engendered by the multiple bus bombings by Hamas. Likud wanted to secure the centre ground vacated by the martyred Rabin and thereby attempted to avoid displays of ideological zeal, thus in the 1996 election there were no pointed references to Judea and Samaria. The successful 'peace with security' slogan of the Likud campaign was indicative of the new politics: the Likud facing in both directions, encouraging hopes and stoking fears.

There was an obvious need for the Likud to synthesise the reality of negotiations with the PLO with an ideological continuity, especially in terms of adherence to Judea and Samaria. Thus a few weeks before the 1996 election, Netanyahu publicly stated that the new facts could not be ignored and that Israel would not return to cities now under the jurisdiction of the Palestinian Authority. Significantly, he did not recognise the Oslo Accord but 'the facts created by the Oslo agreement'.[26] This crucial distinction left open the way to adhere to past ideology in theory but also to deal with the current reality in practice. Like his predecessors, Netanyahu's strategy was to retain territory within the constraints of the political situation, but in this case to embellish it with tactics which publicly projected flexibility. The latter was often portrayed as willingness to compromise on ends rather than simply a more sophisticated approach to means. For many in the Likud and on the right generally, the difference between means and ends was unclear. The political reality forced the Likud to settle for an uneasy hybrid, which gradually mutated towards an increasing Israeli presence in the West Bank.

The Hebron agreement of early 1997 which returned part of the town to Palestinian control touched a raw ideological nerve and the Wye Plantation Accord in 1998 further antagonised many in the Likud. Moreover, the personal animosity, which Netanyahu had aroused amongst his erstwhile colleagues led to ideological schism and fragmentation during the election campaign. Major figures left the Likud to form new parties or join existing ones. The outcome was a resounding defeat by Ehud Barak in the 1999 election and Netanyahu's immediate resignation. In a few short years, Netanyahu had unravelled Menachem Begin's painstaking assembly of an array of differing political tendencies, which emerged as the Likud in 1973.

INTO THE 21ST CENTURY: ENTER SHARON

When Ariel Sharon formally became Prime Minister of Israel at the beginning of March 2001, he was the first Likud leader not to have emerged from a Revisionist-Zionist background. Indeed, this point was hardly mentioned in the polemical press coverage, which greeted his election victory over Ehud Barak. He was deemed to be a master of political expediency – a man without ideology. To some extent this was true, but he was also raised in the Labour Zionist movement – albeit with a sense of Revisionist dissent – in an era of ideological fervour. He came of age during the 1940s and was fashioned politically and militarily by Israel's struggle for independence. Sharon was formally a card-carrying member of Mapai from the late 1950s. He was thus drawn towards the nationalism of Ben-Gurion and Dayan in the early years of the state as opposed to the more liberal attitudes of Moshe Sharett. The relationship was close and significantly, both Ben-Gurion and Dayan refused to take up the complaints against Sharon by his fellow officers regarding the killings at Kibya in 1953 and his breach of discipline at the battle of the Mitla Pass during the Sinai campaign in 1956. The reprisal raids which were promoted by Ben-Gurion, Dayan and Sharon were part of the struggle within Mapai between the hawkish elements more inclined to a hard-line military approach and those who pursued peace with the Arabs through more conciliatory measures such as clandestine diplomacy. Sharett's reaction to Kibya was clear as he recorded in his diary

'There was never a reprisal of this scope and force.
I walked into my office confused, utterly depressed and helpless.'

Sharett and the moderate wing of Mapai had effectively neutralised Ben-Gurion's tendency towards military adventurism for the greater part of twenty years, but this came to an end when the latter returned to government as Defence Minister at the beginning of 1955. It was followed by Sharett's resignation as Prime Minister and then his ousting as Minister of Foreign Affairs in June 1956. In the political wilderness for ten years, a dying Sharett returned in a wheelchair to deliver his last public speech at the Tenth Congress of Mapai in 1965 in which he openly and fiercely attacked Ben-Gurion as a leader and as a policy-maker. This led to Ben-Gurion's exit from Mapai together with his supporters, Dayan, Peres and other notables and the formation of a new party, Rafi.

Yet Rafi did poorly in the 1965 elections and the party split after the Six Day War essentially because a return to the newly formed Labour Party was the only pathway by which prominent figures such as Dayan and Peres could accede to positions of power in national politics. Sharon who occupied senior positions in the IDF identified more with Ben-Gurion and the faction which stayed out of the Labour Party, the State List. This grouping remained small, politically insignificant and finally without Ben-Gurion who retired from political life in 1970.

Sharon's first moves to leave the army and enter the maelstrom of Israeli politics began before the 1969 election. He remained at odds in personal terms with the Chief of Staff Chaim Bar-Lev and many senior military figures. He also disagreed with the construction of the Bar-Lev line to keep the Egyptians at bay. Such was the antagonism that Sharon's retirement was being facilitated by his opponents in the General Staff on the technicality that he had not completed the form requesting a continuation of his army service. Sharon's reaction was to make contact with Menachem Begin and to indicate that he was interested in standing for Gahal in the 1969 elections. Leaked reports in the press that he was offered fifth position on the Gahal list prompted a rethink in Labour circles. There were fears that Sharon's entry into political life would catalyse the breakaway of Dayan and the Rafi faction and thereby initiate a coalescence of the Right. It would also implement the recall of Rabin from Washington who would challenge the old guard in Labour. Pressure on Bar Lev resulted in Sharon's appointment as head of Southern Command and an extension of his tenure in the army. Yet four years later, he was passed over for the post of Chief of Staff and informed that he would have to leave his position by January 1974. This time he actually left the army to join the Liberals within Gahal although both the Rafi wing of the Labour Party and the Free Centre made overtures to him. Within 48 hours of leaving the army, he announced at a press conference that he would seek to create a broad centrist party as an alternative to Labour. This alignment of the centre right would

comprise Herut and the Liberals from Gahal, the Free Centre, the State
List and possibly the Independent Liberal Party. Despite initial opposition within Herut − 'an unworkable polygamy' − Sharon effectively
created the Likud in September 1973. It was even rumoured that he
would be appointed Foreign Minister in Begin's shadow cabinet.

After the Six Day War, Sharon had moved from an essentially hard-
line Mapai position personified by Dayan, Rafi and the State List
towards a more right wing stance. This was motivated by personal
factors as well as ideological ones. There was hostility and enmity
between Sharon and the Labour oriented IDF leadership. His young
son had been tragically killed in a shooting accident outside his home.
In the political sphere, the conquest of the West Bank had brought new
opportunities to resurrect past dreams of Zionist ideology. His belief in
a Jewish presence there for security reasons allowed him to maintain
contact with maximalists who came from different ideological back-
grounds. Although he had joined the Liberals, his views were far more
radical than those of his party colleagues. He also espoused the idea of a
homogeneous unity in Israeli political life such as the dissolution of the
parties within the Likud and their merger. National Unity governments, particularly with those figures to whom he could relate such as
Rabin, Peres and Dayan were another feature of this approach. His
views were tinged with Jabotinsky's concept of national unity during
the breakthrough period to the establishment of the state. The essential
difference was that Sharon projected an Israel in a state of perpetual
crisis, which called for permanent national cohesion with himself
playing a leading role. His leadership model was Ben-Gurion during
the early period of the state. In May 1976, he commented:

> Zionism was a fantastically successful revolution which achieved the estab-
> lishment of the State of Israel, but this revolutionary élan began to peter out
> in the mid-1950s. It is imperative that this revolutionary aspect of Zionism
> be rejuvenated by establishing new goals. But for this you need effective
> leadership; and this requires an urgent change in the political system from
> which leadership arises and functions.

In part, these new goals included new settlements on the West Bank.
Such enthusiasm for 'building' was the Mapai ideological tradition.
Immediately on leaving the army, he commented that 'there has to be
an Upper Jenin, an upper Nablus and an upper Ramallah just as there is
an Upper Nazareth'. In the summer of 1974, he joined Begin and Zvi
Yehuda Kook in visiting new settlements and complained that not
enough was being done to help them. He viewed the occupation of the

West Bank as a continuation of the settlement drive, which had charac-
terised the Zionist enterprise in pre-state days. He pointed out that
between 1967 and 1976 only 74 settlements had been established
whereas between 1930 and 1940 110 had been founded. Jordan was
Israel's eastern border and as early as 1974 he stated that Judea and
Samaria were 'an inseparable part of Israel and from the security point
of view there is no chance of giving them up'.

Although he was appointed Minister of Agriculture in Begin's first
government, of greater importance was his chairmanship of the
government's Ministerial Settlement Committee. His task was to build
five new towns in Judea and Samaria and populate them with 150,000
Jews. In September 1977, Sharon announced that he planned to settle
two million over a period of 20 years. He ridiculed the demographic
argument by deriding statistical projections and suggested that Israel
could easily absorb the West Bank population despite its higher birth
rate and still remain a democratic state. Several areas of settlement were
designated but in particular in the little Triangle (the western slopes of
Samaria to the east) and in a widened Jerusalem corridor which
connected with the Jordan rift valley settlements. Like Dayan and
unlike Begin and the religious settlers, he advocated settlement in all
areas where there was a sparse Arab population.

> If we want a strong independent state we must give up settling just on the
> coastal strip and move elsewhere. Otherwise Israel would consist of a mass
> of concrete from Ashkelon to Nehariya – all within the range of Arab guns
> and having to rely on friendly powers for protection.

Even though he joined Herut in 1977, Sharon's general approach was
thus a maximalist Mapai one, convoluted and radicalised by personal
factors.

His almost pan-Arabist espousal of the view that 'Jordan is Palestine'
emerged as early as December 1974 when he called for Hussein's overthrow and the establishment of a Palestinian state in its stead. During his
brief attempt to don the mantle of a convincing dove as the leader of the
Shlomzion party prior to the 1977 elections, he more than once stated
that he would be prepared to meet PLO representatives. On another
occasion, he spoke about the possibility of a Jordanian-Palestinian state on
both sides of the Jordan. All this vanished when the rival Democratic
Movement for Change captured Labour's disillusioned voters and Sharon
reverted to his former self. He maintained that a cessation of violence
must occur before negotiations could commence with Syria over the
Golan Heights or with the Palestinians regarding the West Bank.

In the years between 1977 and 2001, Sharon consistently continued along this political path. His rejectionist views made him an icon for the far Right and a hate figure for the Left. Moreover when he was in government, the Jewish population in the West Bank increased dramatically. In Jerusalem, he set a personal example by purchasing an apartment in 1987 in the Muslim quarter – in the midst of 20000 Arabs and 40 Jews.

His period as Housing Minister in the early 1990s and the attempt to absorb the Soviet immigration was a disaster. The State Comptroller's report in 1992 spoke about mismanagement, suspected illegalities and overspending. Moreover, his general crudeness and political wheeler-dealing which reflected a general malaise within the Likud helped to further factionalise the party into a collective of warlords with their acolytes. The ostensible party leader, Netanyahu, accused him of 'incessant and tireless subversion'. His far Right stance rejected any rapprochement with the PLO. Speaking at a ceremony to mark the tenth anniversary of Dayan's death he said that 'if Moshe Dayan were alive today, there would be no Intifada and its leaders wouldn't be legitimate partners to peace negotiations.' After the violence inspired by Hamas at the Temple Mount in October 1990, he demanded that Israel assume control of the area and argued for the removal of the keys from the Waqf.

Following his defeat by Barak in 1999, Netanyahu had left the Likud with a mere 19 seats as a result of his enthusiastic support for the dual electoral system for both Prime Minister and party. He had obscured the Likud's ideological focus by withdrawals from the West Bank and his implementation of the Hebron Accord. He had lost to Barak by a huge margin and left the Likud $15 million in the red. Sharon was viewed by his party and the electorate as yesterday's man. He was nothing more than a caretaker leader of the Likud, awaiting Olmert or perhaps the resurrection of a sanitised and seemingly chastened Netanyahu. During his tenure as leader of the Likud, Sharon was virtually invisible. The next elections were scheduled for November 2003 when Sharon would be 76.

One year before his election victory Sharon was 25% behind Barak in the opinion polls. With a semi-rehabilitated Netanyahu hovering in the wings, Sharon therefore understood that he would have to bring down Barak before then. He would have to detach those government parties who leaned ideologically towards the Likud such as the NRP or those whose political demands – justified or not – would not be satisfied by Labour. Such an opportunity availed itself on the eve of the Camp

David summit in the summer of 2000. Barak's determination to settle all outstanding issues – the occupation, the evacuation of settlements, the exchange of land, the right of return as well as Jerusalem – unnerved the Right and the National Religious. Several parties withdrew from the government and others threatened to do so. The Palestinians were similarly politically unprepared and psychologically unwilling to contemplate finality and compromise. They were neither disposed to endorse a Palestinian state, truncated into three blocs connected by roads and bridges nor the suggested division of Jerusalem. Moreover, Arafat was unable to deliver, not simply because the differences between the two sides were too wide and essentially unbridgeable, but also because the corruption of his regime had given birth to an opposition that had to be listened to. In addition, the frustrations of the Netanyahu years, the postponements and prevarications produced a generation of no hope. Sharon's settlement drive moreover had been more than matched by the Barak regime. The lack of any vision of a Palestinian future, bolstered by an educational system which airbrushed out of existence or demonised even the Israeli peace camp, produced the foot soldiers of the new Intifada and the suicide bombers of the Islamists. The dream of Oslo had become a nightmare.

Barak's single-handed attempt to produce 'an end of conflict' badly misfired. It enhanced the inherent instability of a transition situation and furthered the aims of rejectionists on both sides. His government disintegrated, he had disclosed his negotiating position in agreeing to divide Jerusalem – and had received nothing in return. Moreover, this had all been carried out without consulting close allies and coalition partners. Barak was beginning to be perceived not as a brilliant soldier but as an erratic politician and a poor negotiator. His total belief in his own abilities and his projection of total self-confidence were, in the minds of many Israelis, only matched by his predecessor.

When Arafat returned in triumph to the West Bank, having resisted American demands, but also having turned down the best Israeli offer so far, arms dumps were being created, and the training of recruits intensified. In all likelihood, the Intifada would have taken place anyway, but Sharon's visit to the Temple Mount prematurely but predictably ignited a combustible mixture of frustrated ambitions, national politics and Islamic fury. The new uprising – the Israeli inability to utilise conventional riot control against angry youngsters, the shooting of Israeli Palestinians, the 'hot' war between the IDF and armed Palestinian forces – followed an inevitable course. The political outcome was a regression on both sides. As during the first Intifada at the end of the 1980s when Shamir was elected and following the bus bombings by Hamas in early 1996 after which Netanyahu obtained the Premiership, there was a dramatic move to the Right which manifested itself in the election of Sharon. Lightening had struck not twice but three times in the same place. The display of Palestinian violence, regardless of its cause, produced a state of siege in Israeli society. In a Birzeit University Development Studies poll of 1200 Palestinians in the West Bank and Gaza in mid-February 2001, only 11.5% believed that Sharon was serious about reaching a comprehensive and conclusive agreement. Some 77.2% supported military attacks against Israeli targets. When asked about the nature of those targets, 60.4% stated than any Israeli should be considered a target.

The Palestinians restored to prominence the absolute right of return of all four million exiles instead of promoting a two state solution with the return of some exiles plus compensation. Establishing a Palestinian state on the West Bank did not mean an abrogation of the right of return to Israel. Israel was asked to repent and accept the total rather than the shared responsibility for the Palestinian exodus of 1948. The Israeli peace camp fragmented, accompanied by profound soul-searching about the meaning of Oslo. Many like B'Tselem, the Israeli Human Rights organisation analysed and criticised IDF action. Others were confused and immobilised. Palestinian intellectuals, perceiving the lack of symmetry between Israeli power and Palestinian defiance, confined themselves to endorsing and echoing stated official positions rather than attacking the corrupt practices of the Palestine Authority and its lack of democracy. Indeed, it proved difficult to condemn wholeheartedly the suicide bombers of Hamas and Islamic Jihad because it impinged on the sense of 'solidarity with the people'. Palestinian rejectionists such as Edward Said who opposed both Oslo and a two state solution now began to occupy the intellectual high ground.

Sharon thus came to power almost by default with only some 36.69% of the eligible vote, but carried along by a combination of political shrewdness and a degree of luck. It was a remarkable about turn. The Palestinian elite's inability to channel anger and frustration into productive channels had produced an inevitable result. The Palestinian rejectionists had elected the Israeli rejectionists. Any modicum of trust that had previously existed had vaporised.

The new national unity government of Israel was thus headed by the disciples of Ben-Gurion – Sharon and Peres. The former had moved to the Right and been branded as a war criminal by some. The latter had moved to the left and been accused of appeasement by others. Both septuagenarians had been tainted by accusations of political opportunism and cynical pragmatism. Peres, in particular, seemed to have deserted his natural allies of recent years, the heirs of Moshe Sharett's liberal diplomacy.

At the time of writing (October 2001), Sharon, at least publicly, seems to have learned from past errors and has broadly refrained from making rash comments and taking irreversible military actions. His tactics of wearing down the Palestinians through continuous military response and limited incursions into Palestinian territory as well as targeted killings of suspected Islamic and rejectionist planners of suicide missions have won a wide acceptance in Israeli society. Yet while there is a general solidarity on questions of security, opinion polls continually indicate that a majority of Israelis wish to return to the negotiating table to secure an equitable peace with the Palestinians based on the two state solution. This, in a sense, accords well with the reasoning of many non-Likud Israeli electors who voted for Sharon in the elections of 2001. In contrast, a majority of the Palestinian public have indicated in opinion polls that they strongly support the right of return of a postulated four million refugees and their descendants. Moreover, this is seemingly interpreted in the absolutist sense – a right of return to both Israel and Palestine rather than a return to the more ambiguous 'national soil' of Palestine. For all Israelis, including the Left, this is a metaphor for the destruction of Israel and in turn a rejection of a two state solution in favour of a Greater Palestine.

Throughout 2001, Sharon's approach was to hold the Palestinian Authority responsible for all military and terrorist attacks and repeatedly to condemn Arafat's inability or unwillingness to control the suicide bombers of Hamas and Islamic Jihad. This is ironically reflected in a Palestinian determination not to distinguish publicly between Arafat loyalists, secular rejectionists and the Islamists. The 'one people' ambivalence of Arafat's position further allowed Sharon to initially win the support of the new Republican Administration of George W. Bush which had not forgotten the Palestinian leader's dalliance with Saddam Hussein during the Gulf War. Sharon's first major political error occurred during the aftermath of the attacks on the Trade Center and the Pentagon in September 2001, when he attempted to jump on the anti-terrorist bandwagon with further demonisations of Arafat as a Palestinian Bin Laden. Although opinion polls show that American public support for Israel dramatically increased, this throwback to the Likud public relations of the Shamir era did not impress the Americans.

Sharon, it seems, did not anticipate that the Bush Administration wished to repeat the wide coalition of the Gulf War which integrated many Arab and Islamic states. The Americans thus welcomed declarations of support from states such as Syria and Iran and downplayed expressions of solidarity with Bin Laden from Palestinian Islamists. The military regime in Pakistan, a hitherto loyal supporter of the Taliban and thereby a key player in the crisis, stated at an early stage that it had no desire to see Israel included in the war against terrorism.

The Israeli-Palestine conflict of 2000 and 2001 is thus becoming an impediment to a wider goal. The US – much to Sharon's dismay – does not seemingly want a visible and overt Israeli presence in the war against terrorism. Wooing the Arab world and other Islamic states also means turning a blind eye to the policies of Hezbollah, Hamas and Islamic Jihad who in the past organised suicide bombings in Israel. There can now be no self-evident linkage between the suicide bombers of the Trade Center in New York and the Sbarro restaurant in Jerusalem. The Arab world interprets and portrays the campaign of the Palestinian Islamists as part of a national struggle rather than terrorism – and the Americans have not dissented from this. Although supporters of Hamas and Islamic Jihad were demonstrably sympathetic to the Trade Center bombings, their suicide missions in Israel itself – at the time of writing – could be put on hold if they are now perceived to be politically counter-productive.

Under great US pressure, Sharon and Arafat agreed to a tentative ceasefire a week after the bombing of the Trade Center. Arafat was told by the UN's coordinator for the Middle East peace process, Terje Larsen and the European Union's special envoy to the Middle East, Miguel Moratinos that continued violence would bring isolation of the Palestinians and would close all diplomatic doors. A ceasefire, projected as more serious and potentially more stable than its predecessors thus came into a somewhat precarious existence in mid-September 2001 even though it was opposed by both Islamic and secular rejectionists. Any eventual cessation of violence opens the way to negotiations – but the possibility of such negotiations is forcing Sharon to make decisions about the future of the Territories. This, in turn, threatens his double-headed coalition of the far right and messianic national religious who are uncomfortably coupled with the Labour Right which still espouses 'Land for Peace'. Moreover, it was the withdrawal of the former which led to the slow collapse of Barak's government even before the abortive Camp David summit in the summer of 2000. Sharon is also facing the potentially unpopular possibility of implementing the Mitchell Report recommendations which include the freezing of all settlement activity including the 'natural growth' of existing settlements.

Sharon has a difficult personal decision to make: whether to break with the far Right and his previous ideological pronouncements or to embrace the notion of two state solution and thereby cement his reputation as a pragmatist and unlikely peacemaker. Yet both Sharon and Arafat have now begun to comprehend that the destruction of the Trade Center has changed the rules of the game played out in a year of violence. The Israel–Palestine conflict has assumed for the time being a secondary role in US geopolitical concerns. Embracing states such as Iran and making positive comments about the plight of the Palestinians and their future state suggests a shift away from Western 'understanding' of the Israeli position in the name of the greater good of fighting terrorism. The price of enrolling Arab support in this campaign is clearly a harder line against the Sharon government. The Bush Administration may therefore reverse its hitherto isolationist policy. It is a price which the Republican Administration may be more willing to pay ideologically and commercially, given the record of the first President Bush in the early 1990s, than the previous occupant of the White House.

In the unpredictable world of Israeli–Palestinian politics, it is, of course, always possible that an equitable and fair agreement will be arrived at. It would, however, be difficult to sell to disillusioned Israelis and embittered Palestinians. The Jewish settlers, 200 000 strong in early 2001, now fiercely oppose even a partial evacuation. The talk now is of managing the problem rather than solving it, of perhaps leaving it to a new generation of leaders. For many Israelis, the relevance of Jabotinsky's Iron Wall which would protect Israel until such time as negotiations became feasible once more has become the dominating mindset.

> And the leadership (of the Palestinian Arabs) will pass to the moderate groups who will approach us with a proposal that we should both agree to mutual concessions. Then we may expect them to discuss honestly practical questions, such as guarantee against Arab displacement or equal rights for Arab citizens or Arab national integrity. And when that happens, I am convinced that we Jews will be found ready to give them satisfactory guarantees so that both peoples can live together in peace like good neighbours.

The suspicions of both sides, the gap between their political and psychological positions and their mutual antagonism suggests that Jabotinsky's wish for peace – first penned in 1923 – will remain at present little more than a distant aspiration.

NOTES

Prologue

1. *Ma'ariv*, 13 May 1977.
2. Mina Tsemach was one of very few who correctly predicted the result. In the financial journal *Mabat*, two days before the election, she predicted: Likud, 42 seats; Alignment, 30 seats; and the Democratic Movement for Change, 14 seats.
3. *Jerusalem Post*, 18 May 1977.
4. Jimmy Carter, *The Blood of Abraham* (Boston, 1985), p 42.
5. *Jerusalem Post*, 19 May 1977.
6. Malvyn Benjamin, *Jewish Observer*, 23 June 1977.
7. David Ben-Gurion, *Diaries*, 14 September 1948; translation in *Israel: A Personal History* (London, 1971), p 255.
8. Giora Goldberg, 'The Struggle for Legitimacy: Herut's Road from Opposition to Power', in Stuart A. Cohen and Eliezer Don-Yehiya (eds), *Comparative Jewish Politics: Vol II, Conflict and Consensus in Jewish Political Life* (Tel Aviv, 1986), p 149.
9. For an account of Ivan Greenberg's support of the Irgun and the Revisionist cause, see David Cesarani, *The Jewish Chronicle and Anglo-Jewry 1841–1991* (Cambridge, 1994), pp 183–92.

1. The Long and Winding Road

1. Joseph B. Schechtman, *The Jabotinsky Story: Fighter and Prophet – Vol II: The Last Years, 1923–1940* (New York, 1961), p 151.
2. Chaim Weizmann, *Trial and Error* (New York, 1966), p 338.
3. Letter to Bernard G. Richards, 26 July 1931, in *The Letters and Papers of Chaim Weizmann, Series A XV, October 1930–June 1933*.
4. Letter to Baron Edmond de Rothschild, 23 December 1931, in ibid.
5. Letter to Morris Rothenberg 31 January 1931, in ibid.
6. Vladimir Jabotinsky, 'Socialism and the Bible', *Jewish Chronicle Supplement*, January 1931.
7. Vladimir Jabotinsky, 'The Ideology of Betar', Netzivut of Betar (USA).
8. Vladimir Jabotinsky, *The Jewish Call*, vol III, no. 8, August 1935.
9. For a detailed consideration of Arlosoroff's thought, see Shlomo Avineri, *Arlosoroff* (London, 1989); and Shabtai Teveth, *The Killing of Arlosoroff* (Tel Aviv, 1982).

10. Vladimir Jabotinsky, 'The Aims of Zionism', *The Zionist*, vol I, no. 1, 14 May 1926 (New York).

11. From an address Begin gave in 1965, 'Ze'ev Jabotinsky: What Did We Learn from Him?', in Harry Hurwitz, *Menachem Begin* (Johannesburg, 1977), pp 49–50.

12. Schechtman, *The Jabotinsky Story*, Vol II, p 143.

13. Howard M. Sachar, *A History of Israel: From the Rise of Zionism to Our Time* (Oxford, 1976), p 184.

14. Vladimir Jabotinsky, 'The Iron Wall', *Rassviet* 42–43, 4 November 1923; *Jewish Herald* 26 November 1937.

15. Jabotinsky, 'The Iron Wall'.

16. Ibid.

17. Vladimir Jabotinsky, 'The Ethics of the Iron Wall', *Rassviet* 44–45, 11 November 1923; *Jewish Standard*, 5 September 1941.

18. The religious prohibition of *sha'atnez* is the ban on the mixing of wool and linen together in cloth. It is taken from Leviticus 19:19 and Deuteronomy 22:11.

19. Vladimir Jabotinsky, 'Sha'atnez Lo Ya'ale Alekha', *Hadar*, November 1940 (New York).

20. Ibid.

21. Raphaella Bilski Ben-Hur, *Every Individual A King: The Social and Political Thought of Ze'ev Vladimir Jabotinsky* (Washington, 1993), pp 23–34.

22. Vladimir Jabotinsky, 'Speech to the Third World Convention of Betar', *Hadar*, November 1940 (New York).

23. Vladimir Jabotinsky, *The Jewish Call*, vol III, no. 8, August 1935 (Shanghai).

24. *Rassviet*, 18 September 1933, in Schechtman, *The Jabotinsky Story*, Vol II, p 162.

25. Vladimir Jabotinsky, 'Jews and Fascism', *Jewish Echo*, 10 May 1935.

26. Vladimir Jabotinsky, 'Zionist Fascism', *The Zionist*, vol I, no. 4, 25 June 1926 (New York).

27. Vladimir Jabotinsky, 'Zionism and the Land of Israel' (1905), in Ben-Hur, *Every Individual A King*, pp 123–4.

28. David Ben-Gurion, *Diaries I 1923* (Tel Aviv, 1971), pp 267–8, translation in Ronald W. Zweig (ed), *David Ben-Gurion: Politics and Leadership in Israel* (Jerusalem and London, 1991), p 36.

2. The Advocates of Revolt

1. Rafael Scharf, 'Begin: A Talent to Divide', *Jewish Quarterly*, vol 31, no. 3/4, 1984, pp 115–16.

2. J. Bowyer Bell, *Terror Out Of Zion: The Fight for Israeli Independence 1929–1949* (Dublin, 1977), p 45.

3. Emmanuel Katz, *Lehi: Freedom Fighters of Israel* (Tel Aviv, 1987), p 7.

4. Joseph Heller, 'The Stern Gang 1940–49: Ideology and Politics', unpublished manuscript.

5. Tim Pat Coogan, *De Valera: Long Fellow, Long Shadow* (London, 1993), pp 65–6.

6. Jabotinsky, 'Jews and Fascism', *Jewish Echo*, 10 May 1935.

7. Walter Laqueur and Barry Rubin (eds), *The Israel–Arab Reader: A Documentary History of the Middle East Conflict* (London, 1984), p 59.

8. Meir Ben-Horin, 'Max Nordau: A Study of Human Solidarity', Ph.D.

thesis, Columbia University 1953, p 260.

9. Interview with Aryeh Naor, 24 October 1994.

10. Zvi Elpeleg, *The Grand Mufti: Haj Amin Al-Hussaini, Founder of the Palestinian National Movement* (London, 1993), pp 56–63.

11. Eri Jabotinsky, Letter to the Editor of *Zionnews*, 27 March 1942, Jabotinsky Archives, Tel Aviv.

12. I. Alfassi (ed), *Irgun Zvai Leumi: Collection of Archival Sources and Documents April 1937–April 1941*, cited by Yaakov Shavit in the *Journal of Israeli History*, vol 15, no. 1 (Spring 1994), p 114.

13. Joseph Heller, *The Stern Gang: Ideology, Politics and Terror 1940–1949* (London, 1995), p 162.

14. Menachem Begin, *The Revolt* (New York, 1977), p 61.

15. Ibid., p 233.

16. In 1983, the weekly *Koteret Rashit* unearthed the testimony of Yehuda Lapidot, the Irgun deputy commander at Deir Yassin, in the Jabotinsky Archives at the Likud headquarters. Lapidot suggested that the idea for the massacre came from the Lehi contingent in the Irgun unit with the express aim of destroying Arab morale. According to Lapidot, the Irgun headquarters had vetoed the idea. See *Guardian*, 9 April 1983.

17. Natan Yellin-Mor, 'The British Called Us the Stern Gang', *Israel Magazine*, February 1973.

18. *He'Hazit*, no. 2, August 1943.

19. Israel Eldad, 'Five Years after the Assassination of Yair', *Lehi Bulletin*, no. 4, February 1947.

20. P. S. O'Hegarty, *The Victory of Sinn Fein* (Dublin, 1924).

21. Begin, *The Revolt*, p 284.

22. David Ben-Gurion, 'Terrorism or Constructive Effort', an address to the first session of the Annual Conference of the Histadrut, 20 November 1944, in *Rebirth and Destiny of Israel* (London, 1959), p 144.

23. Bowyer Bell, *Terror Out of Zion*, pp 106–7.

24. Richard Crossman, lecture given in Rehovot in April 1959, 'The End of Mandate: Ernest Bevin', published in *A Nation Reborn: The Israel of Weizmann, Bevin and Ben-Gurion* (London, 1960), p 69.

25. Richard Crossman, *Palestine Mission: A Personal Record* (London, 1947), p 19.

26. David A. Charters, *The British Army and Jewish Insurgency in Palestine 1945–47* (London, 1989), p 48, Appendix III.

3. A Jewish State in the Land of Israel

1. Transcript of Begin's address on Irgun Radio, 15 May 1948, Jabotinsky Archives, Tel Aviv.

2. Ibid.

3. Herut Movement 'Motherland and Freedom' (Tel Aviv, June 1948), Jabotinsky Archives, Tel Aviv.

4. *Ha'mashkif*, 6 August 1948.

5. Y. Kosoi at Sitting Five of the Provisional Council of State, 23 June 1948, in Nataniel Lorch (ed), *Major Knesset Debates*, Vol I (Jerusalem, 1992), p 143.

6. Ibid., p 167.

7. *New York Times*, 9 December 1948.

8. Menachem Begin, Speech at Carnegie Hall, 29 November 1948, Jabotinsky Archives, Tel Aviv.

9. Menachem Begin, Statement at a press conference, 19 September 1948, Jabotinsky Archives, Tel Aviv.

10. Menachem Begin, Speech at Rishon L'Zion, 8 September 1948, Jabotinsky Archives, Tel Aviv.

11. *Jerusalem Post*, 19 October 1948.

12. Bibi Netanyahu, who was elected leader of Likud in 1993, similarly projects the idea that the military actions of the Irgun and Lehi 'joined for a time by the Haganah under David Ben-Gurion ... broke the will of the British Government to retain its hold on the country' (Benjamin Netanyahu, *A Place Among the Nations: Israel and the World* (London, 1993), pp 75–6).

13. Herut Manifesto for the first Knesset, Jabotinsky Archives, Tel Aviv.

14. Avi Shlaim, *Collusion across the Jordan: Abdullah, the Zionist Movement and the Partition of Palestine* (Oxford, 1988), p 420.

15. Herut Manifesto for the first Knesset.

16. Herut Movement, 'Motherland and Freedom'.

17. 8 March 1949, in Lorch (ed), *Major Knesset Debates*, Vol II, p 395.

18. Ibid.

19. Ibid.

20. Yonathan Shapiro, *The Road to Power: The Herut Party in Israel* (New York, 1991), p 74.

21. Shmuel Tamir made serious attempts to depose Begin in 1952 and 1966. Ezer Weizmann tried the same in 1972. These attempts were carried out at times when Herut's political fortunes were at a low ebb due to Begin's perceived misjudgement of sensitive situations. All were unsuccessful.

22. Shapiro, *The Road to Power*, p 106.

23. Herut Movement, 'Motherland and Freedom'.

4. Looking for Partners: Revisionism in Transition

1. 7 January 1952, in Nataniel Lorch (ed), *Major Knesset Debates*, Vol III (Jerusalem, 1992), pp 730–31.

2. Interview with Tom Segev, 24 October 1994. See Tom Segev, *The Seventh Million: The Israelis and the Holocaust* (New York, 1993), pp 223–6.

3. 7 January 1952, in Lorch (ed), *Major Knesset Debates*, Vol III, pp 730–31.

4. Menachem Begin, Address to the Fifth Congress of the Herut Movement, 24 November 1958, Jabotinsky Archives, Tel Aviv.

5. 16 March 1965, in Lorch (ed), *Major Knesset Debates*, Vol IV (Jerusalem, 1992), pp 1432–3.

6. 20 March 1963, in ibid., p 1349.

7. Giora Goldberg, 'The Struggle for Legitimacy: Herut's Road from Opposition to Power', in Stuart A. Cohen and Eliezer Don-Yehiya (eds), *Comparative Jewish Politics: Vol II, Conflict and Consensus in Jewish Political Life* (Tel Aviv, 1986), p 147.

8. Yochanan Bader, *The Knesset and I* (Jerusalem, 1979), p 191.

9. Peter Y. Medding, *The Founding of Israeli Democracy 1948–1967* (Oxford, 1990), p 192.

10. 24 November 1952, in Lorch (ed), *Major Knesset Debates*, Vol III, p 766.

11. Michael Bar-Zohar, *Ben-Gurion: A Biography* (Jerusalem, 1978), p 73.

12. Programme for a National Liberal Government Headed by Tenuat Ha'Herut, 1959, Jabotinsky Archives, Tel Aviv.

13. Menachem Begin, 'Discours prononcé au Palais Bourbon devant MM. les

députés et Senateurs de L'Intergroupe pour L'Unité Française', 12 September 1956, Jabotinsky Archives, Tel Aviv.

14. 27 November 1961, in Lorch (ed), *Major Knesset Debates*, Vol IV, p 1246.

15. Mordechai Bar-On, *The Gates of Gaza: Israel's Road to Suez and Back 1955–1957* (London, 1994), pp 6–7.

16. 7 November 1956, in Lorch (ed), *Major Knesset Debates*, Vol III, pp 980–81.

17. Menachem Begin, Address to the 24th Zionist Congress, 25 April 1956, Jabotinsky Archives, Tel Aviv.

18. Harry Hurwitz, *Menachem Begin* (Johannesburg, 1977), p 78.

19. Michael Brecher, *The Foreign Policy of Israel* (New Haven, 1972), p 173.

20. Interview with Shulamith HarEven, 23 October 1994.

21. Guide for Lecturers and Canvassers in the Electoral Campaign for the Fifth Knesset (Herut Movement–Central Committee Information Department 1961), Jabotinsky Archives, Tel Aviv.

22. Rael Jean Isaac, *Party and Politics in Israel: Three Views of a Jewish State* (New York, 1981), p 147.

5. The End of the Socialist Zionist Dream

1. In 1954, Israeli agents were arrested in Egypt for attempting to attack American targets in order to smear Nasser's regime in Western eyes. Pinchas Lavon as Minister of Defence claimed that he knew nothing about this action, despite a claim by the head of military intelligence that he had been ordered to proceed by the Minister. The findings of a judicial inquiry which, although inconclusive, broadly supported this claim were contradicted by evidence that seemed to exonerate Lavon. Ben-Gurion's opposition to Lavon's political rehabilitation resulted in the formation of a Cabinet subcommittee headed by the Minister of Justice. The committee effectively cleared Lavon, a decision that was ratified subsequently by the Cabinet. Ben-Gurion, outvoted, was outraged and the Lavon affair became a source of schism and passionate infighting in Mapai throughout the 1950s and 1960s. The affair was at least one factor in the eventual formation of Rafi by Ben-Gurion in 1965.

2. Terence Prittie, *Eshkol of Israel* (London, 1969), p 331.

3. Michael Brecher, *The Foreign Policy of Israel* (New Haven, 1972), p 249.

4. Shimon Peres, *Battling for Peace: Memoirs* (London, 1995), p 96.

5. Moshe Pearlman, *Ben-Gurion Looks Back* (London, 1965), p 209.

6. The following broad definitions operate: Centre-Right: Herut; General Zionists/Liberals; Free Centre; State List; ShlomZion (the Progessives and Independent Liberals are not included since they always opposed a joint list with Herut). Centre-Left: Mapai; Achdut Ha'avoda; Mapam; Rafi; Sheli; Citizens Rights Movement; the Democratic Movement for Change.

7. Interview with Zalman Shoval, 28 October 1994.

8. Principles and Programme: The Platform of Gahal for the Seventh Knesset, Jabotinsky Archives, Tel Aviv.

9. Ibid.

10. Interview with Zalman Shoval, 28 October 1994.

11. *Jerusalem Post*, 12 December 1973.

12. Menachem Begin, 'Confusion and Whitewash', *Ma'ariv*, 14 December 1973.

13. Ephraim Torgovnik, 'Party Organisation and Electoral Politics: The Labour Alignment', in Howard R. Penniman and Daniel J. Elazar (eds), *Israel at the Polls 1981* (Washington, 1986), p 49.

14. *Jerusalem Post*, 24 December 1973.
15. *Ma'ariv*, 15 February 1977.
16. Letter from Eliezer Berkovits, *Jerusalem Post*, 27 March 1977.
17. *New Outlook*, May–June 1987.

6. The First Begin Government

1. Significantly, Rabin, in his memoirs, makes no reference to having considered Dayan for Cabinet office. *The Rabin Memoirs* (Boston, 1979), pp 241–2.
2. Moshe Dayan, *Story of My Life: An Autobiography* (New York, 1976), p 599.
3. Interview with Benny Begin, 24 October 1994.
4. *Ha'aretz*, 28 March 1977.
5. 'Foreign and Defence Policy and the Effort to Assure True Peace', Likud Platform for the Ninth Knesset (1977), Jabotinsky Archives, Tel Aviv.
6. *Le Nouvel Observateur*, 23 April 1977.
7. 'Foreign and Defence Policy and the Effort to Assure True Peace'.
8. Ibid.
9. Moshe Dayan, *Breakthrough: A Personal Account of the Egypt–Israel Peace Negotiations* (London, 1981), p 361.
10. Jimmy Carter, *Keeping Faith* (London, 1982), p 274.
11. William Quandt, *Peace Process* (Washington DC, 1993), p 255.
12. Dayan, *Breakthrough*, p 58.
13. Mordechai Bar-On, *The Gates of Gaza: Israel's Road to Suez and Back 1955–1957* (London, 1994), p 232.
14. *Jerusalem Post*, 9 January 1978.
15. Interview with Anwar Sadat, *New Outlook*, July–August 1978.
16. Carter, *Keeping Faith*, p 300.
17. Yuval Ne'eman was a member of the left-wing 'greater' Mapam between 1949 and 1952 when it was in alliance with Achdut Ha'avoda. He left because of Mapam's stand on the Slansky trial.
18. Interview with Uzi Landau, 21 October 1994.
19. *Jerusalem Post*, 6 October 1978.

7. The Cost of Camp David

1. Moshe Dayan, *Breakthrough: A Personal Account of the Egypt–Israel Peace Negotiations* (London, 1981), p 323.
2. Interview with Yuval Ne'eman, 25 October 1994.
3. William Quandt, *Peace Process* (Washington DC, 1993), p 282.
4. Eric Silver, *Begin: A Biography* (London, 1984), p 203.
5. Those who either voted against or abstained on the Knesset vote on the Camp David framework included Yitzhak Shamir, Moshe Arens, Ehud Olmert, Yoram Aridor, Zalman Shoval, Dov Shilansky and Michael Dekel.
6. Shimon Peres, *Battling for Peace: Memoirs* (London, 1995), p 294.
7. Menachem Begin, Speech on Signing the Camp David Accords, Israel Press Office, 26 March 1979.
8. Interview with Shulamith Hareven, 23 October 1994.
9. *Ha'aretz*, 18 May 1979.
10. *Jerusalem Post*, 9 October 1977.
11. *New Outlook*, May–June 1979.

12. La'am split in November 1978 into pro- and anti-Camp David factions. Yigal Hurvitz's faction reverted to its origins by taking the name of Rafi – The State List.

13. Yuval Ne'eman, interviewed by Yosef Goell, *Jerusalem Post*, 12 October 1979.

14. Interview with Moshe Katzav, 24 October 1994.

15. The 48 Knesset seats gained by Likud in the 1981 elections were distributed thus: Herut – 25, Liberals – 18, and La'am – 5. This represented a proportionate increase in Herut's representation due to the split in La'am.

8. Lebanon: The Escape of the Golem

1. Ze'ev Schiff and Ehud Ya'ari, *Israel's Lebanon War* (New York, 1984), p 301.

2. Sheli was the product of a merger of left-wing Zionists and the far left. It originated in the split in the Israeli Communist Party in 1965. Its more open wing, Maki, merged with Moked, a socialist grouping, in 1975. This became Sheli in 1977 when several members of the Zionist left joined. Ratz, or the Civil Rights Movement, was founded in 1973 by Shulamit Aloni, a former Labour Party member, following a personal and ideological altercation with Golda Meir. Ratz embraced the separation of state and religion, women's rights, human rights and the peace movement. It formed Meretz with Shinui and Mapam to fight the 1992 elections.

3. The June 1982 figure is taken from a Modi'in Ezrachi poll of 1236 interviewees. The other figures are from Michael Jansen, *Dissonance in Zion* (London, 1987), p 91.

4. *New Outlook*, editorial, September–October 1981.

5. Interview with Eliahu Ben-Elissar, 25 October 1994.

6. Interview with Aryeh Naor, 24 October 1994.

7. Ariel Sharon, *Warrior: The Autobiography of Ariel Sharon* (New York, 1989), p 354.

8. Interview with Uzi Landau, 21 October 1994.

9. *Jerusalem Post*, 26 June 1981.

10. Gideon Rafael, *Jerusalem Post*, 20 December 1981.

11. Aryeh Naor (Begin's secretary), in Ned Temko, *To Win or to Die: A Personal Portrait of Menachem Begin* (New York, 1987), p 441.

12. One popular version of the golem story was the creation of a 'man' out of clay by Judah Loew ben Bezalel, the Maharal of Prague, to serve him and his community. The golem developed a will of his own, independent of his master's, and developed anarchic behaviour. The Maharal was forced to return the golem to the inanimate state of matter from which he had originated.

13. Likud Platform for the Tenth Knesset of 1981, in Yehuda Lukács, *Documents on the Israeli–Palestinian Conflict 1967–1983* (Cambridge, 1986), p 121.

14. *Yediot Aharonot*, 28 September 1981.

15. Rashid Khalidi, *Under Siege: PLO Decision-making during the 1982 War* (New York, 1986), p 195.

16. *Ha'aretz*, 4 November 1981.

17. *Ma'ariv*, 7 April 1982.

18. Raphael Israeli, *PLO in Lebanon: Selected Documents* (London, 1983), p 7.

19. *Ha'aretz*, 16 July 1982, quoted in Michael Jansen, *Battle of Beirut* (London, 1982), p 130.

20. *Yediot Aharonot*, 14 May 1982.

21. Begin and the right often referred to Jewish blood in a quasi-Biblical sense.

Yet there is no mention of 'Jewish blood' in traditional Jewish thought.

22. Ian Black and Benny Morris, *Israel's Secret Wars: The Untold History of Israeli Intelligence* (London, 1991), p 374.

23. Begin's use of the term *havlagah*, 'self-restraint', had a profound resonance in Zionist history since it was used to describe the Yishuv's desire not to respond to provocation by Arab nationalists.

24. Brian Urquhart, *A Life in Peace and War* (London, 1987), p 338.

25. Yossi Melman, *The Master Terrorist: The True Story behind Abu Nidal* (London, 1987), p 114.

26. The three Abu Nidal terrorists probably served a higher master such as Iraqi or Syrian intelligence. The writer Patrick Seale, a long-time sympathizer of the Palestinian cause, suggested a scenario whereby they could have been in the service of the Mossad, given Begin's need to confront the PLO. This was a view held by some in the PLO itself. Yet it is unlikely that Begin himself would have initiated this. His knowledge of ancient Jewish history and his own example mitigated against the possibility that he would condone the killing of one Jew by another for political advantage. See Patrick Seale, *Abu Nidal: A Gun for Hire* (London, 1992), pp 226–7.

27. Schiff and Ya'ari, *Israel's Lebanon War*, p 98.

28. *Guardian*, 7 March 1983.

29. *The Times*, 6 July 1982.

30. Ibid. Israeli Document 108 is listed under its author's heading: 'PLO Attacks on Jewish Targets'. It is, in fact, the report, dated 20 June 1982, of an IDF spokesman, who speaks about attacks on Jewish targets by 'Arab terrorist groups' – which is, of course, a much wider category. The IDF spokesman specifically listed three attacks by Abu Nidal: Spain (3 March 1980) and Austria (1 May and 29 August 1981). This clearly contradicts the author's heading, as the Abu Nidal was devoutly anti-PLO. (See Israeli, *PLO in Lebanon*.)

31. *Jerusalem Post*, 7 June 1982.

32. Schiff and Ya'ari, *Israel's Lebanon War*, p 240.

33. Interview with Aryeh Naor, 24 October 1994.

34. *Ha'aretz*, 9 June 1982.

35. *Yediot Aharonot*, 18 June 1982.

36. *Jerusalem Post*, 13 June 1982.

9. Defeat from the Jaws of Victory

1. *The Times*, 14 July 1987.

2. *Jerusalem Post*, 28 June 1982.

3. Rabin had referred to the deteriorating situation in laying siege to Beirut as a *'plonter'* – a Yiddish word implying an imbroglio or tangle – on 24 July 1982 on the *Mabat* news programme.

4. *Jerusalem Post*, 8 August 1982.

5. Ehud Olmert was elected Mayor of Jerusalem in 1993. As a student in 1966, he asked Begin to step down as Herut leader. He then followed a political odyssey through the Free Centre and La'am and eventually returned to Herut.

6. *Jerusalem Post*, 7 July 1982.

7. *Davar*, 14 July 1982.

8. *Ma'ariv*, 17 July 1982.

9. *Davar*, 13 May 1982.

10. *Yediot Aharonot*, 17 September 1982, in Shai Feldman and Heda Rechnitz-

Kijner, *Deception, Consensus and War: Israel in Lebanon* (Tel Aviv, 1984), p 23.
11. *Jerusalem Post*, 9 July 1982.
12. *Davar*, 9 July 1982.
13. Interview with Uzi Landau, 21 October 1994.

10. Begin's Holocaust Trauma

1. Menachem Begin, press conference, 19 September 1948, Jabotinsky Archives, Tel Aviv.
2. Menachem Begin, Broadcast on emerging from the Irgun underground, 15 May 1948, Jabotinsky Archives, Tel Aviv.
3. Tom Segev, *The Seventh Million: Israelis and the Holocaust* (New York, 1993), pp 255–95.
4. 11 April 1974, in Nataniel Lorch (ed), *Major Knesset Debates*, Vol V, (Jerusalem, 1992), pp 1891–5.
5. 20 May 1974, in ibid., pp 1915–18.
6. 14 January 1976, in ibid., pp 2016–18.
7. 20 December 1973, in ibid., p 1850.
8. *New York Times*, 10 June 1981.
9. Interview with Shulamith Hareven, 23 October 1994. She published an article entitled 'The High Priest of Fear' shortly after Begin had stepped down.
10. Eric Silver, *Begin: A Biography* (London, 1984), pp 7–8.
11. *Jerusalem Post*, 15 June 1982.
12. *Jerusalem Post*, 3 August 1982.
13. *Yediot Aharonot*, 21 June 1982.
14. *New Outlook*, November 1982.
15. Ze'ev Mankowitz, *Jerusalem Post*, 4 August 1982.
16. *Ha'aretz*, 11 August 1982.
17. *Davar*, 10 September 1982.
18. Walter Laqueur and Barry Rubin (eds), *The Israel–Arab Reader: A Documentary History of the Middle East Conflict* (London, 1984), pp 652–6. Moreover, Begin had defined the Six Day War as 'a defensive war' in a Knesset speech on 23 January 1978.
19. Ibid.
20. Thomas Friedman, *From Beirut to Jerusalem: One Man's Middle East Odyssey* (London, 1990), p 128.
21. *The Times*, 29 July 1982.
22. Jonathan Randal, *The Tragedy of Lebanon* (London, 1990), pp 189–95.
23. There is a certain degree of confusion and uncertainty as to the location of boundaries and sites arising from the Biblical account. See *Encyclopaedia Judaica*, Vol III (Jerusalem, 1977), p 700.
24. J. David Bleich, *Contemporary Halakhic Problems*, Vol III (New York, 1989), pp 291–2.
25. The Amalekites were the hereditary enemies of the Jews since the wanderings in the wilderness. They were a desert people that lived in the Negev.
26. *The Jewish Encyclopaedia*, Vol VII (New York, 1925), p 189.

11. The Massacre at Sabra and Shatilla and its Consequences

1. *Ha'aretz*, 20 September 1982.
2. *Al Hamishmar*, 21 September 1982.

3. *Jerusalem Post*, 21 September 1982.
4. *Jerusalem Post*, 3 October 1982.
5. Interview with Yossi Beilin, 20 October 1994.
6. *Jerusalem Post*, 15 July 1982.
7. David Cesarani, *The Jewish Chronicle and Anglo-Jewry 1841–1991* (Cambridge, 1994), p 244.
8. *Yediot Aharonot*, 17 October 1982.
9. Statement of the Board of Deputies of British Jews, June 1982.
10. *New York Times*, 26 September 1982.
11. *New York Times*, 2 October 1982.
12. Jonathan Sacks, 'Religious and National Identity: British Jewry and the State of Israel', in Eliezer Don-Yehiya (ed), *Comparative Jewish Politics: Israel and Diaspora Jewry* (Tel Aviv, 1991), p 55.
13. 'Final Report of the Commission of Inquiry into the Events at the Refugee Camps in Beirut 1983', in *Jerusalem Post*, 9 February 1983.
14. 'War-conduct in the 1982 Lebanon War', in William V. O'Brien, *Law and Morality in Israel's War with the PLO* (London, 1991), p 209.
15. Ibid., p 210.
16. Jacobo Timmerman, *The Longest War* (London, 1982), pp 152–3.
17. *Ha'aretz*, 5 July 1982.

12. Shamir: The Man from Lehi

1. Asher Arian and Michal Shamir (eds), *The Elections in Israel 1984* (Tel Aviv, 1986), p 217.
2. Yitzhak Shamir, *Summing Up* (London, 1994), p 135.
3. Ibid., p 86.
4. *Jerusalem Post*, 7 September 1983.
5. *Jerusalem Post* 1 February 1980.
6. Shamir, *Summing Up*, p 30.
7. In his memoirs, Shamir follows the general line expounded by other former members of Lehi: that a central purpose of this policy of negotiations with the Nazis was to liberate Jews from further oppression in occupied Europe.
8. Shamir, *Summing Up*, p 34.
9. *Jerusalem Post*, 1 February 1980.
10. The number 18 is considered symbolically important in Judaism. The number value of the Hebrew word *chai* – 'life' – adds up to 18.
11. Emmanuel Katz, *Lehi: Freedom Fighters of Israel* (Tel Aviv, 1987), pp 18–19.
12. Tim Pat Coogan, *Michael Collins: A Biography* (London, 1990), p xxii.
13. Katz, *Lehi*, p 79.
14. Nachman Ben-Yehuda, *Political Assassinations by Jews: A Rhetorical Device for Justice* (New York, 1993), pp 175–6.
15. Alex Weissberg, *Advocate for the Dead: The Story of Joel Brand* (London, 1958), pp 166–7.
16. *Parliamentary Debates. Lords 1941–42*, Vol 123, 2 June–22 July (London, 1942).
17. Bernard Wasserstein, 'New Light on the Moyne Murder', *Midstream*, March 1980.
18. *Davar*, 8 November 1944.
19. Fifty years after the assassination of Lord Moyne, reverberations from the act were still felt. James Buchan, who married Lord Moyne's granddaughter, wrote a scathing review of Shamir's biography. See *Spectator*, 30 April 1994.

20. Ben-Yehuda, *Political Assassinations*, p 397.
21. Dov Joseph, *The Faithful City: The Siege of Jerusalem 1948* (London, 1961), p 38.
22. Shamir, *Summing Up*, p 86.
23. Ben-Yehuda, *Political Assassinations*, p 180.
24. Ibid., pp 178–85.
25. Teudot L'Mediniyut ha'chuts shel medinat Yisrael, Israel State Archive, May–September 1948 (Jerusalem, 1981), p 603.
26. Shimon Peres, *Battling for Peace: Memoirs* (London, 1995), p 71.
27. Joseph Heller, 'Avraham (Yair) Stern 1907–1942: Myth and Reality', *Jerusalem Quarterly* 49 (Winter 1989), p 126.
28. *Jerusalem Post*, 23 June 1989.
29. *Jerusalem Post*, 29 October 1979.
30. Leonard Schroeter, *The Last Exodus* (Seattle, 1979), pp 60–83.

13. Above and Below Ground

1. Nicholas Bethell, *The Palestine Triangle: The Struggle between the British, the Jews and the Arabs 1935–1948* (London, 1979), p 277.
2. Nataniel Lorch (ed), *Major Knesset Debates*, Vol V (Jerusalem, 1992), pp 2032–3.
3. *Jerusalem Post*, 1 February 1980.
4. Colin Shindler, *Ploughshares into Swords? Israelis and Jews in the Shadow of the Intifada* (London, 1991), pp 162–6.
5. Interview with Yuval Ne'eman, 25 October 1994.
6. *Ha'aretz*, 18 December 1989.
7. Eliezer Don-Yehiya, 'Jewish Messianism, Religious Zionism and Israeli Politics: The Impact and Origins of Gush Emunim', *Middle Eastern Studies*, vol 23, no. 2 (April 1987).
8. Interview with Moshe Levinger, *Nekuda*, 22 July 1988.
9. Aviezer Ravitsky, 'Religious Radicalism and Political Messianism in Israel', in Emmanuel Sivan and Menachem Friedman (eds), *Religious Radicalism and Politics in the Middle East* (New York, 1990), pp 17–28.
10. Gershom Scholem, *Sabbatai Sevi: The Mystical Messiah 1626–1676* (London, 1973), pp 88–93.
11. Ehud Sprinzak, *The Ascendance of Israel's Radical Right* (New York, 1991), pp 93–6.
12. Uri Zvi Greenberg, from 'For the Tearing of the Mind', translated by Robert Friend in S.Y. Penneli and A. Ukhmani (eds), *An Anthology of Modern Hebrew Poetry*, Vol II (Jerusalem, 1966), p 281.
13. Joseph Heller, *The Stern Gang: Ideology, Politics and Terror 1940–1949* (London, 1995), p 105.
14. For an understanding of this genre of poetry, see Hannan Hever, 'Poetry and Messianism in Palestine between the Two World Wars', in Jonathan Frankel (ed), *Jews and Messianism in the Modern Era: Metaphor and Meaning, Studies in Contemporary Jewry*, Vol VII (Jerusalem, 1991), pp 128–58.
15. *Ha'aretz*, 1 June 1984.
16. *Ma'ariv*, 23 May 1984.
17. *Ha'aretz*, 15 July 1983.
18. *Jerusalem Post*, 16 May 1984.
19. *Ha'aretz*, 3 May 1984.

20. *Jerusalem Post*, 16 May 1984.
21. Rabbi Avraham Weiss, *Jerusalem Post*, 12 July 1984.
22. *New Outlook*, February 1984. The quotation is taken from the addition to the Mincha – afternoon prayer – for Tisha B'Av, which commemorates the destruction of both Temples.
23. *Nekuda*, October 1984.
24. Sprinzak, *The Ascendance of Israel's Radical Right*, p 270.
25. *Al Hamishmar*, 5 September 1984.
26. *Jerusalem Post*, 2 May 1984.
27. Yitzhak Shamir, *Summing Up* (London, 1994), p 151.
28. *Nekuda*, 6 July 1984.
29. *Davar*, 3 August 1984.

14. Outlawing the Palestinians

1. *New Outlook*, May–June 1986.
2. *Ha'aretz*, 24 April 1984.
3. *International Herald Tribune*, 1 February 1985.
4. Laor-L'ma'an Achai V'Reai – For the Sake of My Brothers and Friends.
5. *Guardian*, 25 May 1985.
6. *Yediot Aharonot*, 24 May 1985.
7. Interview with Uzi Landau, 21 October 1994.
8. Shimon Peres, *Battling for Peace: Memoirs* (London, 1995), pp 305–12, 361–2.
9. *Guardian*, 6 November 1985.
10. Ariel Merari, Tamar Prat, Sophia Kotzer, Anat Kurz, Yoram Schweitzer, *Inter 85: A Review of International Terrorism* (Tel Aviv, 1986), p 33.
11. Yehoshafat Harkabi, *Israel's Fateful Decisions* (London, 1988), p 109.
12. Moshe Arens, *Hadar*, vol 5, no. 1, June 1948.
13. Interview with Moshe Arens, 26 October 1994.
14. Benzion Netanyahu, 'Jabotinsky's Place in the History of the Jewish People', lecture given at the University of Haifa, 13 January 1981, Jabotinsky Archives, Tel Aviv.
15. Moshe Decter, *Midstream*, March 1987.
16. Benjamin Netanyahu, *Terrorism: How the West Can Win* (London, 1986), p 8.
17. Benjamin Netanyahu, *A Place Among the Nations: Israel and the World* (London, 1993), p 383.

15. Between Information and Propaganda

1. 'The Nineteenth America–Israel Dialogue; Hasbara: Israel's Public Image – Problems and Remedies', *Congress Monthly*, vol 51, nos 2–3, 1984.
2. *Jerusalem Post*, 25 May 1986.
3. Yitzhak Shamir, 'Israel's Role in a Changing Middle East', *Foreign Affairs*, vol 60 (Spring 1982), p 791.
4. *Wall Street Journal*, 5 April 1983.
5. Daniel Pipes and Adam Garfinkle, 'Is Jordan Palestine?', *Commentary*, vol 86, no. 4, October 1988.
6. 'The Nineteenth America–Israel Dialogue'.
7. Benjamin Netanyahu, *A Place Among the Nations: Israel and the World* (London,

1993), pp 375–6.
8. Ibid., p 204.
9. *New York Times*, 18 October 1985.
10. Netanyahu, *A Place Among the Nations*, p 214.
11. *Ha'aretz*, 18 October 1982.
12. *The Economist*, 9 October 1982.
13. *Jerusalem Post*, 30 December 1988.
14. Colin Shindler, *Ploughshares into Swords? Israelis and Jews in the Shadow of the Intifada* (London, 1991), pp 167–71.
15. Yitzhak Shamir, *Summing Up* (London, 1994), p 179.
16. *Jerusalem Post*, 6 April 1984.
17. Yehoshafat Harkabi, *Israel's Fateful Decisions* (London, 1988), p 125.
18. Interview with Ari Rath, 31 October 1994.
19. *Jerusalem Post*, 7 June 1989.
20. Details of donations above 23,000 shekels received during the Election Campaign for the Thirteenth Knesset, State Comptroller's Report for 1992 (Jerusalem, 1993).

16. The Year of Reckoning

1. Interview with Yossi Beilin, 20 October 1994.
2. *Yediot Aharonot*, 16 December 1988.
3. *Al Hamishmar*, 9 May 1988.
4. *FBIS*, 8 August 1988.
5. Benjamin Netanyahu, *A Place Among the Nations: Israel and the World* (London, 1993), pp 212–13.
6. *Yediot Aharonot*, 23 December 1988.
7. *Jerusalem Post*, 15 March 1988.
8. *Jerusalem Post*, 16 December 1988.
9. *New York Times*, 24 October 1989.
10. *Ha'aretz*, 21 March 1990.
11. *FBIS*, 22 March 1990.

17. The Shamir Plan

1. Yitzhak Shamir, *Summing Up* (London, 1994), p 198.
2. Interview with Yossi Beilin, 20 October 1994.
3. Interview with Moshe Arens, 26 October 1994.
4. Colin Shindler, *Ploughshares into Swords? Israelis and Jews in the Shadow of the Intifada* (London, 1991), pp 129–32.
5. *Jerusalem Post*, 2 March 1989.
6. *New York Times*, 2 April 1989.
7. *Jerusalem Post*, 6 April 1989.
8. *New York Times*, 9 April 1989.
9. Interview with Benny Begin, 24 October 1994.
10. *Ma'ariv*, 15 May 1989.
11. Interview with Eliahu Ben-Elissar, 25 October 1994.
12. Keesings Contemporary Archives (London, 1990), p 370303.
13. *FBIS*, 5 April 1990.
14. Ibid.

18. Forward to the Edge

1. *Ha'aretz*, 1 May 1990.
2. *Ma'ariv*, 27 March 1990.
3. *FBIS*, 13 March 1990.
4. *Yediot Aharonot*, 22 September 1988.
5. *Ha'aretz*, 17 August 1990.
6. *Yediot Aharonot*, 14 August 1990.
7. Yitzhak Shamir, *Summing Up* (London, 1994), p. 225.
8. *FBIS*, 24 January 1991.
9. *FBIS*, 4 February 1991.
10. *Hadashot*, 19 March 1991.
11. Interview with Avishai Margalit, 31 October 1994.
12. *FBIS*, 21 October 1991.
13. *Yediot Aharonot*, 20 October 1991.
14. *Ha'aretz*, 24 October 1991.
15. *Yediot Aharonot*, 25 October 1991.
16. *Davar*, 25 October 1991.
17. Interview with Zalman Shoval, 28 October 1994.
18. *Hadashot*, 28 June 1992.
19. *Ha'aretz*, 27 December 1991.
20. Interview with Zalman Shoval, 28 October 1994.
21. *Jerusalem Report*, 27 February 1992.
22. *Jerusalem Post*, 6 June 1992.
23. *Yediot Aharonot*, 22 June 1992.
24. *Jerusalem Report*, 26 March 1995
25. Michael Karpin and Ina Friedman, *Murder in the Name of God : The Plot to Kill Yitzhak Rabin* (London, 1999), pp. 244-5.
26. *Ha'aretz* 22 April 1996.

SELECT BIBLIOGRAPHY

Abbas Mahmoud, *Through Secret Channels: The Road to Oslo* (London, 1995).

Alexander, Yonah, and Joshua Sinai, *Terrorism: The PLO Connection* (New York, 1989).

Arens, Moshe, *Broken Covenant: American Foreign Policy and the Crisis between the US and Israel* (New York, 1995).

Arian, Asher, *Politics in Israel: The Second Generation* (Chatham, 1989).

Arian, Asher, and Michael Shamir (eds), *The Elections in Israel 1984* (Tel Aviv, 1986).

Arian, Asher and Shamir, Michal (eds.), *The Elections in Israel 1992* (New York, 1995)

Aronoff, Myron J., *Israeli Visions and Divisions* (New Brunswick, 1989).

Aronson, Geoffrey, *Israel, Palestinians and the Intifada* (London, 1990).

Avineri, Shlomo, *The Making of Modern Zionism: The Intellectual Origins of the Jewish State* (London, 1981).

—————— *Moses Hess: Prophet of Communism and Zionism* (New York, 1987).

—————— *Arlasoroff* (London, 1989).

Avishai, Bernard, *The Tragedy of Zionism: Revolution and Democracy in the Land of Israel* (New York, 1985).

—————— *A New Israel: Democracy in Crisis* (New York, 1990).

Bader, Yochanan, *The Knesset and I* (Jerusalem, 1979).

Bar-On, Mordechai, *The Gates of Gaza: Israel's Road to Suez and Back 1955–1957* (London, 1994).

Bar-On, Mordechai, *In Pursuit of Peace: A History of the Israeli Peace Movement* (Washington, 1996)

Bar-Zohar, Michael, *Ben-Gurion: A Biography* (Jerusalem, 1978).

Begin, Menachem, *The Revolt* (New York, 1977).

—————— *White Nights* (London, 1977).

Benvenisti, Meron, *The West Bank Handbook* (Jerusalem, 1986).

Ben-Yehuda, Nachunan, *Political Assassinations by Jews: A Rhetorical Device for Justice* (New York, 1993).

Benziman, Uzi, *Sharon: An Israel Caesar* (London, 1987).

Bethell, Nicholas, *The Palestine Triangle: The Struggle between the British, the Jews and the Arabs 1935–1948* (London, 1979).

Black, Ian and Benny Morris, *Israel's Secret Wars: The Untold History of Israeli Intelligence* (London, 1991).

Bleich, J. David, *Contemporary Halakhic Problems*, Vol III (New York, 1989).

Bowyer Bell, J., *Terror Out of Zion: The Fight for Israeli Independence 1929–1949* (Dublin, 1977).

Brecher, Michael, *The Foreign Policy of Israel* (New Haven, 1972).

Butt, Gerald, *Behind the Star: Inside Israel Today* (London, 1990).

Carter, Jimmy, *The Blood of Abraham* (Boston, 1985).

——— *Keeping Faith* (London, 1982).

Caspit, Ben and Kfir, Ilan *Netanyahu: The Road to Power* (London, 1998)

Cesarani, David, *The Jewish Chronicle and Anglo-Jewry 1841–1991* (Cambridge, 1994).

Chaliand, Gerard, *The Palestinian Resistance* (London, 1972).

Charters, David A., *The British Army and Jewish Insurgency in Palestine 1945–47* (London, 1989).

Chomsky, Noam, *Peace in the Middle East?* (London, 1975).

——— *The Fateful Triangle: The U.S., Israel and the Palestinians* (Boston, 1983).

Cohen, Aharon, *Israel and the Arab World* (London, 1970).

Cohen, Michael J., *Palestine and the Great Powers 1945–1948* (Princeton, 1982).

——— *Truman and Israel* (Berkeley, 1990).

Cohen, Stuart A., and Eliezer Don-Yehiya (eds), *Comparative Jewish Politics: Vol II, Conflict and Consensus in Jewish Political Life* (Tel Aviv, 1986).

Coogan, Tim Pat, *Michael Collins: A Biography* (London, 1990).

——— *De Valera: Long Fellow, Long Shadow* (London, 1993).

Crossman, Richard, *Palestine Mission: A Personal Record* (London, 1947).

——— *A Nation Reborn: The Israel of Weizmann, Bevin and Ben-Gurion* (London, 1960).

Curtis, Michael, *The Middle East Reader* (New Brunswick, 1986).

Darwish, Adel, and Gregory Alexander, *Unholy Babylon: The Secret History of Saddam's War* (London, 1991).

Dayan, Moshe, *Story of My Life: An Autobiography* (New York, 1976).

——— *Breakthrough: A Personal Account of the Egypt–Israel Peace Negotiations* (London, 1981).

Don-Yehiya, Eliezer (ed), *Comparative Jewish Politics: Israel and Diaspora Jewry* (Tel Aviv, 1991).

Drezon-Tepler, Marcia, *Interest Groups and Political Change in Israel* (New York, 1990).

Eban, Abba, *An Autobiography* (New York, 1977).

Efrat, Elisha, *Geography and Politics in Israel since 1967* (London, 1988).

Eisentadt, S.N., *The Transformation of Israeli Society* (London, 1985).

Elazar, Daniel J. and Sandler, Shmuel, *Israel at the Polls 1996* (London, 1998).

Eliav, Liova, *New Heart, New Spirit: Biblical Humanism for Modern Israel* (Philadelphia, 1988).

Elon, Amos, *The Israelis: Founders and Sons* (London, 1972).

Elpeleg, Zvi, *The Grand Mufti: Haj Amin Al-Hussaini, Founder of the Palestinian National Movement* (London, 1993).

Evron, Boas, *Jewish State or Israeli Nation?* (Bloomington, 1995).

Feldman, Shai, and Heda Rechnitz-Kijner, *Deception, Consensus and War: Israel in Lebanon* (Tel Aviv, 1984).

Fisch, Harold, *The Zionist Revolution* (London, 1978).

Flamhaft, Ziva, *Israel on the Road to Peace: Accepting the Unacceptable* (Boulder, 1996)

Flapan, Simha, *When Enemies Dare to Talk* (London, 1979).

——— *The Birth of Israel: Myths and Realities* (New York, 1987).

Freedman, Lawrence, and Efraim Karsh, *The Gulf Conflict 1990–1991* (London, 1993).

Freedman, Robert O. (ed), *The Middle East after Iraq's Invasion of Kuwait* (Florida, 1993).

—— *Israel under Rabin* (Colorado, 1995).

Friedman, Thomas, *From Beirut to Jerusalem: One Man's Middle East Odyssey* (London, 1990).

Gorney, Yosef, *The British Labour Movement and Zionism* (London, 1983).

—— *Zionism and the Arabs 1882–1948* (Oxford, 1987).

—— *The State of Israel in Jewish Public Thought: The Quest for Collective Identity* (London, 1994).

Gowers, Andrew, and Tony Walker, *Behind the Myth: Yasser Arafat and the Palestinian Revolution* (London, 1990).

Grossman, David, *The Yellow Wind* (London, 1988).

Ha'am, Ahad, *Nationalism and the Jewish Ethic: Basic Writings of Ahad Ha'am* (New York, 1962).

Halpern, Ben, *The Idea of a Jewish State* (Harvard, 1969).

Harkabi, Yehoshafat, *Arab Attitudes to Israel* (London, 1972).

—— *Israel's Fateful Decisions* (London, 1988).

Heller, Joseph, *The Stern Gang: Ideology, Politics and Terror 1940–1949* (London, 1995).

—— *The Birth of Israel 1945-1949: Ben-Gurion and his Critics* (Florida, 2000).

Heller, Mark A., *A Palestinian State: The Implications for Israel* (London, 1983).

Hertzberg, Arthur, *Jewish Polemics* (New York, 1992).

Hurwitz, Harry, *Menachem Begin* (Johannesburg, 1977).

Isaac, Rael Jean, *Israel Divided: Ideological Politics in the Jewish State* (Baltimore, 1976).

—— *Party and Politics in Israel: Three Views of a Jewish State* (New York, 1981).

Israeli, Raphael, *PLO in Lebanon: Selected Documents* (London, 1983).

Jakobovits, Immanuel, *If Only My People: Zionism in My Life* (London, 1984).

Jansen, Michael, *Dissonance in Zion* (London, 1987).

Joseph, Dov, *The Faithful City: The Siege of Jerusalem 1948* (London, 1961).

Karpin, Michael and Friedman, Ina, *Murder in the Name of God: The Plot to Kill Yitzhak Rabin* (London, 1999)

Karsh, Efraim (ed.), *From Rabin to Netanyahu: Israel's Troubled Agenda* (London, 1997).

Katz, Emmanuel, *Lehi: Freedom Fighters of Israel* (Tel Aviv, 1987).

Katz, Shmuel, *Lone Wolf: A Biography of Vladimir Ze'ev Jabotinsky* Vol I and II (New York, 1996)

Kaufman, Gerald, *Inside the Promised Land* (London, 1986).

Keller, Adam, *Terrible Days* (Amselveen, 1987).

Khalidi, Rashid, *Under Siege: PLO Decision-making during the 1982 War* (New York, 1986).

Kimmerling, Baruch, *The Israeli State and Society: Boundaries and Frontiers* (New York, 1989).

King, John, *Handshake in Washington: The Beginning of Middle East Peace?* (London, 1994).

Kornberg, Jacques, *Theodor Herzl: From Assimilation to Zionism* (Bloomington, 1993).

Landau, David, *Piety and Power: The World of Jewish Fundamentalism* (London, 1993).

Langer, Felicia, *An Age of Stone* (London, 1988).

Laqueur, Walter, *The Road to War: The Origin and Aftermath of the Arab-Israeli Conflict 1967–8* (London, 1968).

Laqueur, Walter, and Barry Rubin (eds), *The Israel-Arab Reader: A Documentary History of the Middle East Conflict* (London, 1984).

Leibowitz, Yeshayahu, *Judaism, Human Values and the Jewish State* (London, 1992).

Liebman, Charles S., *Pressure without Sanctions* (New Jersey, 1977).

Lissak, Moshe, *Israeli Society and its Defence Establishment* (London, 1984).

Lockman, Zachary, and Joel Beinin, *Intifada: The Palestinian Uprising against Israeli Occupation* (London, 1990).

Lorch, Nataniel (ed), *Major Knesset Debates*, Vols I–VI (Jerusalem, 1992).

Lukács, Yehuda, *Documents on the Israeli-Palestinian Conflict 1967–1983* (Cambridge, 1986).

Lucas, Noah, *The Modern History of Israel* (London, 1974).

Makovsky, David, *Making Peace with the PLO: The Rabin Government's Road to the Oslo Accord* (Boulder, 1996)

McDowall, David, *Palestine and Israel: The Uprising and Beyond* (London, 1989).

Medding, Peter Y., *Israel: State and Society 1948–1988* (Oxford, 1989).

—— *The Founding of Israeli Democracy 1948–1967* (Oxford, 1990).

Melman, Yossi, *The Master Terrorist: The Time Story behind Abu Nidal* (London, 1987).

Mishal, Shaul, *The PLO under Arafat* (New Haven, 1986).

Morris, Benny, *The Birth of the Palestinian Refugee Problem 1947–1949* (Cambridge, 1987).

—— *1948 and After: Israel and the Palestinians* (Oxford, 1990).

Netanyahu, Benjamin, *Terrorism: How the West Can Win* (London, 1986).

—— *A Place Among the Nations: Israel and the World* (London, 1993).

Newman, David, *The Impact of Gush Emunim: Politics and Settlement in the West Bank* (London, 1985).

O'Brien, Conor Cruise, *The Siege* (London, 1986).

O'Brien, William V., *Law and Morality in Israel's War with the PLO* (London, 1991).

O'Hegarty, P.S., *The Victory of Sinn Fein* (Dublin, 1924).

Oz, Amos, *In the Land of Israel* (London, 1983).

Ofer, Dalia, *Escaping the Holocaust: Illegal Immigration to the Land of Israel 1939–1944* (Oxford, 1990).

Oren, Michael B., *The Origins of the Second Arab-Israeli War: Egypt, Israel and the Great Powers 1952–1956* (London, 1992).

Pappe, Ilan, *The Making of the Arab-Israeli Conflict 1947–1951* (London, 1992).

Pearlman, Moshe, *Ben-Gurion Looks Back* (London, 1965).

Penniman, Howard R., *Israel at the Polls: Knesset Election of 1977* (Washington, 1979).

Penniman, Howard R., and Daniel J. Elazar, *Israel at the Polls, 1981* (Bloomington, 1986).

Peres, Shimon, *Battling for Peace: Memoirs* (London, 1995).

Peretz, Don, *Intifada: The Palestinian Uprising* (London, 1990).

Peri, Yoram, *Between Battles and Ballots: Israeli Military in Politics* (Cambridge, 1983).

Perlmutter, Amos, *Israel: The Partitioned State* (New York, 1985).

Porat, Dina, *The Blue and Yellow Stars of David: The Zionist Leadership in Palestine and the Holocaust 1939–1945* (London, 1990).

Porath, Yehoshua, *The Palestinian Arab National Movement 1929–1939: From Riots to Rebellions* (London, 1977).

Prittie, Terence, *Eshkol of Israel* (London, 1969).

Pryce-Jones, David, *The Closed Circle: An Interpretation of the Arabs* (London, 1989).

Quandt, William, *Peace Process* (Washington, 1993).

Rabin, Yitzhak, *The Rabin Memoirs* (Boston, 1979).

Rabinovich, Itamar, *The Brink of Peace: The Israeli-Syrian Negotiations* (Princeton, 1998)

Randal, Jonathan, *The Tragedy of Lebanon* (London, 1990).

Reinharz, Yehuda, *Chaim Weizmann: The Making of a Zionist Leader* (Oxford, 1985).

Rose, Norman, *Chaim Weizmann: A Biography* (London, 1986).

Roth, Stephen J., *The Impact of the Six Day War* (London, 1988).

Rubin, Barry, *Revolution until Victory: The Politics and History of the PLO* (London, 1994).

Rubinstein, Ammon, *The Zionist Dream Revisited* (New York, 1984).

Sachar, Howard M., *A History of Israel: From the Rise of Zionism to Our Time* (Oxford, 1976).

——— *A History of Israel, Vol II* (Oxford, 1987).

Sadat, Anwar, *In Search of Identity* (London, 1978).

Sahliyeh, Emile, *In Search of Leadership: West Bank Politics since 1967* (Washington DC, 1988).

Said, Edward, *The Question of Palestine* (London, 1981).

Sarig, Mordechai (ed.) *The Political and Social Philosophy of Ze'ev Jabotinsky: Selected Writings* (London, 1999)

Sayigh, Rosemary, *Too Many Enemies: The Palestinian Experience in Lebanon* (London, 1994).

Schechtman, Joseph B., *The Jabotinsky Story: Rebel and Statesman – Vol I: The Early Years, 1880–1923* (London, 1956).

——— *The Jabotinsky Story: Fighter and Prophet – Vol II: The Last Years, 1923–1940* (New York, 1961).

Schenker, Hillel, *After Lebanon* (New York, 1983).

Schiff, Ze'ev, and Ehud Ya'ari, *Israel's Lebanon War* (New York, 1984).

——— *Intifada* (London, 1990).

Scholem, Gershom, *Sabbatai Sevi: The Mystical Messiah 1626–1676* (London, 1973).

Schnall, David, J., *Radical Dissent in Contemporary Israeli Politics* (London, 1979).

——— *Beyond the Green Line* (New York, 1984).

Schroeter, Leonard, *The Last Exodus* (Seattle, 1979).

Schweitzer, Avram, *Israel: The Changing National Agenda* (London, 1986).

Seale, Patrick, *Abu Nidal: A Gun for Hire* (London, 1992).

Segev, Tom, *The Seventh Million: The Israelis and the Holocaust* (New York, 1993).

Segre, Dan V., *Israel: A Society in Transition* (Oxford, 1971).

——— *A Crisis of Identity: Israel and Zionism* (Oxford, 1980).

Shamir, Yitzhak, *Summing Up* (London, 1994).

Shapiro, Yonathan, *The Road to Power: The Herut Party in Israel* (New York, 1991).

Sharfman, Daphna, *Living without a Constitution: Civil Rights in Israel* (London, 1993).

Sharon, Ariel, *Warrior: The Autobiography of Ariel Sharon* (New York, 1989).

Shavitt, Yaakov, *Jabotinsky and the Revisionist Movement: 1925–1948* (London, 1988).

Sheffer, Gabriel, *Moshe Sharett: Biography of a Political Moderate* (Oxford, 1996)

Shimon, Gideon, *The Zionist Ideology* (Brandeis, 1995)

Shindler, Colin, *Ploughshares into Swords: Israelis and Jews in the Shadow of the Intifada* (London, 1991).

Shipler, David, *Arab and Jew: Wounded Spirits in a Promised Land* (New York, 1986).

Shlaim, Avi, *Collusion across the Jordan: Abdullah, the Zionist Movement and the Partition of Palestine* (Oxford, 1988).
—— *The Iron Wall: Israel and the Arab World, 1948-98* (London, 2000).
Shultz, George P., *Turmoil and Triumph: My Years as Secretary of State* (New York, 1993).
Silver, Eric, *Begin: A Biography* (London, 1984).
Simon, Leon, *Ahad Ha'am: A Biography* (London, 1960).
Sivan, Emmanuel, and Menachem Friedman (eds), *Religious Radicalism and Politics in the Middle East* (New York, 1990).
Spiegel, Steven L. (ed), *The Arab-Israel Search for Peace* (London, 1988).
Sofer, Sasson, *Begin: An Anatomy of a Leadership* (Oxford, 1988).
—— *Zionism and the Foundations of Israeli Diplomacy* (Cambridge, 1998)
Sprinzak, Ehud, *The Ascendance of Israel's Radical Right* (New York, 1991).
Stone, I.F., *Underground to Palestine* (London, 1979).
Sykes, Christopher, *Crossroads to Israel* (Bloomington, 1973).
Talmon, J.L., *Israel Among the Nations* (London, 1970).
Tamir, Avraham, *A Soldier in Search of Peace* (London, 1988).
Temko, Ned, *To Win or to Die: A Personal Portrait of Menachem Begin* (New York, 1987).
Teveth, Shabtai, *The Killing of Arlosoroff* (Tel Aviv, 1982).
—— *Ben-Gurion and the Palestinian Arabs* (Oxford, 1985).
Thomas, Hugh, *The Suez Affair* (London, 1967).
Timmerman, Jacobo, *The Longest War* (London, 1982).
Urquhart, Brian, *A Life in Peace and War* (London, 1987).
Viorst, Milton, *Sands of Sorrow: Israel's Journey from Independence* (London, 1987).
Wasserstein, Bernard, *The British in Palestine: The Mandatory Government and the Arab-Jewish Conflict 1917-1929* (London, 1978).
Weisburd, David, *Jewish Settler Violence* (London, 1989).
Weissberg, Alex, *Advocate for the Dead: The Story of Joel Brand* (London, 1958).
Weizmann, Chaim, *Trial and Error* (New York, 1966).
Wilson, Mary C., *King Abdullah and the Making of Jordan* (Cambridge, 1987).
Yaniv, Avner, *Dilemmas of Security: Politics, Strategy and the Israeli Experience in Lebanon* (New York, 1987).
Zipperstein, Steven J., *Elusive Prophet: Ahad Ha'am and the Origins of Zionism* (London, 1993).
Zweig, Ronald W. (ed), *David Ben-Gurion: Politics and Leadership in Israel* (Jerusalem and London, 1991).

INDEX

Abbas, Abul, 213, 226, 227, 248; request for
expulsion from PLO, 248
Abdullah, King, 11, 21, 36, 37, 43, 44, 45, 60,
193; contact with Israel, 43
Abramovich, Aharon, 136
Abu Iyad, 241
Abu Musa, 209, 217, 227
Abu Nidal, 117, 118, 214, 217, 226, 228, 229;
break with Yasser Arafat, 119; protected
by Syria, 228
Abu Nidal group, 119, 120
Abuhatzeira, Aharon, 105
Achdut Ha'avoda, 9, 18, 64, 66, 67, 77, 94,
105, 191
Achille Lauro, hijacking of, 213, 226, 227, 248
Achimeir, Abba, 17, 183; trial of, 174
Achimeir, Yossi, 211
Achituv, Avraham, 201
Acre prison, 14, 31
Administrative Council, under autonomy
plan, 90
Agranat Commission, 76, 83
Agudat Yisrael party, 200, 207, 238, 239, 258,
260, 261, 277, 278
Algeria, 151; under French, 55, 56
Ali, Rashid, 26
aliyah, see immigration of Jews
Alkalai, Rabbi, 194
Allon, Yigal, 3, 4, 67, 77, 81, 86, 139, 191
Allon Plan, 76, 84, 264
Aloni Shulamit, 2, 107, 142, 205
Altalena affair, 4, 32, 37, 44, 113
Altman, Aryeh, 42
Amalekites, 156, 157, 158
American Jewish Committee, 79, 192, 231,
232, 251
American Jewish Congress, 231, 251, 253
American Jews, 155, 162, 164, 208, 215, 216,
219, 231, 239, 242, 245, 247, 249, 251, 252,
253, 254, 260, 266; zealotry among
settlers, 201

Amikam, Eliahu, 138
Amir, Yigal, 280
Amirav, Moshe, 211
anarchism, 15, 29
Anders, Wladyslaw, 27
Anglo-American Commission of Inquiry, 34
anti-communism, 54, 182
Anti-Defamation League, 163, 231, 245, 246,
247
anti-fascism, 34, 40
anti-Nazism, 22
anti-racism bill, 229
anti-Semitism, 23, 25, 164, 178, 218
Arabs, 43, 169, 272; alleged plan to
exterminate Israel, 148; alliance with
Jewish workers, 13; Israeli, 73, 153 (rights
denied, 237; seen as foreigners, 101);
opposition to Zionism, 12; organization
of labour, 10; refugees, taken by Ben-
Gurion, 45; seen as Europeans, 146; *see
also* Palestinians
Arafat, Yasser, 117, 119, 120, 130, 137, 147,
209, 211, 213, 222, 226, 227, 235, 237, 240,
241, 242, 244, 245, 246, 250, 252, 256,
264, 267, 268, 286, 287, 289, 290, 291;
death sentence on, 119; interview
banned from broadcast, 230; likened to
Hitler, 252; manoeuvrability of, 226;
rapprochement with King Hussein, 226;
urged to initiate new policy, 240; US
visa opposed, 247
Arens, Moshe, 94, 114, 172, 208, 212, 215,
220, 225, 229, 239, 245, 250, 251, 255, 256,
257, 258, 259, 273, 274; resignation of,
274 (call for, 270)
Argentina, 168
Argov, Shlomo, attempted killing of, 119, 133
Aridor, Yoram, 106, 111, 192, 202
Ariel, Yisrael, 200
Arlosoroff, Chaim, assassination of, 10, 174,
196

312

Armistice Agreement (1949), 45
arms imports of Israel, 82
Asher, tribe of, 155
Ashkenazi, Motti, 83
Ashkenazim, 1, 103, 148, 156, 178
Ashrawi, Hanan, 270, 273
al-Assad, Hafiz, 126
assassinations, 29, 176, 177, 180, 181; of
  Avraham Vilenchik, 181; of Count
  Bernadotte, 181; of Eliahu Giladi, 181; of
  governor of Vilna, 180; of Israel Pritsker,
  181; of Semion Petlyura, 180
Ateret Cohanim yeshiva, 262
attacks on Israel, statistics for, 118
Attlee, Clement, 33
autonomy for Palestinians, 88–90, 116, 236;
  as compromise, 100; for Gaza, 96; for
  West Bank, 96
Avneri, Uri, 119; meeting with Yasser
  Arafat, 138, 143
Axis powers, Israel as satellite of, 24

Bader, Yochanan, 49, 173
Baker, James, 248, 250, 253, 254, 256, 257,
  259, 265, 269, 276; presence in Israel,
  269; speech by, 254, 255
Baker Plan, 260; opposition to, 258
Balfour Declaration, 7, 22, 223
banks, and subsidy system, 79
Bar-Illan, David, 233
Bar-Kochba, Shimon, 194, 195
Bar-Lev, Chaim, 143, 210, 283
Bar-Simantov, Yaakov, killing of, 118
Baruk, Ehud, 281, 282, 286, 287, 290
Baram, Uzi, 142, 162
Bazak, Ya'akov, 200
Begin, Menachem, 1, 6, 10, 11, 15, 18, 29, 32,
  37, 38, 39, 41, 42, 44, 45, 49, 50, 52, 54, 55,
  63, 64, 65, 67, 68, 69, 70, 71, 73, 74, 75,
  82, 85, 86, 87, 90, 91, 92, 110, 111, 117, 118,
  123, 125, 126, 127, 130, 131, 132, 134, 139,
  142, 143, 144, 147, 156, 157, 159, 161, 162,
  163, 166, 170, 174, 182, 186, 191, 192, 196,
  198, 199, 201, 206, 207, 221, 224, 225, 241,
  250, 253, 272, 275, 279, 281, 283, 284, 285;
  adulation of, 172; arrival in Palestine, 27;
  attack on Germany, 51; attack on Geula
  Cohen, 107; attack on partition, 37;
  attitude to PLO, 147; attitude to Sinai,
  94; call for Golda Meir to resign, 75;
  compared with Hitler, 149; demonization
  of, 5; effect of Kahan Commission
  report, 169; elected as head of Herut, 2;
  elected prime minister, 27; escaped Nazi
  invasion, 149; execution of father, 148;
  first government of, 83–95; Holocaust
  trauma of, 145–58; labelled as terrorist, 3;

letter to Ronald Reagan, 150; Nobel
  Prize for, 52; obsessive relation with past,
  149; opposed by Shamir, 188; populism
  of, 101; refusal of Sabra and Shatilla
  inquiry, 153; refusal to renounce Camp
  David, 192; relation with Sharon, 122;
  resignation of, 170, 171, 172 (call for, 164);
  rhetoric of, 20, 27, 36, 38, 40, 42, 43, 47,
  53, 58, 109, 136, 140, 145, 151, 173, 218;
  traditionalism of, 238; triumphalism of,
  111; visit to USA, 40
Begin, Benny, 274, 280
Beilin, Yossi, 141, 162
Beirut, 151; bombing of, 110, 116, 156, 166;
  evacuation of, 208; siege of, 128, 134,
  136, 142, 143, 149, 164, 167; see also West
  Beirut
Bekaa Valley, 110, 123, 126, 129
Bellow, Saul, 230
Ben-Aharon, Yossi, 233
Ben Bichri, Sheva, 156, 157
Ben-Eliezer, Aryeh, 56
Ben-Gal, Avigdor, 101, 121
Ben-Gera, Ehud, 180
Ben-Gurion, David, 2, 3, 4, 5, 8, 9, 10, 12,
  13, 18, 20, 21, 32, 33, 36, 37, 39, 40, 41,
  44, 48, 51, 53, 55, 56, 57, 58, 62, 63, 65,
  66, 68, 69, 72, 77, 84, 92, 94, 113, 139,
  155, 187, 191, 197, 198, 202, 215, 241, 282,
  283, 288; acceptance of partition, 45;
  animosity to Herut, 54, 64; antipathy to
  Begin, 63; egocentrim of, 64; opposition
  to Irgun, 35; view of Lenin, 18
Ben-Ner, Yitzhak, 136
Ben-Porat, Yeshayahu, 132
Ben Shoshan, Yeshua, 190, 195
Ben-Yair, Elazar, 22, 180
Ben-Yosef, Shlomo, 21
Ben Zeruiah, Yoav, 156, 157, 158
Berlin, Isaiah, 230; call for Sabra and Shatilla
  inquiry, 164
Berman, Julius, 163
Berman, Yitzhak, 162
Bernadotte, Count, assassination of, 41, 181,
  182
Betar youth group, 9, 11, 12, 14, 16, 17, 18, 19,
  31, 47, 90, 114, 149, 184, 215; Hymn of,
  20; rise of, 20–7; World Conference (in
  1935, 20; in 1938, 15, 21)
Bevin, Ernest, 34, 43, 177
Bialkin, Kenneth, 163
Bin Laden, Osama, 289, 290
Biton, Charlie, 211
Black September, 146, 211
Black, Conrad, 232
Bleich, J. David, 155
Bnei Brak, 262

Board of Deputies of British Jews, 3, 119, 120, 163, 164
Brand, Joel, 178
Brezhnev Plan, 211
Brit Ha'Biryonim, 18, 90, 196
Brit Ha'Canaim, 199
British government, 3, 11, 13, 14, 21, 27, 45, 60, 175, 210, 222, 223, 250; compared to Nazis, 145, 176; cooperation with, 32; intelligence services, 213; relations with, 7, 33, 34; revolt against, 20, 21, 23, 24, 28, 30, 36, 38, 43, 174, 182; view of Shamir, 179
British Army, Jews in, 25
Broadcasting Act (1965), 135, 136
Broadcasting Authority, inefficiency of, 80
broadcasting staff dismissed, 100
Bronfman, Charles, 234
Brun, Natan, 138
Brzezinski, Zbigniew, 91
B'Tselem, 288
Buber, Martin, 14, 15
Buchenwald camp, 22, 150
Burg, Avrum, 140, 156
Burg, Yosef, 99, 121, 141, 188
Bus 300 incident, 189, 193
Bush, George, 243, 244, 245, 247, 248, 249, 251, 252, 253, 265, 266, 269, 271, 276, 277, 291; pressure to end West Bank occupation, 252; relations with Shamir, 253, 267; suspension of dialogue with PLO, 248
Bush, George W., 289, 290, 291

Camp David Accords, 91, 103, 105, 113, 121, 153, 154, 188, 191, 195, 196, 208, 211, 215, 222, 225, 227, 250, 263, 270; cost of, 96–108; interpretation of, 264; opposition to, 99; public support of, 98, 102;
Camp David 2000, 287, 290
Campaigning Group for the Golan Heights, 271
camps, Palestinian, 242; demolition of, 159
Carter, Jimmy, 2, 90, 91, 93, 96, 97, 98, 154, 208, 249, 253; administration, 78; Christianity of, 91
ceasefire with PLO, 116, 117, 125, 142
Ceausescu, Nicolae, 88
censorship of media, 134, 135
Chamberlain, Neville, 57
Chile, 169
Churchill, Winston, 22, 33
Circle of Herut Loyalists, 92
Citizens for Zahal organization, 138
Civil Rights Movement, 2
class conflict, 10; proposed deterrence of, 9

cluster-bombs, embargoed for Israel, 78
coalition-building, of right, 107, 114
Cohen, Ariel, 136
Cohen, Geula, 105, 107, 144, 192, 268, 271
Cohen-Avidov, Meir, 135, 204
Cohen-Orgad, Yigal, 200
Cold War, 182, 249
Collins, Michael, 30, 31, 174, 177
Committee Against the War in Lebanon, 127, 137
Committee for the Renewal of Jewish Settlement in Hebron, 190
Committee for the Sanctity of Human Life, 199
communism, 22, 55, 182, 214; demise of, 235, 249, 265
Communist Party, 107
Conference of Jewish Solidarity with Israel, 252
Connolly, James, 23
consumerism in Israel, 273
corruption scandals, 77, 78, 80, 82, 275; concern about, 79; under Labour, 106
Council of Settlements in Judea, Samaria and Gaza, 203, 262, 271
Cranston, Senator Alan, 164
cross-border attacks, 245, 246, 247, 248
Crossman, Richard, 34
Czechoslovakia, 151, 270; arms deal with Egypt, 56

Dachau camp, 22
Daily Telegraph, 232
Dalton, Hugh, 33
David's Tower, 37
David, King, 156, 157, 158
Davidesku, Joseph, 181
Davis, Sammy, Jr, 135
Dayan, Moshe, 63, 65, 66, 67, 68, 70, 71, 72, 76, 83, 84, 85, 86, 90, 91, 93, 97, 99, 100, 104, 112, 114, 144, 195, 282, 283, 284, 285, 286; resignation of, 99, 188; unpopular in Israel, 87
death penalty proposed for Arab terrorists, 209
declaration of a Palestinian state, 246
Declaration of Palestinian Independence, 241
defence spending of Israel, 81
Degel Ha'Torah party, 238, 239, 260, 277, 278
Deir Yassin massacre, 3, 29, 182
Dekel, Mikhail, 139, 274
democracy, 10, 14, 40
Democratic Alliance, 209
Democratic Front for Peace and Equality, 142

Democratic Front for the Liberation of Palestine (DFLP), 116, 146, 209, 213, 228, 245

Democratic Movement for Change, 1, 2, 5, 82, 99, 104, 107, 112, 285

Democratic Party (US), 249, 253

demonstrations: against war, 153, 166, 168; in support of war, 141

deportees, question of delegation rights, 258, 259

Diaspora Jewish community, 2, 67, 115, 133, 162, 163, 184, 214, 220, 224, 225, 227, 229, 231, 232, 233, 239, 244, 251, 252, 270; confusion among, 230–4; East European, 147; see also American Jews

Dirac, Paul, 101

dissidents: role of, 28; Russian, 184

distribution of wealth, 104

Dome of the Rock, plan to blow up, 195

Druckman, Chaim, 154, 165, 203

Dulzin, Arye, 87

East Bank, 2, 21, 36, 37, 43, 44, 55, 57, 93, 141, 222, 268

Easter Rising (Ireland), 22, 26, 31, 177

Eban, Abba, 86, 136, 163, 202

egalitarianism, 63

Eglon, King, assassination of, 180

Egypt, 73, 97, 99, 100, 105, 106, 121, 184, 188, 207, 247, 257; arms deal with Czechoslovakia, 56; eliminated as enemy threat, 99; German scientists working in, 51; peace with, 95; treaty with, 98

Ehrlich, Simcha, 82, 102, 192

Ein Vered Group, 71, 93, 105

Einstein, Albert, 40

Eitan, Raphael (Raful), 101, 111, 115, 116, 117, 119, 125, 126, 131, 136, 140, 142, 151, 159, 161, 165, 168, 189, 192, 269

El Al, attacks on airport counters, 214

Eldad, Israel, 29, 30, 38, 93, 94, 105, 176, 181, 182, 183, 185, 191, 197, 199

elections: 1965, 62, 69, 283; 1969, 62, 283; 1973, 74; 1977, 85, 87, 285; 1984, 201–5, 201; 1988, 235, 236, 237; 1992, 272, 273–9; 1996, 280, 281; 1999, 281, 286; 2001, 282, 288; of Palestinian negotiators, 251, 255, 256; to first Knesset, 42–8, 182; to second Knesset, 49; to third Knesset, 55; to fourth Knesset, 54

electronic media, role of, 218, 223

Eli, Ovaadia, 106

Eliav, Liova, 119, 191, 211

Eliyahu of Vilna, 194

Elon, Amos, 197

embezzlement scandals, 77

Entebbe operation, 216

Eretz Israel, 45, 46, 47, 55, 57, 60, 70, 72, 85, 88, 92, 94, 95, 100, 141, 155, 156, 185, 187, 204, 208, 222, 241, 255, 262, 269, 272

Eretz Israel Front, 255

Eshkol, Levi, 58, 62, 63, 65, 67, 68, 184

ethnic rights, 89

Etzion, Yehuda, 190, 195, 196, 197

European Community (EC), 132

European Union, 290

Fahd Plan, 138

far right, 113, 252, 255, 259–60, 261, 262, 263, 272, 280; absorbed into Herut, 94; break with, 96–108; resurrection of, 191–7

Fascism, 18, 40, 41, 148, 207; Italian, 16, 24; Jewish, 9, 24

Fatah organization, 116, 117, 209, 226, 241, 242, 245, 246, 247; attacks by, 246

Fatah Revolutionary Council, 229

Fatherland Front, 181

Fighters' Party, 182, 183

Final Solution, 25, 176

Fonda, Jane, 135

Force 17 organization, 213, 226

foreign currency bank accounts, 102 (abroad, 78)

40-kilometre clearance in Lebanon, 123, 125, 126, 131, 132, 133, 136

Foxman, Abe, 231, 245

France, 46, 55, 56, 151, 222

Frangieh, Tony, 151

Free Centre, 72, 73, 75, 99, 283, 284

Friedman, Milton, 102

Front for Eretz Israel Loyalists, 86

Gahal see Gush Herut Liberalism

Galei Zahal radio station, 136

Galilee, Judaization of, 112

Galili, Israel, 71, 76, 85, 162

Galili document, 84

Gamiram, Yitzhak, 190

Gaza, 71, 72, 90, 92, 98, 105, 153, 203, 204, 250, 256; Israeli withdrawal from, 57; pacification programme, 111; population's support for peace process, 271

Gaza Strip, capture of, 56

Gemayel, Bashir, 122, 124, 125, 151, 154, 159; assassinated, 153; elected president of Lebanon, 152

General Zionists, 49, 53, 54, 55, 56, 57, 58, 61

German scientists working for Egypt, 184

Germany, 26, 49–52, 103, 147, 175; approaches to, 25; feeling against, 50; industry, 51; negotiations with, 26; question of reparations, 49, 52, 54, 145; responsibility for Holocaust, 170;

scientists working in Egypt, 51; Avraham
    Stern's contact with, 176; West, 50, 145
    (Nazi personnel in, 51; relations with,
    50)
Geva, Eli: relieved of command, 140;
    renounces command, 131
Giladi, Eliahu, 187; assassination of, 181
Gilead, 37, 45
Givat Ze'ev settlement, 265
Golan, 71, 72, 105, 117, 195, 203, 285; attack
    on, 144; call to annex, 121, 187;
    colonization of, 271; retention of, 271;
    Syrian command of, 116
Golda Meir Foundation, 234
Goldman, Nahum, 164
Goldstein, Baruch, 205
Goren, Shlomo, 156, 157
Greater Israel, use of term, 254
Greece, 183
Green Line, 266
Greenberg, Ivan M., 5
Greenberg, Uri Zvi, 17, 18, 45, 174, 180, 183,
    196, 197
Gross, Martin, 234
Grossman, Chaika, 150
growth rate of Israel, 81, 82
guerilla warfare, 176, 177, 187
Gulag, 184; Begin's experience in, 42, 54,
    100
Gulf War, 243, 249, 264, 267, 270, 272, 289;
    cost to Israel recompensed, 269
Gur, Motta, 111, 141, 142
Guri, Chaim, 63
Gush Emunim, 94, 105, 165, 190, 191, 193,
    194, 195, 198, 200, 201, 203, 204, 238
Gush Herut Liberalim (Gahal), 5, 41, 59, 62,
    65, 67, 68, 71, 72, 73, 74, 84, 144, 146,
    283, 284; close to disintegration, 69, 70
Guterman, Yaakov, 170
Gutman, Israel, 151

Ha'am, Ahad, 14, 15
Habash, George, 117, 147, 209, 217, 226, 241
Habib, Philip, 118, 126, 167
Habib Plan, 129
Ha'Etzni, Eliakim, 204
Haganah, 32, 35, 54, 175, 177, 179, 180, 182,
    197, 198
Haig, Alexander, 122, 153
Hamas, 280, 286, 288, 289, 290
Hammami, Said, 119
hanging of British army sergeants, 3, 31
Ha'olam Hazeh, 77
Hapoel Hatzair, 9
heredim, 238, 239
Harel, Isser, 183
Harkabi, Yehoshafat, 214, 231

hasbarah, 232; industry, 220–25
Hashomer Hatzair, 18
Hassan, King, 88
Hassan, Prince, 222
Haviv, Avshalom, 31
Hawatmeh, Naif, 187, 209, 217, 226, 241
Hazit Ha'Moledet, 41
He'Hazit publication, 29
health care, cost of, 103
health service, 63
Hebrew language, 20; revival of 176
Hebron, 56
Hebron Agreement, 281, 286
Hebron Islamic College, attack on, 189, 190
Hebron massacres: in 1929, 196; in 1994, 205
Hecht, Reuben, 26
Heineman, Benzion, 190
Helms Amendment, 247
Helsingfors Declaration, 89
Herut, 2, 42, 44, 45, 46, 47, 51, 53, 54, 58, 59,
    60, 61, 62, 63, 64, 69, 70, 72, 73, 87, 93,
    94, 95, 101, 103, 112, 113, 115, 117, 136, 140,
    145, 151, 155, 169, 171, 172, 183, 185, 203,
    206, 207, 208, 211, 231, 236, 265, 284, 285;
    activities in USA, 40; attitude to South
    Africa, 56; birth of, 5, 36–41; coalition-
    building, 64; Fifth National Conference,
    50, 57; founding conference of, 42;
    image of, 59; leadership challenge, 193;
    loss of seats, 49; parliamentary stability
    of, 52
Herut publication, 28
Herzl, Theodor, 11, 12, 24, 42, 194
Herzog, Chaim, 65, 143, 198, 210, 261
Hezbollah, 290
Histadrut, 10, 47, 55, 57, 59, 233, 279;
    conference (1944), 31; elections, 58, 73
Hisadrut Housing Corporation, 77
Hitler, Adolf, 10, 17, 22, 23, 24, 25, 26, 30,
    42, 51, 143, 149, 150, 170; urge to
    resurrect, 150
Hoess, Commandant, 51
Hofi, Yitzhak, 111
Hollinger Corporation, 232, 233
Holocaust, 25, 91, 115, 170, 218, 250, 285;
    reparations for, 49; survivors of, 50, 103;
    trauma of Begin, 145–58
Hurvitz, Yigal, 5, 103, 104, 106, 114
Hussein, King, 122, 146, 211, 212, 227, 241,
    263, 264, 268, 285; Menachem Begin's
    refusal to meet, 221; withdrawal from
    West Bank, 250
Hussein, Saddam, 222, 228, 243, 248, 249,
    266, 267, 268, 269, 289
Husseini, Faisal, 240, 251, 268, 270, 273

immigrant ships, turned back, 22, 29

immigration of Jews, 9, 33, 79, 184;
absorption of, 262; and unemployment,
276; from Eastern Europe, 21; from
Morocco, 58; from USSR, 184, 185, 264,
270, 276 (paying for, 265–7); limited by
White Paper, 19, 22, 34
Independent Centre, 99
Independent Liberal Party, 61, 62, 65, 284
inequality, increase of, in Israeli society, 103
inflation, 82, 102, 104, 106, 202, 207
Intifada, 235, 237, 240, 246, 249, 250, 255,
256, 257, 278; control of, 246; intention
to suppress, 236
Intifada 2000, 287, 288, 289
Iran, 122
Iraq, 119, 120, 122, 209, 217, 222, 226, 228,
229, 248, 264, 269; bombing of nuclear
reactor, 106, 117, 148, protection of Abu
Nidal, 228
Irgun Zva'i Leumi (National Military
Organization), 3, 4, 5, 19, 21, 22, 26, 27–
35, 37, 40, 41, 43, 46, 47, 53, 59, 90, 93,
95, 98, 123, 141, 145, 147, 170, 172, 174,
175, 176, 177, 179, 180, 186, 197, 198, 215,
241; split in, 175
Irgun Zva'i Leumi b'Israel see Stern Group
Irish struggle, 174, 177; interest in, 23, 30, 31
Iron Fist policy, 235, 244
Islamic fundamentalism, 214, 247, 249
Islamic Jihad, 226, 288, 289, 290
Israel Aircraft Industries, 215
Israel Broadcasting, 100
Israel Corporation, 77
Israel Defence Force (IDF), 45, 113, 115, 122,
131, 132, 133, 135, 137, 139, 142, 155, 157,
160, 167, 168, 190, 246, 257, 267, 268; as
hallowed institution, 140; as police
squad, 236; cooperation with Phalange,
161; entry into West Beirut, 153, 159
(question of, 134, 143); reputation of,
160, 161; soldiers resisting Lebanon war,
139
Israel lobby in USA, 266
Israel Television, 135, 138
Israel Workers' Party see Mapai
Israel–British Bank, 77
Israeli Air Force, 117, 126, 132; attack on
Syrian missiles, 124; bombing of
Lebanese coast, 118; bombing of West
Beirut, 120
Israeli pound, floating of, 102
Italian Jews, position of, 24
Italy, 25

Jabotinsky, Ze'ev Vladimir, 5, 7–8, 9, 10–19,
20, 24, 28, 29, 31, 34, 36, 41, 42, 44, 45,
46, 47, 57, 59, 87, 88, 89, 90, 93, 94, 95,

114, 146, 150, 172, 174, 175, 179, 182, 184,
210, 216, 218, 231, 250, 284, 291; death of,
22, 28; issue of return of body, 54, 63;
resignation from Zionist Executive, 12
Jabotinsky, Eri, 26, 46
Jarring, Gunnar, 88
Jerusalem, 38, 180, 255, 287; Arab, 37;
creation of suburbs, 265; destruction of,
180; East, residents of, question of
delegation rights, 257, 258, 259;
expansion into territories, 266;
internationalization of, 45; proposed
placement under Vatican, 24
Jerusalem Post, 120, 127, 135, 140, 232, 285;
sale of, 233
Jewish Agency, 86, 179, 215, 274
Jewish army, establishment of, 25
Jewish conspiracy, image of, 266
Jewish majority to be created in Palestine, 11
Jewish Revolt: First, 32, 180; Second, 194
Jewish state, 7, 8, 10, 13, 14, 25, 28, 33, 36–48,
56, 87, 95, 169, 174, 175, 178, 179, 183, 278
Jewish Underground, 187–91, 203, 209;
amnesty, 210
Jewishness: castigation of, 163; issue of, 232,
239
Jews: definition of, 260; killing Jews, 38
Jibril, Ahmed, 117, 147, 209, 214, 227
Joint Israel Appeal, 131
Jonathan Institute, 233
Jordan, 2, 11, 43, 57, 72, 75, 84, 88, 106, 141,
154, 213, 223, 236, 268, 270, 272;
citizenship of, 90; election of
parliament, 46; marginalization of, 263;
negotiation with, 44, 211, 212, 213;
option eliminated, 264; peace treaty
with, 215
Jordan is Palestine position, 159, 221, 222,
223, 285; committees, 221
Jordanian–Palestinian delegation, 273
Joseph's Tomb, Nablus, 262
Josephus, 180
jubilee-year principle, 9
Judea, 43, 71, 76, 90, 97, 100, 105, 146, 147,
153, 172, 194, 203, 210, 230, 253, 256, 281,
285; absorption of funding, 273–4;
conquest of, 185, 191; control of, 282;
proposed state of, 251; retention of, 85,
87, 94, 96, 99, 100, 204, 211, 217, 254;
settlement of, 208
Jung, Guido, 24

Kach party, 201, 204, 251
Kadoumi, Farouk, 147
Kahan Commission, 153, 164, 173;
condemnation of Sharon, 166; report,
165, 169

Kahane, Meir, 105, 201, 229, 231, 251; elected to Knesset, 193, 205
Kalisher, Rabbi, 194
Kastner trial, 145
Katz, Shmuel, 92, 93
Katzav, Moshe, 74
Kaufman, Chaim, 95
Kela, settlement, 272
Kenan, Amos, 112
Kessar, Yisrael, 279
Khomeini, Ruhollah, 249
kibbutzim aid, abuse of, 79
Kibya, attack on, 111, 282
killing: in response to killing, 200; of Palestinians, within Jewish religious law, 190
King David Hotel, bombing of, 3, 29, 33, 35
Kirkpatrick, Jeane, 215
Kiryat Arba settlement, 189, 190, 200, 280
Kiryat Malachi, 74
Kiryat Shemona settlement, attack on, 146
Kishinev pogrom, 25
Kishon, Ephraim, 138
Kleiner, Mikhail, 140
Klutznick, Philip, 164
Knesset: first, 42–8; second, 49; third, 55; fourth, 54
Kohl, Helmut, 170
Kollek, Teddy, 65
Kook, Avraham Yitzhak, 194
Kook, Hillel, 26, 46
Kook, Zvi Yehuda, 105, 190, 193, 196, 203, 284
Koor Industries, 233
Kupat Holim, 78
Kurds, Iraqi atrocities against, 267
Kuwait, 267; invasion of, 268

La'am faction, 5, 86, 98, 99, 112, 155, 203
Labour Alignment, 1, 2, 4, 6, 52, 66, 67, 69, 71, 73, 75, 77, 107, 115, 141, 142, 144, 191, 205, 207, 210, 234, 235, 237, 259, 271, 283; decline in vote of, 237; disillusion with, 5
Labour Party (Israel), 2, 33, 52, 66, 71, 72, 73, 74, 75–82, 84, 85, 86, 87, 89, 90, 92, 96, 98, 101, 102, 105, 106, 109, 111, 139, 142, 143, 145, 147, 148, 156, 162, 168, 169, 202, 203, 205, 207, 208, 210, 218, 220, 221, 225, 229, 234, 236, 239, 246, 250, 254, 257, 258, 263, 264, 279; and Peace Now protest, 141, 162; ballot for candidates, 80; fragmentation of, 52, 62–82; internal reform of, 277, 278; promise to freeze settlements, 277
Labour Party (UK), 33, 34, 175, 212

Labour Zionism, 3, 6, 33, 41, 54, 76, 77, 100, 174, 178
Lamerhav group, 47
land, Jewish right to buy, 85, 90, 212
land for peace formulation, 76, 84–5, 97, 108, 210, 211, 254, 257, 272, 290
Land of Israel movement, 71, 72, 75, 93, 99, 191
Landa, Max, 234
Landau, Chaim, 49, 98
Larnaca, killing of Israelis, 213
Larsen, Terje, 290
Lavon affair, 62, 65
Law for the Prevention of Terrorism, 229
Law of Return, 239
League of Nations, 223
Lebanese Armed Revolutionary Brigades, 118
Lebanon, 45, 131, 236, 270; Israeli invasion of, 123–8, 128–44, 148 (justified by Shamir, 153; opposition to, 166); Israeli withdrawal from, 141, 193, 206, 207; soldiers' pledge not to serve in, 139; war in, 109–27, 218 (Begin's rationale for, 152; cost of, 202); criticism of Israeli conduct, 224; dead in, 202; débâcle of, 172; opposition to, 140–4; preparation for, 115–24; religious arguments for, 154–8; Yitzhak Shamir's attitude to, 173; support for, 110, 130, 132, 134, 167
Lehi (Fighters for the Freedom of Israel), 27–35, 37, 41, 93, 95, 105, 114, 171–86, 187, 188, 197, 198, 199, 241, 280; assassination attempts by, 177; difference with Irgun, 179; operatives proposed to work as prostitutes, 181
Leibowitz, Yeshayahu, 138; pressure for trial of, 138
Lekert, Hirsch, 180
Lenin, V.I., 46, 174; as focus of respect, 18, 22
letter-bomb campaign against German scientists, 184
Levi, Yehuda Arie, assassination of, 180
Levinger, Moshe, 190, 191, 194, 195, 198, 203, 279
Lévi-Strauss, Claude, 206
Levy, David, 160, 192, 206, 171–2, 203, 254, 255, 258, 265; as Foreign Minister, 263, 274; call for resignation, 270; relations with Shamir, 274
Levy, Yehuda, 233
Liberal Party, 58, 59, 60, 61, 62, 70, 72, 86, 89, 102, 112, 121, 284
Libya, 119, 229
Lie, Trygve, 181–2

Likud bloc, 1, 5, 41, 76, 85, 86, 87, 89, 102, 106, 110, 112, 132, 134, 135, 136, 138, 144, 147, 153, 162, 167, 168, 171, 192, 198, 200, 201, 202, 204, 205, 206, 208, 210, 211, 212, 214, 217, 218, 219, 220, 223, 225, 227, 228, 229, 230, 231, 232, 233, 237, 238, 239, 243, 244, 245, 246, 247, 248, 249, 250, 251, 254, 255, 258, 259, 260, 264, 266, 269, 270, 272, 274, 275, 276, 278, 279, 284, 286, 289; attitude to media, 134 (foreign, 137); attitude to PLO, 89; decline of pragmatic wing, 263; defeat of, 280; falling popularity of, 273, 279; fear of Palestinians, 218; formation of, 68–75; increased vote of, 74, 106, 107, 108; opposition to, 169; political donations to, 233, 234; Ronald Reagan's tolerance of, 253; reservations about Madrid Conference, 271; response to criticism of war in Lebanon, 140–4; Statement of Principles, 72; support for, 132; US loss of confidence in, 276; Netanyahu as leader, 280, 281
Lior, Dov, 200
Litani river, 155
Lithuania, 46
Livni, Menachem, 190
loan guarantees, US, withholding of, 266, 276
Lockerbie bombing, 229
lockouts, proposed as treasonable to Zionism, 9
Lod, Arabs expelled, 183
Lubavitcher movement, 193, 231, 239, 277

Ma'ale Adumium, 265
Ma'a lot, attack, 133, 146, 187
Ma'arach see Labour Alignment
Mabat programme, 135
Machpela, cave of, 45
Machteret Malchut Yisrael, 191
Machteret Yehudit see Jewish Underground
Mack-Lieberman legislation, 248
Madrid Conference, 270, 271, 272, 274, 276
Magen, David, 144
Mandatory Palestine, 11, 13, 37, 47, 57, 60, 145, 223, 243, 250, 280
Mapai, 4, 5, 8, 9, 10, 36, 40, 41, 44, 46, 47, 48, 50, 52, 53, 54, 57, 58, 62, 63, 64, 66, 67, 68, 69, 71, 73, 76, 77, 84, 94, 145, 174, 184, 282, 283, 284; coalition against, 69; decline of, 55, 71
Mapam, 39, 66, 67, 139, 142, 143, 150, 277
Marcus, Andre, 234
Margalit, Dan, 78
Martin, Sergeant, killing of, 31, 187
Masada, 22, 180
Maxwell, Robert, 233

mayors of Nablus and Ramallah, bomb attacks on, 189, 198
McMahon Correspondence, 222
McMichael, Harold, 21; attempted assassination of, 177
media: press regarded as fifth column, 135, 136; responsibility of, 134–7
Meimad, 239, 278
Meir, Golda, 58, 67, 71, 73, 76, 83, 84, 86, 88, 139, 146, 185, 187, 218, 221, 238; call for resignation, 75
Mekel, Aryeh, 232, 233
Mendes-France, Pierre, 164
Meretz, 278, 279
Merridor, Dan, 208, 250, 251, 256, 258, 280
Meridor, Yaakov, 26, 28, 57
Meshiach Ben David, 194, 197
Meshiach Ben Yosef, 194, 197
messianism, 193, 194, 195, 196, 225, 238, 277
Mevo Dotan settlement, inauguration of, 266
Middle East Peace conference, 269
military Zionism, 42
Milstein, Marshall, 51
minimum wages law, 58
Misgav Am, attack on, 133
Mishcon, Lord, 212
Mitchell Report, 290
Mitla Pass, attack on, 111, 282
Mitterrand, François, 149
Mitzna, Amram, 162
Mizrachi, 9, 194, 238
Modai, Yitzhak, 98, 254, 255, 258
Moledet, 255, 268, 269, 271, 273, 279
Morasha, 200, 201, 204, 205
Moratinos, Miguel, 290
Moravia, Alberto, 206
Mordechai, Eliahu, 199, 200
Morocco, emigrants from, 58
Moshav movement, 72
Mossad, 173, 183, 185
Moyne, Lord: assassination of, 31, 32, 33, 177, 179, 199; hostility to Zionism, 178
Moynihan, Daniel, 215
Mubarak, Hosni, 253, 256
Mubarak Plan, 257
Mufti of Jerusalem, 26
Mussolini, Benito, 23, 24, 30

Nahariya, shelling of, 116
Namir, Ora, 221
Narodnaya Volya organization, 22
Nasser, Gamal Abdel, 51, 55, 56, 184
Nathan of Gaza, 195
Nathan, Abie, 230
National Council for Soviet Jewry, 184

National Guidance Committee (Palestinian), 189, 190, 198
National Labour Federation, 57
National Party (Syria), 159
National Religious Party, 65, 67, 76, 82, 98, 99, 107, 121, 141, 154, 164, 165, 188, 192, 193, 200, 205, 255, 278, 286, 287
National Unified Command (Palestinian), 240
National Unity government, 65, 68, 69, 70, 71, 75, 84, 87, 171, 193, 205, 207, 208, 218, 220, 226, 231, 235, 237, 239, 250, 251, 252, 254, 256, 257, 262, 263; end of, 257, 278
National Workers' Federation, 47
National Zionist Organization, 29
nationalism, 109, 168, 186, 193; Arab, 13, 26, 30; Palestinian, 88, 90, 154, 218, 225, 226; Polish, 41
Navon, Yitzhak, 81, 162, 165, 202
Nazism, 17, 20, 23, 25, 26, 40, 50, 51, 89, 175, 188; acquiescence in, 51; Begin's experience of, 100; use of term as label, 145, 146, 147, 148, 150
Nechaev, Sergei, 18
Ne'eman, Yuval, 94, 105, 155, 192, 198, 199, 269, 271
Neot, David, 262
Netanyahu, Benjamin, 208, 215, 218, 220, 221, 223, 224, 225, 226, 227, 228, 229, 233, 236, 243, 244, 245, 248, 255, 259, 269, 271, 274, 280, 286, 287, 288; as spin doctor, 219; campaign against terrorism, 214–19; disagreement with Shimon Peres, 220; opposition to Oslo Agreement
Netanyahu, Yonatan, 216
Netivot Shalom (Paths to Peace) movement, 165
new left, 147
New Zionist Organization, 18, 19, 179
Nissim, Moshe, 201
Nitzanim beach, attack on, 248
Nobel Peace Prize, 173
Nordau, Max, 25
Nusseibeh, Sari, 268

occupation, term used by George Bush, 253
Ofer, Avraham, suicide of, 77
O'Hegarty, P.S., 31
oil price: fall in, 207; increase in, 81, 102, 104
Olmert, Ehud, 137, 138, 203, 208, 220, 223, 224, 233, 263, 286
Ometz group, 143
Ometz party, 200, 205
open underground, proposed by Begin, 31
Operation Big Pines, 121, 122, 123, 126, 145, 151, 153
Operation Little Pines, 122, 126

Operation Peace for Galilee, 109, 123, 127, 132, 140, 150, 152, 277
opinion polls, 1, 2, 102, 111, 130, 132, 133, 134, 166, 201, 205, 207, 232, 237, 252, 263, 268, 271, 273, 286
Oslo Agreement, 280, 281, 287, 288
Oz, Amos, 138, 150, 237

pacifism, accusation of, 139, 140
Paice, Mervyn, hanged by Irgun, 31
Pakistan, 290
Palestine, delineation of, 223
Palestine Liberation Front, 213, 245; attack on sea resort, 248
Palestine Liberation Organization (PLO), 109, 118, 120, 132, 133, 137, 154, 167, 191, 199, 208, 210–14, 216, 229, 240, 241, 242, 243, 247, 248, 250, 255, 259, 260, 264, 267, 270, 271, 273, 285, 286; agrees to absence from peace negotiations, 270; and oil-state funding, 243; as nerve centre of Palestinian politics, 226; attacked (in Beirut, 123, 128, 129; in Lebanon, 117; in Southern Lebanon, 110, 116); attacks on Israeli targets, 133; attacks on Northern Israel, 116, 118, 120, 128; ban on contact with, 230; blamed for all terrorism, 228; ceasefire with, 125, 142; contact with individual members, 229; demonization of, 225; determination to eliminate, 110, 118, 121, 123, 130, 142, 159, 163, 212; dialogue with USA, 242, 244, 245, 246, 248, 249, 251; evacuation from Beirut, 124, 143, 145, 153, 163, 167; failure to condemn Saddam Hussein, 267; funding of, 233, 267; meetings with British Jews, 232; negotiation with, 110, 112, 134, 164, 169, 183, 211, 227, 237, 247, 251, 252, 256, 269; presence in Southern Lebanon, 116; presence in West Beirut, 130, 131; rejection of terrorism, 241; retaliatory attacks on, 189; reunification of, 227; shelling of Northern Israel, 125; sinking of, 225–30; strategy, 246; viewed as terrorist organization, 89, 118, 119, 120, 225, 226, 240, 268; war material of, 133
Palestine National Alliance, 209
Palestine National Council, 213, 226, 236, 241, 270
Palestinian Authority, 281, 289
Palestinian state, 85, 86, 99, 106, 112, 147, 242, 251, 255, 256, 272, 287
Palestinian Right of Return, 288, 289
Palestinian terrorism, 109, 117, 146
Palestinians, 91, 98, 137, 166, 213; and peace process, and USA, 78; autonomy for, 88; changes among, 240–4; conflict with,

fatigue with, 192; determination to eliminate, 277; dialogue with, 224, 257; transfer of population, 212, 222, 237, 268; in joint Jordanian delegation, 270; labelled as Nazis, 146; negotiation with, 84, 103, 183, 190, 217, 236, 257, 264, 269, 281; non-existence averred, 238; outlawing of, 206–19; participation at UN, 147; recognition of, 73; reconciliation with, 235; relations with, 7, 12, 13, 14, 22, 25, 44, 63, 87, 88, 89, 96, 146, 178, 189, 254, 255; rights of, 67, 188; seen as 'cancer', 101; self-determination, 222; self-government, 273; support for invasion of Kuwait, 268; treatment of, 101 see also nationalism, Palestinian

Palmach organization, 35, 54

Papo, Aharon, 139

partition, 11, 13, 20, 36, 37, 44, 45, 70, 93, 178, 187, 210, 215, 241, 242

Peace for Peace rally, 271

peace movement, 240, 252, 254, 267–8

Peace Now movement, 92, 110, 137, 138, 139, 140, 141, 144, 145, 162, 202, 204; influence on White House, 254

Pearse, Padraig, 23

Peel Commission, 21

Peli, Gilad, 190

Pentagon attack, 289

Peres, Shimon, 2, 63, 65, 70, 71, 77, 79, 80, 82, 84, 85, 86, 105, 106, 114, 142, 144, 162, 182, 184, 200, 202, 206, 207, 211, 212, 218, 221, 231, 235, 236, 237, 250, 251, 252, 258, 259, 260, 261, 263, 264, 270, 274, 279, 280, 283, 284, 288; ousted as party leader, 278

Peron, Juan, 168

Petliura, Semion, 25; assassination of, 180

Phalange (Lebanon), 110, 123, 124, 130, 151, 154, 159; cooperation with Israel, 122; entry into Sabra and Shatilla camps, 153, 160

Pinto, Danny, 101

Poland, 9, 12, 18, 25, 38, 58, 149, 151, 174, 195; Nazi occupation of, 149

policemen, Jewish, 10, 27

political donations: identification of, 233; taxation of, 234

Popular Front for the Liberation of Palestine (PFLP), 117, 146, 147, 209, 213, 228, 241, 245

Popular Front for the Liberation of Palestine-General Command (PFLP-GC), 117, 209, 214

Porat, Hanan, 289

premiership, direct elections to, 286

Presidents' Conference of Major Jewish Organizations, 151, 231, 245, 253

prisoner exchanges, 209, 221

Pritsker, Israel, assassination of, 181

Progressives, 60, 62

Project Renewal, 106

Provisional Government, 39, 41, 42, 43

Purple Line, 265, 266

Rabin, Leah, 78, 79, 80

Rabin, Yitzhak, 5, 76, 77, 78, 79, 80, 83, 85, 106, 112, 114, 118, 141, 142, 143, 144, 202, 208, 209, 218, 221, 235, 236, 240, 245, 250, 251, 257, 258, 260, 263, 274, 278, 279, 283; economic deterioration under, 102; handshake with Arafat, 280

Radler, David, 232, 233

Rafi see Reshimat Poalei Israel

Ramlawi, Nabil, 120

Ramle, Arabs expelled, 183

Ratosh, Yonatan, 174, 280

Ratz group, 107, 110, 143, 205, 277

Raziel, David, 26, 28, 31, 42, 175

Reagan, Ronald, 109, 111, 125, 129, 153, 166, 208, 218, 244, 249, 250, 253; Begin letter to, 150

Reagan Plan, 124, 152, 154, 227; rejected by Israel, 153

Red Crescent (Lebanese), 137

refusal to serve in armed forces, 287

Reich, Seymour, 253

religious parties, 239, 263; rising vote of, 238

Religious Zionist Movement see Mizrachi reparations see Germany

Reshimat Poalei Israel (Israel Workers' List) (Rafi), 62, 65, 66, 67, 68, 70, 77, 84, 94, 99, 104, 283, 284

Revisionist Party, 47

Revisionist Zionism, 3, 4, 5, 6, 7, 8, 9, 10, 11, 12, 14, 17, 20, 23, 24, 26, 27, 28, 29, 34, 36, 39, 41, 42, 44, 46, 53, 54, 69, 93, 96, 105, 109, 184, 185, 186, 210, 215, 216, 218, 219, 223, 230, 250, 256, 268, 282; crisis in, 18; growth of, 16; in transition, 49–61

Revisionist Zionist Conference, Fifth, 16

Richter, Yehuda, 205

Riga, 185; as stronghold of Revisionist Zionism, 184

Rogers Plan, 71, 146

Roman Empire, Jewish accommodation with, 180

Romania, 211

Rosenblum, Herzl, 138

Rothschild, Baron Edmond de, 8

Russia, 89; revolution, 174

Russian immigrants, voting power of, 277

Sabra and Shatilla camps, massacre at, 124, 153,
    202; as war crime, 160; call for inquiry
    into, 164; consequences of, 159–70;
    inquiry into, 165; responsibility for, 165
Sacks, Jonathan, 165
Sadat, Anwar, 88, 91, 93, 96, 97, 98, 106, 188;
    Nobel prize for, 52; visit to Jerusalem,
    88, 94
Saguy, Yehoshua, 122
Said, Edward, 288
Samaria, 43, 71, 76, 90, 97, 100, 105, 146,
    147, 153, 172, 194, 203, 210, 230, 253, 256,
    281, 285; conquest of, 185, 191; retention
    of, 85, 87, 94, 96, 99, 100, 204, 211, 217,
    254; settlement of, 208
Sapir, Pinchas, 76, 81
Sapir, Yosef, 66
Sarfatti, Margherita, 24
Sarid, Yossi, 112, 127, 137, 142, 143, 145, 268
Sartawi, Issam, 119
Saudi Arabia, 140, 267
Savinkov, Boris, 22
Schach, Eliezer Menachem, 239, 260, 277
Schiff, Ze'ev, 109, 160
Schmidt, Helmut, 170
Schneerson, Menachem, 231, 239, 277
schools, Palestinian, re-opening of, 254
Schwartzbard, Shalom, 180
Scud missiles, 268
security, uses of, 210–14
Segal, Hagai, 190
Sephardim, 58, 105, 106, 108, 148, 172, 178,
    199, 211, 238, 239, 260, 277; falling vote
    for Labour Alignment, 74; gap with
    Ashkenazim, 103
settlements, 70, 85, 100, 112, 117, 189, 203,
    208, 262; ban on, 97; cessation of, linked
    to peace process, 265; continuation of,
    256; expansion of, 97; freeze proposed,
    154, 291; funds available for, 204; hint of
    corruption in construction, 274; in
    Territories, 96, 99, 103, 113, 220, 275,
    284, 285; Israeli support for freeze, 274;
    Labour Party promise to freeze, 277;
    mass, 265; momentum of, 267; new, 262,
    266, 274; on Golan Heights, 272;
    pressure from USA to halt, 276;
    requirement to cease, 254; 'security',
    279; West Bank, 188
settlers, 251, 276; religious, 225; violence of,
    280, 291
Sevi, Sabbatai, 195
Shamir, Yitzhak, 28, 29, 30, 99, 113, 114, 137,
    153, 165, 171–86, 187, 192, 197, 198, 199,
    201, 203, 204, 211, 212, 215, 220, 221, 224,
    225, 228, 229, 230, 231, 232, 235, 236, 237,
    239, 240, 241, 245, 246, 247, 265, 268,

269, 270, 272, 273, 276, 279, 280, 288,
    289; admiration for Gush Emunim, 204;
    and settlement programme, 266; as
    Knesset Speaker, 188; autocratic style of,
    192; domestic problems of, 206–10; falls
    in no-confidence vote, 260; involved in
    killing of Eliahu Giladi, 181; last
    government of, 262–81; opposition to
    Begin, 188; relations with Bush, 253, 267;
    relations with David Levy, 274; relations
    with left, 182; visit to USA, 252, 258
Shamir, Moshe, 72, 188
Shamir Plan, 249–61, 278, 280
Shapira, Yosef, 200
Shapiro, Yonathon, 47
Sharett, Moshe, 46, 64, 155, 182, 238, 282,
    283, 288, 289
Sharif, Bassam Abu, 241
Sharon, Ariel, 72, 86, 93, 101, 114, 117, 118,
    122, 123, 125, 126, 131, 132, 134, 135, 136,
    137, 138, 140, 142, 144, 151, 153, 157, 159,
    160, 161, 162, 163, 168, 169, 171, 172, 205,
    206, 212, 254, 255, 265, 266, 269, 274,
    277, 280, 283, 284, 285, 286, 287, 288,
    289, 290, 291; advocacy of settlement
    expansion, 285; as 'fighting Jew', 115; as
    Minister of Agriculture, 112; as Minister
    of Defence, 115, 121, 221; as Minister of
    Housing, 262, 266, 275, 286 (hint of
    corruption, 274); attitude to media, 135;
    call for resignation, 164; calls for
    dismissal, 139; candidate for premiership,
    286; censorship by, 122; challenge for
    Herut leadership, 193; commanders'
    rebellion against, 162; damage to IDF,
    160; deprived of initiation of action, 129;
    devious tactics of, 127, 137, 168, 224, 130;
    left's detestation of, 111; needed by
    Begin, 113; opposition to, 168;
    responsibility for Sabra and Shatilla
    massacre, 166; relations with Begin, 122,
    168; as Likud leader, 282, 286; as Prime
    Minister 282, 288; resignation of, 258,
    259 (called for, 139); rise of, 111–15; thirst
    for power, 113
Sharq-al-Awsat newspaper, 120
Shas party, 207, 234, 239, 258, 260, 261, 263,
    277, 279
Shaw, George Bernard, 31
shelling of Northern Israel, 115, 116, 117, 118,
    120, 125, 128, 161
Shikun Ovdim corporation, 77
Shilansky, Dov, 136, 144, 151, 204
Shiloah, Zvi, 72
Shilon, Dan, 136
Shinui party, 107, 205, 277
Shitrit, Meir, 106

Shlomzion party, 86, 112, 285
Shomron, Dan, 236, 246, 267
Shostak, Eliezer, 99
Shoval, Zalman, 72, 104, 276
Shultz, George, 153, 208, 236, 244, 249
Shultz Plan, 230, 236
Sicarii, 18
Signoret, Simone, 206
Silone, Ignazio, 206
Sinai, 56, 71, 72, 192; evacuation of, 97, 105, 115; eviction of settlers, 113; proposed development of harbour, 84; withdrawal from, 92, 99, 122, 195, 236
Six Day War, 62, 65, 67, 68, 70, 71, 72, 84, 97, 144, 148, 152, 156, 184, 185, 194, 224, 238, 240, 255, 279
Slansky trial, 54
Slovina, Leah, 184, 185
Sobol, Yehoshua, 161, 201
socialism, 2, 9, 10, 14, 17, 54, 58, 182
Socialist Zionism, 42, 62–82, 85
Sokolov, Nahum, 8
Soldiers Against Silence organization, 139
Solomon, King, 158
Soloveitchik, Joseph, 164
South Africa, 56
sovereignty, 43, 90, 212; Egyptian, 96; Israeli, 91, 154, 225, 254 (in territories, 273); joint, 84
Stalin, Joseph, 30
State List, 71, 72, 73, 75, 98, 99, 103, 104, 283, 284
State of Independent Palestine, proposed, 240
Stern, Avraham, 17, 22, 26, 28, 29, 31, 42, 95, 105, 174, 175, 180, 181, 183, 185, 193, 196, 197; approaches to Nazi Germany, 175, 182; death of, 27, 30; mythologization of, 176; Eighteen Principles of National Renewal, 30, 176, 181
Stern, Isaac, 230
Stern Group, 22, 23, 24, 176, 187; disintegration of, 176; robberies by, 27
strikes, 10, 103; viewed as treasonable to Zionism, 9
subsidies, 102; cutting of, 104
Sudetenland, 147
Suez Canal, 83; crisis, 56
Sulam journal, 94
Sykes–Picot Agreement, 222–3
Syria, 88, 94, 116, 119, 123, 124, 125, 126, 127, 128, 132, 135, 142, 143, 151, 200, 209, 214, 217, 226, 228, 229, 236, 267, 270, 285; missiles in Lebanon, 116, 117, 121, 124, 129; negotiations with, 211, 270

Taasa-Glezer, Miriam, 136
Taba, negotiations over, 207

Tabenkin, Yitzhak, 64, 105, 191
Taliban, 290
Tami party, 105
Tamir, Shmuel, 70, 72
taxation, 58; indirect, 103; reduction of, 106
Techiya, 103, 104, 107, 108, 155, 188, 198, 200, 201, 204, 205, 255, 261, 268, 271, 273, 279; formation of, 192
Tel Hai fund, 78, 234
Telem party, 104, 155
telephone system, inadequacy of, 79
Temple Mount, 286, 287; Jewish services not allowed, 87
Tenuat Ha'Herut, 37
Tenuat Ha'Meri Ha'Ivri (United Resistance Movement), 34
Territories, Occupied, 78, 240, 246; conquest of, 70, 224; control of, 88; economic integration of, 76; Israeli sovereignty over, 225; population growth in, 275; retention of, 71; settlement in, 76, 90, 113, 194, 220, 265, 275; status of, 251; withdrawal from, 211
terrorism, 3, 29, 31, 32, 53, 109, 124, 130, 131, 154, 181, 209, 211, 212, 216, 221, 227, 240; indiscriminate, 198; individual, 177, 187, 190, 198; international, 146, 216, 227, 228 (renounced by Fatah, 217; renounced by PLO, 217); Irgun accused of, 28; Islamic, 280, 287; Jewish, 190, 199, 209, 280; mass, 190; monitoring of, 246; Netanyahu's campaign against, 214–19; of PLO, 213, 216, 242 (Arafat's abandonment of, 245); Palestinian, 199, 214, 216, 235; (fear of, 209); questioned by Palestinians, 217; required renunciation of, 227, 242 US war against terrorism, 289, 290, 291 see also Palestinian terrorism
Thatcherism, 102
Third Temple, 200; building of, 176, 196, 199
Timmerman, Jacobo, 168
Topf and Sons company, 51
Torah Research Institutions, 79
Trade Center, 289, 290, 291
Trotsky, Leon, 174
Tsomet, 192, 255, 261, 279
Tsouri, Bet, 177, 178
Tsouri, Hakim, 177, 178
two-state solution, 211, 243

Ukraine, Jews massacred in, 25
unemployment, 104, 276; insurance, 58
Union of Soviet Socialist Republics (USSR), 30, 147, 182, 183, 243; demise

of, 243, 270; severs diplomatic ties with
    Israel, 185; support for Arab countries, 81
United Jewish Appeal, 132
United Kingdom (UK) *see* British
    government
United Nations (UN), 43, 181, 216, 221, 290;
    Palestinian participation at, 147
UN General Assembly, 36, 242
UN Resolution 181, 241, 242; Resolution
    242, 71, 73, 75, 87, 96, 97, 212, 226, 227,
    236, 241, 250, 270; Resolution 338, 75,
    212, 250, 270
UN Security Council, 120, 147, 211, 212
United States of America (USA), 33, 78, 115,
    116, 118, 119, 121, 124, 126, 132, 143, 153,
    154, 164, 166, 208, 212, 214, 215, 216, 220,
    221, 227, 229, 232, 234, 241, 242, 243,
    244, 247, 253, 254, 257, 258, 259, 266,
    269, 270, 272, 273, 276, 289, 290, 291;
    aid from, 207; dialogue with PLO, 242,
    244, 245, 246, 248, 249, 251; economic
    aid to Israel, 104; Israeli economic
    dependency on, 103; loss of confidence
    in the Likud, 276; pressure on Shamir
    government, 267; State Department, 43,
    248, 265
Uris, Leon, 218
Uruguay, 169
Uzis, exported to Germany, 51

Vance, Cyrus, 98
Vatican, 24
Versailles Peace Conference, 222
Verwoerd, Hendrik, 56
Vietnam War, 231
Vilenchik, Avraham, assassination of, 181
Voice of Damascus, 136
Voice of the Silent Majority, 138
Volkischnationalen Hebraertum, 25

wage freeze, 104; proposed, 59
Waksman, Michael, 181
Warsaw Ghetto, 41, 150
Weinberger, Caspar, 153
Weiss, Avraham, 199
Weizmann, Chaim, 2, 6, 7, 8, 10, 29, 33, 34,
    36, 44, 45, 97, 99, 104, 114, 215
Weizmann, Ezer, 72, 97, 99, 103, 104, 112,
    113, 114, 171, 190, 205
welfare services, postponed, 102

West Bank, 2, 43, 44, 45, 46, 55, 57, 88, 92,
    96, 98, 117, 141, 154, 169, 190, 210, 237,
    241, 250, 255, 281, 284; retention of, 101,
    221, 264; settlements in, 97, 188, 225, 285
West Beirut, 131; bombing of, 120, 143;
    Israeli advance into, 129, 134, 143, 153,
    159; PLO presence in, 130; shelling of,
    123, 128, 129, 130, 131; siege of, 131; water
    supplies (cut, 128, 143; restored, 128, 129)
World Jewish Congress, 248
World Zionist Organization, 6, 11, 12, 16, 19,
    208; elections in, 8
Wye Plantation Accord, 281

Ya'ari, Ehud, 230
Ya'ari, Meir, 85
Yad Vashem: army visits banned, 151; hunger
    strike by Holocaust survivors, 150
Yadin, Yigal, 114, 188
Yadlin, Asher, 78
Yahad organization, 205
Yahadut Ha'Torah list, 277, 279
Yariv, Aharon, 218
Yehoshua, A.B., 138
Yellin-Mor, Natan, 29, 30, 176, 180, 181, 182,
    183, 185, 187
Yesh Gvul, 139, 287
yeshivot, 79; funding of, 238, 239
Yiddish culture, 12, 15
Yoffe, Avraham, 72
Yom Kippur War, 73, 75, 76, 77, 83, 88, 141,
    144, 145, 152, 188, 201; inflation
    accompanying, 81
Yosef, Ovadia, 239, 260, 263, 277
Yotvat, kingdom of, 92

Zabledovitch, Shlomo, 234
Zadok, Chaim, 77
Zahle, siege of, 110, 151
Zar, Moshe, 190
Ze'evi, Rehavam, 200, 268, 269, 271
Zelnik, Yitzhak, 177
Zionism, 2, 146, 149, 184, 191, 193, 194, 223,
    225, 238, 241, 242, 260; defined as racism,
    254; military, 31 *see also* Labour Zionism
    and Revisionist Zionism
Zionist Congress: 17th, 7, 11, 13, 45; 24th, 56
Zionist Organization of America, 244
Zippori, Mordechai, 122, 123, 125, 165